D0916918

From First Words to Grammar

From First Words to Grammar

Individual Differences and Dissociable Mechanisms

Elizabeth Bates

University of California, San Diego

Inge Bretherton

Colorado State University, Fort Collins

Lynn Snyder

Denver University

in collaboration with

**Marjorie Beeghly, Cecilia Shore, Sandra McNew,
Vicki Carlson, Carol Williamson, Andrew Garrison,
Barbara O'Connell**

Cambridge University Press

Cambridge
New York   New Rochelle   Melbourne   Sydney

Published by the Press Syndicate of the University of Cambridge
The Pitt Building, Trumpington Street, Cambridge CB2 1RP
32 East 57th Street, New York NY 10022, USA
10 Stamford Road, Oakleigh, Melbourne 3166, Australia

First published 1988

Printed in the United States of America

Library of Congress Cataloging-in-Publication Data
Bates, Elizabeth.
From first words to grammar.
Bibliography: p.
1. Language acquisition.   2. Learning, Psychology of.
I. Bretherton, Inge.   II. Snyder, Lynn S. (Lynn
Sebestyen)   III. Title.
P118.B29   1988   401′.9   87–9367

British Library Cataloguing in Publication Data
Bates, Elizabeth
From first words to grammar: individual
differences and dissociable mechanisms.
1. Grammar, Comparative and general—
Syntax   2. Language acquisition
I. Title   II. Bretherton, Inge
III. Snyder, Lynn
415   P291

ISBN 0 521 34142 6

To our children
Julia
Christopher, Monica, and Ruth
Jimmy and Joshua

CONTENTS

Part III: A Summary View

PREFACE

A few years ago, we published a book about the transition from gesture to the first word, trying to show how linguistic and nonlinguistic symbols emerge through the interaction of more primitive cognitive systems (Bates, Benigni, Bretherton, Camaioni, and Volterra, 1979). In this book we have moved a step further, tracing the passage from first words to grammar in another sample of healthy middle-class children. Once again, we have focused on the way that a complex system emerges from simpler beginnings. In both works, we have argued that nature and children both create new machines out of old parts. The capacity to name things is built out of several converging nonlinguistic skills. The capacity to acquire a grammar relies on a reworking of the same mechanisms that are used to build a lexicon. The emphasis in both cases is on continuity rather than discontinuity, construction rather than maturation.

In the 1970s this interactive view of language development was so popular that we were preaching among the converted. In the 1980s things have changed, and a different view of language is fashionable once again. The emphasis now in many quarters is on discontinuity rather than continuity, maturation rather than construction—a view of language as special and separate from the rest of cognition, perception, and learning. Some old notions about the autonomy of grammar have appeared in a revised and more explicit form called Modularity Theory, a theory of the way things come apart at the boundary between cognitive systems, including some boundaries that separate components within language proper (e.g., phonology, grammar, and lexical semantics).

Because Modularity Theory presents the old view in such an explicit form, we can conduct a direct test of competing hypotheses about the emergence of grammar. For one thing, things do come apart in interesting ways during the early stages of language development. In the last 15 years we have discovered that children do not all learn language the same way. There are qualitative as well as quantitative variations in the learning process, suggesting that at least two partially dissociable learning mechanisms are at work during the passage from first words to grammar. The question is how to characterize the dissociable mechanisms that underlie individual differences in language development. Will they break down along the "vertical," language-specific lines suggested by Modularity Theory? Or do the dissociations reflect a split between "horizontal" mechanisms that cut across cognitive domains?

We think that our results come down resoundingly in favor of an interactionist view of language development. Just as well, or this book would have to serve as a recantation of previous statements. But we have taken the modular point of view seriously, given it a run for its money, and pointed out some ways that the two theories could compete and perhaps converge at later stages of development. After all, in two separate volumes we have not yet gotten beyond the dawn of language, leaving our children long before their third birthdays. Children and believers in modularity still have a lifetime to find the crucial flaws in our approach.

ACKNOWLEDGMENTS

We owe our greatest debt to the parents and children who participated in this longitudinal study. As the reader will see, we have obtained very good evidence for the validity of parental reports in the study of early language. This occurred because the parents who collaborated with us listened to their children and knew them very well, and because they handled our endless queries with patience and insight.

We are also grateful to an army of graduate and undergraduate research assistants who helped us make the critical transition from video-taped observations to high quality data. The seven graduate students listed on the first page played a particularly important role in data collection. They are listed in an order that reflects the amount of time spent on the project, the closest we could come to a quantification of blood, sweat, and tears.

The long phase of data collection and preliminary analysis was carried out at the University of Colorado, supported by grants to Bates and Bretherton from the National Science Foundation and the Spencer Foundation. The even longer phase of final analyses and writing took place at the University of California, San Diego, with support from the John D. and Catherine T. MacArthur Foundation Research Network on the Transition from Infancy to Early Childhood, and from a grant to the senior author from the National Institute of Neurological and Communicative Disorders and Stroke.

There are those who participated in many other ways that are harder to describe. Our thanks go to Katherine Nelson, Ann Peters, and Catherine Snow for their response to an earlier version of the manuscript and for many fruitful conversations about the nature of individual differences in language development. Several other colleagues helped shape our thinking through creative opposition in long and lively debates about modularity, innateness, and the componential structure of mind. They each retain very different views from ours, and cannot be held responsible for a failure to dissuade us from the ideas presented here. But they deserve our thanks nonetheless. A partial list includes Ursula Bellugi, Melissa Bowerman, Eve Clark, Herb Clark, Angela Friederici, Howard Gardner, Judith Johnston, Brian MacWhinney, Jean Mandler, Michael Maratsos, Gabriele Miceli, David Rumelhart, Dan Slobin,

Lorraine Tyler, Virginia Volterra, Eric Wanner, and Edgar Zurif. Beverly Wulfeck and Barbara O'Connell took on far more tasks than they had time to do, to help this manuscript come into the world a little at a time. Finally, this book would never have been finished at all if George Carnevale had not made coffee, taken Julia to the zoo, shopped for groceries, and held his wife's hand when she was ready to give up the whole enterprise.

Part I
Background

Chapter 1
Introduction

Children do not all learn language the same way. It isn't just that some are slow and some are fast, or that some learn French and some learn Arabic. Rather, there seem to be some qualitatively different ways to make the transition from first words to grammar.

This finding came as a brutal surprise to many psycholinguists in the 1970s. It was surprising because of a series of nested assumptions and conclusions that had characterized child language research in the previous decade.

1. **Creativity.** Children are active and creative participants in the acquisition process. They make errors and innovations that cannot be found in their linguistic environment, in an apparent effort to forge a coherent albeit temporary theory of their language. Investigators may debate about the nature of the child's intermediate theories, e.g., whether they have to be represented in terms of rules and whether those rules are probabilistic or deterministic in nature (Rumelhart and McClelland, 1986; Pinker, 1986). But few students of child language would argue with the premise that children somehow go beyond the data provided by their caretakers.

2. **Predispositions.** Children can go beyond their data, because they are equipped with prior clues of some kind about the possible forms that a natural language can take. The debate then and now has focused not on the existence or nonexistence of these predispositions, but on their "domain specificity." Does the child come into the world with constraints on learning that are specific to the domain of language (e.g., Bickerton, 1984)? Or does s/he apply more general cognitive principles to the specific problems posed by language acquisition (e.g., Bates and MacWhinney, 1982)? In either case, the existence of prior constraints is recognized.

3. **Biological Bases.** Whether they are specifically linguistic or not, these predispositions must be based on some kind of biological structure shared by every normal member of the species. Whether or not other species share this structure to any interesting degree is a more

controversial matter, closely related to the domain-specificity issue. If our prior knowledge is uniquely linguistic in nature, it is probably unique to our species as well; if our prior knowledge is based on more general cognitive principles, then other species may share at least some part of that preparation for language (though apparently not enough to finish the task). In either case, however, we assume that these predispositions have a biological base.

4. **Universality.** Because these predispositions are biologically based, they should result in universal patterns of language acquisition, i.e., a linguistic embryogenesis of sorts. That is, we should all acquire language in the same way.

We believe that the first three conclusions are by now incontrovertible, nor are they challenged by new information on individual differences in language development. But the fourth assumption is clearly invalid. What is biological is not necessarily universal; and what is universal is not necessarily biological (Hardy-Brown, 1983). Biological factors can be responsible for variation across individuals (e.g., blue versus brown eyes). And environmental constraints can be responsible for attributes that all of us share (e.g., we all have to learn ways to adjust to gravity, as long as we are bound to planet Earth). And yet the psycholinguists' romance with biology has led to a profound belief in universal sequences of language development (Lenneberg, 1967; Dale, 1976; Slobin, 1979; Gleitman and Wanner, 1982). Differences in rate of development have always been expected. And we knew that some differences in content and structure would be partially dictated by the language that a particular child must learn. Until quite recently, however, we believed that universal stages would become apparent, once we were able to factor out the "local details" of acquisition within and across natural languages.

As pioneered by Slobin and his colleagues (e.g., Slobin, 1982 and 1985), cross-language research seemed to offer a powerful tool for separating universal from particular, like wheat from chaff, laying bare those aspects of development with a "true" biological base. And yet, as this research program has progressed, the particulars of acquisition across languages have begun to eclipse the universals that we first set out to find (Braine, 1976; Varma, 1979; Hakuta, 1982; Slobin and Bever, 1982; Erbaugh, 1982; Bates, McNew, MacWhinney, Devescovi, and Smith, 1982; Bates, MacWhinney, Caselli, Devescovi, Natale, and Venza, 1984; MacWhinney, 1986; Clark, 1985; Newport and Maier, 1985).

Even in the earliest stages of grammar, there are marked differences from one language to another in the nature of first word combinations (Braine, 1976; Bates, 1976; MacWhinney and Bates, 1978). For example, Turkish children seem to make productive use of case inflections from the very beginning of multiword speech—and perhaps slightly before, raising serious questions about the validity of the term "one-word stage" (Slobin, 1985). The same is true, to a lesser extent, for children acquiring Hindi (Varma, 1979) and Polish (Weist, 1983; Weist & Koniecanza, 1985). By contrast, Russian and Serbo-Croatian children seem to avoid acquiring grammatical morphology until they have exhausted a series of other possibilities (e.g., acting for a brief period as though they were acquiring a rigid word-order language like English—Slobin, 1979; Radulovic, 1975). English children tend to leave verbs out of their early telegraphic speech (Bloom, 1970); but Italians rarely omit the verb, preferring (like Italian adults) to omit the subject of the sentence (Bates, 1976; MacWhinney and Bates, 1978). And this is only a partial list of cross-language variation in very early grammar.

Children also differ radically, from language to language, in the strategies that they use to interpret adult sentences (Slobin and Bever, 1982; Bates et al., 1984; MacWhinney, Pleh, and Bates, 1985). For example, English children are sensitive to the meanings encoded by word order by 28 months of age (Bates et al., 1984) and may even be making a limited use of word order during the so-called one-word stage (Golinkoff, 1983; Golinkoff and Kerr, 1978). Turkish children attend to the case markings on nouns as a clue to sentence meaning from the earliest stages tested; they show no interest at all in word order until they are 4 or 5 years old, and even then word order plays only a very small role in their behavior. Serbo-Croatian, Hungarian, and Italian children offer a series of points between these two extremes. They ignore word order in sentence comprehension for many months or years, and word order never becomes their major source of information (Bates and MacWhinney, 1987; MacWhinney, Pleh, and Bates, 1985; Caselli and Devescovi, in preparation). However, they all seem to begin sentence processing by attending primarily to meaning, including a tendency to treat animate nouns as the agents of actions. The use of morphological cues comes in at different points in each language, depending on how difficult those cues are to perceive and to process in real time (Bates and MacWhinney, 1987).

To account for all this new information about cross-language variation, the search for universals has been reformulated in two ways.

First, insofar as universals can be stated at all, they are expressable in terms of a set of clues or hints about processing that help the child discover the peculiarities of his own language. Slobin (1973, 1979, 1985) discusses these universal processes in terms of a list of operating principles like "Pay attention to the ends of words." Bates and MacWhinney (1987) handle the same universal effects somewhat differently, explaining them in terms of garden variety notions like frequency, perceivability, memory load, and semantic transparency. In either case, however, there has been a shift in focus from *universal content* to *universal mechanisms* or *processes*.

Second, the very concept of a "universal" has been redefined, in ways that are compatible with Chomsky's (1981) notion of "parameter-setting" (see also Keenan, 1976; Slobin, 1985; Pinker, 1986; Hyams, 1983). According to the theory of parameter setting, natural languages vary too much in their basic structure to permit a definition of universals entirely in terms of some intersect, i.e., the set of structures that *every* language has to have. Linguists now speak of "implicational universals," a pool of structural possibilities in which any choice carries important structural consequences of the "If X, then Y" variety. Each individual language has charted a path through this set of possibilities; however, given the many implicational constraints within the system, the total set of possible pathways is finite, and rather small. Hence language acquisition can be viewed as a process of setting successive parameters and living with their preordained consequences, e.g., "Since my language seems to permit omission of sentence subjects, then the following constraints on pronoun use must follow. . . ." Biology provides the universal parameters; language input triggers a set of constrained choices within that pool of possibilities.

This new view of language universals permits much more variation across natural languages. However, it still predicts universal sequences *within* a given language. Parameters are set as soon as the relevant data are encountered, and by definition these must be data that are available to every child. Furthermore, once a parameter is set, there are no mechanisms for turning back; the child's linguistic future is determined. Given this situation, there is very little room for variation in the way that any single language is acquired. There may be variations in rate of development—either because a particular child is slow in attending to the input or because the environment is so impoverished that it takes longer for the critical information to appear. But the sequence and nature of development should be the same for every child acquiring that language.

What are we to do, then, with the discovery that English is not always acquired the same way? There is a textbook picture of early language development that goes as follows (e.g., Gardner, 1983, p. 79): Children begin with single words (especially names for things), and then pass through a telegraphic stage of first word combinations (with sentences made up of content words stripped of their morphology), and end in a burst of grammatical development in which bound morphemes and function words take their places among the major constituents of sentence structure like "ivy growing in between the bricks" (Brown, 1973). But subsequent research has revealed an uncomfortable number of exceptions to this supposedly universal pattern, even among middle class children acquiring standard dialects of English.

For example, Nelson (1973) found a wide range of variation in the one-word stage, in the content and structure of early vocabularies. Some children do begin primarily with names for things, plus a few routines like "bye-bye." Others begin with very heterogeneous vocabularies that defy any kind of orderly characterization by form class; furthermore, their "one-word" vocabularies often contain whole phrases. Bloom, Lightbown, and Hood (1975) reported a similar range of variation at the stage of first-word combinations. Some children do pass through a telegraphic stage, hooking together content words in their least marked form, with little if any use of grammatical morphology. Others use grammatical function words from the very beginning, referring to themselves and the listener in pronominal form, with variable use of bound morphology (see also Nelson, 1975). Research by Horgan (1981) suggested that early "noun lovers" carry their preferences over into the later stages of grammatical development, concentrating primarily on means for expanding noun phrases; early "noun leavers" remain uninterested in noun phrase development, concentrating primarily on verb morphology. And so on. As we shall see in more detail below, the list of linguistic features that vary markedly across children is now very long, covering aspects of phonology, syntax, morphology, semantics, and pragmatics. And the list of candidate explanations for these differences has grown accordingly.

For those who equate universality and biology, the only possible explanation for variation is *environmental*: Children learn language in different ways, because they receive different kinds of input. But we think that a study of individual variation can tell us even more about the *biological* substrates of language. In the studies described below, we are investigating individual differences in language development from 10 to 28 months of age, during the transition from first words to grammar. Our goal is to identify associations and dissociations, synchronies and asynchronies, packages of abilities that "hang together" over time. The underlying assumption in all this work is the following:

> Individual differences in language development can be brought about by the differential strength and/or differential timing of two or more underlying mechanisms responsible for language acquisition and language processing.

Hence individual differences in the *content* of early language development will ultimately lead to the identification of universal *mechanisms* responsible for that content. To paraphrase Kempler (1984, p. 1):

> Sometimes when things come apart, we can see more clearly how they were put together.

In pursuit of this goal, we will apply some of the techniques of psychometric theory to the analysis of language measures that are firmly grounded in recent child language research: measures of total comprehension and production, to be sure, but also measures of flexibility in the use of object naming, imitation and acquisition of novel words, semantic relations, utterance complexity, grammatical productivity, and qualitatively different "styles" of lexical and grammatical acquisition. We are not proposing that language is "caused" by mental age—although this possibility usually springs to mind as soon as the word "psychometrics" is mentioned. Rather, the very concept of general intelligence may need to be redefined when more is learned about its relationship to the different mechanisms responsible for language acquisition in the early stages. What we hope to show is that psychometric methods can be fruitfully applied to the study of language acquisition, using individual differences to tell us something interesting about the nature of the Language Acquisition Device (McNeill, 1970).

Using this method, we will show that the language processor can be decomposed into "natural" processing components that are at least partially dissociable in the course of normal language acquisition. This idea itself is hardly new. Various proposals for the "modular" status of language processing are available, and will be considered in some detail below. However, we believe that our conclusions about componential nature of language processing will come as a surprise to many linguists and psycholinguists. Languages have traditionally been analyzed into separate levels, corresponding roughly to phonology (the sound system), lexical semantics (the relationship between words and their meanings), and grammar (a set of principles for mapping meaning into sound). Following this tradition, psycholinguists have generally assumed the existence of language processors devoted to each level of linguistic structure, e.g., one or more phonological analyzers, one or more devices for handling lexical and relational semantics, and at least one parser (and perhaps several subsystems) for dealing with grammatical analysis. We will present evidence suggesting that children divide language up in an entirely different way, at least at the earliest stages of language learning. Mechanisms responsible for rote reproduction of forms can be separated from mechanisms for segmenting and analyzing the internal structure of those forms. Mechanisms responsible for comprehension can be dissociated from the mechanisms responsible for production. However, these partially dissociable mechanisms seem to cut across the traditional linguistic levels of grammar and semantics.

Because they are not uncontroversial, the *logical, methodological*, and *empirical* underpinnings of this work need to be spelled out in more detail before we can proceed. These are covered in the following three chapters.

In Chapter 2, we will present the logical grounds for this work in terms of what is currently called the "modularity hypothesis" (Chomsky, 1980, 1981; Fodor, 1983; Gardner, 1983). This will include a discussion of what linguists and psycholinguists mean by "the language faculty," and the "components," "modules," or "subsystems" that make up that faculty.

In Chapter 3, we will present the methodological grounds for the present study, discussing some uses and abuses of correlational research in language development, as a tool for investigating the underlying structure of the language processor.

In Chapter 4, we will provide some of the empirical groundwork for our current research in a review of the literature on individual differences in language development. This will lead directly into an overview of the design of our own longitudinal study.

The next twelve chapters each contain one substudy within the structure of our longitudinal project. When this journey is complete, we will return to the issues outlined in Chapters 2–4, summarizing what individual differences in early language have told us about language learning and the architecture of the Language Acquisition Device.

Chapter 2
Modules and Mechanisms

The research presented in this volume rests on two assumptions:

1. The language faculty has a componential structure. That is, it consists of identifiable and partially dissociable mechanisms for perceiving, learning, and using a natural language.
2. Individual differences in normal language development can be used to learn about the componential structure of the language faculty.

The first of these assumptions is fairly uncontroversial, though much blood has been shed over the nature of the components or modules that make up the language faculty (as we shall see in more detail below). The second assumption has a long and respectable history in psychology, but it is surprisingly unpopular among linguists and psycholinguists— particularly those linguists and psycholinguists who believe that language is "special," based on innate structures and processes that bear little resemblance to those that are required for garden variety learning and memory.

By embracing both of the above assumptions, we align ourselves with the so-called "faculty psychology" movement pioneered in the nineteenth century by Gall, carried over into intelligence testing in the twentieth century by Thurstone, Spearman, Cattell, and others (e.g., Thurstone, 1938; Spearman, 1937; Cattell, 1971; see Sternberg and Powell, 1983, for a review). Faculty psychology has undergone a modern revival, celebrated in an influential book called *Modularity of Mind* by Jerry Fodor (1983; see also Fodor, 1985). However, Fodor and many of his colleagues have taken great care to distance themselves from the psychometric tradition in faculty psychology, in particular from the multivariate statistical methods that first evolved to test claims about the componential structure of mind. In the next chapter, we will present a more detailed defense of the correlational method, and the ways in which that method can and cannot be applied in the study of language development. In this chapter, we want to present some historical background leading to the modern modularity movement, to clarify our own position on the role of individual differences in the study of mental structure.

Modularity versus Interactionism: Some Working Definitions

Let us begin with the following definition of modularity in modern cognitive psychology, with a particular emphasis on its implications for language development:

> Cognitive modules are self-contained components of mind. Each module can be characterized in terms of the processes and/or representations needed to operate in a specific content domain that is particularly important for the organism.

Several implications for language processing and language development follow from this definition. First, although modules may interact with one another in mature real-time processing, they are sufficiently bounded in time and space that they can develop independently in children (out of synchrony with other aspects of intelligence), and they can break down independently under various forms of brain damage. Second, claims about modularity can have several different loci. For example, they have been applied to the boundary between language and the rest of cognition, and to the boundaries between specified subcomponents of language (e.g., phonology, grammar, and lexical semantics). If these components and subcomponents define the seams and joints of a modular language processor, they should also be the units most likely to "come apart" when there are asynchronies in normal or abnormal language development.

As we shall see later, this is not the only possible form of the modularity argument. It is, for example, far less restrictive than the version proposed by Fodor (1983, 1985). But it is the most eclectic and widely recognized form of the argument, and the one that we will be testing here.

The opposite of this modular approach is usually called *interactionism*. Applied to the domain of language (where the opposition between interactionism and modularity is particularly clear), this approach can be summarized as follows:

> Language is an interactive system that depends crucially on processes and representations from a variety of cognitive domains. The acquisition of language will be shaped and timed by the emergence and development of these requisite cognitive systems.

For proponents of this interactionist view, language development may differ from other forms of learning in content and organization, but not in the processes that are applied to that content, i.e., a common stock of mechanisms for perception, storage, recognition, and retrieval of information. Hence interactive constraints on language development will apply not only to the emergence of single words and their meanings (a process that obviously has to depend on the contents of perception and cognition), but also to the more "strictly linguistic" areas of phonology and grammar.

Notice that there is really only a partial opposition between these versions of modularity and interactionism. An interactionist must accept the existence of general but nevertheless self-contained processes for perceiving, learning, and remembering. And to the extent that such general mechanisms have definable boundaries, asynchronous development is possible. In fact, there is no such thing as a totally *nonmodular* theory of mind, since this would be tantamount to the claim that mind and brain are unbounded objects with no internal structure whatsoever. Even the most rabidly empiricist/associationist approach to the mind must assume the existence of "tiny modules," i.e., nodes or stored responses that can be connected to one another via some kind of associative process (e.g., Hull, 1943). The argument between proponents of modularity and interactionism revolves instead around four much more subtle questions:

1. The size of the modules that are most relevant for human mental activity (i.e., micromodules and macromodules)
2. The extent to which those modules map onto familiar content domains like language, music, mathematics, spatial knowledge, face recognition
3. The nature and timing of interactions between mental modules (i.e., are modules completely encapsulated, or do they "leak?")
4. Whether modular structures are innate and/or hard-wired in the brain

The research on individual differences presented in this volume is most relevant to Questions 2 and 4.

Question 2. We will examine which component processes "come apart" in asynchronous language development. If the processes break down along language-specific lines (e.g., lexical versus grammatical development), there is more support for the domain specificity of language acquisition mechanisms. Alternatively, if asynchronies in normal language development reflect general components of processing (e.g., rote versus analytic modes of learning), we have more evidence for an interactionist approach.

Question 4. We will be examining the very first stages in language acquisition, in the passage from first words to grammar. It is possible for innate systems to "kick in" fairly late in development, e.g., the events associated with puberty. However, the converse is unlikely; if a dissociation between mechanisms is evident at the earliest stages of development, before experience has played a major role, the dissociation probably reflects innate and species-specific factors. To the extent that we find very early dissociations between language-specific components (e.g., lexical versus grammatical development), results are compatible with the argument that these components are innate and/or hard-wired. To the extent that these language-specific components fail to dissoci-ate in the early stages (despite evidence for dissociations among more general processing components), claims about the innate and hard-wired status of domain-specific modules are attenuated.

This brings us to a problem that will be crucial for the interpretation of our individual difference findings: the logical and empirical relationship between *modularity* and *nativism*. This important issue is best understood against an historical background.

Modularity and the Analogy-Anomaly Debate

Like almost everything else of interest in cognitive psychology, the debate between modularists and interactionists can be traced back to early Greek philosophy. With regard to the nature and origins of language, the Greeks were divided on two issues that tend to be conflated in the modern literature (Robins, 1968): Nature versus Con-vention, and Analogy versus Anomaly.

The Nature-Convention issue bears a striking resemblance to the modern nature-nurture controversy. The Stoics and the Skeptics argued that language is given in nature, an instinctual system that we know in the same way that we know how to walk and breathe. The Aristotelians argued, instead, that language is a product of human reason and social agreement. It is acquired through the senses, and passed on from one generation to another through demonstration.

The Analogy-Anomaly debate focused on a related but logically independent issue: the relationship between language and cognition. For the Analogists, including Aristotle, language was viewed as a lawful sys-tem produced by the powers of human reason. They believed, for exam-ple, that there are reasons why particular words are assigned to their meanings, even though the rational origins of the word-referent link may have become opaque with time and use. To prove their point, they set about trying to uncover the rational underpinnings of apparently arbi-trary sound-meaning relationships. For example, they noted that the name Poseidon seems to decompose (at least obliquely) into the Greek words for "foot" and "sea"; for this reason, then, it is reasonable to assign this particular name to the God of the Sea. In contrast, the Anomalists (including the Stoics and the Skeptics) argued that language is neither lawful nor rational in its structure. It is an arbitrary system that cannot be reduced to or explained by the principles of human reason. Hence language must be studied and described in its own right, *sui generis*.

Because of their stress on the rational nature of language, Analogists also tended to embrace the notion of Convention. If language is a rational system, produced by human reason, then it could certainly be acquired by the same powers of reason through a process of social transmission. Conversely, given their stress on the irrationality of language, Anomalists tended to accept the idea that the system is given in nature. As we shall see shortly, this alignment between Anomaly and nativism continues in the twentieth century, illustrated most clearly in the work of Chomsky and his followers (e.g., Chomsky, 1981; Gleitman, 1983; Pinker, 1982 and 1986; Wexler and Culicover, 1980). But the alignment is not logically necessary. That is, we can find nativist versions of the Analogy position, and nonnativist versions of the Anomaly position.

In Greek times, these two debates revolved primarily around the nature and origins of the link between words and their meanings. Why do we use this sound, and not some other sound, to stand for a particular object or event? There was much less interest in the nature and origins of grammar, i.e., the theme that has dominated modern linguistics and psycholinguistics. From our comfortable modern vantage point, we now know that the Anomalists were largely right on the sound-meaning issue, but the nativists were necessarily wrong. Languages vary enormously in the sounds that they assign to particular meanings (e.g., "dog," "chien," "cane," and "perro" can all refer to the same fuzzy mammal). There are some pockets of onomatopoeia in natural languages, i.e., sounds like "bang" or "sneeze" that bear a marginal resemblance to their meanings. In addition, the Analogists are partially right about the rational nature of the lexical processes that create word compounds. Productive compounds like "apple juice" and "shoemaker" have a transparent rational base. And we have learned through several centuries of etymological research that most complex words have an underlying structure. This structure can usually be traced to simpler elements that were once combined in a productive way, demonstrating that there is a certain amount of rationality/regularity of patterning in lexical history. But with regard to the origins and nature of lexical roots, it looks very much as though the Anomalists have won the argument: The relationship between root words and their meanings is arbitrary and irrational.

However, precisely because so many variants are possible in human natural languages, it is difficult to argue that word-referent relationships are given in nature. To account for the enormous variability in lexical assignments across natural languages, we have to conclude that the links between words and their meanings are established by convention and acquired through some form of social transmission. In other words, they have to be learned. Hence, even though the ancient Anomalists believed that the irrational language system is given in nature, the evidence suggests that they were wrong.

This break in the alignment between Anomaly and Nature was carried over into research on phonology and grammar in twentieth century American linguistics (e.g., Bloomfield, 1933). The American structuralist school grew up in response to a pressing historical need: to document the nature and variety of a large number of dying American Indian languages. Many of these languages were radically different in phonological and grammatical organization from the Indo-European languages that had dominated Western thinking, leading many members of the structuralist school to believe that the range of possible variation in human language may be infinite. They sought both a theory and a method that would fit with their conviction that the forms of language are arbitrary at every level of analysis.

The strongest possible form of this relativist view can be seen in the work of Benjamin Whorf (e.g., Whorf, 1956). According to the famous Whorfian hypothesis, the categories and boundaries of language determine the categories and boundaries of cognition and perception. And to the extent that languages can vary in their structure, human reason can vary accordingly. So, for example, if a given language has no word to mark the boundary between blue and green, a native speaker of that language will see blue and green as variations within a single continuously shaded color category. The linguistic determinism hypothesis runs directly counter to the Aristotelian view that language is determined by the universal properties of human reason. In its strong form, the Whorfian hypothesis is probably wrong (see Brown, 1968, for a discussion). But it is important historically in demonstrating just how far the Anomalist approach can be taken, within an epistemological framework emphasizing the role of the environment in determining the categories of thought and language.

In the second half of the twentieth century, the original alignment between Anomaly and nativism has been reintroduced by theorists concerned primarily with the nature and origins of grammar. For nigh on thirty years, Chomsky and his co-workers have tried to elucidate those properties of grammatical organization that are shared by natural languages (Chomsky, 1957, 1965, 1981). Although the issue is still controversial, there do appear to be certain general principles that are shared by human languages, enough to postulate the existence of a Universal Grammar (Bickerton, 1984).

The renewed belief in Universalism has brought about another lively version of the Analogy-Anomaly debate. Chomsky's theory of transformational grammar has undergone extensive revision (Chomsky 1957, 1965, 1981). Its most recent form, Government and Binding Theory, is radically different in many ways from the versions of transformational grammar that became familiar to psycholinguists in the sixties and seventies. But one principle has remained intact in every version of the theory: the autonomy of grammar. According to the autonomy doctrine, the categories and principles of grammar are completely independent from the categories and principles of semantics, pragmatics, and other related conceptual systems. The grammar has an exquisite and orderly internal structure, so in that sense it is neither irrational nor arbitrary. Nevertheless, grammatical structure is so eccentric and domain specific that it cannot be derived from or reduced to the principles of any other cognitive system. In that sense, this is a strong modern version of the Anomaly position. However, it differs from the Anomalist approach of the earlier American structuralists in two important ways. First, the grammar is based on universal principles that supposedly underlie all human languages. So the relativism of linguists like Bloomfield and Whorf is soundly rejected. Second, the grammar involves abstract structures and principles that cannot be derived through any kind of simple inductive procedure. In other words, it cannot be learned—unless the learner already knows a great deal about the target language, replacing inductive procedures with a deductive approach, based on a series of a priori hypotheses about the range of languages that could be "out there" (Wexler and Culicover, 1980). In this fashion, Chomsky follows the Stoics and the Skeptics, claiming that the anomalous structures of language are the way they are because they are given in nature.

Throughout his career, Chomsky has been at war with the empiricists, i.e., with those who claim that knowledge derives from the environment. The war began in his review of Skinner's *Verbal behavior* (Skinner, 1957; Chomsky, 1959). The battle raged again more recently in a published debate between Chomsky and Piaget (Piatelli-Palmerini, 1980). In our view, however, Chomsky's one great flaw lies in his inability to grasp the important differences that distinguish his opponents. There is very little of interest in common in the views of Piaget and Skinner, although both do indeed grant the environment a role in shaping the course of development. For Skinner, the role of the environment is an absolute, far stronger than any of the predispositions that the organism brings into the situation. For Piaget, the inherent structure of the organism at Time 1 is a critical determinant of the outcomes that are possible at Time 2, given any environmental input. Indeed, Piaget was pilloried by American behaviorists in the 1950s and 1960s, when his work began to disseminate in this country, precisely because he placed such a heavy emphasis on the role of organismic factors in learning.

We suggest that Piaget's views on language acquisition constitute a modern version of the Analogist view that language is an inherently rational system, a product of human reason. However, as we have argued elsewhere (Bates, Benigni, Bretherton, Camaioni, and Volterra, 1979), Piaget also offered a new kind of nativist approach to the structure of natural language. In other words, he represents an alignment between Analogy and Nature. Language is an innate system, but the innate outcomes do not require the operation of domain-specific factors.

To explain what we mean, let us offer just one metaphor from another part of the animal kingdom: the notorious stickleback fish (Tinbergen, 1951). The stickleback fish is famous for a rather eccentric characteristic, a zigzag dance that is performed during courtship. Tinbergen entertained two hypotheses about the possible source of this zigzag behavior, two different kinds of control mechanisms that could each bring about the same outcome. We can paraphrase these control systems crudely as follows:

1. **The hard-wired approach**. This kind of mechanism would operate by giving out precise instructions for each zig and each zag in the complete dance, e.g., "Move five centimeters to the right, then make a 90 degree turn to the left and move five centimeters, then make a 90 degree turn to the right and move five centimeters. . . . " Of course we assume that such instructions are unconscious and unverbalized. If they exist at all, they probably involve a set of low-level sensorimotor connections that are "triggered" by an internal organismic state. The point is that each eccentric detail in the zig-zag dance is insured by genetic factors.
2. **The by-product approach**. By this account, the zigzag outcome is the product of two much simpler approach and avoidance systems that are locked together in a way that insures their alternation, e.g., "I'm scared, I'm leaving. . . . I'm less scared, I'm attacking. . . . I'm scared again, I'm leaving. . . . " The zigzag dance itself is eccentric and species-specific, but the genetic route by which that outcome was attained involves very general factors that are shared by many species.

By a series of experimental manipulations designed to throw approach and avoidance motivations out of balance, Tinbergen was able to show that the complex dance does involve the juxtaposition of approach and avoidance states and their associated behavioral patterns. The stickleback "builds" its new adaptation by the interlocking of simpler, preexisting systems. Hence the zigzag dance is only *indirectly* innate, the emergent product of simpler inputs combined in a particular way.

Using biological metaphors of this kind, we have argued that the universal aspects of human language, including Universal Grammar, could derive from this kind of phylogenetic and ontogenetic pattern: simpler and more ancient cognitive and perceptual systems that come together in our species in a new way. Languages represent the full set of stable, workable solutions to a common set of problems encountered when we try to map particular nonlinear conceptual structures (e.g., reference, agent-action relations) onto a linear channel with certain perceptual, motor, and memory constraints. Universal aspects of language acquisition reflect the successive solutions that children find as the mapping effort develops and new problems are encountered (Bates and MacWhinney, 1979, 1982). This is a strong interactionist view that may be entirely wrong. But it is not an inherently "antibiological" approach, as its critics sometimes claim (e.g., Gleitman, 1983; Curtiss and Yamada, 1978). The route that children take in acquiring language is strongly conditioned by biological factors. However, those factors are not necessarily domain specific—even though their effects may be seen most clearly in the language domain. In other words, we are trying to separate the questions of innateness and domain specificity.

Our views on innateness and domain specificity developed through the 1970s, before the most recent version of the modularity argument emerged in the literature. The debates on Analogy versus Anomaly and on Nature versus Convention have now been recast in a somewhat different language. In particular, Chomsky's views on the autonomy of language have been refined and extended to other aspects of cognitive functioning—including spatial relations, face recognition, and many other candidates for an autonomous, modular mental status. In the process, investigators have become much more precise in their efforts to characterize the difference between modular and nonmodular systems. As a result, we are closer to an empirical test of these very old ideas. Let us move on now to examine some alternative versions of the modern modularity position, to see exactly where we stand on the issue.

Modularity in Modern Times

Fodor (1985, p. 3) provides the following rather opaque definition of a psychological module:

> A module is (inter alia) an informationally encapsulated computational system—an inference-making mechanism whose access to background information is constrained by general features of

cognitive architecture, hence relatively rigidly and relatively permanently constrained. One can conceptualize a module as a special-purpose computer with a proprietary database. . . . It is a main thesis of *Modularity* that perceptual integrations are typically performed by computational systems that are informationally encapsulated in this sense.

This definition resembles the one we provided earlier in its emphasis on domain-specificity (i.e., "informationally-encapsulated" and "proprietary"). The species-specific nature of a module is also underscored by terms like "special-purpose" and "rigidly and relatively permanently constrained." Notice, however, that Fodor is restricting his discussion to *perceptual* modules. In applying the doctrine of modularity to language acquisition, we will instead examine aspects of both comprehension and production.

In Fodor (1983), we find the same stress on perceptual mechanisms. But the concept of modularity is much more loosely defined, through a lengthy list of characteristics that could apply to both sensory and motor systems (and to some integrated systems responsible for both sensory and motor computations within a single domain). To highlight his preferred version of the modularity argument, Fodor distinguishes four different approaches to the componential structure of mind. These are worth reviewing, because they have very different implications for the work to be presented here.

Fodor's least favorite approach is the "associationist account," an antimodular view of mind as an unbounded set of myriad tiny units connected through a large web of associations (e.g., Hebb, 1949; Hull, 1943). This is the view presumed to underlie Spearman's notion of general intelligence or "g" (Spearman, 1937), and Lashley's twin concepts of "equipotentiality" and "mass action" in the relationship between brain and behavior (Lashley, 1950). Some version of associationism or connectionism can be found in theories of learning and memory since Hull, including such recent formulations as Anderson and Bower's Human Associative Memory (Anderson and Bower, 1973), various proposals involving Spreading Activation Networks (e.g., Loftus and Loftus, 1976), and modern theories of Parallel Distributed Processing (Rumelhart and McClelland, 1982, 1986). Without belaboring Fodor's own criticisms of the associationist approach, we find it difficult to imagine how an unconstrained connectionist theory could account for qualitative differences in language development, except by recourse to some heavy-handed form of environmental shaping. Connectionism has to be constrained in some fashion to account for the fact that the same input can result in qualitatively different patterns of learning from one child to another (Bates and MacWhinney, 1986; McClelland and Rumelhart,

1986). When such constraints are offered, they tend to incorporate at least one of the remaining three approaches to modularity outlined by Fodor.

The next approach, which Fodor attributes to Chomsky, is "Neocartesianism" or "the structure of the mind viewed as the structure of knowledge." According to Fodor, Chomsky views our innate predisposition to learn language in terms of *content* rather than *process*.

> It turns out, upon examination, that what Chomsky thinks is innate is primarily *a certain body of information*: the child is, so to speak, "born knowing" certain facts about universal constraints on possible human languages. It is the integration of this innate knowledge with a corpus of "primary linguistic data" (e.g., with the child's observations of utterances produced by adult members of its speech community) that explains the eventual assimilation of mature linguistic capacities. (p. 4)

This particular account of mental structure is quite compatible with cross-linguistic differences in language acquisition, according to the parameter-setting theory outlined earlier. But it is also hard to reconcile with the literature on individual differences within a single language. If linguistic content is universal, then differences must necessarily reside in the child's primary linguistic data. There is no mechanism that would permit such differences to originate inside the child.

In the two remaining accounts, the boundaries of mind are located at the level of *process*, or more specifically, *processors*. Here Fodor distinguishes between *horizontal faculties* and *vertical faculties*. He defines a horizontal faculty as a "functionally distinguishable cognitive system whose operations cross content domains." Putative mechanisms like "short term memory" or "judgment" are typical examples. By contrast, a vertical faculty is a mechanism or processor that has developed to meet the demands of one particular bounded domain of knowledge. The so-called language organ is a paradigm case, but others might include face recognition, and whatever mechanism handles information about three-dimensional space.

Fodor's notion of vertical faculties corresponds almost exactly to Gardner's (1983) concept of multiple intelligences, and both books are devoted primarily to a characterization of this last type of module. Neither of these theorists denies the possibility that a certain amount of horizontal architecture exists. But they find it relatively uninteresting and largely irrelevant to a characterization of our most important mental organs—in particular human language.

If the language processor can be characterized in terms of *modular processes*, rather than *modular content*, the individual differences observed in language acquisition could shed light on the horizontal and/or vertical nature of these modules. If these modules do have a biological base in the developing central nervous system, it should be possible (at least in principle) for one subsystem to mature slightly out of synchrony with another. This could occur entirely because of innate differences in timing; or the slight asynchrony might be encouraged by differences in the environmental conditions that "trigger" or support one system versus another. Regardless of the cause, asynchronies in the development of universal mechanisms should be observable in asynchronies among the linguistic and/or nonlinguistic behaviors controlled by those mechanisms.

Gardner agrees explicitly with this conclusion and lists it among his eight criteria for the identification of a separate intelligence. Let us review his criteria briefly, to determine how they might apply to individual differences in the development of language.

1. **An identifiable core operation or set of operations.** Linguists have already determined that certain domains of language can be effectively described as separate systems, e.g., phonology, syntax, semantics, and pragmatics. The fact that languages are easier to describe if we can break them down into pieces leads to the suggestion that such divisions are "natural," i.e., not just properties of the linguist, but properties of the mechanism(s) responsible for language. Whether or not children will see things that way is a separate issue (and one that we will address here).

2. **Susceptibility to encoding in a symbol system.** This criterion is related to the last one, revolving around the identifiability and "describability" of a given domain. In this case, however, Gardner is talking not about the operations identified by specialists, but about the symbol systems that we have developed for ourselves to cope with different kinds of content. This includes language, musical notation, and mathematical symbols for describing spatial relations. If mankind has had to develop a special system of representation to describe a domain, perhaps that domain is "unique" in some natural and organic way. We will simply accept this criterion as a given, but one that is less relevant to research on very young children.

3. **An evolutionary history and evolutionary plausibility.** Modular or bounded systems are more likely to have appeared quite suddenly in evolution (all of a piece). The same is true of systems that appear in only a few related species, as though one either does or does not choose to develop such a mechanism (i.e., there is no such thing as half a module). As Gardner notes, "this is an area where sheer speculation is especially tempting, and firm facts especially elusive."

It is, in any case, one that we will not address here (but see Bates et al., 1979, for a further discussion of ontogeny and phylogeny in language development).

4. **Potential isolation by brain damage.** "To the extent that a particular faculty can be destroyed, or spared in isolation, as a result of brain damage, its relative autonomy from other human faculties seems likely." (p. 63) We will go back to this criterion later, comparing our findings with normal children to evidence for dissociability of language functions in the aphasia literature.

5. **The existence of idiots savants, prodigies, and other exceptional individuals.** Of particular interest here are some rare reports of retarded children who develop language far in advance of their general cognitive level. This is another criterion that we will examine in more detail later, for comparison with data on normal children.

6. **Support from experimental psychological tasks.** Here Gardner invokes techniques that are relevant primarily to research on adults, showing that one particular content area (e.g., syntax) can be impervious to or encapsulated from information in another content area (e.g., semantics or phonology). This is another area to which we will return much later, for comparison with our own findings on normal children.

7. **A distinctive developmental history, along with a definable set of expert "end-state" performances.** Gardner introduces a potpourri of developmental issues here, concerning the degree to which a given domain can pull ahead or fall behind in normal development. This is certainly germane to our enterprise, since this kind of developmental asynchrony is presumed to underlie individual differences in language.

8. **Support from psychometric findings.** This is the most relevant criterion for our purposes, and the point of greatest disagreement between Gardner and Fodor. Support for the structural integrity of a modular process is provided "To the extent that the tasks that purportedly assess one intelligence correlate highly with one another, and less highly with those that purportedly assess other intelligences."

Gardner's last criterion is entirely consonant with the approach to the identification of mental faculties taken by Gall and Thurstone. Both investigators used variation among individuals as a means of identifying "packages" of mental abilities. In his long battle with Spearman, Thurstone (1938) tried to prove the evanescence of "general intelligence" on strictly empirical grounds, showing that intelligence tests invariably factor down into (at least) seven separate sources of variance. Spearman worked just as hard to show that tests of purportedly separate mental faculties share enormous amounts of variance when scores are subjected to factor analysis. It is now a truism in differential psychology that both men were right and both men were wrong (Sternberg and Powell, 1983; Carroll, 1985). A battery of intelligence tests, properly administered, can usually be shown to yield an hierarchical structure: a significant proportion of shared variance (Spearman's "g"), qualified by orthogonal factors and subfactors that stubbornly refuse to go away. The oft-cited division between verbal and visual-spatial intelligence is a case in point—a conclusion reached in the psychometric literature long before we developed theories of "left-brain" and "right-brain" processes that provide a neural basis for such a division. In our view, this hierarchical approach to individual differences is entirely compatible with Fodor's useful distinction between horizontal and vertical faculties (see also Carroll, 1985).

Fodor disagrees. To see exactly how and why he disagrees, let us compare his list of modularity criteria with Gardner's. There are in fact two lists: one set of general characteristics (largely analytic in nature) and a second, much more concrete set of empirical criteria. The first set is briefly summarized as a set of questions that we can ask about modules: Are they domain specific, or do they operate across content domains (i.e., are they vertical or horizontal)? Are they innate, or are they formed by some kind of learning process? Must they be "assembled" from a stock of elementary units, or are they mapped directly into their neural implementation? And insofar as they do have a neural implementation, are they hard-wired (i.e., localized in different parts of the brain)? Finally, is the system computationally autonomous (unaffected by the resources or lack of resources in other systems), or must they share horizontal resources?

From this a priori set of questions, Fodor moves on to derive nine criteria that have a more direct empirical test, and spends the rest of the book exploring their consequences. Each of these nine criteria should permit us to identify what he calls an "input system," i.e., a special-purpose device for analyzing the information relevant to a particular content area. Only a subset of these are relevant to developmental work, so we will risk oversimplification and review the list briefly.

1. **Domain specificity.** Once again, a true vertical faculty or input system should be specialized for one kind of content.
2. **Mandatory operation.** Once an input system is up and running, it will (like a sneezing reflex) obligatorily respond to the stimuli in its domain no matter what else is going on around it.
3. **Limited access to mental representations.** The inner workings of a modular input system should be very hard to "think about" or subject to consciousness (just as it is difficult to think about the features

that go into recognition of a familiar face, or the various bits of information that comprise perception in three dimensions).

4. **Speed.** Because information is handled efficiently by special-purpose devices that need not consult the rest of mind, modular input systems work very fast.

5. **Informational encapsulation.** Not only is it difficult to get information *out* of the intermediate stages of a modular processor (criterion #3), it is also difficult to get information *in*. Instead, we have to wait until the module is finished and then either accept or reject its product.

6. **Shallow outputs.** Modular input systems hand out simple, shallow products, often of the yes/no or go/stay variety. This makes sense, because if an input system handed us a complete report of everything it did, it would no longer be efficient or useful. Indeed it would no longer be a module.

7. **Neural architecture.** Modular input systems are associated spatiotemporally with particular, fixed areas of the brain.

8. **Characteristic patterns of breakdown.** Because modules tend to be localized in the brain, they break down in very specific ways. They can be, for all practical purposes, selectively eliminated and/or selectively spared.

9. **Characteristic pace and sequencing in ontogeny.** Modules tend to appear, develop, and reach adult levels of functioning on a fixed schedule. This criterion, of course, is absolutely critical to a developmental study of individual differences in language.

There is a peculiar cleavage in Fodor's list of nine criteria. The first six characteristics are typical of all overlearned skills: typing, driving, skiing, working on an assembly line, etc. They are the characteristics that define the difference between *automatic* and *controlled* processes, a difference that can be induced experimentally in the laboratory for any arbitrarily specified set of perceptual-motor behaviors (Shiffrin and Schneider, 1977; Posner and Snyder, 1975; Norman and Shallice, 1980). The last three characteristics are, by fiat, biological ones, and surely are not relevant to learning to tie one's shoes or driving home from work. Fodor has essentially grafted six criteria that are true of many *learned* systems onto three criteria that define *innate* systems, to describe the kind of system that he finds interesting.

Nevertheless, we believe that *all* of these nine criteria are compatible with a correlational methodology. That is, they all lead to the prediction that the behaviors associated with modular systems should "hang together" or correlate with one another more than they correlate with behaviors controlled by other systems. And yet Fodor insists that modularity is a property of differences between *species*, but not differences between *individuals*—unless those individuals have suffered some kind of brain damage. He criticizes Gall for failing to make this point, as follows:

> Gall's fascination with, and insistence upon, degrees of individual difference is a most striking feature of his writings. Yet it sits badly with another of Gall's favorite themes: the repeated analogizing of faculties to instincts. . . . To put it in a nutshell, what is instinctive is genetically determined, but the reverse clearly doesn't have to hold. In fact, if what you have in mind by a vertical faculty is something like what the ethologist has in mind by an instinct, you probably will *not* want to postulate vertical faculties corresponding to parameters of individual differences; not even where such differences are inherited. On the contrary, in the study of instincts, the natural theoretical idealization is to a genetically and neurologically homogeneous population; instincts are forms of *species*-specific behavior. If one takes the analogy between instincts and fundamental powers seriously, one must suppose—precisely contrary to the methodology that Gall endorses—that vertical faculties are to be inferred from the discovery of competences that are relatively *in*variant across subject populations. (p. 20)

On the basis of this passage, we can see why Gardner and Fodor, agreeing on almost everything else, part company on the applicability of individual differences in normals to the discovery of mental modules. Fodor, astute observer that he is, is certainly not guilty of equating biology and universality. However, as far as he is concerned, individual differences are simply not interesting even if they do have a biological base: "Aptitude for baseball playing, even if inherited, is patently not interestingly like an instinct" (p. 20).

At the same time, however, Fodor does believe that individual cases are relevant, if dissociations are created by some kind of neural pathology. The paradigm case is, of course, language breakdown in aphasia, a phenomenon that has been used for many years to argue strongly in favor of (1) dissociations between language and the rest of cognition, and (2) dissociations within the language processor, in particular between grammar and semantics (Caramazza and Berndt, 1978, in press; Zurif and Blumstein, 1978; Zurif and Caramazza, 1976). Presumably the aphasia evidence is admissable, while individual differences in normals are not admissable, because we know that the former involves an insult to the brain's hard-wired neural architecture. Fodor seems to be assuming that the range of variation observed in normal individuals does *not* involve variations in neural architecture. But do we really know enough to make that assumption? It is entirely possible (as Gall believed) that differences among normal individuals are produced by asynchronies and/or asymmetries in the development of "mental organs" (to use Chomsky's favorite term). In fact, we will show later that the dissociations observed among normal children bear a nontrivial resemblance to patterns of breakdown observed in adult aphasia.

In short, we think that Fodor's dislike of research on individual differences in normals is based entirely on aesthetic criteria, and not on sound scientific argumentation. The key word is "interesting," a word that recurs every time Fodor confronts the difference between innate and learned systems. He admits the strength and nature of this aesthetic bias in the following passage (Fodor, 1985, p. 5):

> All these ideas imply a sort of relativistic holism. . . . The thing is: I *hate* relativism. I hate relativism more than I hate anything else, excepting, maybe, fiberglass powerboats. What it overlooks, to put it briefly and crudely, is the fixed structure of human nature. [italics Fodor's]

This kind of aesthetic is perfectly understandable. Asked why she so *dislikes* the notion of domain specificity, one of our authors has been known to respond that she "hates obscurantism," i.e., a kind of academic scorched earth policy whereby one proves the domain specificity of one's subject matter by casting it in opaque and impenetrable terms. But with all due respect, we see no reason why anyone should be influenced in their choice of methodology by this kind of aesthetic bias.

Assuming for the moment that there is an innate vertical faculty for language, how might it be organized? There is in fact little agreement on this point. For example, Fodor discusses a single "language module" without regard to the possible structure of subsystems within language. In fact, he quite explicitly argues that lexical semantics falls "inside" the language module. Hence debates about the dissociability of grammar and semantics are relatively unimportant in Fodor's version of the argument. This is actually ironic, since the MIT version of modularity owes so much historically to Chomsky's position on the autonomy of grammar. Furthermore, in the opening pages of *Modularity of Mind*, Fodor credits Merrill Garrett with inspiring the whole effort in Garrett's remark that "Parsing is just a reflex" (1983, p. iv).

Gardner places his bets differently, opting for the existing of submodules within the language faculty:

> Syntactic and phonological processes appear to be special, probably specific to human beings, and unfolding with relatively scant need for support from environmental factors. Other aspects of language,

however, such as the semantic and pragmatic domains, may well exploit more general human information-processing mechanisms and are less strictly or exclusively tied to a "language organ" (p. 81).

Compared with either Fodor or Gardner, Chomsky draws a much finer set of vertical boundaries within the language faculty. For example, he would separate the module that handles thematic relations (i.e., "who did what to whom") from modules that deal with interpretation of pronouns and assignment of co-reference relations within a sentence. Indeed, the list of candidate modules changes in each successive version of Chomsky's grammatical theory, as more and more evidence accrues regarding the nature of Universal Grammar.

In short, even though the concept of modularity is currently quite fashionable, there is little consensus regarding the nature of linguistic modules. The doctrine is greatly in need of more empirical work to determine which boundaries are relevant to natural language processing, and to the various stages of language development.

Modularity—Where We Stand

The work presented here falls squarely within the tradition of faculty psychology, or modularity as it is currently known. However, in our search for the component processes that control individual differences in language, we are open with regard to the horizontal or vertical nature of these dissociable mechanisms. In contrast with the explicit "vertical" biases of most modern proponents of modularity, we have been engaged in a search for horizontal modules, i.e., component processes that language shares with other aspects of cognition, and processes that grammar shares with phonology, lexical semantics, and pragmatics. In other words, we think horizontal architecture is "interesting."

Fodor has argued that cognitive science is doomed if the mind is not best characterized by vertical modules. Because their boundaries are knowable, vertical modules are amenable to study. By contrast, horizontal faculties of mind are so vague and unbounded that they present intractable problems for empirical investigation. We believe otherwise. Progress *can* be made in the study of horizontal mental architecture, if we have a reasonable theory to guide that research and if we can identify promising areas of development where the operation of horizontal modules is revealed.

In our earlier work on the passage from gesture to the first word, we concentrated on the boundary that Fodor places between language and nonverbal cognition (Bates, Camaioni, and Volterra, 1975; Bates, Benigni, Bretherton, Camaioni, and Volterra, 1977 and 1979; Bates,

Bretherton, Shore, and McNew, 1983; Bates and Snyder, 1987). The work was inspired by Piaget's claim that language emerges at the end of the sensorimotor period as just one manifestation of a more general symbolic function with implications for many other aspects of cognition (e.g., inferred causality and spatial relations, deferred imitation, mental imagery, symbolic play—cf. Piaget, 1962). There is of course no known (or acceptable) method for excising the hypothetical symbolic function and observing its effects on verbal and nonverbal domains. Hence the only methodology open to proponents of the Piagetian view is correlational: When language first appears, what other cognitive functions are reliably by its side? And if language is delayed, what other cognitive functions are notably lacking in the child's performance? Using this methodology, we were forced to a revision of Piaget's original claims. The relationship between very early language development and nonverbal cognition appears to involve what we called *local homology*, i.e., a series of skill-specific relationships that hold only for certain *aspects* of language and cognition, at certain points in development. For example, the emergence of single words is predicted by (1) earlier reorganizations in gestural communication (e.g., pointing, giving, showing), (2) the age of emergence of tool use and means-end relations (changes between 9 and 11 months that predict linguistic performance at 10–13 months), (3) the concomitant emergence of "gestural naming," i.e., recognitory gestures with familiar objects (e.g., drinking from an empty cup, putting a shoe to one's foot), and (4) some limited aspects of vocal and gestural imitation. Aspects of early cognition that did *not* predict the emergence of naming included spatial relations and object permanence—thus raising problems for the classical Piagetian notion of a unified stage shift from sensorimotor to representational functioning (see also Corrigan, 1978; Fischer, 1980).

We concluded that several different "modules" or mechanisms contribute to the passage from preverbal communication to the productive use of naming: the social factors that underlie preverbal gestural communication, the analytic mechanisms responsible for early tool use (which also contribute to aspects of preverbal communication), and the imitative mechanisms that permit the child to pick up arbitrary symbol-referent bonds in language and in symbolic play. These factors all play a role in the emergence of symbols, but they seem to involve partially dissociable sources of variance. Since these earlier studies, we have found evidence for other unique relationships between language and cognitive development, including a shift from single to multigesture symbolic play that seems to accompany the passage from single to multiword speech at 20 months of age (Shore, O'Connell, and Bates, 1984; Shore, 1986). All of these very specific findings challenge the notion that "All is one," and everything changes together in cognitive development. At the same time, they suggest that reorganizations in early language reflect factors that cut across cognitive domains, i.e., what Fodor would call "horizontal modules."

We are not trying to argue that this is a particularly elegant example of cognitive research. But it does show that general claims about the horizontal architecture of mind can be tested, and falsified. In this volume, we take up the horizontal/vertical question again. But this time, we are looking entirely within the general domain of language, trying to identify and characterize the factors that operate during the passage from single words to grammar. In our review of the literature on individual differences in language, a variety of candidate horizontal and vertical faculties will present themselves, as explanations for the patterns of dissociation observed in early language learning. The four with the most important implications for current controversies about modularity are the following:

1. **Grammar versus semantics**, an explicitly vertical form of dissociation, referring entirely to a division between components of the language processor.
2. **Form versus function**, another language-specific form of dissociation, though it is one that blurs some traditional lines between linguistic content areas (where phonology and syntax may be regarded as components of form, while semantics and pragmatics are regarded as components of meaning or function—see above citation from Gardner).
3. **Comprehension versus production**, a dissociation that may or may not be restricted entirely to language, but one which certainly cuts across linguistic components like phonology, semantics, and grammar.
4. **Rote versus analytic processing**, an explicitly horizontal kind of dissociation, involving many aspects of cognitive processing other than language proper.

We have given a fair test to these and several other candidate explanations for patterns of individual variation among normal children. However, the results come down clearly in favor of horizontal modules: dissociations among comprehension and production, rote and analytic processing, but no evidence whatsoever for early dissociations between the traditional content domains of language (in particular grammar versus semantics). If proponents of modularity accept our methodology, they should accept the work presented here as evidence *against* an innate or in any case an early dissociation between linguistic modules. Instead, asynchronies in early language development seem to involve processes that cut across the various subdomains of language.

But in fact many proponents of a nativist and language-specific version of the modularity hypothesis quite pointedly do *not* accept our methodology—which brings us to the next chapter, where we will do our level best to explain and defend the use of correlational statistics to ask interesting questions about the structure of a developing mind.

Chapter 3
Individual Differences and the Correlational Method

Once reliable, believable patterns of association and dissociation are established, we can use those patterns as clues to the identification of separate underlying processing mechanisms in language acquisition. Multivariate statistics are crucial to this enterprise, permitting us to distinguish between true correlation and mere coincidence. We have been surprised, however, at the resistance that many colleagues in child language have shown to correlational techniques (e.g., Harris, 1983). It may be useful to consider for a moment why this is the case, so that we can clarify exactly what can and cannot be learned from the techniques adopted here.

There is probably no area in developmental psychology that is further removed from the psychometric tradition than the study of child language. Since the early 1960s, training in child language research has emphasized both the methods and theories of formal linguistics and/or linguistic anthropology; there has been considerably less emphasis on quantitative techniques. A check through randomly selected issues of *The Journal of Child Language* will reveal how little use of statistics characterizes research in our field, compared, for example, with comparable issues of *Child Development*.

There are good reasons why this situation has persisted. For one thing, many investigators identify correlational techniques with the "bad old days" from the 1930s to the 1950s, when child language research was essentially atheoretical, and empirical studies often consisted of a "shot-gun search" for correlational relationships among such variables as total number of words produced, birth order, and social class (see McCarthy, 1954, for a representative review). Furthermore, for many of the questions that interest child language researchers, there has been no need for high powered inferential statistics. Roger Brown's book, *A First Language* (1973), showed us how much can be learned from detailed descriptions of naturalistic data for only three children. This landmark work has served as a prototype for research inside and outside of English, in virtually any new content area that has arisen within the field.

31

But child language researchers are beginning to ask different questions—about the range of variation that is possible within a given population. These questions require a methodology that is familiar to many of our colleagues but relatively unfamiliar and indeed unwelcome within our own field. It is pointless to insist that hammers are more important than handsaws. No single tool is adequate to all tasks. For some questions, the use of descriptive techniques with small samples is precisely the way to begin. For others, we are forced to use larger samples, turn our observations into numbers, and manipulate those numbers with correlations, multiple regression, and other multivariate techniques.

Let us first consider some questions for which inferential statistics are generally unnecessary. In the classic small-sample studies (e.g., Brown, 1973; Miller and Ervin, 1964; Braine, 1976), three kinds of issues predominate.

1. **Sequencing and timing of different forms.** An excellent example here is Brown's work on the sequence of acquisition for fourteen basic English morphemes. Although this sequence was originally derived from only three children, it that was replicated later by DeVilliers and DeVilliers (1973) with a much larger sample. Furthermore, a similar sequence is found in adults acquiring English as a second language—a surprising finding that poses a challenge to many extant theories of first versus second language acquisition (Dulay and Burt, 1974; Hakuta and Diaz, in press).

2. **Intermediate stages in the acquisition of single forms.** In studying the acquisition of a single adult form (e.g., Bellugi, 1967, on the acquisition of negation in English), it has often proven useful to identify one or more "precursors," early versions that represent the child's first approximations of the adult target. Sometimes the intermediate forms are ungrammatical from an adult point of view (e.g., "Why not cracker can't talk?"). In other cases, the child relies on simpler substitute forms that are functionally related to a more complex acquisition target. For example, one child studied by Slobin and Welsh (1973) was asked to imitate embedded sentences like "A boy who cried came to my party;" she reproduced the target sentence by substituting a sentence with two simple conjoined clauses, e.g., "A boy cried and he came to my party." Whether or not every child produces the same intermediate versions of a given target form is really beside the point. Any detailed formal model of the learning process should be able to account for single case studies like these.

3. **Error patterns.** Prior to full mastery of a form—or in some cases, after a period of appropriate and error-free performance—children begin to make creative errors that seem entirely unrelated to their

language input. Overgeneralizations like "foots" or "goed" are common examples. There are, however, many more elaborate examples of errors and outright inventions in grammar and semantics that provide clues to the operation of deep analytic processes and theory-building procedures in the child (Bowerman, 1982; Clark, 1983; Karmiloff-Smith, 1979). For these illustrative but rare events, statistical techniques are often out of the question. Each individual example constitutes a challenge that must be accounted for by any theory of language acquisition.

Precisely because these initial studies have been so successful, they have led to another set of questions: How general are the errors, intermediate forms, and acquisition sequences uncovered in case studies? And what are the causal mechanisms that underlie these patterns? Why do certain sequences occur in language acquisition? Why does A precede B, and why do C and D invariably come in together? The best way to determine cause and effect relationships is to manipulate a putative cause directly and observe its effect on other events. But in child language research, we rarely have either the knowledge or the power necessary for true experimental tests. More often, we must infer cause from the co-occurrence between events—events that happen simultaneously, and/or events that occur in a reliable sequence. More specifically, we must examine the shared properties of naturally co-occurring events to infer something about the mechanisms responsible for their timing.

Haven't we all been taught that correlation and cause are not the same thing? A number of old chestnuts are cited to make this point, e.g., the correlation between foot size and mental age, or the correlation between Amy Carter's height and the rate of inflation in the late 1970s. The point of these examples is that foot size could not possibly cause mental age, and the rise in Amy Carter cannot be held responsible for the concomitant rise in prices. There are, however, more subtle causal inferences that are not so outlandish. Foot size and mental age are undoubtedly related to one another via some third causal mechanism (e.g., rate of maturation). And the correlation between Amy Carter's height and the rate of inflation is no accident: Both were chosen because they were known to change across the shared tenure of her father's administration. Some observers believe that only one of these variables is *caused* by Carter's administration; others believe that *neither* change is causally related to Carter's policies. But both are tightly bound to a common temporal reference point and were selected to reflect that reference point. So the covariance between the measures is in fact not random.

The point is this: One *can* infer cause from correlation, but only within the framework of a complex model of reciprocal causal influences, together with a large amount of information about the properties that the correlated variables do and do not have in common. Patterns of correlation do not in themselves constitute a theory. But they can be interpreted and used within well-structured theories. And they may help us move beyond description to mechanisms.

To offer a chestnut of our own, consider the set of primary and secondary sex characteristics that define the global event called "puberty." These events are unquestionably intercorrelated. Moreover, some of them (e.g., budding breasts) reliably precede the others (e.g., the onset of menstruation). Using this example, we can respond to some of the more common criticisms of correlational research as follows:

Correlation is not cause. Indeed, we cannot conclude that budding breasts cause menstruation, despite the sequential and correlational information at our disposal. But we can conclude that they form part of an interesting system.

Just because two variables are correlated does not mean that they are the same thing. Of course the disparate content areas that constitute puberty are not "the same thing." Many different subsystems are involved, each with its own intrinsic properties and causal mechanisms (e.g., axillary hair, mammary glands, ovaries). They are, however, all apparently sensitive to some common triggering mechanism. In that sense, they do constitute an abstract entity of sorts.

When everything is changing at the same time, correlations are not interesting. This is the criticism that really underlies the mental age and foot size example. Since children are getting better at everything over time, of what possible use is correlational research (e.g., Harris, 1983)? The puberty example helps here as well. The set of events that make puberty unique are certainly correlated with general rate of maturation. However, the particular components of the puberty system are correlated with *one another* much more strongly than they are with the rest of the developing body. One could, in principle, partial out the variance shared with the rest of maturation and still find significant correlations among the primary and secondary sex characteristics of puberty.

In sum, correlation can be used to identify variables that form a system. This includes correlations that are defined *synchronically* (e.g., X and Y always come in together) and correlations that are defined *diachronically* (e.g., high levels of X are usually followed by high levels of Y). Once the system has been identified, we can examine the properties the various components have in common to figure out exactly why they work together. For example, physiologists used the correlations among the disparate events of puberty to postulate the existence of some abstract controlling mechanism. The discovery of hormones (i.e., "the" cause that unites various primary and secondary sex characteristics) followed an initial stage of research that was at least implicitly correlational. By the same logic, we can use patterns of association and dissociation to identify coherent subsystems in language acquisition. Just because Language Event A and Language Event B are correlated does not mean that A causes B or that A and B are the same thing. But if A and B are correlated with one another, even after more general factors of maturation or mental age are partialed out, we can conclude that they are sensitive to some common mechanisms. Our problem then becomes the identification of the underlying mechanisms responsible for that system.

Whether psycholinguists like correlations or not, many current lines of research assume correlational methods either explicitly or implicitly. Whenever an investigator notes that "A and B happened at the same time," or "B seems to happen soon after A," he is making a correlational statement. Similarly, claims that "Mothers who produce a lot of A have children who produce a lot of B" are based on correlational data. But the correlational nature of the claims are often left implicit. Implicit correlational studies can be dangerous, when "co-occurrence profiles" are presented on the basis of very few observations. In a recent critique of small sample methodologies in child language research, Hardy-Brown (1983) points out how easy it is to obtain a high correlation entirely by chance in a small sample study. At the same time, correlations that hold for the population as a whole may be difficult to detect. Small sample studies are extremely useful in showing us what is *possible.* They cannot tell us whether the same patterns are general or reliable.

Some recent areas of research that involve correlational questions include the literature on parent-child interaction, i.e., "motherese" and "scaffolding" (see Bates, Bretherton, Beeghly-Smith, and McNew, 1982, for a review), research on cognitive bases of language (for reviews see Bates and Snyder, 1987, and Johnston, 1985), and studies of individual differences in language acquisition (reviewed by Nelson, 1981; Kempler, 1980; Bretherton, McNew, Snyder, and Bates, 1983). In the first two fields, studies of "coincidences" in very small samples were quite common in the initial stages—and appropriately so. The special adjustments that mothers make in speech directed to children first needed to be described in detail. Once a characterization of these speech adjustments became available, it could be used in larger studies with more mother-child pairs, to determine whether amount and quality of motherese really do have a facilitative effect on language learning. The samples used in motherese studies have still been relatively small. One of the largest is Newport, Gleitman, and Gleitman's 1977 study of fifteen children. However, their sample spanned a broad age range, so that degrees of freedom and large amounts of variance were lost in partialing age out of correlations; even then, the behaviors that were measured in mothers and in children could mean very different things at different ages within the sample (Furrow, Nelson, and Benedict, 1979). Nevertheless, the problem of sampling is now openly discussed, and the field seems to have reached a healthy realization of the limits and benefits of these methodological decisions (Gleitman, Newport, and Gleitman, 1984).

In the area of cognition-language relations, the first round of studies were also based on descriptions of co-occurring events in a very few children. For example, based on a sample of only three children, Bates, Camaioni, and Volterra (1975) noted that intentional communication through the use of vocal and gestural conventions (e.g., using an adult to obtain an object, or using an object to obtain adult attention through giving and pointing) appeared simultaneously with instances of means-ends relationships and tool use outside of communication (e.g., using a support to rake in an object). They concluded that both social and nonsocial tool use are manifestations of a more general change in cognitive abilities, corresponding to Piaget's Sensorimotor Stage V. Here, too, however, the need for a stronger statistical test has been recognized, and many more substantive studies have been carried out. For example, Bates et al. (1979) replicated the 1975 finding with a sample of twenty-five American and Italian children. Other investigators have found similar effects, occasionally in still larger samples (e.g., Harding and Golinkoff, 1978).

In the study of individual differences in language acquisition—a psychometric problem if ever there was one—the same evolution has yet to take place. At the initial stages of description, this was again an appropriate research strategy. For example, Bloom, Lightbown, and Hood (1975) found two distinct patterns of first-word combinations in a sample of only four children. Two of the children showed the canonical pattern of telegraphic speech, with omission of grammatical function words and inflections (i.e., Roger Brown's Stage I). The other two, however, used pronouns and a high proportion of grammatical morphemes in their speech from the very beginning, never displaying those Stage I speech patterns that were previously thought to be universal. In a study of only one child, Peters (1977) described a "holistic" pattern of grammatical development, consisting in the pervasive use of large and apparently unanalyzed phrases rather than the morpheme-by-morpheme constructions that were usually reported in the literature. These studies served as an important challenge to prevailing theories of language learning, showing us how much diversity is possible at the early stages.

The problem is that the list of characteristics that define alternative styles has now grown tremendously, although to our knowledge there has been no unified study previous to our own in which all or most of these postulated characteristics were examined in one sample (Bretherton et al., 1983). Furthermore, claims about the causes of alternative language styles have often been based on "correlations" in groups of two to four subjects. For example, Bloom et al. note that their two telegraphic or "nominal" children were both girls; the two "pronominal" children were boys. This finding has been cited by other investigators as evidence of a gender-associated difference in early grammatical style. But with a sample of four children, it is quite possible that such a distribution of styles might occur by chance. Assuming that any single child has a 50/50 chance of developing nominal or pronominal style, the gender-related differences observed by Bloom et al. correspond to a chance baseline of 1 in 16. This outcome is sufficiently unlikely that it is certainly worth pursuing in larger-sample studies; but a probability of 1 in 16 does fall below the conventional .05 cutoff point for significance of results.

Even within more traditional descriptive studies, multivariate statistics have begun to prove useful in drawing causal inferences. In fact, a particularly useful example can be found in Brown's original monograph (1973). Having described the order of acquisition for fourteen grammatical morphemes, Brown went on to ask why this particular order should occur. He postulated three possible causal influences: frequency, semantic complexity (i.e., conceptual difficulty), and formal grammatical complexity (i.e., the number of units that have to be coordinated, as well as the number of inflectional agreement and/or ordering procedures required to use each morpheme properly). He then rank-ordered the fourteen morphemes along four corresponding dimensions: order of acquisition by children and frequency of use by parents (both determined from his own transcripts) and both semantic and formal complexity (determined through the author's own intuitive judgments). Rank-order correlations were then computed among these four dimensions. Note that this is an analysis *across materials,* contrasting with the more common correlational technique of analysis *across subjects* (Clark, 1973). Hence the sample size for the correlations is fourteen (whereas the sample for a correlation across subjects would have to be only three). Results indicated that frequency bears no relationship to order of acquisition; both semantic and formal complexity correlate significantly with acquisition order, but to approximately the same degree. Brown concludes from this correlational analysis that semantic and formal complexity both have a causal role in the acquisition of morphemes, where frequency in parental speech does not.

There are other ways to ask the frequency question. For each morpheme, for each individual child, it would be possible to compute frequency in parental speech and time of onset in child speech. Pearson product–moment correlations, across children rather than across materials, could then tell us whether parents who produce more of a given form also have children who acquire that form earlier. For a few aspects of English morphology, particularly use of verbal auxiliaries, there is some evidence that this is the case (Gleitman, Newport, and Gleitman, 1984; Furrow and Nelson, 1984).

There are also other ways to analyze Brown's own data, as Moerk (1980) and Block and Kessel (1980) have pointed out. For example, Moerk notes that significant rank-order correlations can be found in Brown's data if some of the morphemes in his list are eliminated. After all, perhaps some morphemes are frequency-sensitive while others are not. As Pinker (1981) notes in a published critique of Moerk and of Block and Kessel, this assumes that we have some noncircular, a priori basis for eliminating morphemes from the list. However, Moerk's general point is well taken. It may well be the case that two active causal mechanisms effectively cancel each other out, leaving us with the mistaken impression that neither variable plays a role. For example, high-frequency forms tend to be low in information value, precisely because they are so predictable. Frequency and informativeness of grammatical morphemes may both influence order of acquisition, but in opposing directions (Slobin, 1979). This information could be lost if we were to restrict ourselves to simple correlational data.

To examine converging and competing influences on a single variable, some kind of multivariate approach is needed. Block and Kessel offer one such approach, worth considering in detail because it introduces the use of multiple regression, a procedure that we will use extensively in the present study. With Brown's original analyses, we cannot tell which of the two correlated "causes," semantic or formal complexity, is contributing most to order of acquisition. Of course if there were large differences in the two correlations (e.g., semantic complexity correlates with acquisition at $+.90$, whereas formal complexity correlates at $+.40$), we might conclude immediately that the relationship with semantics is more powerful. What we would have done to reach this conclusion is an eyeball version of multiple regression. That is, we would have guessed that the variance due to formal complexity is significantly smaller than the variance contributed by semantics. But there are many logically possible relationships among overlapping variables that cannot be determined so easily by visual inspection of a simple correlation matrix. Suppose, for example, that the two predictor variables correlate at roughly equal rates with the target (which is, in fact, the case in Brown's data). Fig. 1 illustrates two different situations that might underlie these numbers. Predictor A and Predictor B might be contributing the *same* variance to Target C (i.e., all the overlap with the target is contained within the overlap between A and B). If this were the case, all the

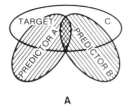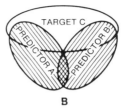

A   B

Figure 1a and b: Two possible patterns that might underlie a set of inter-correlated variables.

significant variance would be accounted for in the first step of a stepwise regression; providing a second variable would add nothing significant to the equation, regardless of the order in which variables are entered (Fig. 1a). There are also situations in which A and B each contribute *unique, independent* variance (Fig. 1b). In this case, each variable increases the prediction significantly when it is entered on the last step.

If the first situation held in Brown's data, we would have to conclude that, *for the purpose of predicting order of acquisition,* semantic complexity and formal complexity are the same thing. If the second situation held, we could conclude that semantics and formal complexity each bear an independent relationship to order of acquisition, perhaps based on the contribution of independent mechanisms. In Block and Kessel's analysis, the first result was found. They infer from this pattern that formal complexity is an epiphenomenon of semantics, supporting theories of grammar that are semantically based. Of course, as Pinker (1981) points out, one could just as easily conclude the opposite: that semantic complexity is an epiphenomenon of grammar. Pinker concludes that we have learned nothing whatsoever from Block and Kessel's analysis that was not already obvious in Brown's original conclusion, i.e., that we simply cannot tell which variable plays a causal role.

While we agree with Pinker's point that the direction of causality is unclear in these regression analyses, we do not agree that the analysis is useless. It has been established that *semantics and grammar make inter-dependent contributions to the order of acquisition of morphemes.* As Figure 1b illustrates, this did not have to be the case. The two hypothetical causes could have operated independently. Instead, from the point of view of sequencing in acquisition, they operate "as if" they were the same thing. One can never *disprove* independence, any more than one can *disprove* the existence of fairies, or subatomic particles. All that we can do is to give independence (or existence) a fair chance to show itself. Toward this end, multiple regression is a useful tool.

Having argued that psychometric techniques can make a contribution to developmental psycholinguistics, we hasten to add that the converse is also true. One reason it has been easy for child language researchers to ignore psychometric research is that large-sample studies of infant and adult intelligence have been markedly uninformed by psycholinguistic theory. For example, the Bayley Test of Infant Intelligence contains questions like "Does the infant speak in sentences?"—thus covering twenty years of child language research in a single item. In all fairness, the Bayley Test was developed long before the flowering of psycholinguistics in the 1960s. Even so, more current tests of verbal ability are also relatively uninformed by research in child language from 1970 onward—in particular, recent findings on qualitatively different patterns in language acquisition, which are surely pertinent to the establishment of language norms.

In a recent reanalysis of the Fels and Berkeley longitudinal studies, McCall, Eichorn, and Hogarty (1977) provide data that underscore the potential contribution of an enriched psycholinguistic perspective to the field of differential psychology. First, they addressed the issue of continuity over time. Previous studies had concluded that infant intelligence tests were unrelated to intellectual functioning beyond the preschool years. McCall et al. found instead that infant tests have considerable predictive value, if correlational analyses are based on the first principal component at each age instead of total scores. Hence there is continuity in rate of intellectual development from the first few months of life through at least 5 years of age. More importantly for our purposes, McCall et al. found that, after 12 months of age, the first principal component of these tests is defined primarily by verbal/symbolic items. This trend begins early in the second year, and apparently increases into adulthood (when, as we know, the vocabulary subscales of the Wais and the Stanford-Binet correlate so highly with total IQ that they can be used as a short form to estimate IQ for many purposes). This means that language is at the core of those intellectual abilities that remain stable over time.

Second, McCall et al. found evidence for a qualitative reorganization in the content of the first principal component at four distinct age levels: 9 months, 12–13 months, 20–21 months, and again around 30–31 months. These stagelike shifts in content were also accompanied by exceptionally wide variation among children in the sample, which decreased sharply when the qualitative reorganization was complete. It is particularly interesting to us that three of these psychometric boundaries coincide with well-known boundaries in language and communicative development. At 9–10 months, on the average, we find the first clear evidence of language comprehension, and intentional communication through conventional signals; 12–13 months is the average onset time for the production of meaningful speech. The average age for the passage from single- to multiword speech is 20–21 months. It is not entirely clear whether the 30–31 month shift matches an equivalent boundary in language. However, we do know that the "grammaticization" process begins after 20 months and is virtually complete in most children by 3 years of age. Hence 30 months seems to stand in the middle of an amazingly rapid period of grammatical development. We are not suggesting that the McCall et al. events "cause" changes in language; nor can we conclude that the shifts in language are responsible for concomitant reorganizations in the rest of intelligence. It does, however, seem reasonable that the two research bodies are yoked together in some meaningful way. It would surely be useful for psychometricians to attend more carefully to new information about individual differences in language development, since language is so clearly implicated during major transitions in intellectual functioning.

One last lesson from the psychometric literature is particularly important for a longitudinal study like ours. How shall we interpret correlations that hold across developmental stages, when so many things have changed between measurements? The stability of individual differences reflected in a correlation does mean that *something* is continuous; but that "something" is not always obvious from a superficial look at the content of two measures. Both Kagan (1971) and McCall (1981) distinguish between *homotypic continuity* and *heterotypic continuity* in longitudinal research. Homotypic continuity holds when we find cross-age correlations in the same content domain—for example, a correlation between vocabulary totals at 1 and 3 years of age. Heterotypic continuity holds when we find correlations between content domains—for example, a correlation between vocabulary totals at 1 year and grammatical complexity two years later. In the first instance, we might be tempted to interpret the correlation in fairly shallow terms, postulating the existence of some unitary vocabulary acquisition device. In the second instance, the connection is less obvious, and we are forced to consider explanations at a more abstract level.

Still more distressing is something we might call *homotypic discontinuity*, where the "same" measure is uncorrelated, or perhaps even negatively correlated, from one stage to another. For example, the repetitious behavior of filling and emptying containers is a positive index of intellectual development in a 9-month-old child (Bates et al., 1979). However, if a child is still fascinated by this repetitious game at 3 years of age, we may begin to worry that something is wrong. In short, superficially similar behaviors can mean very different things at different points in development. The same message holds within language development. For example, we will provide evidence later on showing that certain aspects of grammatical morphology at 20 months are negatively correlated with the "same" measure eight months later.

When the element of time is added to correlational research, all the attendant problems of interpretation are increased; on the other hand, the opportunity to identify interesting systems becomes even greater. Let us move on now to a review of the literature on individual differences in language, where some candidate "systems" are provided.

Chapter 4
Review of the Individual Differences Literature

Fortunately for us, the burgeoning literature on individual differences in language development has now been reviewed in considerable detail in several published books and papers (Nelson, 1981; Nelson, 1985; Kempler, 1980; Goldfield and Snow, 1985; Bretherton, McNew, Snyder, and Bates, 1983). We can restrict ourselves here to a task-oriented discussion of major points, divided into two sections a review of linguistic and associated non-linguistic phenomena that show individual variation, and a review of mechanisms proposed to account for these patterns.

Individual Differences: Evidence

Lexical Development

Nelson (1973) was the first to point out just how much children can vary in vocabulary composition during the one-word stage. Using a combination of maternal diary data and taperecordings made in the home, Nelson followed eighteen children longitudinally from approximately 1 to 2 years of age. In her first report, based primarily on the first fifty words acquired by each child, she described a dimension of variation from *referential style*, (i.e., vocabularies with a high proportion of common object names) to *expressive style*, (i.e., heterogeneous, vocabularies containing items from a variety of form classes, including some frozen phrases like "Stop it" and "I love you"). The term "referential" derives from the tendency for children at this end of the dimension to focus on the process of object naming. The term "expressive" captures the tendency for children at the other extreme to focus more on the social/regulatory uses of language. The referential/expressive dimension was quantified through simple proportion scores: total object names divided by total vocabulary. These scores were normally distributed, with most children falling somewhere in the middle. And yet, for children at extreme ends of the distribution, linguistic behavior was so strikingly different that it seemed to reflect the operation of qualitatively different acquisition mechanisms and/or linguistic environments.

43

Since Nelson's original report, a host of separate studies have shown variation in noun use, of one sort or another. This includes reports by Bloom (1973) of four children in the one-word stage, Dore (1974) of two children in the one-word stage, Starr (1975) of twelve children from 1 to 3 years, Peters (1977) of one very atypical child from 7 to 22 months, and several reports by Horgan including one study of thirty children from 2 to 4 years (Horgan 1978, 1979) and a case study of one very unusual child from 15 to 36 months (Horgan, 1981). The interactive of "noun emphasis" with grammar in several of these studies will be discussed shortly.

In addition to the noun finding, Horgan also reports a higher number of adjectives in nominal/referential children. Since adjectives modify nouns, this finding is perhaps not surpising. However, Lieven (1980) suggests that the referential child also has a greater *variety* of items *within* lexical categories (based on two case studies between 18 and 25 months). This suggests that "nouniness" may be just one aspect of a richer and more varied approach to lexical development, typical of precocious and verbally fluent children.

Some of Nelson's original data support this inference. Referential style proportion scores in Nelson's study were correlated with *rate of development,* with referential children reaching the fifty-word boundary weeks or months earlier than children with more heterogeneous vocabularies. The greater precocity of referential children is also reported in Horgan's study of thirty children (1978, 1979) and in a study of seven children from 13 to 27 months by Ramer (1976).

But rate of development is not the only correlate of referential/expressive style. Nelson also reports a positive relationship between expressive style and imitation, in an elicited imitation task administered between 18 and 21 months. There is, then, at least one aspect of language in which expressive children excel. Similar findings are reported by Bloom and colleagues (Bloom, Hood, and Lightbown, 1974, 1975) in a longitudinal sample of five children (see below), and by Clark (1974, one child from 33 to 36 months) and Ferguson and Farwell (1975, three children from 11 to 24 months).

However, some qualifications are also in order. Leonard, Schwartz, Folger, Newhoff, and Wilcox (1979) introduced novel object names to a sample of twenty children between the ages of 14 and 24 months. Using a criterion similar to Nelson's, Leonard et al. classified nine of the children as referential and eleven as expressive. Their findings for elicited imitation ran directly counter to expectations: more imitation of object names by referential children. A similar finding has since been reported by Nelson, Baker, Denninger, Bonvillian, and Kaplan (1985) for twenty-four children at 22 months of age; however, by 27 months their results had reversed back to the more typical finding of an association between imitation and expressive style. Why are there so many paradoxical findings concerning the relationship between lexical style and imitation? As several investigators have noted, imitation is not a single function. Children may imitate with or without understanding (Clark, 1977; Bates et al., 1979; MacWhinney, 1982; Snow, 1981, 1983); and they may repeat an adult utterance for a variety of reasons, including a desire just to keep the conversation going (Keenan, 1977). For now, we can only conclude that the relationship between lexical style and imitation deserves further investigation (see Study 5).

Finally, in Nelson's study referential style was positively correlated with parental education level and with first-born status. Because these same variables tend to be correlated with the child's IQ, this kind of finding leads to the suspicion that referential style is nothing other than a byproduct of differences in intelligence. We will have a great deal more to say about this later (see especially Study 9).

Our own first contribution to the literature on individual differences in lexical development was a study of thirty-two children from middle-class families, at 13 months of age (Snyder, Bates and Bretherton, 1981). Twenty-seven of these children went on to participate in the longitudinal project to be described here, so that the Snyder et al. study provides some of the variables that we will track up through the early stages of grammar. In the initial study, we concentrated entirely on the results of a detailed maternal interview, based on a checklist of words and phrases likely to occur in the comprehension and production vocabularies of children in the second year of life (see Snyder et al., and Study 1, below, for further details on procedure). Briefly summarized, the findings of Nelson and other investigators were replicated and extended in several new directions. First, we found evidence for a referential/expressive style dimension (i.e., proportion of object names in the child's total vocabulary) from the very beginning of language acquisition (when production vocabularies averaged only ten to twelve words). Second, this range of variation occurred in both comprehension and production. Although comprehension and production totals were not significantly correlated in this sample (because of a group of children who understood far more than they produced), the referential style proportion scores for comprehension and production *were* significantly related. In other words, children who are referential in their expressive speech show a similar bias for object names in receptive language. Third, we confirmed Nelson's finding that referential children are more advanced overall in lexical development. And again, this was true for both comprehension and production. Fourth (and finally), we used detailed anecdotal information from the mothers to classify vocabulary items along a dimension of "contextual flexibility." For example, if a child produced the word "doggie" only in the presence of the family dog, or only in response to one picture in a favorite book, that word was classified as "context bound." If, instead, the child used "doggie" to label or recognize different dogs, in a variety of contexts, the same word would be classified as "context flexible." In our view, children with a high proportion of context-flexible object names in their vocabulary have probably passed an important milestone in language acquisition: They have obtained some insight into "the idea that things have names." In fact, correlational analyses showed that the more precocious, referential children were also more likely to use their words for common objects in this context-flexible way.

To summarize so far, referential style in lexical development is characterized by a bias toward object-naming in particular and use of nouns in general, with more use of adjectives later on, greater variety and flexibility within lexical categories, and a faster rate of development overall (in both comprehension and production). Expressive style is characterized by more heterogeneous vocabulary from the very beginning of language development (in both comprehension and production), the inclusion of some formulaic expressions even in the one-word stage, perhaps a greater propensity toward imitation, but slightly slower development overall.

Grammatical Development

Bloom (1970) was the first to point out a contradiction in the extant literature on "universal" patterns of early grammar. Some studies concentrated on the telegraphic nature of first word combinations, i.e., utterances built entirely out of uninflected content words. Other studies emphasized the "pivot-open" structure of early grammar, i.e., frame/slot constructions made up of a high-frequency function word (e.g., NO, MORE) and a slot that can be filled by several different content words (e.g., NO MILK, MORE SHOE). Bloom suggested that telegraphic speech and pivot-open constructions may reflect two different approaches to early language learning, raising problems for the theory that all children make use of a single Language Acquisition Device.

In the first major empirical study of individual differences in early grammar, Bloom et al. (1975) introduced a contrast between *nominal style*, i.e., multiword constructions composed primarily of nouns and other content words, and *pronominal style*, i.e., multiword constructions in which the same meanings are conveyed with nonspecific pronominal forms. All four children in the Bloom et al. study produced some pivot-open constructions. In particular, negation was expressed with the formula NO + X, and recurrence was expressed with word-based formulas like MORE + X or 'NOTHER + X. However, to encode semantic relations involving action, location and possession, two of the children (both of them girls) produced telegraphic combinations of content words, such as "Kathryn sock," "touch milk." One of the major differences lay in the tendency for these children to refer to themselves by name. To express the same meanings, the two boys were more likely to use nonspecific forms of reference: "I finish," "My truck," "Play it." In particular, these children referred to themselves with first-person pronouns.

By the time all four children reached a Mean Length of Utterance of 2.5 morphemes, the differential use of pronouns had disappeared. Hence, unlike referential/expressive style, the nominal/pronominal contrast seems to have a short half-life. It is, nevertheless, a robust finding, reported in several other studies, including Peters (1977), Branigan (1977), Goldfield (1982), and a follow-up of the original referential/expressive sample by Nelson (1975, 1981).

Nelson's follow-up study yielded several other grammatical characteristics associated with pronominal/expressive style. For example, the formulaic expressions or frozen forms reported in the one-word stage (e.g., "I love you") seem to continue through the early stages of grammar (see also Ramer, 1976; Lieven, 1978; Clark, 1974; Branigan, 1977; Goldfield, 1982).

Another characteristic of the nonnominal approach to early grammar is the use of "dummy terms," meaningless sounds that some children seems use as "fillers" to increase sentence length and give their utterances a more "grown up" shape. The most famous example is the mysterious word "wida" used by Bloom's daughter Allison late in the one-word stage (Bloom, 1973). Before Allison produced any true multiword utterances, she managed to create the impression of sentencehood by adding this apparently meaningless sound to her single words, e.g., "Mommy wida." This tendency persists for many children well into the first stages of multiword speech, as reported in Nelson's followup study and in the studies by Ramer (1976), Peters (1977), Branigan (1979), Horgan (1978), and Leonard et al. (1979).

Although all children used some pivot-open constructions in the Bloom (1975) study, Horgan reports a greater proportion of such lexically based combinations in her nonnominal children or "noun leavers," compared with her nominal children or "noun lovers." A similar pattern can be found in Braine's (1976) review of first-word combinations across natural languages. Hence, in addition to their use of frozen forms, pronouns and dummy terms, pronominal/expressive children seem to use more "rules" based on a single lexical item; e.g., NO + X, MORE + X,

X + ALLGONE. Furthermore, their pivot-open constructions tend to include a variety of grammatical function words—not only pronouns, but also interrogatives, articles, and auxiliary verbs (Nelson, 1975; Branigan, 1977; Horgan, 1978; Ramer, 1976).

We have already noted that pronominal/expressive children are more likely to engage in imitation. This tendency seems to hold in both single and multiword speech, reintroducing an old question in the language development literature: Does imitation play a role in the acquisition of grammatical rules? In the late 1960s, we had come to accept the conclusion that imitation is *not* a means of acquiring new grammatical patterns, although it may play a role in acquiring new words. If new rules do come in via imitation, the imitative utterances of small children should be at least a bit more sophisticated grammatically than their own spontaneous speech. Studies by Ervin (1964) and Slobin and Welsh (1973) suggested, instead, that children will only imitate forms that are already in their repertoires. In fact, they cite instances in which a child was unable to repeat on command a sentence that she had produced herself the day before. The new individual differences literature qualifies this conclusion considerably. For nominal/referential children, the old argument is valid: Those imitations that do occur tend to be filtered through the child's current rule system in spontaneous speech. However, for children at the nonnominal end of the continuum, imitative utterances often contain forms that have not yet occurred spontaneously (e.g., Bloom et al., 1974). This difference provides still more support for the notion that different acquisition mechanisms underlie that contrast between pronominal and nominal style.

Finally, there is a suggestion in the literature that pronominal/expressive children are less consistent than nominal/referential children in their use of word order (as reported by Lieven, 1980, and more recently by Vihman and Carpenter, 1984; see also Braine, 1976, for some related arguments). This does *not* refer to word order patterns based on single lexical items (e.g., MORE + X). If anything, pronominal/expressive children are *more* consistent in their ordering of word-based patterns. However, when investigators analyze word-order regularities at a more abstract level, e.g., Agent-Action-Patient or Subject-Verb-Object, the telegraphic utterances of a nominal child seem to provide a better fit to some kind of abstract ordering principle. A similar argument may pertain to a tendency that we have noted in our own samples: Morphological overgeneralizations seem to be more common in nominal/telegraphic children, once those children finally begin to produce grammatical morphemes at all (see especially Study 12, this volume). This seems to be a morphological analogue to the claim that nominal style is associated with more consistent use of word-order principles—suggesting that this mode or style of language learning involves more consistent application of rules across the board.

We entered into the literature on individual differences in early grammar in a follow-up study at 20 months of the same children studied by Snyder et al. (Bretherton et al., 1983). We wanted to look at many of the semantic/syntactic variations described so far in a single sample of children, in an empirical test of the "two-style" picture that had emerged in the literature to date. Both interview and observational data were employed. The maternal interview involved a series of detailed probes into the way that children used various kinds of single and multi-word utterances: rates of imitation and labeling, ability to answer questions and engage in conversation, ability to talk about absent referents (past, future, or "pretend"), different semantic "case" relations expressed with single and/or multiword sentences (e.g., agent-action, action-patient, object-location, possessor-possession). In addition, we asked about the kinds of multiword constructions that each child used: pivot-open patterns (e.g., MORE + X), telegraphic patterns with two nouns (e.g., MOMMY SOCK) or with a noun and one other content word (e.g., TINY BABY), constructions involving pronouns and other grammatical function words, plus the presence or absence of various noun and verb inflections in the child's speech (e.g., singular/plural contrasts, past-tense markers). The same categories used in the interview were then applied to transcripts of spontaneous speech (from video-recordings made at home and in the laboratory). Hence the interview and the observations could be used to conduct independent tests of the two-style theory.

The interview and observational codings were subjected to separate cluster analyses–a technique similar in many respects to factor analysis, except that it permits the emergence of correlated clusters, and it is better suited to the kind of data derived from adding up "yes/no" answers in an interview (Tryon and Bailey, 1970). In the interview, four separate clusters emerged. A *Nominal/Referential cluster* was defined primarily by the number and variety of constructions with content words reported by the mother (especially noun-noun constructions) and by the variety of semantic case relations expressed in multiword speech. A *Grammatical Morpheme cluster* reflected the child's use of utterances with pronouns instead of noun phrases, and by utterances using verb inflections, articles, prepositions, and auxiliaries. So far these clusters seem to confirm the nominal/pronominal dimension that other investigators had described with smaller samples. However, not all the variables tested here fell into the "two-style" picture. Two additional clusters emerged in the interview analysis. A *Dialogue cluster* reflected *both* labeling and imitation rates as well as the child's tendency to participate in conversation and answer questions. This was something of a surprise, since the literature led us to expect labeling to fall under nominal style, with imitation falling under pronominal style. The fourth and final dimension, termed the *Semantic-Cognitive cluster,* involved "decontextualized" language (i.e., talking about absent referents in various ways) and the range of semantic case relations conveyed with single words. The Bretherton et al. (1983) analysis of free-speech data yielded similar results: a referential-nominal cluster, a grammatical morpheme cluster, and a third cluster that combined the third and fourth above into a single *Semantics-Dialogue* dimension.

To summarize, then, Bretherton et al. confirmed the split between nominal and pronominal style in early grammar in two independent data sets. But the two-style picture that had emerged in the literature up to that point had to be modified in several ways. For one thing, pronominal style actually seemed to extend to the child's tendency to use *any* inflections or grammatical function words at 20 months. And several dimensions presumed to fall under either nominal or pronominal style went off to form clusters of their own: imitation and labeling, participating in conversation, and the sophisticated use of single words to express different semantic relations and to talk about absent referents. The interview results have since been replicated in a separate sample of thirty 20-month-old infants studied by Shore (1981; see also Shore, 1986). We feel fairly confident, then, that these cluster analyses are tapping into something both reliable and real.

In the present study, we will follow twenty-seven of the children studied by Snyder et al. (1981) and Bretherton et al., from a 10-month data set that has not been presented elsewhere, through to the productive use of grammar at 28 months of age. A large number of additional measures at 13 and 20 months will also be included. But the Bretherton et al. cluster variables will play an important diagnostic role throughout the study.

Pragmatic Development

Compared with the findings on semantics and grammar, there is considerably less evidence on individual differences in pragmatics, defined as differences in the range of communicative functions that children choose to express with their single and multiword speech. The literature that does exist is difficult to interpret, primarily because there are so many confounds between form and function.

In her original study, Nelson pointed out that referential children are by definition more involved in the labeling functions of language, while expressive children make greater use of social/regulatory expressions like "Stop it." This conclusion is based not only on the different forms that children used, but on the way they allocated their time before the cameras. Referential children spent significantly more time engaged in bouts of object play; expressive children made more bids for adult attention and generally spent more time involved with other human beings. Some related evidence is provided in later studies (Nelson 1981, based on Ross, Nelson, Wetstone, and Tanouye, 1980, and Furrow, 1980; Dore, 1974; Starr, 1975; Branigan, 1977; Peters, 1977; Lieven, 1980; Nelson, 1985). In her case studies, Lieven paid especially close attention to the pragmatic character of expressive/pronominal speech. She reports more comments about existence and recurrence, more bids for attention, and (a curious note) a generally greater tendency to make statements that are irrelevant to the conversation.

In contrast, Bloom et al. emphasize that their children are using different *forms* to convey precisely the same *meanings*—although they did find greater evidence for imitation by pronominal/expressive children, which presumably means that these children were apt to repeat an adult utterance for no obvious communicative purpose. Bretherton et al. are also skeptical about the claim that pronominal/expressive children are more communicative. They point out that the utterance "Mommy sock" can be just as effective in social regulation as the command "You do it." And the act of labeling an object for another human being is, in itself, a very social act—perhaps more social in function than simple imitation (see also Bates et al., 1975, on the "declarative" function of pointing, giving, and showing objects). Furthermore, the evidence from Leonard et al. and from Bretherton et al. on labeling and imitation at 20 months seems to be at odds with the claim that referential/nominal children like to go around naming things, whereas expressive/pronominal children repeat what they hear instead. As Nelson (1981) suggests, some of the disparity between studies might depend on the age at which children were tested. In fact, we will present evidence later that many aspects of lexical style are age dependent (see especially Studies 1, 3, and 7).

In any case, two pragmatic differences do seem to be fairly well established: Expressive children produce a greater variety of speech act forms, and they spend more time directly engaged in social interaction that does *not* involve objects. The question is not whether these differences exist, but what they mean.

First, in her critique of Dore's speech-act coding system, Chapman (1981) points out that function and form are frequently confounded. If a given child does produce a large number of imitative utterances, she might entirely by accident hit upon a greater variety of adult speech acts (e.g., promises, warnings, requests). In other words, by reproducing more linguistic *forms* without regard to their meaning, a pronominal/expressive child could give the impression of pragmatic sophistication. Lieven's point that expressive children's speech is often "irrelevant" provides some support for this view.

Second, the greater use of social/regulatory expressions might be a byproduct of temperament and cognitive style variables that are related only indirectly to language. Note, first of all, how many of the social/instrumental expressions reported in the early stages are really quite negative in intent: "Stop it," "Don't do dat," "Mine!" (although, in all fairness, "I love you" appears in the same list). These expressions might occur more often, in front of visiting experimenters, when a child is tired or cranky or unable to get interested in the experimental toys. Which brings us to the point about time spent with toys versus people. Suppose that a referential/nominal child is somewhat more introspective, and/or that she has a greater attention span? These decidedly nonlinguistic factors might result in what appears to be a "less" communicative style, as the child avidly explores the new toys laid out by the experimenter. In this light, evidence that the referential/expressive child engages in more labeling (at least at the earliest stages) suggests that she is at least trying to share her enthusiasm with the audience.

Our point is simply this: Compared with the growing evidence for dissociations within both semantics and grammar, current evidence for variation in pragmatics is not very strong. It is difficult to know whether the greater pragmatic variety in the language of expressive/pronominal children is based on true differences in function or whether the differences are byproducts of cognitive style and temperament and/or the way that children analyze linguistic forms. We hope to provide some evidence relevant to this point in the present study.

Phonological Development

The evidence for variation in phonology is still slim, but the findings to date are consistent. Particularly important is the dimension of "intelligibility" or "good articulation." Several studies have reported that the speech of pronominal/expressive children is difficult to understand and transcribe (Nelson, 1981; Peters, 1977; Branigan, 1977; Horgan, 1979, 1981; Ferguson, 1984; Ferguson and Farwell, 1975; Leonard, Newhoff, and Masalem, 1980). Indeed, some frustrated investigators have been driven to use the term "mushmouth." Researchers in the Stanford Child Phonology Project have tried to explicate this poorly specified notion of intelligibility. Vihman (1981) reports that subjective ratings of intelligibility are highly correlated, in the one-word stage, with the number and variety of identifiable consonants that a child manages to use. But this is not all. From the one word stage through 3 years of age, there seems to be a reliable and continuous dimension of "phonological consistency," i.e., whether or not a child pronounces a given word type the same way across instances. By 3 years of age, this variability in phonology is also associated with greater variability or inconsistency in the child's grammatical rule system (Vihman and Carpenter, 1984).

However, these intelligibility and consistency ratings do not mean that the child is "bad" at phonology. Rather, children at the extreme expressive/pronominal end of the continuum seem to be emphasizing different aspects of phonology, concentrating on prosody or intonation at both the word and sentence level. In other words, pronominal/expressive style involves a focus on whole forms, sketching out the broad outlines of a word or sentence and working on the details later; by contrast, nominal/referential style involves a focus on segmentation, breaking out the phonemic/syllabic/lexical units and building them up gradually into whole forms.

There is a terrible irony in these findings on variation in phonology, if they prove to be robust in future studies. As Goldfield and Snow (1985) point out, the "new generation" of language acquisition studies in the 1960s gave us the impression that all children pass through a course of development from naming, to telegraphic speech, to grammar. We now know that this style of development is only half the story. Apparently the early studies picked up children who would currently be classified as referential or nominal in their approach to early grammar. Why is this the case? Ursula Bellugi (personal communication, 1984) has described the early phases of Roger Brown's research project, when children were selected for participation in their landmark longitudinal study. Although many children were considered, the three who were ultimately chosen had one thing in common: They spoke clearly enough to facilitate transcription and coding of audiotapes. No one dreamed then that individual differences in intelligibility would prove to be associated in any interesting way with qualitative differences in early grammar.

Cross-Domain Relationships

In Table 1, we have summarized most of the individual differences in language development suggested in the last decade, divided into different linguistic and nonlinguistic content areas: semantics, grammar, pragmatics, phonology, and demographic characteristics that cut across content areas and age levels. Table 1 is further organized into two columns, with each column reflecting one extreme in a series of bipolar dimensions.

This two-column format corresponds to a hypothesis that appears, implicitly or explicitly, throughout the individual differences literature: The variables in each column reflect the operation of some common

Table 1. *Individual Differences in Language Development: Summary of Claims in the Literature*

Strand 1	Strand 2
Semantics	
High proportion of nouns in first 50 words	Low proportion of nouns in first 50 words
Single words in early speech	Formulae in early speech
Imitates object names	Unselective imitation
Greater variety within lexical categories	Less variety within lexical categories
Meaningful elements only	Use of "dummy" words
High adjective use	Low adjective use
Context-flexible use of names	Context-bound use of names
Rapid vocabulary growth	Slower vocabulary growth
Grammar	
Telegraphic in Stage I	Inflections and function words in Stage I
Refers to self and others by name in Stage I	Refers to self and others by pronoun in Stage I
Noun-phrase expansion	Verb phrase expansion
Morphological overgeneralization	Morphological undergeneralization
Consistent application of rules	Inconsistent application of rules
Novel combinations	Frozen forms
Imitation is behind spontaneous speech	Imitation is ahead of spontaneous speech
Fast learner	Slow learner
Pragmatics	
Object-oriented	Person-oriented
Declarative	Imperative
Low variety in speech acts	High variety in speech acts
Phonology	
Word-oriented	Intonation-oriented
High intelligibility	Low intelligibility
Segmental emphasis	Suprasegmental emphasis
Consistent pronunciation across word tokens	Variable pronunciation across word tokens
Demographic Variables	
Female	Male
Firstborn	Later-born
Higher SES	Lower SES

cause or mechanism, creating two (and only two) separate and coherent strands of variation in language development. This is a very strong claim, with serious implications for our understanding of the modular structure of language. Because the two strands in Table 1 cut across content areas and age levels, evidence for a Two-Strand theory would provide support for the view that the componential structure of language is *horizontal* rather than *vertical*. But the apparent unity in Table 1 is still a matter of speculation. The Two-Strand claim rests on the results of many separate studies, most of them based on only a small subset of these many and disparate variables, usually with a small sample of children, studied over a relatively brief span of development. An adequate test of the theory requires a unified study, examining all (or most) of these factors in a single sample of children, across the relevant age range.

The Bretherton et al. (1983) paper is to our knowledge the single most comprehensive study of individual differences to date in a sample large enough to permit a statistical test of cohesion among variables. This study already suggests that the Two-Strand theory is in trouble. At least three clusters fell out of their analyses: two aspects of multiword speech, and a third cluster reflecting sophisticated use of single words. This suggests a potential separation between variations in single word speech and variability in early grammar.

On the other hand, there are scattered findings in support of a horizontal, cross-domain model of the mechanism(s) underlying individual differences in language. Nelson and colleagues have shown that referential children are more likely to elect a nominal style when they pass from single words to sentences; conversely, the expressive child in the one-word stage is more likely to use a pronominal style in early grammar. Although this is a short-term finding, from late in the one-word stage to first-word combinations only a few weeks later, it does provide support for the view that individual differences are continuous from semantics to grammar. Similarly, the various studies on phonology suggest that the formulaic/Gestalt approach to grammar occurs in children who apply a similar strategy to the sound system; and the referential/nominal/analytic approach to semantics and grammar co-occurs with a consistent and analytic approach to phonology. Hence three major "modules" of language—semantics, grammar, and phonology—may be paced by the same underlying mechanisms.

In the studies presented below, we set out to test the Two-Strand theory implicit in Table 1 in more detail in a single longitudinal study. Although ours is perhaps the most complete study to date, we still fall short in several crucial ways. First of all, limits on our resources (both technical and financial) precluded a detailed study of phonological variation. The Stanford Child Phonology Project has produced important new results on parallels between phonology and grammar, suggesting that our omission is a serious one. We will have to restrict our conclusions here entirely to lexical/grammatical development and to a few relevant non-linguistic measures. Second, we had to stop our study at 28 months of age, when grammatical development was in full flower. We cannot know, then, how the patterns of variation will change later on. Findings reviewed by Goldfield and Snow (1985) suggest that some version of referential/expressive style persists through adulthood, manifested in the different ways that adults approach second-language learning. We will provide data from first words to the beginning of grammar—a useful enterprise, but hardly the whole story.

Before we begin our story, we have one more task: a survey of the many explanations that have been offered so far to explain the patterns of variation in Table 1.

Individual Differences: Explanations

Table 2 summarizes the alternative explanations that have been offered for the two putative styles of language acquisition. These explanations are not mutually exclusive. And though it has been useful to organize them in two columns, corresponding to the Two Strands in Table 1, each proposed mechanism could be responsible for some separate portion of the variance. We engage in this exercise simply to demonstrate the range of causal mechanisms that have been proposed so far. Four levels of explanation are proposed: social, linguistic, neurological, and cognitive.

Social explanations

Both *exogenous* and *endogenous* social factors are relevant here. Proposed exogenous factors include maternal style, as well as some demographic or "biosocial" variables such as gender, birth order, and social class.

In Nelson's original monograph, maternal style was proposed as a likely cause for the range of variation in lexical style observed in the one word stage. She noted that some mothers spent more time engaging their children in interactions involving objects; while others spent more time in more direct interpersonal transactions. A related social hypothesis has been offered by Lieven (1980), who noted a greater tendency for the mother of an expressive child to "imitate" or repeat the child's own statements. If there is a link between expressive/pronominal style and imitation, it might thus result from a tendency for children to pick up their parents' conversational strategy.

Table 2. *Individual Differences in Language Development: Alternative Explanations*

	Social Explanations
Exogenous	Maternal style and input
	• Object vs. person focus
	• Does or does not imitate the child
	Social class
	• Elaborated vs. restricted code
Endogenous	Temperament
	• Object vs. person orientation
	• Reflective vs. impulsive approach to problems
	Linguistic Explanations
Within language proper	• Language function vs. language form
	• Open vs. closed class lexicon or semantics vs. grammar
	• Word order vs. morphology
Between language and cognition	• Environmentally sensitive and insensitive processes
	Neurological Explanations
Interhemispheric	• Right vs. left hemisphere emphasis
Intrahemispheric	• Anterior vs. posterior emphasis within the dominant hemisphere
	Cognitive Explanations
Unidimensional	• General intelligence
	• Field dependence—independence
Multidimensional	• Analytic vs. Gestalt/holistic processing
	• Analytic vs. imitative learning mechanisms
	• Patterners vs. dramatists
	• Information sensitive vs. frequency-sensitive
	• Comprehension-driven vs. production-driven
	• Analysis for understanding vs. analysis for reproduction

Furrow and Nelson (1984) have offered some of the most detailed evidence to date for environmental correlates of language style. Using transcripts from Nelson's original study, they analyzed the maternal language of expressive and referential children at two stages of language development (in the 2–2½ year old range). In line with earlier observations by Bloom et al. (1975), mothers of expressive and referential children did not differ in their own relative use of nouns versus pronouns. Hence the noun/pronoun difference in the children cannot be attributed to modeling in any straightforward sense. However, they did find differences in the *communicative functions* expressed by mothers of the two style groups: more reference to objects by referential mothers, and more reference to persons by expressive mothers. Furthermore, this difference between mothers interacted with developmental level, occurring entirely within the lower MLU range. Recall that the noun/pronoun difference between children is also restricted to the first stages of grammar and disappears (at least temporarily) once all children are acquiring productive control over grammatical morphology. Because the object/person difference between mothers tracks the noun/pronoun difference between children, it seems possible that mother and child are collaborating in the child's development of a language style.

Associations between maternal style and child outcome have also been reported by DellaCorte, Benedict, and Klein (1983) and by Tomasello and Todd (1983). Mothers who followed up the child's attention to objects by providing a description or some other comment tended to have children who acquired a larger number of object names. By contrast, mothers who provided a particularly high proportion of directives tended to have children with a smaller proportion of nominals in their vocabulary.

It is not clear, however, whether these data really do support an environmental–causal view. In any naturalistic dyadic interaction, we are confronted with the problem of bidirectional effects (cf. Bates, Bretherton, Beeghly-Smith, and McNew, 1982; Bohannon and Marquis, 1977; Barnes, Gotfreund, and Wells, 1983). Is the referential child created by an object-oriented mother? Or is the mother simply responding to her child's inherent preference? Who is in charge? As far as we can tell, there is no way out of this causal dilemma, at least in the literature available so far. Furrow and Nelson (1984) admit this possibility, but point out that

> The existence of child-to-mother influences does not weaken . . .
> the position that parental modeling of functions contributes to indi-
> vidual differences. Correlations are no more likely to reflect
> exclusively child-to-mother than they are mother-to-child influences.
> (p. 533)

In other words, bidirectional effects are quite likely. Parents are not entirely responsible for individual differences, but they can play some role (however indirect) in the establishment and/or the enhancement of a particular language style.

A recent dissertation by Goldfield (1985) provides a useful compromise on the issue of environmental effects on style. Goldfield followed twelve infants from the prespeech stage, through acquisition of their first fifty words around 18 months of age. She did not replicate the finding that referential children engage in longer bouts of solitary object play, but she did find that such children were more likely to use a toy to initiate a social exchange (see also Ross, Nelson, Wetstone, and Tanouye, 1980). This is an individual difference dimension with roots deep in the prespeech period, beginning with giving and showing objects around 9 months of age. And as Bates et al. (1975) and Bates et al. (1979) have shown, such "proto-declarative" communications are good predictors of progress in lexical development many months later. From this point of view, we could argue that the initial bias toward referential communication originates in the child in the earliest stages of intentional communication. However, Goldfield (1985) provides additional information to suggest that parents can augment or damper this initial object orientation in the course of lexical development. She concludes that

> A highly referential lexicon is not the necessary outcome of a child intent on object exploration or a mother who tends to label objects, but rather of a dyad which uses objects as topics of mutual interest, interaction and conversation. Referential contexts emerge from joint attention to a physically present referent; the child who tends to use objects to engage mother, and the mother who exploits such episodes to provide object labels each contributes to the maintenance of such contexts in the history of the dyad. (p. 30)

Other claims for a parental role in language development are based on such traditional sociological dimensions as gender, birth order, and social class. These variables have always had a peculiar status as "explanations." They are presumably shorthand for a vast array of poorly understood causal mechanisms. There is, in any case, some evidence that pronominal/expressive style occurs more often in laterborns, suggesting that quality and quantity of adult input may have an effect. The hint of a gender-related difference could also be due to social/environmental factors, but the biological versus social origins of gender-related differences are so controversial that we shall consider this point unanswerable for now.

There is also a small amount of evidence that pronominal/expressive style is common among children of the working classes, where parental education is at or below average (e.g., Nelson, 1973; Parisi and

Giannelli, 1974). Furthermore, there is an interesting parallel between nominal/pronominal style in children and the distinction between Elaborated Code and Restricted Code proposed by Bernstein and colleagues (e.g., Bernstein, 1970). This last distinction is based on studies of language use among working-class and middle-class adults in Britain. Briefly summarized, the "restricted code" is a type of language spoken in both classes, characterized by a high pronoun/noun ratio and by frequent use of formulas and semiproductive conversational forms. It is the language of intimacy, spoken by those who can take a great deal for granted. The "elaborated code" is a type of language spoken primarily by middle- to upper-class speakers, characterized by a much greater use of explicit nominal forms and a greater variety of novel and well-structured syntactic forms. This code works well in any setting in which little shared knowledge can be taken for granted, including written discourse. Bernstein suggests that children of the middle classes are exposed to both codes, hence have an easier time of it when they encounter written modes of discourse in school settings. Although it is entirely speculative at this point, the greater use of pronouns and formulas by expressive/pronominal children would be consistent with differences in input of the kind that Bernstein describes.

Turning to endogenous social factors, we find several claims concerning the role of temperament. The object-oriented/person-oriented contrast described in many of the earlier studies might be a characteristic that the child brings to bear on language acquisition with or without the mother's help (Nelson, 1973, 1981). And there are certain compelling similarities between the nominal/pronominal dimension and the dimensions of reflectivity/impulsivity and shyness or vigilance versus sociability discussed by Kagan, Reznick, and colleagues at Harvard (Kagan, 1981). Some of this revolves around the notion of "risk-taking"— though it is not always obvious who is taking the risks! On the one hand, expressive/pronominal style seems to be associated with "leaping before you look," moving quickly into the use of a new phrase for communicative purposes and worrying about its internal structure later (cf. Fillmore, 1979). In this sense, pronominal children could be viewed as the uninhibited risk-takers in the crowd. On the other hand, at some stages of development referential/nominal children seem to make a greater number of errors, perhaps in their drive to find and apply rules (Goldfield and Snow, 1985). If this means that referential children aren't afraid to make a mistake, then perhaps they are the risk-takers. We will present some evidence germane to this vexed point in Study 12, though much of the answer will depend on research still in progress (including an ongoing study of language differences and temperament at Harvard, by Reznick, Snow, and Wolf, 1985).

Linguistic explanations

There are two kinds of domain-specific linguistic explanations: models that emphasize different mechanisms *within* language proper, and models that emphasize a contrast between linguistic and nonlinguistic processing.

Horgan (1981) considers a contrast between *function-oriented* and *form-oriented* learning, suggesting that the "noun lovers" in her studies care more about the content of language (i.e., semantics, pragmatics), whereas the "noun leavers" are more interested in levels of form (i.e., syntax, morphology, phonology). A similar suggestion can be found in Dore's (1974) distinction between code-oriented and message-oriented babies. Presumably this theory would predict continuity in style between phonology and grammar (as discussed above), but a discontinuity between single-word semantics and early grammar (in contrast with the findings reviewed by Nelson).

An alternative is discussed by Gleitman and Wanner (1982), who are primarily interested in the autonomy of grammar compared with other aspects of lexical processing. They stress, in particular, a contrast between the *open-class lexicon* (i.e., meaning-bearing content words like nouns, verbs, and adjectives) and the *closed-class lexicon* (i.e., grammatical function words and, perhaps, inflectional markers like the plural "s" or the progressive "ing"). One lexicon is involved in semantic interpretation; the other is involved in parsing, and hence belongs within the grammar "module" (Berndt and Caramazza, 1980; Caramazza and Berndt, in press). Evidence for a developmental dissociation between open- and closed-class vocabulary (latent in some of the evidence on nominal/pronominal style) could be construed as support for this view. However, strong longitudinal correlations between lexical style in the one-word stage and grammatical style later on could pose a problem for the theory that open- and closed-class items are acquired by separate mechanisms.

A third linguistic proposal was introduced by Bloom et al. (1975) in their original discussion of the nominal/pronominal contrast. They suggested that nominal children are concentrating on the word-order properties of language (consistent with evidence discussed above by Lieven and Ramer). Pronominal children, instead, are starting their grammatical careers with an emphasis on morphology (closed-class items, both bound and free-standing). This would constitute a claim for modularity within the boundaries of grammar, i.e., a dissociation between syntax and morphology. If this characterization is correct, we would expect pronominal children to excel over time in the production and comprehension of morphology, building on their "headstart" in Stage I; nominal children should, instead, show a better grasp of word-order principles in the later stages of grammatical development.

In another kind of "modular" approach to individual differences, a line is drawn between processes peculiar to language (vertical faculties in Fodor's terminology), and processes shared with other aspects of cognition (i.e., horizontal faculties in the Fodor framework). Gleitman and colleagues have, for example, discussed a contrast between *environmentally sensitive* and *environmentally insensitive* aspects of language (Newport, Gleitman, and Gleitman, 1977; Gleitman and Wanner, 1982; Gleitman et al., 1984; see also Goldin-Meadow and Mylander, 1985). Environmentally insensitive elements are those structures that are universal to all natural languages (including the communicative systems invented by deaf children with restricted input). These structures are presumably acquired via a robust and biologically based set of language-specific processing mechanisms, and hence should prove impervious to statistical variations in linguistic input or "motherese." By contrast, environmentally sensitive elements are those structures that vary across natural languages, additions or modifications that particular languages make to the hypothetical Universal Grammar. These structures should be quite sensitive to fluctuations in a given child's experience. The dimension of environmental sensitivity is obliquely correlated with the above contrast between grammar and lexical semantics. That is, one would expect the environment to have a greater effect on the development of content words. But the dimension also applies within the closed class. For example, Gleitman et al. (1984) cite several studies showing that the development of verbal auxiliaries is affected by the statistical distribution of auxiliaries in maternal speech. In particular, mothers who produce a large number of sentence-initial auxiliaries (as in "Are you drawing a man?") tend to have children who make greater progress in the use of sentence-internal auxiliaries (as in "Yeah, I'm going draw his nose"). Because this auxiliary system is a peculiar property of English, it cannot belong to the stock of innate linguistic hypotheses. It follows that auxiliaries have to be picked up by some kind of frequency-sensitive general learning mechanism. By this line of argument, the contrast between nominal and pronominal style might reflect the extent to which a given child makes use of environmentally sensitive, frequency-driven acquisition mechanisms. Nominal children are sticking primarily to the exercise of innate linguistic hypotheses; pronominal children are relying more on some kind of general-purpose learning device. But if this explanation is to be noncircular, there must be some independent motivation for predicting those aspects of grammar that will and will not be affected by the environment.

Neurological explanations

Although there is no real evidence one way or the other, two different kinds of neurological models are at least compatible with the data so far: inter-hemispheric and intra-hemispheric.

The inter-hemispheric explanation is rooted in the ubiquitous contrast between "left-brain" and "right brain" processes (Kempler, 1980; Bates et al., 1979; Horgan, 1979; Goldfield and Snow, 1985). The current wisdom has it that the left cerebral hemisphere of most right-handed individuals is specialized for sequential/analytic modes of processing, whereas the right hemisphere is specialized for tasks requiring some kind of simultaneous/holistic analysis. In general, the left hemisphere seems to be ideally suited for language. However, evidence has accumulated in the last few years suggesting that the right hemisphere plays a major role in at least two aspects of language: formulaic speech (e.g., Van Lancker, 1975; Kempler, Van Lancker, and Hadler, 1984) and prosody (e.g., Ross, 1981). The association of pronominal/expressive style with early use of intonation, and a greater reliance on formulas and frozen forms, invites speculation that this style of language reflects a relatively greater use of right hemisphere processes.

The intrahemispheric explanation is quite different, based on a puzzling similarity between the dissociation of language styles in childhood and the breakdown of language in adult aphasics, in particular the contrast between Broca's and Wernicke's aphasia. The typical Broca's aphasic is described as "agrammatic," producing slow or nonfluent telegraphic utterances that leave out function words and grammatical inflections. This syndrome generally occurs with lesions in the anterior portion of the left hemisphere. Wernicke's aphasia is sometimes proposed as a virtual mirror image: hyperfluent speech that is superficially well formed from a grammatical point of view, but frequently senseless or "empty," with heavy use of pronouns and a reliance on formulaic expressions. This syndrome tends to occur with lesions in the posterior portion of the left hemisphere.

Suppose that we present a neurologist with transcripts of child speech taken from the extreme ends of the nominal/pronominal style continuum, without giving away the age or mental status of our "patients." If he were to follow the usual profiles for Broca's and Wernicke's aphasia (e.g., Goodglass and Kaplan, 1972), our neurologist might classify an extreme case of nominal style as an instance of agrammatism, whereas the extreme pronominal child could well receive a diagnosis of Wernicke's aphasia. Although the matter is purely speculative, it seems reasonable that the respective mechanisms subserved by Broca's area and Wernicke's area could develop slightly out of synchrony in a perfectly normal child, producing "Broca-like" and "Wernicke-like" effects in early grammatical development.

Cognitive explanations

Finally, among the cognitive explanations, we again find two kinds of proposals: explanations in terms of a single dimension, and theories that postulate the existence of two or more dissociable processes.

The most obvious unidimensional explanation is the old-fashioned notion of IQ. Given the existing evidence that referential/nominal style is characteristic of more precocious children, one might argue that variations along the referential/expressive dimension reflect nothing other than the relative presence or absence of hard mental work. Smart children discover rules faster; slow children do the best they can to sound like a grownup until they can get to the same point in rule acquisition. We will provide evidence against this interpretation later on (see especially Study 8). However, even at face value, something is missing. Pronominal/expressive style, as it is described in the literature, seems to involve a positive approach to language that is not captured by some vague notion of "slow growth." The postulated reliance on imitation, memory for large phrasal units, and greater sociability (e.g., Peters, 1977 & 1983) suggest that this style reflects a mode of analysis that is qualitatively rather than quantitatively different from an idealized nominal/referential style.

The cognitive dimension of field independence has also been named as a potential source of linguistic variation, with greater field independence associated with a more "context independent" and rule-driven approach to language development. Here too, however, the two styles would have to reflect points along a single mental dimension. This approach is mathematically incompatible with the kind of evidence that we will present here, where two or more orthogonal factors vary independently with some children scoring high or low on both (see especially Study 11).

The kind of explanation that is offered most often by investigators in this field is couched in terms of two qualitatively distinct modes of analysis. We find terms like analytic versus Gestalt (Peters, 1977), analytic versus holistic processing (Bretherton et al., 1983), and analytic versus imitative learning (Kempler, 1980). A variant on this contrast is provided by Wolf and Gardner (1979), who distinguish between Patterners and Dramatists. Across symbolic modalities (e.g., language, play, art), Dramatists are interested in reproducing reality; Patterners, by contrast, like to play with the possibilities, creating permutations of the reality and discovering abstract organizing principles along the way. Although all these proposals differ in emphasis, they share the view that language learning depends on at least two kinds of analysis: from part to whole, and from whole to part. To acquire a natural language properly, everyone will have to do a little of both. But children may differ in the extent to which they rely on one or the other.

As stated so far, these two hypothetical modes of analysis would apply in any cognitive domain. And, of course, they overlap to a considerable extent with the left/right hemisphere arguments described above. However, one can be considerably more specific about the consequences of these or related dimensions for language. For example, Snow and Bates (1984) have considered at least three slightly different versions of the analytic/holistic distinction that are particularly germane to language acquisition.

1. **Content versus frequency.** Nominal/referential style may reflect an "information-sensitive" mode of processing, whereas pronominal/referential style may be "frequency sensitive." Under this interpretation, the two putative underlying mechanisms respond to different aspects of the input.
2. **Comprehension versus production.** In the same vein, we might argue that the First Strand of variance in language is "comprehension driven," while the Second Strand is "production driven." In other words, nominal/referential children are primarily interested in figuring out what language is for and what people are trying to say; pronominal/expressive children are trying to sound like other people. But this comprehension/production characterization could be misleading, since most of the evidence for individual differences can be found within production.
3. **Understanding versus reproduction.** Putting the case rather differently, we could explain variations in style with a contrast between *analysis for understanding* and *analysis for reproduction*. This terminology covers much of the same territory. But it has the advantage of incorporating the word "analysis" twice! That is, it stresses the idea that at least two kinds of analysis must go on for a language to be successfully acquired.

As we have said, few of these explanations are mutually exclusive. And most of them are really little more than descriptions of the basic phenomena at a slightly more general level. But until we have a more solid empirical test of the Two-Strand theory, it is probably safe to say that all of them are premature.

One last cautionary note, before we proceed to the data: In most individual-difference studies, we find ourselves deriving typologies from

unimodal distributions. For example, Nelson operationalized refer-
ential/expressive style as a simple proportion score: the total number of
common nouns in each child's vocabulary divided by the total number of
words from any form class. Because these ratios were normally distributed, with most children falling somewhere in the middle, she was able
to carry out a series of correlational analyses (e.g., the relationship
between referential style and birth order). Such analyses would be inappropriate if referential/expressive style classifications came from a bimodal distribution. Nevertheless, many secondary sources have treated
referential style as a dichotomy, i.e., as a bimodal distribution with all
children classified into one of two types.

We certainly do not want to lay this error at Nelson's door (since she
has taken every reasonable precaution to avoid it). But we do want to
keep it away from our own. It is very difficult to discuss individual
differences without slipping into typological terms. The two columns
listed in Table 1 are meant to reflect *dimensions*. Nevertheless, every
time we label two ends of a dimension, we create two tags. And whenever we create two tags, we are tempted to pin those tags onto the
t-shirts of small children—even our own children! It is occasionally useful to talk about children with extreme scores (on one end or the other
of a continuous dimension). However, throughout this review and
throughout this monograph, we hope to make the following point clear:
*We are using individual variation to discover something useful about the
mechanisms that underlie language learning; we are not interested in developing a typology of children, nor do we think that it would be useful to do so.*

With that warning delivered, we can now turn to the twelve substudies
that comprise our own effort to test some of the explanations laid out in
Table 2.

PART II
Individual Studies

Overall Design of the Longitudinal Study

The twelve studies reported in the next twelve chapters are all based on a single longitudinal study of twenty-seven children at four age levels: 10, 13, 20, and 28 months. At each age level, data were collected in two sessions. The first session was always held in the home, followed by a session in the laboratory no more than 7 days later.

Procedure

Throughout the study we used a mixture of parental interviews and observations of free speech and free play, supplemented by a set of much more structured and standardized experimental tasks for eliciting particular linguistic/symbolic behaviors. In many instances, we used different measures to get at the same underlying construct, e.g., a maternal interview on word comprehension together with a single-word comprehension task. Although the resulting proliferation of measures does complicate things statistically, it also gives us the opportunity to cross-validate our results and to converge on the same idea from several points of view.

All our procedures have ample precedents in the developmental literature. However, we have relied particularly heavily on parental interview techniques in the earlier sessions. Our previous experience suggests that parental interviews, if conducted properly, can provide a much more valid perspective on emerging language skills than 2 or 3 hours of itinerant observation. Several caveats about the use of parental reports are in order.

1. Parents should only be asked about current behaviors; retrospective reports tend to be much less reliable.
2. The interview should focus on skills that are just emerging, with enough frequency to be noticed but still within the limits of a casual albeit intimate observer. Thus, it may make sense to ask the mother of a one-year-old about her child's productive vocabulary; but by the time the child's vocabulary exceeds 300 to 400 words, the task is probably hopeless.

69

3. We have found it useful to rely more on recognition memory than on recall. So, for example, instead of asking the parents "What animal words does your child know?" we present them with a list of animal words that are common in early vocabularies and ask whether any of those words have shown up yet in their own child's receptive and/or expressive vocabulary.
4. Finally, a much more valid body of information can be gathered from parents if the interviewer probes for anecdotal information about the way that a particular word is used. In this way, we focus not only on whether the child has a given form, but how, where, and when he uses it.

Further details on the various interview techniques, and on our structured and spontaneous observations, are provided in the method sections for each individual study.

Subjects

To select our initial longitudinal sample, we drew the names of potential subjects from birth announcements in the local paper. Infants with birth weights greater than 5.5 pounds and addresses reasonably near the University were selected. Parents were then contacted through an introductory letter describing the project, with a followup phone call a few days later. This technique resulted in a 70% acceptance rate.

The children in the longitudinal study were all originally participants in a study of causal understanding in infancy (Carlson-Luden, 1979) involving an initial group of forty-eight infants averaging 10 months, 11 days (with a range from 10:0 to 10:28). At the end of the Carlson-Luden study, parents were asked if they would be willing to participate in our longitudinal study of language and symbolic development, up through 28 months of age. The parents of thirty-two children agreed, resulting in a starting sample of sixteen boys and sixteen girls.

These infants were next seen at 13 months of age. Five children subsequently moved away. At 20 months, three new children were therefore invited to participate in the project, to bring the sample up to fifteen boys and fifteen girls. This sample of thirty children all participated in the final sessions at 28 months. Although the total sample thus varied from one session to another, twenty-seven children participated at all four age levels. All the statistics to be reported in this monograph are based on this constant sample of twenty-seven, including thirteen boys and fourteen girls. Thirteen children were firstborn, ten were secondborn, and four were thirdborn or later. Their average birthweight was 7.2 pounds, with a range of 5.5 to 9.0. Average age in days at the initial 10-month session was 311, with a range of 300–324. At all subsequent sessions, children were within 2 weeks on either side of the target range. (For more details regarding demographic variables, see Study 12.)

Some of the measures to be discussed below were developed and reported in other publications, where the data are based on the full sample of infants at those particular age levels (i.e., thirty-two children at 13 months and thirty children at 20 and 28 months). When results from those papers are cited, here or elsewhere, they refer to the larger samples (e.g., Snyder et al., 1981; Bretherton et al., 1983; Beeghly, 1981; Beeghly and Bates, 1984; Bretherton and Bates, 1984).

A final note regarding the demographic makeup of this sample. Although we did not select subjects systematically on the basis of race or socioeconomic level, the demographic characteristics of Boulder, Colorado, are such that these selection criteria resulted in a sample of middle- to upper-middle-class Caucasian children (with the exception of one black child from a middle-class family). This is, then, a very homogeneous and privileged group of children, a fact that limits the generalizability of our findings. And yet, as we shall see, we did still find a robust range of individual differences in this sample. The very fact that such qualitative and quantitative differences can be found in a healthy, homogeneous group of children suggests that we may indeed find out something important about the biological factors responsible for individual variation.

Chapter 5: Study 1

Comprehension and Production
at 10 and 13 Months

Just how soon can we begin to see evidence for a dissociation between language learning mechanisms? The results presented here suggest that dissociations are evident from 10 to 13 months, in the comprehension and production of first words.

In this study, we will build on an earlier report by Snyder et al. (1981), taking their results in two new directions.

First, the Snyder et al. 13-month maternal interview measures will be compared with observational data at the same age level. This comparison provides an important methodological clarification for readers who are skeptical of parental reports, as it demonstrates once again that parents do know what they are talking about (see also Bates et al., 1979). In particular, the dissociation between comprehension and production cross-validates in both the interviews and the observational data.

Second, the Snyder et al. results are traced back to 10 months of age, demonstrating the origin of this dissociation between modalities at the earliest stages of language learning.

Method

With regard to the 10-month data, in this report we will focus exclusively on a brief interview administered to the mother during the 10-month home session, dealing with language and communication. This interview was included in Carlson-Luden's protocols in anticipation of our subsequent longitudinal study of language (Carlson-Luden, 1979); results of the language and communication interview are not discussed in her dissertation.

The interview focused on two areas. First, in the comprehension section mothers were asked to list all the phrases and/or words that the child seemed to understand. Second, mothers were asked to list any words that the child produced, divided into (1) words that were produced by the child spontaneously, and (2) words that the child only said in imitation of someone else. Since virtually all words that the mothers reported were entered into both categories, we subsequently combined the data for spontaneous and imitative production at this age level. Note that this interview involved a "recall method," in contrast with the recognition checklists and detailed probes for anecdotes that we used at later ages. Furthermore, in the 10-month interview we tended to be more generous than we were 3 months later in the sounds that were counted as "words." For example, a consistent sound made in the context of requesting (e.g., "MMMMMM!") was included in the production word count at this level; the same item would not be included in the word count later on.

At 13 months, our maternal interview data include five measures taken from Snyder et al.: total comprehension and production vocabularies, referential style in both comprehension and production (i.e., proportion of the reported vocabulary consisting of common nouns), and referential flexibility in production (i.e., proportion of the expressive vocabulary consisting of common nouns used flexibly across a variety of contexts). We did not use their measure of referential flexibility in comprehension, since Snyder et al. had concluded that the flexibility coding scheme simply does not work well when applied to comprehension data.

Since the 13-month home session was not videorecorded, observational measures of language were taken primarily from the videotaped session in our laboratory. The single exception is a very short word count during one home-session task in which the Experimenter silently modeled familiar gestures with appropriate and inappropriate objects (e.g., drinking from a cup vs. drinking from a comb—for details, see Bates et al., 1983). During or after modeling, some children spontaneously named the experimental objects. These words were recorded manually if both the Experimenter and the Recorder agreed on the child's production.

The 13-month laboratory session involved a series of standard tests and structured play situations, all of which were videotaped and transcribed. These procedures included a segment of the child engaged in free play with the mother with a standard set of laboratory toys, elicited symbolic play with the Experimenter, and a language-comprehension task. Transcriptions of these segments were combined with the single-word count taken during the home session, yielding an average of 1–1½ hours' worth of language observations for each child. In such a limited period, the amount of speech likely to be produced by a 13-month-old is relatively small. For this reason, we kept our observational measures appropriately simple: a total count of all the different recognizable words produced by the children, divided into (1) spontaneous productions, and (2) imitations. Imitations are operationalized here as any word produced by the child that had occurred in the immediately preceding adult utterance. Note that these are both measures of types rather than tokens, since any given word produced by the child counted only once despite possible repetitions.

The only observational measure of comprehension, and the only structured language test we used at this age level, was a "multiple choice" measure, described by Bretherton, Bates, McNew, Shore, Williamson, and Beeghly-Smith (1981a). In this task, three familiar objects were presented in random positions from left to right in a transparent plastic box with three wells. The side of the box facing the child was covered with a transparent door hinged at the top, preventing the child from touching or grabbing objects while they were set in place on each trial. After the objects were placed, the Experimenter obtained the child's attention and asked for the target object twice, e.g., "Where's the car, Eric? Get the car." The transparent door was then lifted and the child was free to choose one of the three objects. Eight different common objects were used, each appearing as the target object on two trials and as one of the two distractors on a random subset of the other trials. The eight objects included a bottle, cup, shoe, doll, car, telephone, spoon, and teddy bear. There were sixteen trials total, permitting scores for correct object choice ranging from 0 to 16 (with chance performance standing at 33%).

To summarize, the 13-month language measures that we will adopt in the present study are the following: from the interview, *total comprehension vocabulary, referential style in comprehension* (i.e., proportion of the comprehension vocabulary consisting of common nouns), *total production vocabulary, referential style in production* (i.e., proportion of the production vocabulary consisting of common nouns), and *referential flexibility* (i.e., proportion of the production vocabulary consisting of context-flexible common nouns); from the observations, *total words produced spontaneously* and *total words produced in imitation;* from the structured comprehension test, *total correct matches of name and object.*

Results and Discussion

The results are divided into two sections: a comparison of interview and observational data at 13 months, and an examination of the 10-month data as they relate to language 3 months later.

Interviews and Observations at 13 Months

Table 3 lists the Pearson product-moment correlations among all the 10- and 13-month language measures. Note that here, as in all the studies to be reported subsequently, we examined the descriptive statistics

Table 3. *Correlations Among 10- and 13-Month Measures*

	10-Month Interview		13-Month Observations			13-Month Interview				
	Production	Comprehension	Production		Comprehension	Production		% Flexible	Comprehension	
	Total	Total	Spontaneous	Imitative	Total	Total	% Nouns	Nouns	Total	% Nouns
10-Month										
Production	—									
Comprehension	*.40	—								
13-Month Observed										
Spontaneous production	*.41	-.13	—							
Imitative production	*.40	.22	**.63	—						
Comprehension	.07	.23	.04	.32	—					
13-Month Interview										
Total production	**.72	.22	**.72	**.59	.15	—				
% Nouns production	**.52	**.59	.32	*.45	~.33	**.51	—			
% Flexible Nouns	**.49	**.54	.20	*.38	*.49	**.50	**.84	—		
Total comprehension	~.35	**.52	-.03	.10	**.52	~.27	*.42	**.56	—	
% Nouns comprehension	.27	~.37	.11	~.33	**.61	.27	~.37	**.62	**.77	—

~$p<.10$
*$p<.05$
**$p<.01$

for each variable to determine whether it met the assumptions necessary for linear regression. Measures with more than 60% zero entries were always excluded from consideration, and highly skewed measures were normalized before use in correlational analyses.

We should begin by pointing out that the results reported by Snyder et al. for the maternal interview, with the full sample of thirty-two children, were maintained within our longitudinal subsample of twenty-seven:

1. First, the correlation between comprehension and production totals at 13 months does not reach significance ($+.27$), due primarily to a group of children who reportedly understand far more than they produce (see also Goldin-Meadow, Seligman, and Gelman, 1976).

2. Within comprehension, there was a range in variation along the referential style continuum similar to the range in production. In comprehension, the percentage of the reported vocabulary made up of common nouns averaged 34%, with a range of 14 to 66%. In production, the average was 27.6%, with a range of 0 to 77.8%. Within both comprehension and production, this referential style dimension was positively and significantly correlated with vocabulary size. So referential style is characteristic of more precocious development even in very young children, in both modalities.

3. The referential style advantage is further clarified by looking within each child's common noun vocabulary (for expressive language only), at the proportion of items that could be classified as *contextually flexible*. Performance on this measure covered the full range from 0 to 100%, with an average of 32.3%. Contextual flexibility was clearly associated with overall progress in language development: with total vocabularies in both comprehension and production, and with referential style. Hence, comprehension does correlate with particular *aspects* of production, in particular with flexible object naming.

To summarize these results, we offer once again the conclusion reached by Snyder et al.: *Flexible object naming unites comprehension and production because this measure seems to reflect the extent to which the child really understands the idea that things have names.*

In the interview, the production totals averaged 12.0 (from 0 to 45), and the comprehension totals averaged 48.25 (from 17 to 97). With regard to comprehension, some investigators have argued that a receptive vocabulary of fifty or more words represents an important boundary in language development, perhaps marking a "vocabulary burst" in comprehension that is equivalent to the burst in expressive vocabulary typically observed in the second half of the second year (e.g., Benedict, 1979). If this view is correct, it is worth noting that thirteen children, or approximately one half the longitudinal sample, have a reported receptive vocabulary of fifty words or more. None of the children has crossed the fifty word boundary in production, although one child comes surprisingly close.

Much lower levels of language production are evidenced in the observations, as we might expect. An average of only 1.69 spontaneous word types was observed (ranging from 0 to 9), with imitative words averaging .69 (ranging from 0 to 3). Eleven children produced no recognizable, meaningful speech at all during our home and/or laboratory sessions. Should we conclude that parents overestimate their children's language abilities, and that our interview data reflect only the parents' wishful thinking? There are two ways to control for this possibility with the data we have available: (1) determine whether the *pattern* of results in the meager observational data is consistent with the pattern obtained by maternal report, and (2) examine correlations between observational and interview data.

The observational data are of course too few to subcategorize according to either content or style. We do, however, find the same pattern of dissociation between comprehension and production totals that occurred in the interview data. In particular, although the imitation and spontaneous production measures were significantly correlated, neither was related to the multiple-choice test of comprehension.

Furthermore, the respective comprehension and production totals in the interview and the observations cross-validate one another: Interview-comprehension totals correlate with comprehension testing in the laboratory (+.52) but not with observed production; interview-production totals correlate with both of the observed production measures (+.59 with imitations and +.72 with spontaneous vocabulary) but not with comprehension testing.

Finally, the laboratory-comprehension test did correlate significantly with a particular aspect of reported production: a correlation of +.49 with referential flexibility. This provides a particularly comforting validation of the interview technique. If we are correct in our inference that the flexibility measure reflects "understanding of the idea that things have names," we should expect children high on referential flexibility to perform well when asked to match names with objects in the laboratory.

To summarize so far, in comparing the interview and observational data at 13 months we find that comprehension measures "hang together" with each other and with those aspects of production that seem to reflect a deeper understanding of reference. However, beyond this relationship between comprehension and what we might call "analyzed productions," we find a remarkable degree of dissociability between receptive and expressive vocabularies.

Back to the Beginning: Correlations from 10 to 13 Months

Recall that we have only two measures of language development at 10 months: total comprehension and total production, both taken from a brief maternal interview. We cannot validate these maternal reports against observational data at this age level—although Bates et al. (1979) did validate similar interview data against observations from 9 to 12 months in a different sample.

If we are willing to accept these parental reports of their infants' achievements, it is striking just how much progress many of the children have made in language by only 10 months of age. The average number of words or phrases reported in comprehension was 17.9, with a range of 6 to 35. Of course much of this consists of language comprehension within routines in which there is considerable contextual support for language: e.g., "Let's have a bath" while the water is running, "Don't bite" during breast-feeding, "Spit it out" said with hand held to mouth after the child has picked something off the floor.

According to the parents, the average number of words produced at 10 months was 5.7, with a range of 1 to 13. Most of these reported productions also occurred within well-practiced routines: "hi," "bye," "yum," "mama" (usually as an all-purpose request), and so forth. Also, these totals include "wordlike" sounds like an MMMM request, forms that function in a conventional manner but that do not bear any systematic relationship to actual words in the adult language. Nevertheless, given the fact that 12 months is usually reported as the average onset time for first words (e.g., Lenneberg, 1967), it is interesting that mothers did report so much linguistic activity fully 2 months earlier.

It is possible that, between the ages of 10 and 13 months, many parents raised their criteria for what properly qualifies as a "word." For example, the parents of four infants actually reduced their estimates of language production from 10 to 13 months—including one mother who reported four words at the first session and no words at all 3 months later. Nevertheless, whether or not we accept the *absolute* number of words and phrases reported by these parents, it may still be the case that their enthusiastic 10-month reports give a valid estimate of the *relative* abilities of children in both comprehension and production. This can be determined, at least in part, by considering the correlations among measures (see Table 3).

First, in contrast with the pattern of findings three months later, the 10-month comprehension and production totals were significantly correlated $(+.40, p < .05)$. However, the cross-age correlations suggest that 10-month comprehension and 10-month production will project off into separate directions. That is, early comprehension is most strongly related to later comprehension; conversely, early production relates most strongly to later production.

Furthermore, even though 10-month comprehension does not predict later production *totals,* it does correlate quite highly with those aspects of 13-month language that seem to reflect "analyzed production," in particular referential style and flexible object naming.

In this study and in the studies that follow, we want to use such patterns of association and dissociation to make rather strong inferences about the underlying mechanisms that may be responsible. We would like to suggest that there are two partially dissociable "strands" in language development, based on two kinds of acquisition mechanisms: (1) a mechanism responsible for comprehension and for productive, analyzed use of the same forms in speech; and (2) a mechanism responsible for picking up new forms in the sound stream for immediate use in language production, before extensive analysis has taken place. So far, however, our claims are based on "eyeball" comparisons between correlation coefficients. Through regression analysis, it is possible to pull apart the separate contributions that correlated variables make to one another. This permits a closer estimate of the separate contributions from hypothetical underlying mechanisms.

Our first effort in this direction was a series of regression analyses examining the joint contributions of 10-month comprehension and 10-month production to language at 13 months. In each of these regressions, we can determine both the *joint* and the *unique variance* contributed by early comprehension and production. A summary of the regressions that we are about to describe is presented in Table 4.

In the first analysis, the target variable was total reported production at 13 months. 10-month comprehension and production jointly predict 53.35% of the variance in this measure $(R = .73, p < .01)$. However, when this regression is performed with 10-month comprehension added last, the total variance accounted for increases by less than 1%, compared with a significant increase of 48.5% when 10-month production is added last. In other words, all of the variance in this analysis seems to fall within a single production-to-production strand.

Analogous regressions were performed with each of the 13-month observed language measures as targets. For observed imitation, neither the joint nor the unique contributions by 10-month language reached

Table 4. *Regressions of 10-Month Measures on 13 Months*

	10-Month Predictors		
	Joint Variance (r^2)	Unique to Comprehension (r^2)	Unique to Production (r^2)
13-Month targets			
Observed			
Spontaneous production	*.274	.103	*.256
Imitative production	.168	.005	.116
Comprehension	.054	.047	.000
Interviews			
Total production	**.533	.007	**.485
% Nouns production	**.450	*.175	~.094
% Flexible Nouns	**.392	*.142	~.091
Total comprehension	.302	*.178	.022
% Nouns	.160	.085	.017

~ $p < .10$.
* $p < .05$.
** $p < .01$.

significance. However, for observed spontaneous speech the total variance accounted for did reach significance. Furthermore, early production uniquely accounted for a significant proportion of that variance, while early comprehension did not. To summarize, then, the relationship between 10-month production and 13-month production has very little to do with comprehension processes—at least as we have assessed them here.

When we regress these two 10-month measures on 13-month comprehension, the picture is reversed. The equation involving the multiple-choice comprehension task failed to reach significance—which follows from the rather low raw correlations in Table 3 involving this relatively "noisy" measure. However, the regression using reported comprehension vocabulary as the target yielded very clear results.

Here the total amount of variance accounted for is 30.20% ($R = .55$, $p < .05$). When production is entered into the equation last, the variance changes by a non-significant 2.2%. When 10-month comprehension is entered last, the variance increases by 17.8% ($p < .05$). In other words, from 10- to 13-months we also find a single comprehension-to-comprehension strand.

Putting these analyses together, we can conclude that, across the 10 to 13 month period, *comprehension predicts comprehension, and production predicts production, with very little overlap between the two modalities.*

The results of these particular regression analyses are not surprising, since the simple correlation coefficients involving comprehension and production totals were already quite far apart. Regression becomes more useful in exploring the contributions of the 10-month variables to 13-month measures of style and strategy, since most of the correlations involving these variables were significant. The question is: Do all these significant relationships reflect the operation of joint comprehension and production variance (i.e., something that we could call "verbal fluency" or "linguistic maturity")? Or do either of the 10-month variables make unique contributions?

Let us begin with referential style in production. When the 10-month measures are both regressed on this variable, the total variance accounted for is 44.98% ($R = .67$). When production is entered into the equation last, the change in variance totals 9.4% ($p < .054$). When comprehension is added last, the corresponding increase is 17.5% ($p < .01$). In other words, comprehension makes a greater contribution to referential style in production. When the same regression is performed on referential style in comprehension, results are in the same direction but fall below significance (see Table 4).

Finally, 10-month comprehension and production were regressed on the 13-month measure of referential *flexibility* in production. This time the total variance accounted for was 39.23% ($p < .01$). Again the largest unique contribution comes from 10-month comprehension (an increase of 14.2%, $p < .05$), compared with a nonsignificant increase of 9.1% when 10-month production is added to the equation last ($p < 0.07$). To summarize, the so-called comprehension strand also encompasses certain key aspects of production at 13 months—in particular, the use of object names in a flexible and general way across contexts.

Conclusion

The 10- to 13-month regression analyses corroborate our earlier interpretation of the correlation matrices: the style and strategy measures at 13 months load highly on comprehension, supporting our view that these measures of expressive language reflect "analyzed production." By contrast, the 10- and 13-month production totals seem to involve a different aspect of speech output, one that is relatively independent of referential analysis and understanding.

Assuming that we are correct in delineating two partially separable strands in early language development, how shall we characterize the second strand? Since it seems to involve variance in language output after comprehension variance has been removed, we could simply define it in negative terms: unanalyzed, or perhaps, holistic production. And yet why should the *absence* of analysis predict anything consistent at all? Perhaps the second strand should be more properly characterized in terms of another *kind* of analysis, in the service of some other goal. The literature on individual differences in language contains two related suggestions to characterize this other kind of production: *imitation* and *sociability*.

With regard to imitation, we did differentiate between spontaneous and imitative speech in our 13-month observations. However, both aspects of observed production correlated with the "second strand" to exactly the same degree (see Table 3). Other investigators (e.g., Keenan, 1977; Clark, 1974; Leonard et al., 1979; Stine and Bohannon, 1983) have pointed out that imitation can serve a variety of functions. Thus, predictions about the relationship between imitation and other aspects of language development should require very careful consideration of how and why the child repeated someone else's words. Our simple distinction between imitative and spontaneous speech in this study fails to capture any of these functional dimensions. In the next set of studies, we will be in a better position to assess the contribution of imitation to the "second strand" in language development.

It has also been suggested that the second style of acquisition involves language in the service of goals that are more social than cognitive (e.g., Furrow and Nelson, 1984; Lieven, 1980). We have no data to test such an hypothesis at this age level, although relevant measures are available in the 28-month session, to be discussed in Study 10.

To identify the mechanisms responsible for these first dissociations in language development, we need to move ahead to later stages, when the children apply their acquisition mechanisms to a new and different set of problems. In the next study, we will focus on Mean Length of Utterance and first-word combinations at 20 months of age. This will be our first look at the passage from first words to grammar.

Chapter 6: Study 2
The Meaning of Mean Length
of Utterance at 20 Months

In the modern psycholinguistic era, one of the most widely used measures of structural development is Mean Length of Utterance (MLU) in morphemes (Brown, 1973). This measure has recently come under fire, particularly when it is used for children at relatively advanced stages of development, i.e., from 3 years of age onward (see Bowerman, 1973). However, in the 20- to 28-month age range, the measure has considerable validity. In the next few studies, we will provide still more evidence suggesting that MLU is a valid and important measure. But we will also show that it means entirely different things between one age level and another.

Many studies are devoted to the content and form of first-word combinations, in English and in other languages (e.g., Bloom, 1970; Bowerman, 1973; Brown, 1973; Braine, 1976; Bates, 1976). In this study, we will instead examine the internal structure of 20-month MLU from a psychometric point of view. This will include multivariate analyses using a set of semantic/syntactic cluster scores derived from Bretherton et al. (1983) in their study of our sample (see Chapter 4). Bretherton et al. used cluster analysis to test many of the existing claims about individual differences in semantics and in the use of grammatical forms at 20 months of age. Here we will build on their findings in two ways.

First, we will use the various observational and interview clusters that emerged in that study as predictor variables in order to explore in more detail the internal composition of the classic MLU measure. This analysis will demonstrate that individual variation in 20-month MLU is controlled primarily by rote factors. In other words, 20-month-old children can buy a high score rather inexpensively, through ample use of formulas and unanalyzed expressions.

Second, after mapping out the synchronic relationship between MLU and the various cluster scores, we will consider cross-age relationship between first words and first sentences. This analysis will give us more insight into the mechanisms underlying the "two strands" of development discussed in Study 1. In particular, we will show that the rote content of 20-month MLU is continuous with a "pure" or unanalyzed production strand stretching back to 10 months of age.

Method

By 20 months of age, most children were producing considerably more spontaneous speech in our home and laboratory sessions than they did at 13 months. For this reason, there was now a better balance between interview and observational measures.

In contrast with the 13-month procedure, both the home and laboratory visits at 20 months were completely videotaped. Since each session lasted between 1–1½ hours, this yielded from 2 to 3 hours of videorecording for each child, supplemented by audiorecording to assist in the resolution of unclear utterances. In the home session, a detailed interview was carried out with the mother concerning aspects of the child's single and multiword language (described by Bretherton et al., 1983). During this interview, we taped the child engaged in free play alone with a set of standard toys that we had brought with us. Other segments carried out in the home included a test for comprehension of lexical combinations, and the introduction of a novel object concept (discussed in Studies 4 and 5, respectively). In the laboratory session, segments included mother and child engaged in free play (with the same objects the child had manipulated alone in the home session), a repetition of the "multiple choice" test of language comprehension administered at 13 months (discussed by Bretherton et al., 1981a and in Study 4), and elicited symbolic play with the Experimenter.

Orthographic transcriptions were made of the videotaped data (supplemented by the audiorecordings where necessary). Transcripts included the child's speech, the nonverbal context in which it occurred, and adult utterances directed to the child (i.e., conversation between the parents and the Experimenter was excluded unless the child responded directly to something he or she overheard). When child-speech was taken from structured experimental tasks in which the Experimenter's speech and the nonverbal context were completely standardized (e.g., the elicited symbolic play procedures), then transcription was restricted to the child's speech (recorded within protocols noting the point in a standard procedure during which each child utterance occurred).

This transcription process was preceded by a lengthy period of training for each transcriber, on a randomly selected subset of tapes. Our goal was a minimum of 80% agreement with one other observer. However, many of the 20-month olds were producing a relatively high proportion of unintelligible utterances of seemingly greater than single-word length (as described by Vihman, 1981). For this reason, we could not quite attain the projected 80% agreement despite lengthy training. Hence we made the decision to code all 20-month data twice, independently, and to make use only of those utterances on which both raters agreed. Note that this conservative procedure is likely to *reduce* the amount of individual variation that we are likely to observe in children at this age, insofar as unintelligible utterances may be the ones that contain the largest amount of formulaic or unanalyzed speech. We will return to this point in the final chapter.

Following Brown (1973), we calculated MLU in morphemes for each child. Our goal had been to use what has become a traditional minimum of fifty intelligible utterances for each child (e.g., Miller and Chapman, 1981). There were several cases, however, in which the number of intelligible utterances that a child produced fell well below this criterion. Most of these were children who produced only single-word utterances during the home and laboratory sessions; if the mother also reported that her child did not yet use sentences, we assigned the child an MLU score of 1.00. The smallest number of utterances used for an MLU calculation was twenty.

Four interview cluster scores and three corresponding observational cluster scores were taken directly from calculations reported by Bretherton et al. (1983). The resulting seven measures include the nominal multiword clusters for both interview and observations, the grammatical morphology clusters for both interview and observations, the semantic-conceptual and the dialogue clusters from the interview, and the combined semantics-dialogue cluster from the observations. For two children, a substantial portion of the audiorecording in the laboratory was lost due to equipment failure. For these two cases, we retained the MLU score; however, the more detailed observational cluster analyses are not available for these children, so that the sample size for all analyses involving the observational clusters is twenty-five. Finally, we used the full set of 10- and 13-month comprehension and production measures described in Study 1.

Results and Discussion

The results will be discussed in two sections: (1) the relationship of 20-month MLU to the 20-month cluster variables, and (2) cross-age relationships from 13 to 20 months.

MLU and the Semantic and Grammatical Clusters

The average MLU obtained at 20 months with the above procedures was 1.14, with a range of 1.00 to 2.11. Seven of the children were still in the single-word stage, with MLUs of 1.00. One child would be classified within Brown's Late Stage I (MLU 1.5–2.0), and one other child falls within Stage II (MLU 2–2.5). The others all fall within the range described as Early Stage I (MLU 1.01–1.50). This distribution is quite close to norms reported by Chapman (see Miller and Chapman, 1981) for MLU in this age range, for a sample of children in Madison, Wisconsin (a small university community quite similar to Boulder, Colorado).

Given this MLU distribution, several inferences can be drawn from the literature. First, Stage I is the point at which Bloom et al. (1975) report maximum differentiation among children in their sample along the nominal-pronominal continuum discussed earlier. However, according to Brown (see also Maratsos, 1983), grammatical morphology has not reached criterion for productivity among Stage I children. In light of both the Bloom and the Brown findings, we can expect to find strong individual differences in our 20-month sample (as the Bretherton et al. cluster analyses have already suggested); in addition, however, we might also expect variation in MLU to reflect factors other than productive understanding of grammatical morphemes. As we shall see, our results strongly support the prediction that 20-month MLU derives primarily from rote or relatively unanalyzed production.

The correlations between MLU and the seven cluster variables are generally high and positive—so much so that they are relatively uninformative by themselves (see Table 5). For this reason, we turn directly to multiple regression to learn more about both the unique and joint variance contributed to MLU by the cluster scores (summarized in Table 6). First, we carried out analyses using the four interview clusters as predictors. This involved four stepwise regressions, in which each of the four clusters was entered last, in turn. In this way, we could determine the unique contribution of each cluster when the effects of all the others had been removed. Second, we carried out an analogous set of regressions using the three observational clusters as predictors, again with each cluster entered last in one analysis to determine its unique contribution to MLU.

Results of the four regression analyses with the interview clusters are quite straightforward (see Table 6). The total variance in MLU accounted for by the four interview clusters was substantial: 47.6% ($R = .69; p < .01$). However, interview morphology was the only predictor to contribute unique variance when entered last: a significant increase of 27.1%.

When three analogous stepwise regressions were carried out using the three observational clusters as predictors, the results were similar (also summarized in Table 6). An impressive 90% of the variance in MLU is

Table 5. *Correlations of the 20-Month Cluster Variables with 20-Month Mean Length of Utterance*

Interview		Observations	
1. Nominal multiword	*.43	1. Nominal multiword	**.70
2. Grammatical morpheme	**.64	2. Grammatical morpheme	**.92
3. Semantic-conceptual	.26	3. Semantics-dialogue	*.39
4. Dialogue	.18		

$*p<.05.$
$**p<.01.$

Table 6. *Cluster Score Regressions on 20-month MLU*

Interview Clusters		Observation Clusters	
Joint variance (r^2)	**.476	Joint variance (r^2)	*.900
Unique variance to		Unique variance to	
1. Nominal multiword	.000	1. Nominal multiword	*.032
2. Grammatical morpheme	*.271	2. Grammatical morpheme	**.384
3. Semantic-conceptual	.002	3. Semantics-dialogue	*.036
4. Dialogue	.039		

$*p<.05.$
$**p<.01.$

accounted for by the three observational clusters taken together. This is perhaps not surprising, since MLU and the observational clusters were all derived from the same transcripts. However, the pattern of unique contributions by the three clusters is much more interesting: 38.4% is contributed when observational morphology is entered last, compared with a reliable but very small 3.1% for the observational nominal multi-word cluster and 3.5% for the observational semantics-dialogue cluster.

Recall that the two morphology clusters reflect use of closed-class morphology, both free standing function words (e.g., articles, auxiliaries, prepositions, pronouns) and bound morphemes (e.g., plural marking, progressive "-ing," past tense "-ed"). This leads clearly to the following conclusion:

> Variance in MLU at 20 months is associated almost exclusively with variation in the use of function words, for both the interview and the observational data.

If Brown and Maratsos are correct in their argument that the use of these closed-class items at 20 months is nonproductive, then we are forced to a second, related conclusion:

> Variance in Mean Length of Utterance at 20 Months is accounted for primarily by formulaic, unanalyzed use of grammatical morphemes.

This conclusion receives further support as we turn to a consideration of how early combinatorial speech maps onto the two "strands" in language development at the earlier stages.

From First Words to First Sentences

Table 7 summarizes cross-age correlations, from the 10- and 13-month vocabulary measures to both MLU and the cluster scores at 20 months. The 10-month measures have relatively weak predictive validity across this age span. None of the correlations involving 10-month comprehension reaches significance; 10-month production is unrelated to MLU, although it does correlate reliably with several of the cluster variables.

The 13- to 20-month relationships are more reliable and more informative. In particular, MLU seems to be related primarily to total production at the early stages, but not to comprehension or to the various proportion scores for style and flexibility in early word use. This pattern is clarified by a series of regression analyses, summarized in Table 8.

In the first pair of regressions, the two predictors of MLU were observed production (using the measure of words produced spontaneously) and observed comprehension (from the multiple choice task). The regression was performed twice: once with comprehension entered last, and once with production entered last. The total variance accounted for was a significant 30.3%. However, comprehension contributed no unique variance whatsoever when entered last, whereas

Table 7. *10- to 13-Month Variables with 20-Month MLU and Cluster Scores*

	MLU	Interview Clusters				Observational Clusters		
		Nominal Multiword	Grammatical Morpheme	Semantic-Conceptual	Nominal Dialogue	Grammatical Multiword	Semantics-Morpheme	Dialogue
10-Month								
Comprehension	-.10	.08	-.10	~.34	.21	-.06	-.04	.29
Production	.08	~.37	~.33	*.44	*.41	.11	.17	.25
13-Month								
Observed								
Spontaneous	**.55	*.43	*.46	.28	.17	*.43	**.57	.29
Imitative	~.37	*.46	*.44	*.39	.20	-.35	*.50	.28
Comprehension	.00	.18	~.34	.40	**.49		.12	-.39
Interview								
Total								
production	**.50	*.42	**.56	*.42	*.43	-.34	**.63	*.41
% Nouns production	.11	.38	.23	**.56	*.39	.09	.23	*.49
% Flexible nouns	.21	**.49	*.44	**.61	**.52	.22	.31	**.57
Total comprehension	.01	.20	.19	**.54	~.34	.03	-.01	-.35
% Nouns	.12	~.36	~.34	**.64	*.42	.13	.15	*.42

~p< .10.
*p< .05.
**p< .01.

Table 8. *13-Month Regressions on 20-Month MLU and Cluster Scores*

20-Month Targets	Observed			Interview			Interview		
	Comp. Only	Prod. Only	Joint r^2	Comp. Only	Prod. Only	Joint r^2	Prod. Totals Only	% Flex. Nouns Only	Joint r^2
1. MLU	.000	**.303	**.304	.018	**.272	**.273	**.237	.006	**.278
Interview Clusters									
2. Nominal multiword	.025	*.184	.217	.007	*.148	.188	.043	.088	**.267
3. Grammatical morpheme	.107	*.197	*.320	.002	**.279	*.318	*.145	.032	**.341
4. Semantic-conceptual	*.153	.071	*.236	**.192	.081	**.371	.024	*.185	**.380
5. Dialogue	*.241	.022	*.271	.054	*.124	*.242	.025	*.145	*.320
Observational Clusters									
6. Nominal multiword	.027	*.181	.213	.005	.124	.126	.073	.002	.123
7. Grammatical morpheme	.010	**.330	*.345	.001	**.453	**.454	**.309	.000	**.407
8. Semantics-dialogue	~-.148	.078	.234	.058	.106	.233	.019	*.180	**.355

~p< .10.
*p< .05.
**p< .01.

production uniquely accounted for the full 30.3% when it was entered second. We then repeated the analyses using comprehension and production totals from the 13-month interview. The results were almost identical: The total variance accounted for was a significant 27.3%; only 1.8% of this was contributed uniquely by comprehension, compared with a 27.2% increase when production was entered last. *Hence variation in 20-month MLU is continuous with early production, but not with early comprehension.*

Another pair of analyses demonstrate that the link between MLU and early production is based almost on the "second strand," i.e., production that involves relatively little analysis. This time the two predictor variables were referential flexibility and total production vocabulary (again taken from the interview). The total variance accounted for was 27.8%; 23.7% of this was contributed uniquely by vocabulary totals, compared with less than 1% by referential flexibility. *Hence variation in 20-month MLU seems to be continuous with rote, unanalyzed aspects of production from the very beginning of language acquisition.*

There is an alternative interpretation for the findings reported so far: Perhaps comprehension and referential flexibility are too unreliable to predict anything that happens 7 months later. In order to support our notion of "two strands" in language development, we need to demonstrate a *double dissociation,* wherein both groups of early variables predict different aspects of language over time. The various 20-month cluster scores reflect quite different aspects of grammar and semantics, including both single- and multiword speech. Hence they provide a test for the two-way dissociation of rote versus analyzed language across the second year.

Table 8 summarizes the results of a series of stepwise regressions involving the same 13-month predictors just described. Each of the seven 20-month cluster scores served as the target for one set of six regressions: One pair compared the contributions of observed comprehension and production, another pair compared reported comprehension and production, and a third pair compared production totals with referential flexibility.

First, the two grammatical morphology clusters show results identical to those just described for MLU. Whether morphology is assessed by observations or by parental report, virtually all of the variance shared with first words comes from production rather than comprehension. Furthermore, within 13-month production, prediction of early morphology comes exclusively from vocabulary totals after referential flexibility is removed. *In short, the use of grammatical morphemes at 20 months is continuous with rote or unanalyzed production of single words at the early stages.*

The two nominal multiword clusters are based on first sentences of a different kind: telegraphic combinations of content words, reflecting a variety of different semantic relations. These clusters show much less evidence for continuity with *either* strand in early language (see Table 8). For both the interview and observational versions of the nominal multiword cluster, early comprehension contributes no unique variance at all. For three out of the four regressions in which comprehension is entered first and production is entered second, there is a significant contribution from production. However, this overlap with early production does not decompose neatly into analyzed versus rote speech. In fact, neither aspect of 13-month production contributes unique variance to the nominal multiword clusters.

To summarize so far, MLU and morphology are continuous with rote aspects of production at the early stages, i.e., with the so-called second strand. Nominal or telegraphic speech does not clearly belong to either strand.

So far this does not look much like the double dissociation that we sought to clarify our findings. However, the picture does become clearer when we consider longitudinal predictions for the remaining 20-month clusters. *The semantic-conceptual-dialogue clusters all seem to be continuous with the first, more analytic strand. Hence we do have the desired double dissociation between strands of development from 13 to 20 months.*

First consider the semantic-conceptual cluster from the interview. This variable reflects a variety of sophisticated things children can do with either single- or multiword utterances: talking about the past or future, using language to indicate "pretend," expressing a variety of semantic case relationships with sentences or with single words. In a sense, then, this variable reflects many of the same *meanings* conveyed in the nominal multiword cluster, except that the child is not required to express those meanings in a sentence. When 13-month comprehension and production are both used as predictors (in both the interview and observational versions), the only significant unique variance comes from comprehension. Furthermore, in the regressions comparing rote versus analyzed production at 13 months, the unique contribution by referential flexibility is significant (18.5%, $p < .05$), but the unique contribution from total production is not.

The interview dialogue cluster shows a more mixed pattern. This variable reflects several aspects of language use at 20 months: labeling objects, imitating language by others, answering questions, and making new comments in dialogue. In the regression involving observed comprehension and production, the total variance accounted for (27.1%) is composed primarily of unique variance from comprehension

(24.1%). However, when the corresponding reported vocabulary scores are used, the only significant unique contribution comes from reported production. This apparent disparity is resolved in the third pair of regressions involving the two different aspects of reported vocabulary: With 32% of the variance accounted for overall, referential flexibility makes a significant unique contribution of 14.5% compared with 2.4% from production totals. *In other words, the dialogue cluster also has more in common with the first, more analyzed strand in language development.*

Finally, the semantics-dialogue cluster in the observations represents a conflation of the variables tapped separately by the respective semantic-conceptual and dialogue clusters in the interview. In the regression analyses involving early comprehension and production, none of the unique or joint predictions reached significance. However, the final pair of regressions was more informative: When production totals and referential flexibility are the predictors, the total variance accounted for is a significant 35.5%. A significant 18% of the variance is uniquely contributed by referential flexibility, compared with 1.9% by production totals. *Given this finding, we can conclude that the three semantic-conceptual-dialogue clusters all belong to the first strand in language development, on a continuum with early comprehension and flexible object naming.*

Conclusion

We now have the evidence required to postulate a double dissociation between the two strands in language development. The "first strand" seems to involve comprehension, as well as those aspects of production that have been analyzed and understood by the child. This strand runs from the earliest stages of word comprehension and productive object naming through sophisticated use of single- or multiword utterances to express relational meanings, talk about the outside world, and participate at least minimally in conversation. However, we do not yet have any evidence that this strand of development connects up with *grammar.* It does not tie in clearly, as we thought it might, with telegraphic combinations of content words as reflected in the nominal multiword clusters. In fact, these nominal combinations seem to fall somewhere outside the developmental picture we have painted so far—a point to which we must return in subsequent studies.

By contrast, the second strand does tie into grammar, but only at a rote and superficial level. This strand begins in early production but seems to reflect variance in speech output that is unrelated to comprehension or to productive naming. It connects up at 20 months with MLU and with the use of grammatical morphology. However, there is good reason to believe that these measures of "grammar" are really nonproductive. That is, some 20-month-old children are "cheating," obtaining higher MLU's than their peers by loading their speech with inflections and function words that are poorly understood.

At this point, we cannot decide between two competing hypotheses. On the one hand, the two strands of language development may reflect the dissociation of mechanisms that will eventually turn into separate modules for semantics and grammar, respectively. On the other hand, they may reflect analytic versus rote learning mechanisms that cut across traditional content areas in language. This issue will be clarified later, when we have completed our examination of 20-month language and followed the two dissociable strands of language development into productive acquisition of grammar at 28 months. There we will see that first words and grammar are inextricably tied together. The dissociations observed in early language do not reflect a split between linguistic levels, but rather a dissociation among the mechanisms responsible for acquiring *both* semantics and grammar.

Chapter 7: Study 3
Lexical Development and Lexical Style at 20 Months

In this study we will switch temporarily from structure (reflected in MLU and clusters of first word combinations) to content (reflected in various measures of lexical development at 20 months). We will consider lexical development at 20 months from several points of view.

Composition. We will examine changes in the composition of vocabulary at this critical stage, when children pass from first words to sentences. This will include some new but very basic normative information about changes in the major lexical form class categories. For example, we will see a shift from an emphasis on referential language (e.g., object names) to predicative language (e.g., verbs and adjectives).

Style. These normative changes will be related to the issue of "lexical style," i.e., individual differences in vocabulary composition. At 13 months, the more precocious children tended to specialize in object names. However, we will show that at 20 months, "nouniness" is no longer a hallmark of language progress; instead, the more precocious children are expanding all aspects of the open class, particularly verbs. In other words, lexical style reflects basic normative changes in the composition of the lexicon.

Relationships between Grammar and the Lexicon. Here we will focus on how these 20-month lexical measures relate to grammar and meaning as discussed in Study 2. In multivariate analyses involving both MLU and the various cluster scores, we will demonstrate very strong links between lexical and grammatical development, in both the observations and the interview data. In addition, we will see that the lexical shift from nouns to verbs correlates with the structural shift from single words to word combinations. This is a sensible finding, and a longstanding topic of speculation in the field, but it is documented here for the first time in a large sample.

Longitudinal relationships. We will end by examining links between the 20-month lexicon and the first-word measures described in Study 1. This will provide still more evidence for continuity between stages.

A cross-cutting theme in all these analyses is the relationship between observational and interview assessment. The two data sets are highly correlated overall. But there are also some subtle contrasts in their composition—differences in content and differences in psychometric structure. These differences seem to be related to the contrast between what the child *knows* (as reported by the parent) and what the child prefers to *use* (as demonstrated in the home and laboratory sessions).

Finally, we will continue our consideration of the "two-strand" approach to language that emerged in the first two studies. These two strands will feed into aspects of lexical development and lexical style at 20 months, but their content will change markedly from one age to another. For example, referential style was part of the analytic/conceptual strand at 13 months; non-nominal expressions fell within the rote production strand. At 20 months, when children are meeting the challenges of predication, "nouniness" no longer characterizes either strand of development. The analytic/conceptual strand connects up with variation in the range of verbs that are under a child's control, according to maternal report; the rote strand connects instead with a tendency to make greater use of verbs in the laboratory observations. This split between verb knowledge and verb use complicates our story, demonstrating (among other things) the *heterotypic* nature of early language development—a theme that will continue through the next few studies. It will also force us to consider some alternative characterizations of the two-strand idea, with implications for the modular nature of language-learning mechanisms.

Method

At 20 months, we have information on expressive vocabulary from free speech and from parental report. Observational assessments were taken from the same transcripts described in Study 2 (i.e., the transcripts used to derive MLU and the observational clusters). Parental reports on lexical development were taken in the home session, in conjunction with the interview described in Study 2.

The parental reports were based on a 400-item checklist of words that might be produced by children in the 20-month age range, based on our own previous research and studies by other investigators. The checklist was divided into familiar nominal categories such as food, animal names, furniture, and clothing, as well as lists of common action verbs, adjectives, functors, proper nouns, and routine expressions like "bye-bye." Parents read over the checklist and indicated which items they remembered hearing in their own child's speech. In contrast with the vocabulary interview at 13 months, we did not request anecdotal information for those items that the parents checked. Indeed, given the large vocabularies evidenced by many of our 20-month-olds, such a detailed procedure would have been intolerably long. However, this means that we have no measure of referential flexibility equivalent to the one reported at 13 months.

In addition, there was no effort to assess lexical comprehension by parental report. Pilot work had suggested to us that parents are simply unable to keep track of word comprehension by this age. We do have several observational measures of comprehension, elicited within structured situations or "tests"; but these are fairly complex in their own right and will be discussed separately in studies below.

All vocabulary totals and subtotals were calculated separately for free-speech and for parental report. The disadvantage of this procedure is that it doubles the number of relationships we might obtain by chance. The advantage is that a separation between free-speech and interview data permits us to test the validity of any patterns we do find by replicating them in two data sets. Subtotals were calculated within the following categories: "open-class" items (i.e., content words broken down into common nouns, verbs and adjectives), "closed-class" items (including all grammatical function words and bound inflections), and a miscellaneous class that included proper nouns, routines like "hello," and a few adverbials and other items that were difficult to classify by an open-closed-class distinction. The decision to exclude proper nouns from the open-class count was based on the Snyder et al. finding that proper names are unrelated to any other language variable, including other nouns.

These subtotals were used to derive a number of proportion scores for use in an exploration of lexical style. We began by calculating the same style measure used in Study 1: *referential style,* i.e., the proportion of the child's vocabulary consisting of common nouns. Horgan (1981) has suggested that "noun lovers" and "noun leavers" retain their respective preference for or avoidance of nouns thoughout the language learning years. If she is correct, we would expect high positive correlations between referential style at 13 months and the same measure 7 months later. Furthermore, since referential style was characteristic of the most advanced children at 13 months, we might expect the more advanced children to continue in their "noun specialization" at 20 months. This kind of pattern would be an example of what Kagan (1971) called "homotypic progression," i.e., continuity over time within the same content area.

However, other researchers have noted that vocabulary changes in composition as well as size in the second year (e.g., McCarthy, 1954; Bloom, Hafitz and Lifter, 1980; Gentner, 1982). For one thing, some children begin to use closed-class items, i.e., grammatical function words and inflections. At the same time, there is also an increase within the open class in the verb and adjective categories. Since these new forms are "the thing to do" around 20 months of age, we may find that "closed-class style" and/or "verbiness" are typical of the more advanced children at this stage. Furthermore, the more precocious children at 13 months (who tended to specialize in nouns) may switch lexical preferences when they encounter all the relevant new lexical/grammatical material to be acquired at 20 months. This pattern would be an example of what Kagan calls "heterotypic progression," in which two different content areas are correlated over time because they depend on some common underlying mechanism.

To test these competing hypotheses, we constructed several proportion scores in addition to referential style. One was *closed-class style,* consisting of the total number of different function words and inflections divided by total vocabulary. This was pitted against *open-class style,* i.e., the total number of content words (common nouns, verbs, and adjectives) divided by total vocabulary. The remaining style variables all reflect the child's preferences *within* the open class: *noun density* (common nouns/content words), *verb density* (open-class verbs/content words) and *adjective density* (open-class adjectives/content words).

To summarize, we derived a total of fourteen lexical scores for each child, seven each in the respective interview and observational assessments: total vocabulary, referential style, closed-class style, open-class style, noun density, verb density, and adjective density.

Results

As we promised, the results are divided into four parts: size and composition of the lexicon, lexical style, relationships between the lexicon and grammar, and lexical style from first words to the 20-month onset of grammar.

Size and Composition of the 20-Month Lexicon

According to the parental reports, single-word vocabularies have increased enormously: from a 13-month mean of 12 words to a 20-month mean of 142, ranging from 1 to 404. The boundary for the oft-cited vocabulary burst in the second year is usually placed at fifty words (Nelson, 1973; Kagan, 1981). Following this convention, we can conclude that nineteen of the twenty-seven children in our sample have now passed this frontier.

The language observations provide a much lower estimate of the children's single-word repertoires, although the average is still considerably higher than corresponding observations at 13 months: from a 13-month mean of 1.7 to a 20-month mean of 36 different words, ranging from 4 to 121. Only five children actually displayed fifty or more distinct morphemes across the home and laboratory visits. The disparity between reports and observations is not surprising. What adult could display his entire vocabulary in 2 to 3 hours of spontaneous conversation? The crossvalidation between parental report and observations resides not in a comparison of totals but in the relationships between these two estimates—in this case, a large and reliable correlation of +.83 ($p < .01$).

Despite this large overlap in variance, there are further differences between parental reports and free speech beyond the obvious differences in size. In particular, the *composition* of 20-month vocabulary differs in the two data sets. Parental reports break down as follows: 71.8% open-class items (including 56% common nouns, 8.9% verbs, 6.9% adjectives), 5.5% closed-class morphemes, with a remaining 22.7% from the miscellaneous class. The corresponding figures for free speech are 61.8% open-class (including 46% common nouns, 8.3% verbs, 7.5% adjectives), 23.4% closed-class morphology, with a remaining 14.8% in the miscellaneous class. A major difference here lies in the greater proportion of closed-class items in free speech. Here too, a comparison between free speech and total vocabulary would probably look quite similar if we were studying adults. In spontaneous conversation, we can produce only a limited sample of our large open-class vocabularies; however, we may well be called upon to use most if not all of our grammatical function words in order to produce well-formed speech. Nevertheless, this difference also has developmental implications: parental report is more likely to reflect what the child *knows,* whereas free speech reflects those forms that she is more likely to *use.* This difference between knowledge and use may map onto the respective first and second strands of language development that have emerged in our data so far.

Lexical Style

Table 9 presents correlations between the various lexical proportion scores and total vocabulary, in both free speech and interviews. First, consider referential style. In the early stages described in Study 1, and in reports by other investigators studying the one-word stage, referential style was characteristic of the more precocious children (i.e., the children with larger vocabularies overall). At 20 months, this is no longer true: in the interviews, referential style is indeed correlated positively and significantly with vocabulary totals (+.50, $p < .01$); in the observations, however, the correlation between total vocabulary and referential style is nonsignificant, and in the negative direction (-.10).

Table 9. *Correlations of Lexical Style with Vocabulary Totals at 20 Months*

	Vocabulary Totals	
Lexical Style Scores	Reported	Observed
Reported		
1. Referential style	**.50	~.35
2. Open-class style	**.65	*.49
3. Closed-class style	-.17	-.07
4. Noun density	-.06	-.11
5. Verb density	**.55	**.49
6. Adjective density	.25	.19
Observed		
7. Referential style	-.23	~-.39
8. Open-class style	*.49	.27
9. Closed-class style	.00	.14
10. Noun density	-.16	~-.39
11. Verb density	.15	*.43
12. Adjective density	.11	.14

~$p<.10$.
*$p<.05$.
**$p<.01$.

This brings us to consider "closed-class style" as an alternative. We know that the free-speech totals contained a higher proportion overall of closed-class items. Hence we might expect closed-class style to predict vocabulary size in the observations. As can be seen in Table 9, this was clearly not true either. The closed-class proportion scores do not correlate with vocabulary size in *either* the interviews or the observations.

What about the open-class as a whole, including entries within the new categories of adjective and verb? For the parental report data, open class style was an even better predictor of total vocabulary than the traditional measure of referential style: +.65 ($p < .01$), compared with +.50. To test whether this apparent improvement in the prediction was significant, we regressed both referential and open-class style on vocabulary total, in alternating orders: with 45.7% of the variance accounted for overall, open-class style made a significant unique contribution of 22.6%, compared with a nonsignificant 6.5% from referential style. *In other words, the fashionable thing to do at 20 months (i.e., the style associated with greater overall progress) is to expand all aspects of the open class, and not simply object names.*

In the free-speech data, the simple correlation between open-class style and total vocabulary failed to reach significance, although it was at least in the positive direction (+.14, compared with –.10 for referential style). However, regression analyses showed that these low correlations are misleading. When the two style scores are regressed on free speech vocabulary totals, in alternating orders, the results were as follows: With 23.8% of the variance accounted for overall, the open-class score contributes 22.7% unique variance, whereas referential style contributes a smaller but still significant 16.7%. Note that the sum of the two totals for *unique* variance is larger than the total joint variance. This unusual situation represents what have been called "suppressor effects." What this means is that the two style scores are working in opposite directions, effectively canceling each other out! The contribution by open-class style reflects a significant *positive* partial correlation of +.55 ($p < .01$); the contribution by referential style reflects a significant *negative* partial correlation of –.41 ($p < .05$), variance from overall open-class expansion is removed.

It should be quite clear by now that referential style is, in itself, no longer the hallmark of language advancement by 20 months of age. Instead, the more precocious children are the ones who are expanding the open class by adding verbs and adjectives as well as nouns. This opposition between "nouniness" and "verbiness" is responsible for the suppressor effects we just observed.

This conclusion is confirmed and clarified by a final set of style analyses within the open class involving three proportion scores: noun density, verb density, and adjective density. As summarized in Table 9, total reported vocabulary is correlated at +.55 ($p < .01$) with verb density within the open class; similarly, the free-speech measure of verb density correlates with free speech vocabulary at +.45 ($p < .05$). Corresponding density scores for nouns and adjectives are unrelated to overall vocabulary. *We can conclude, then, that the "thing to do" at 20 months, characteristic of the most advanced children, is to acquire open-class verbs.* Referential style is, at least temporarily, "out of fashion." And closed-class usage seems to be irrelevant, at least at this age.

There is only one complication to this otherwise very clear story. Free speech and reported vocabulary totals were, as we noted, highly related (+.83). The two open-class style proportion scores were also highly correlated (+.67, $p < .01$). However, the two corresponding verb density measures were entirely unrelated: +.08. The two verb-style scores

Table 10. *Full and Partial Correlations of 20-Month Vocabulary Scores with MLU and the Cluster Scores*

	Vocabulary Scores			
	Reported	Partialing Out Observed	Observed	Partialing Out Reported
1. MLU	**.54	-.35	**.79	**.74
Interview clusters				
2. Nominal multiword	**.71	~.36	**.67	.21
3. Grammatical morpheme	**.61	.07	**.71	*.44
4. Semantic-conceptual	**.70	*.50	**.57	-.03
5. Dialogue	**.65	~.38	**.57	.08
Observational clusters				
6. Nominal multiword	**.73	.01	**.88	**.72
7. Grammatical morpheme	**.61	*-.40	**.87	**.82
8. Semantics-dialogue	**.72	.24	**.76	*.42

~ $p < .10$.
* $p < .05$.
** $p < .01$.

may reflect very different aspects of verb knowledge—or perhaps, more precisely, some kind of difference between verb knowledge (reflected in parental reports) and verb use (reflected in free speech). This difference is clarified in the next section, where we examine the relationship between lexical development and 20-month grammar and semantics.

Grammar, Semantics, and the Lexicon

Several important events happen around the same time sometime during the second year: the sudden burst in single-word vocabulary, the use of single words to convey semantic relations (e.g., saying "daddy" to indicate the relation of ownership while pointing at daddy's shoes), and the passage from single words to sentences (Greenfield and Smith, 1976; Nelson, 1973; Bloom, 1970; Kagan, 1981). The correlations reported in Table 10 strongly support the idea that these developments may be causally related (although the direction of causation is unclear). Both interview and observational vocabulary totals correlate very highly with MLU and with all seven of the grammatical and semantic cluster scores.

Table 11. *20-Month Lexical Style with MLU and Cluster Scores*

	Lexical Style Scores			
	Reported		Observed	
	Open-Class Style	Verb Density	Open-Class Style	Verb Density
1. MLU	.13	.28	-.03	*.45
Interview clusters				
2. Nominal multiword	**.55	**.59	*.47	.15
3. Grammatical morpheme	~.37	~.33	.26	*.42
4. Semantic-conceptual	**.76	**.64	**.70	.00
5. Dialogue	**.58	.21	.28	-.01
Observational clusters				
6. Nominal multiword	*.43	*.46	.22	~.38
7. Grammatical morpheme	.23	.29	.01	**.51
8. Semantics-dialogue	**.65	**.52	**.60	.18

~ $p < .10$.
* $p < .05$.
** $p < .01$.

The onset of multiword speech is predicted not only by overall vocabulary expansion, but also by certain aspects of lexical style (Table 11), including overall open-class expansion and verb expansion within the open class. This finding is in line with conclusions from several case studies (e.g., Bloom, Hafitz, and Lifter, 1980). The suggestion is that verbs and adjectives lead the child into the discovery of grammar, because they are associated with predicative meanings—that is, with those meanings that motivate grammatical relations at the clausal level (Bates and MacWhinney, 1982). However, the pattern of relationships in Table 11 is very complex, forcing us to confront differences between observational and interview data.

To explore these differences, we carried out a series of partial correlations (also reported in Table 10): one set examined correlations of the grammatical and semantic measures with parental report, controlling for the variance shared with free speech; conversely, the other set examined correlations of the same variables with free speech, controlling for variance shared with parental report. With these controls, interview vocabulary now correlated significantly with only two variables: a positive correlation with the interview semantic-conceptual cluster and a negative correlation with the observational morphology cluster. By contrast, free-speech vocabulary now correlated significantly with all three observational clusters (but especially with the two involving word combinations), with the interview morphology cluster, and with MLU. *These mirror-image results suggest that parental report picks up more variance from the "first strand"; free speech contains more variance from the "second strand."* This is compatible with our contention that the interview reflects what the child knows, while the observations are better assessments of what the child is ready to use.

A similar picture emerges when we examine correlations involving 20-month lexical style, summarized in Table 11. Neither measure of closed-class style related to *any* of the grammatical or semantic measures. In the interviews, open-class style and verb density both correlated with semantic/conceptual/nominal aspects of 20-month language. In the observations, however, open-class style and verb density project off in opposite directions. Open-class style correlated with the semantic-conceptual and nominal clusters, but not with grammatical morphology. Verb density correlated only with MLU and morphology. *In other words, overall open-class expansion is associated with the first strand in both data sets. But the verbs tapped by the interview measure align only with the "first strand," whereas the verbs tapped by free speech align with the "second strand."*

Another way to illustrate this point is through regression analyses on the style scores, using the cluster variables as predictors (Table 12). For the open-class scores, the patterns are essentially the same. Using the observational clusters as predictors, 44.8% of the variance in the interview-style score is accounted for overall ($p < .01$); in the corresponding equation for free speech, 50.6% of the variance is accounted for by three observational clusters combined ($p < .01$). In both regressions, the only significant unique prediction comes from the observational semantics-dialogue cluster: a 25.3% increase in the equation predicting interview open-class style, and a 42.1% increase in the equation predicting observed open-class style ($p < .01$). Regressions using the interview clusters as predictors tell exactly the same story. The total variance accounted for by these four predictors is 63% for open-class style in the interview and 54.6% for open-class style in the observations. The only significant unique contribution to these equations comes from the semantic-conceptual cluster: an increase of 20.8% for interview open-class style and 29.5% for observational open-class style ($p < .01$). *Open-class style is clearly associated with semantic-conceptual sophistication, reflected in the semantic-conceptual-dialogue clusters.*

Table 12. *Regressions of 20-Month Clusters on Lexical Style*

| | Lexical Style Scores | | | |
| | Reported | | Observed | |
	Open-Class Style	Verb Density	Open-Class Style	Verb Density
Interview clusters				
Joint variance	**.630	**.554	**.568	.332
Unique variance				
Nominal multiword	.002	*.096	.025	.008
Grammatical morpheme	.019	.021	.035	**.269
Semantic-conceptual	**.208	*.144	**.314	.016
Dialogue	.040	.060	.025	.042
Observational Clusters				
Joint variance	**.449	*.230	**.506	*.293
Unique variance				
Nominal multiword	.003	.026	.008	.010
Grammatical morpheme	.021	.004	.066	.133
Semantics-dialogue	**.253	.079	**.421	.021

*$p < .05$.
**$p < .01$.

However, the corresponding regressions on verb density look very different. First, when the observational clusters are used as predictors, *no* significant variance is accounted for, joint or unique, in either of the verb-density scores. When the interview clusters are used as predictors, the two-verb-density style scores yield interesting and different results. For observed verb density, the joint prediction fails to reach significance (33.1% total, $p < .10$); there is, however, a significant unique contribution of 26.9% by the morphology cluster when entered last ($p < .01$). Since observed verb density and interview morphology are drawn from different data sets, this is a nontrivial result. *It states that the verbs produced by 20-month-old children across a brief observational period tend to be the "carriers" of whatever grammatical morphology they control at this point.*

In the corresponding regression on interview verb density, a significant 55.3% of the variance ($p < .01$) is accounted for jointly by the four interview clusters. In this case, however, there are *two* unique contributions: 14.4% ($p < .01$) from the semantic-conceptual cluster, and 9.6% ($p < .05$) from the nominal multiword cluster. This is a useful piece of information, suggesting that verb use and verb knowledge are both implicated in the transition into multiword speech, but in different ways. *High-probability verbs carry grammatical morphology; but the broader range of verbs tapped by the interview measure is associated with lexical sophistication in general, and with nominal, telegraphic speech in particular.*

To summarize, both measures of open-class style reflect semantic-conceptual sophistication independent of grammatical form. Verb-density measures are, by contrast, implicated in different aspects of the ability to combine words at 20 months. Verb knowledge is associated with nominal multiword speech; verb use is associated with the grammatical morphology.

The finding that verb expansion predicts early grammar is entirely sensible and reasonable, from a normative point of view. Verbs epitomize the expression of predicative/relational meanings, which in turn are the meanings that underlie and motivate early sentences. But the more detailed aspects of these findings are a bit more mysterious. How do we account for the difference between two style measures that are calculated in exactly the same way? Remember that the two verb-density proportions were entirely unrelated to one another, which already suggested that they involve different verbs, or, at least, different aspects of verb knowledge and verb use. There are two ways that we could interpret these findings at this point.

1. **The grammar/semantics hypothesis.** The verbs observed in free speech are "carriers" for most of the inflectional morphology and many of the function words used by 20-month-old children. The verbs reported by parents are "carriers" of predication and relational meaning, reflected in telegraphic word combinations. In both instances, the contrast between verb density and open-class style reflects a partial dissociation between grammar and semantics.

2. **The rote/analytic hypothesis.** The verbs observed in free speech are particularly frequent, and may reflect to some extent the production of rote or formulaic sentence fragments. The verbs reported by the parents are more extensive and varied, including lower-frequency items, so that the variance in this measure may have more to do with analyzed than rote language, including single- and multiword meanings.

Table 13. *Full and Partial Correlations of 13-Month Measures with Vocabulary Totals at 20 Months*

| | | Vocabulary Scores | | |
| | | Reported Partialing Out Observed | | Observed Partialing Out Reported |
	Reported		Observed	
10-Month				
Comprehension	*.40	**.65	.05	**-.56
Production	*.44	~.35	.30	-.12
13-Month				
Observed				
Spontaneous	.32	-.25	**.53	*.50
Imitative	*.45	.01	**.53	.32
Comprehension	.37	.27	.27	-.06
Interview				
Production	**.50	.00	**.60	~.38
% Nouns in production	**.51	*.48	.31	-.24
% Flexible nouns in production	**.65	**.61	*.40	-.31
Comprehension	*.38	*.48	.13	-.35
% Nouns in comprehension	**.51	**.52	.28	-.29

$\sim p < .10.$
* $p < .05.$
** $p < .01.$

We cannot decide between these alternatives without more information, presented in the next few studies.

Continuity from 13 to 20 Months

Table 13 summarizes correlations between the fourteen 20-month lexical measures and the first-word variables discussed in Study 1. In general, these correlations demonstrate strong continuity in lexical development in the period from first words to first-word combinations. In addition, however, they also demonstrate the complex and heterotypic nature of lexical style as it changes over time. Finally, these data add more support to the notion that reported vocabulary belongs in the first strand (relating more to comprehension, referential style, and referential flexibility), whereas free-speech vocabulary relates more to the second strand (in particular to vocabulary totals at 13 months).

To obtain a clearer picture of these relationships, we conducted two mirror-image sets of partial correlations (also reported in Table 13): total observed vocabulary with the 13-month measures, controlling for reported vocabulary; and total reported vocabulary with the same 13-month measures, controlling for observed vocabulary. The results are unambiguous. When the huge amount of variance shared by the two lexical measures is removed, reported vocabulary correlates significantly only with the first-strand measures at 13 months: comprehension, referential style, and referential flexibility. By contrast, free-speech vocabulary now correlates only with the observed and reported 13-month production totals.

To summarize so far, our two different assessments of vocabulary at 20 months have a great deal of variance in common. However, the non-overlapping portions of these two measures seem to project off in different directions. *Reported vocabulary belongs to the first strand, including the more flexible and analyzed aspects of early speech. Observed vocabulary belongs to the second strand, in particular to those aspects of 13-month vocabulary that are independent of analysis and understanding.*

The same point is made when we consider the relationship between measures of lexical style at 13 and 20 months. The simple correlations in Table 14 can be summarized briefly: 20-month open-class style also belongs in the first strand, correlated with 13-month comprehension, referential style, and referential flexibility. *In other words, the children who were understanding and producing relatively high proportions of nouns from the earliest stages continue to accumulate all content words at a higher rate later on.*

Given this pattern, then, we might also expect a connection between early style measures and verb density. If this were true, we could conclude that children doing the "in thing" at 13 months (i.e., nouns) are switching to the "in thing" several months later (i.e., verbs). But this simply is not borne out by the data. Neither of the 20-month verb-density measures correlated beyond chance levels with first words. In other words, we have found a *discontinuity* between early lexical development and the specific elaboration of verbs in the second year. This is a very different pattern than we have found so far, meriting careful consideration below.

Table 14. *13-Month Regressions on 20-Month Lexical Style*

	Observed			Interview			Interview		
	Comp. Only	Prod. Only	Joint r^2	Comp. Only	Prod. Only	Joint r^2	Prod Totals Only	% Flex. Nouns Only	Joint r^2
Reported									
Open-class style	*.208	.016	*.231	*.198	.014	*.263	.000	.145	.209
Verb density	.031	.031	.000	.133	.023	.203	.035	.005	.075
Observed									
Open-class style	.134	.003	.140	*.211	.000	.227	.012	*.167	.184
Verb density	.011	.025	.038	.049	.131	.148	*.163	.068	.167

*$p < .05$.

Conclusion

This is the most complex of the studies presented so far, and the results at this point are more heterogeneous and difficult to understand than they will seem when we have completed our longitudinal journey. The main findings can be summarized as follows:

1. **The role of verbs in lexical expansion.** Although the vocabulary burst that takes place during the second year involves a very large increase in common nouns, there is a greater *rate* of increase in lexical items that express predicative meanings—adjectives, adverbs, closed-class items, but particularly verbs.

2. **Lexical style: from "nouniness" to "verbiness."** Whereas the most precocious children at 13 months were those with a high proportion of nouns in their vocabulary, by 20 months the most precocious children are expanding all aspects of the open-class. And within the open class, overall progress is predicted by a proportional emphasis on verbs. In other words, "nouniness" is a hallmark of progress at the early stages, while a more general open-class style is characteristic of lexical advance 6–7 months later. And within the open class, "verbiness" is associated with overall rate of development. This underscores the heterotypic nature of language development, a point that we will have to make repeatedly in the next few chapters. It is not the case, however, that early referential style turns into verb style later on. Instead, we find our first evidence of discontinuity in lexical development; children in the middle range are able to use the discovery of verbs to move ahead in several aspects of development. Lexical style is a heterotypic variable.

3. **Lexical/grammatical links.** We find very strong evidence for continuity between lexical and grammatical development—within and between age levels. Our findings confirm two hypotheses with a long history in child language: a link between the vocabulary burst in the second year and the subsequent (or concurrent) appearance of multiword speech and a link between the appearance of lexical predicates (particularly verbs) and the passage from single to multiword speech.

4. **Interview/observation comparisons.** Overall, this study also provides further evidence for the value of interview techniques, exemplified in very high correlations between interview and observational vocabulary totals. Indeed, the magnitude of the correlations compares favorably to intertest and even test–retest reliabilities in the adult psychometric literature (e.g., the correlation between the Stanford-Binet and the Wechsler verbal intelligence scales). Nevertheless, when the large amount of overlapping variance

between measures is removed, our interview and observational assessments do project off in separate directions. In particular, the interviews seem to fall into our first strand of analytic language variables, whereas the observational assessments align more closely with the second strand of rote or "pure production" measures. This is particularly true for verb density scores in the interviews and the observations. These two style scores are uncorrelated with one another, and they each map onto a different strand of acquisition. We suggested that verbs reported by the mother reflect what the child *knows*, while the verbs observed in free speech reflect what the child is likely to *do*.

What do these findings tell us about the relationship between grammar and semantics—hence the more general issue of modularity? Bloom et al. (1980) have argued that verbs play a unique and important role in early language development. At least in English, verbs carry most of the inflectional morphology that needs to be acquired, while at the same time conveying semantic relationships among the various nouns that the child has been acquiring for many months. As such, verbs represent a kind of bridge from semantics to grammar, and their appearance late in the second year reflects a corresponding change in emphasis on the child's part. Our data on lexical style from 13 to 20 months are consonant with Bloom's conclusions, but from a somewhat different perspective.

In the one word stage, referential style and referential flexibility are typical of the more advanced children. At the beginning of the two-word stage, open-class expansion in general and verb expansion in particular are now the hallmarks of language precocity. There is continuity from early referential expansion to later open-class expansion, as we might expect. That is, children who are ahead on one are likely to be ahead on the other. And yet the specific category of verbs seems to represent a discontinuity with early language. The discovery of verbs will of course be important for every child. However, for some children it seems to open new vistas and to present a more rapid way of breaking into the language than that which they had previously used. These children suddenly move from the middle ranks toward the head of the class. This is precisely the situation that is responsible for the lack of continuity between "nouniness" at 13 months and "verbiness" at 20 months. Does this mean that verbs represent the first signs of a new language module, in particular a module devoted to grammar?

The dissociation *within* verbs complicates this interpretation. The more important findings in this study seem to replicate in both the interview and the observational data. However, despite the fact that the two vocabulary totals share considerable variance, the nonoverlapping variance in these measures seems to project off in different directions. Reported vocabulary, which reflects a wider sampling of what the child *knows,* aligns more with the first strand in language development: with productive naming at the early stages, and with semantic-conceptual sophistication later on. This is particularly true for verb-density scores in the interview data. Free-speech vocabulary, which reflects the more frequent forms that the child typically *uses,* aligns more with the second strand: the unanalyzed or less productive aspects of early speech and MLU and grammatical morphology at Stage I. This pattern is particularly marked in the observational data on verbs. If verbs reflect the first stirrings of a separate grammar module, it is not clear why we should find such a sharp demarcation between verb knowledge and verb use.

We cannot yet decide between two competing explanations for the two strands: the grammar/semantics hypothesis or the rote/analyzed hypothesis. The peculiar and discontinuous behavior of the verb-density measures seems to provide more support for a grammar/semantics dissociation. By this argument, noun development reflects the operation of a lexical module primarily devoted to the acquisition of referential meanings. Verb development reflects the appearance of a grammatical module devoted to (perhaps) relational meanings as well as the forms needed to express predication. But the relationship between grammatical morphology at 20 months and unanalyzed production at 13 months provides more support for a rote/analytic distinction. From this point of view, the first appearance of purely grammatical forms in speech (i.e., function words and inflections) seems to be controlled by factors responsible for imitative, rote learning of single words at one year of age. The variance in free-speech verb density reflects the use of high probability verbs that carry much of this rote morphology. Variance in the interview verb-density scores reflects instead the application of semantic/conceptual analysis to verbs and their associated predicative meanings. This issue will be clarified when the same variables are connected up with truly productive use of grammar at 28 months.

A final point regards the status of nominal/telegraphic constructions at 20 months. In the last two studies we have had a difficult time classifying nominal word combinations with either of the two language strands. These telegraphic utterances seem to hang somewhere in between the two groups of measures, changing alignments from one set of analyses to another. Could these word combinations involve some third mechanism? If they do, perhaps this third mechanism is the grammar module that has eluded us so far. The next study, on single- and multiword comprehension at 20 months, should help answer this question.

Chapter 8: Study 4
Single- and Multiword
Comprehension at 20 Months

The purpose of this study is to compare comprehension of single words with comprehension of multiword commands, in relationship to the passage from single- to multiword utterances in expressive language.

We should admit from the outset that this particular study has more than its share of methodological problems. Comprehension is by definition a mental event, one that must be inferred from some combination of overt behavior and context. At 13 months we were able to obtain a reasonably reliable estimate of comprehension abilities by relying on the parents, who observe their own children daily in a host of relevant situations. The 13-month "multiple choice test," our one observational index of comprehension, did give roughly comparable results (see also Bretherton et al., 1981a). But this test was unquestionably a weaker and less reliable measure than the parental reports. Children performed just beyond chance levels, a fact that is not surprising given that this test is also strongly affected by factors such as toy preference and obedience.

By 20 months, most parents have completely lost track of their children's receptive vocabularies. We are thus forced to rely entirely on direct observations. To our knowledge, there are no *standardized* language comprehension tests for single words or sentences that claim to work before 2–2½ years of age. For single-word comprehension, in addition to our own multiple choice test, there are several *experimental* procedures that do work at above chance levels from the end of the first year (e.g., Oviatt, 1979; Kuczaj, 1979; Reznick and Kagan, 1983; Kagan, 1981). However, these procedures function best when used as they were intended to test hypotheses against group rather than individual data. Although a 20-month-old does at least "understand the game" better than a 1-year-old, results of comprehension experiments are still clouded by irrelevant and task-specific sources of noise.

Obviously the same thing holds for assessments of multiword comprehension. Nevertheless, at least one experimental procedure is available that holds promise. Sachs and Truswell (1978) have shown that

113

children in the one-word stage can comprehend and obey commands that require integrating two distinct lexical items in a novel combination, e.g., commands such as "Tickle the cup." The control for novel combinations is an important one, since a child might resolve a command like "Tickle the dolly" *not* by computing a relationship between the two content words "on line," but by processing each word separately and then producing the canonical "scene" that is *usually* associated with those words. We can only be certain that the child comprehends a whole multiword construction if she can obey a command involving two familiar items in a configuration that she has never heard or seen before.

Can we take the Sachs and Truswell findings to mean that children in the one-word stage have receptive control over grammatical rules? Probably not. Grammar can be defined for our purposes as *the ability to produce and understand both novel and ordered combinations of morphemes, in accord with the conventions of one's native language.* The Sachs and Truswell study proves that children in this age range can understand *novel combinations,* but it tells us nothing about *ordering.* In fact, Wetstone and Friedlander (1973) have shown that children who produce ordered strings in their own speech may respond in the same way to both ordered and scrambled sentences, e.g., "Tickle the doll" vs. "Doll the tickle" (cf. Golinkoff, 1983; Golinkoff and Kerr, 1978). How can we account for this disparity between comprehension and production? In Stage I, English children do typically produce a systematic subset of the possible word orders in their language. However, the cross-linguistic generality of this finding has been questioned (Braine, 1976), and the interpretation of the English patterns remains a matter of considerable controversy (e.g., Bowerman, 1973; Golinkoff, 1983; Golinkoff and Kerr, 1978; Howe, 1976; Bates and MacWhinney, 1979). For example, the children may be producing ordered strings based on rote combinations of two words or on rules with a very limited scope based on just a few lexical items (e.g., "In a sentence involving the word 'more', always put 'more' in first position"). In other words, it remains to be proven whether Stage I children have mastered grammatical rules of ordering in *either* comprehension or production.

For present purposes, we will make only the most minimal assumptions concerning the abilities that underlie early word combinations. Fully aware of the methodological problems inherent in early comprehension testing, we propose a test of the following hypothesis:

Combinatorial comprehension and combinatorial production in Stage I speech involve the same kind of "pregrammatical" processing, namely, the ability to plan and interpret two or more content words under a single intonation contour.

As we shall see, there is some support for this hypothesis. The data will also provide a challenge to the two-strand picture developed so far, with further albeit limited evidence for discontinuity from single words to grammar. This apparent discontinuity will not be resolved until all the evidence has been examined, in Studies 11 and 12.

Method

For single-word comprehension testing, we adopted the same multiple-choice test described in Study 1, and by Bretherton et al. (1981a). This task was always administered in the laboratory, at the second 20-month session. The procedure is identical at 13 and 20 months, and the scoring is the same: a possible range from 0 to 16 correct object choices, with a chance level of 33%.

Our test of multiword comprehension was an adaptation of the work by Sachs and Truswell (1978). With their mothers seated behind them, the children were presented with a paired series of purely linguistic commands (i.e., no nonverbal cues) by the Experimenter. The command pairs included both a familiar command (e.g., "Kiss the baby") and an unfamiliar or improbable counterpart to that command (e.g., "Kiss the ball"). Each child received five pairs of commands, that could be somewhat individualized to reflect the naming competence of an individual child. For instance, the "kiss" command might be individualized by substituting a child's more familiar equivalent such as "hug" or "love," and the "baby" might become either a "dolly" or a "teddy bear," depending on maternal assessment of the child's preferred or best-known term for that act or object. Similarly, in another command a truck might be called either a "truck" or a "car," or a sofa might be substituted for a chair, depending on which object or term was more generally familiar to the child.

The five command sets were as follows: "Kiss the baby" paired with "Kiss the ball"; "Tickle the dolly" paired with "Tickle the cup"; "Push the car" paired with "Push the keys"; "Give the book to Mommy" vs. "Give the book to the chair"; and "Put the hat on your head" vs. "Put the hat on your foot."

For each command in a given pair, the two objects specifically contrasted in that pair (e.g., the dolly and the ball) were presented in randomized position equidistant from the child. The mother watched as the Experimenter delivered the two verbal commands, always unaccompanied by gestural support, and always with the probable command first and the improbable second. Each request was made three times (or fewer if the child complied and acted correctly on the specified object earlier). Then, after the improbable command in each set—and regardless of infant compliance—the mother was asked to get her infant to do the unfamiliar act "However you would normally get her/him to understand and do it." The maternal version of each command was scored and analyzed separately, as part of a separate study of maternal teaching style; those data will not be presented here. Considering only the standardized commands delivered by the Experimenter, each child could obtain a score of 0 to 5 on the respective canonical and noncanonical command sets.

Results and Discussion

The Multiple-Choice Test

On the multiple-choice test for single-word comprehension, scores averaged 55%, compared with a chance baseline of 33.3%. As noted by Bretherton et al. (1981a), this is a significant gain over the near-chance performance of 13-month-olds. However, the respective 13- and 20-month versions of this test were *not* significantly correlated with one another (+.18). Bretherton et al. report that the internal reliability of the measure at 20 months is also very low. In the various experimental studies by other investigators using comprehension procedures in the first and second year, internal reliabilities are usually not reported. There is, then, no way of knowing whether our own measure functions particularly badly as a test of individual differences. We suspect, however, that such results are endemic of infant comprehension testing in general.

Not surprisingly, this multiple-choice test also entered in very few significant relationships with the other 20-month language measures. In fact, of the twenty-two variables at this age level that we have discussed so far (MLU, seven clusters, and fourteen lexical measures), only two correlations with single-word comprehension were significant beyond the conventional .05 level: +.38 with the interview semantic-conceptual cluster and +.55 with interview verb density. For what it is worth, these findings do at least align in the predicted direction, i.e., placing single-word comprehension in the "first strand" of language development, where it presumably ought to be.

The Commands Test: Canonical and Noncanonical

On the commands task, scores for canonical commands averaged 2.96 (range: from 1 to 5); the corresponding scores for noncanonical commands averaged 1.69 (range: from 0 to 5). A student's t-test for the difference between these means was significant at $p < .05$. As we might expect, comprehension of multiword commands is easier when the child can map the relationship between two words directly onto her prior world knowledge (see also Chapman and Kohn, 1978). Nevertheless, the correlation between canonical and noncanonical command scores was a high +.73 ($p < .01$). This hardly qualifies as "split-half reliability," since the implausible version of each command was designed to follow and build upon the plausible version. But it does seem fair to conclude that there is less error variance in the multiword comprehension test than there was in our single-word assessment. The multiple-choice task of choosing an object from an array is a simple and natural one for children, but it is also a task that permits a high proportion of "false positives" or chance successes. On the commands task, there is less room for guessing; the child either obeys (having presumably understood at least some part of the message) or ignores the command and does something else.

Let us assume, then, that the canonical portion of the commands task offers a better assessment of single-word comprehension, without *necessarily* implying comprehension of combinations (as Sachs and Truswell have also noted). By contrast, the noncanonical portion of the task *does* imply the ability to hear and compute a novel relationship between two known lexical items. How do these two measures compare in their relationship to grammar and semantics in 20-month production? Table 15 presents the simple correlations between canonical and noncanonical commands and the other 20-month variables: MLU, the seven semantic and grammatical clusters, and the fourteen lexical measures. Most of these correlations are significant. Furthermore, in most of them the relationship with the more difficult, noncanonical commands task is higher. To test this observation further, we carried out partial correlations with the noncanonical measure, removing the variance from canonical command scores (also recorded in Table 15). Very little changed.

To extract more interesting, qualitative patterns from this matrix of significant relationships, we turn again to regression analysis, using the various cluster scores as predictors and the two respective comprehension scores as targets. Given the findings reported in the last two studies, what should we expect?

Overall, we should expect the two comprehension measures to align more with the first strand of language development, i.e., with measures involving semantic-conceptual sophistication. However, for the noncanonical version of the commands task, there is one rather different prediction: If this task does indeed reflect the child's ability to compute a novel relationship between two content words, it ought to be the comprehension "mirror-image" of telegraphic combinations of content words in production. Hence noncanonical command scores should bear a significant and unique relationship to the nominal multiword cluster scores, in both the interview and the observations.

Table 15. *Correlations Involving 20-Month Comprehension*

		Comprehension Measures			
		Single Word (Choice Task)	Canonical Commands	Noncanonical Commands	Noncanonical Partialing Out Canonical
20 months					
1.	MLU	.07	~.33	**.51	*.41
2.	Interview clusters				
	Nom. multiword	~.32	*.47	**.71	**.61
	Gramm. morpheme	.12	.24	*.46	*.44
	Semantic-conceptual	*.38	*.48	**.58	~.38
	Dialogue	.04	.26	*.45	*.40
3.	Observational clusters				
	Nom. multiword	~.34	~.38	**.68	**.65
	Gramm. morpheme	.11	~.36	**.55	*.46
	Semantics-dialogue	.25	**.52	**.75	**.63
4.	Interview lexical				
	Total vocabulary	.29	**.52	**.66	*.48
	Open-class style	~.32	*.45	**.49	.26
	Verb density	**.56	**.55	**.65	*.42
5.	Observed lexical				
	Total vocabulary	.25	*.46	**.69	*.59
	Open-class style	.15	*.45	~.37	.04
	Verb density	.01	.16	.18	.09
13 months					
6.	Interview				
	Production totals	.01	~.37	*.44	.25
	% Nouns prod.	.21	~.34	*.43	.27
	% Flexible nouns prod.	.07	.17	*.41	*.44
	Comprehension totals	.28	.22	~.34	.28
	% Nouns comp.	.16	.00	.24	~.37
7.	Observed				
	Spontaneous production	.05	*.40	*.48	.29
	Imitative production	~.35	.24	*.42	~.38
	Single word comprehension (choice task)	.18	.05	.22	.28

~ $p < .10$.
* $p < .05$.
** $p < .01$.

As described in Studies 2 and 3, we conducted "rounds" of regression analyses, first using the interview clusters and then using the observation clusters, in a series of hierarchical orders giving each cluster an opportunity to be entered last. Hence we can compute both the joint and the unique variance contributed by the various predictor variables. Results are summarized in Table 16.

For the canonical commands (i.e., our best estimate of single-word comprehension), the equation using the four interview clusters fell short of significance ($p < .10$). Furthermore, none of the individual cluster scores contributed unique variance. The same results were obtained with the free-speech clusters. Apparently, canonical commands map onto the various grammatical and semantic clusters via some basic, shared "verbal ability" factor. There are not strong style differences on this particular measure.

For the noncanonical commands, we have a partial confirmation of our predictions. On the interview regressions, the total variance accounted for was a significant 54.8% ($p < .01$). However, the only unique contribution was a significant 17.3% ($p < .01$) from the interview nominal multiword cluster. *Hence comprehension of novel multiword commands does seem to have most in common with production of novel, telegraphic utterances.*

However, these results did not replicate in the observational regressions. This time the total variance accounted for was 62.5%, with the only unique contribution coming from the semantics-dialogue cluster (14.2%). Recall that the nominal and morphological clusters in the observations were much more highly correlated than the corresponding clusters in the interview. Hence the interview clusters probably provide a better test of our predicted "special relationship" between comprehension of noncanonical commands and telegraphic speech in production. Still, we can only regard this as a partial confirmation of our hypothesis.

What can we conclude so far? There is at least some evidence, weaker than we might have hoped, that 20-month comprehension aligns with the first strand in language development that emerged in Studies 1–3. Furthermore, there is some evidence (also weaker than we might have hoped) of a "special" relationship between comprehension and production of lexical combinations. To complete our investigation of single- and multiword comprehension at this age level, we need to consider the longitudinal relationships, from first words to sentences.

Table 15 includes correlations between the 13-month language variables (comprehension and production totals in free speech and in the interview, plus referential style and referential flexibility in the interview only) and the three 20-month comprehension scores. The multiple-choice test, for reasons that should already be clear, shows no continuity with any of the earlier measures. And comprehension of multiword commands seems to present a reversal of the usual "two-strand" pattern, correlating more highly with early production variables. To examine these patterns in more detail, let us move directly to a series of regressions paralleling the ones described in Studies 2 and 3. Results of these regressions are also summarized in Table 16.

First, there were three pairs of analyses using comprehension of canonical commands as the target: two involving observed comprehension and production at 13 months as the predictors, two involving interview comprehension and production, and two comparing the predictive value of referential flexibility and total production. Briefly summarized, these analyses yielded very little. None of the total predictions reached significance, and there was no evidence for a unique contribution from any aspect of 13-month language. In general, then, the canonical multiword comprehension measure shows little continuity with early language.

By contrast, there was evidence for 13–20 month continuity with comprehension of noncanonical commands. However, the direction of the effects constitutes a perplexing exception to the "two-strand" picture that has emerged in our data so far. First, the regression using observed comprehension and production at 13 months as predictors yielded a total of 27.3% of the variance accounted for ($p < .05$). 22.1% of this was uniquely contributed by production, compared with 4.1% by comprehension. This seems to run directly counter to the idea of a stable "comprehension-based" style of language acquisition. On the regressions using interview comprehension and production as predictors, the total equation was significant (with 25.3% of the variance accounted for), but neither of the unique contributions reached significance. The same thing was true for the two regressions looking only at early production: The total equation did reach significance, but there were no unique contributions either from total production or from referential flexibility. *To summarize, multiword comprehension bears no obvious relationship to any of the early language style measures, even though it does bear a coherent relationship to multiword production.*

Conclusion

The main point of this study was to examine the relationship between single- and multiword comprehension, and the passage from single- to multiword speech in production. For the single-word measures, we found weak confirmation for the idea of a "first strand" of language dominated by comprehension and analyzed production. For the multiword measure, we also found partial support for the hypothesis that

Table 16. *Regressions on Canonical and Noncanonical Commands*

	Canonical	Noncanonical
20-Month		
Interview clusters		
Joint r^2	.331	*.549
Unique variance from:		
Nominal multiword	.095	**.173
Grammatical morpheme	.041	.021
Semantic-conceptual	.062	.023
Dialogue	.009	.000
20-Month		
Observational clusters		
Joint r^2	.288	**.625
Unique variance from:		
Nominal multiword	.000	.024
Grammatical morpheme	.009	.005
Semantics-dialogue	.117	*.142
13-Month observations		
Joint r^2	.167	*.273
Unique to comprehension	.001	.041
Unique to production	*.163	*.221
13-Month interview		
Joint r^2	.166	*.252
Unique to comprehension	.013	.052
Unique to production	.117	.132
13-Month interview		
Joint r^2	.153	*.245
Unique to production total	.121	.072
Unique to % flexible nouns	.000	.044

* $p < .05$.
** $p < .01$.

telegraphic speech and telegraphic comprehension are systematically related, via some shared "combinatorial language" function.

We did not, however, find a neat and elegant picture in which *all* measures of comprehension belong to the same "political party," i.e., the first strand of analyzed and comprehended language. Remember, however, that the nominal multiword clusters presented a similar anomaly in Study 2. Like the nominal multiword clusters (i.e., telegraphic speech), comprehension of novel multiword commands (i.e., telegraphic comprehension) seems to stand somewhere in between the two strands in language development that have emerged so far.

Perhaps these two sides of "combinatorial ability" in language are the true precursors of a "grammar module." This grammar module may be independent of both the rote use of grammatical morphemes that lies behind MLU and the morphological clusters, and the semantic-conceptual analysis that lies behind referential flexibility and lexical development through the second year. A test of this hypothesis will come later, when we find out which of the various early language measures lead most directly into productive use of grammar.

At this point, however, there is one further hypothesis that we need to consider. Telegraphic comprehension and telegraphic production may have one very particular, age-dependent mechanism in common: the emerging ability to "chunk" two units instead of one in working memory (e.g., Case and Khanna, 1981). In a separate study with the same longitudinal sample presented here, Shore et al. (1984) investigated the passage from single- to multischeme combinations in elicited symbolic play. They found a transition in the gestural modality that directly paralleled the passage into multiword speech, confirming a hypothesis proposed by Nicolich (1975) in an earlier small-sample study. That is, children move from single to multischeme sequences of gestures around the same time they move from single- to multiword combinations. Furthermore, when other aspects of language and symbolic ability were controlled, Shore et al. found a unique and reliable correlation between novel gestural combinations and the nominal multiword cluster that we have studied here.

Shore (1981) investigated this relationship further with a separate sample of 20-month-olds, replicating the findings from Shore et al. Furthermore, Shore also found that the multiword/multischeme transition involves combinatorial abilities in both semantic and nonsemantic domains (e.g., motor planning in a block-building task). Shore concludes that the passage from single- to multiword speech at 20 months depends at least in part on a developmental increase in either the size or the efficiency of working memory. This abstract notion of "chunking," as discussed by Shore and by Case and Khanna (1981), involves the ability to handle more than one unit in a variety of novel tasks, i.e., tasks in which combinations cannot be retrieved as a whole from long-term memory.

If the findings by Shore and colleagues are correct, the "special relationship" that we have found here between multiword comprehension and multiword production may be based on an age-specific shift in the number of content units that a child can handle in working memory (see Beeghly, Weiss, and Cicchetti, 1985, for parallel findings at a later age in Down's Syndrome children). This would explain why these two aspects of language development at 20 months seem to fall outside the two strands of language acquisition. If this age-specific explanation is correct, we would *not* expect the two combinatorial language measures to be particularly good predictors of grammatical productivity at 28 months, holding rote grammar and/or semantic-conceptual abilities constant. Alternatively, if the appearance of telegraphic speech and multiword comprehension reflects the first true manifestations of a developing grammar module, these twin measures ought to be the best overall predictors of grammatical ability at the later stages.

Chapter 9: Study 5
Acquisition of a Novel Concept at 20 Months

The purpose of this study is to add to our understanding of the partially dissociable mechanisms that underlie individual variation in language development, by investigating the manner in which 20-month-old infants acquire an entirely new lexical concept, in a situation in which we have complete control over the amount of experience each child has with the concept to be acquired.

We have characterized the "first strand" of language variables in terms of an analytic mechanism responsible for comprehension, and for flexible and productive use of speech. If this characterization is correct, children who score highly on variables in the first strand should also show more understanding and generalization of the novel lexical concept when amount of experience is held constant.

We have argued that the "second strand" involves relatively unanalyzed production, perhaps in the service of social goals and/or "sounding like other people." The literature on individual differences has led us to expect this second style variable to load highly on language imitation (but see Leonard et al., 1979; Nelson et al., 1985). So far, we have failed to confirm this prediction with our few measures of imitation. At 13 months, imitation and spontaneous production were in no way differentiable (although they did both tend to align with later second-strand variables). At 20 months, reported and observed rates of imitation failed to align with either the morphological or the nominal multiword clusters, falling instead into separate clusters of items that have more to do with the way children understand and use single-or multiword speech. As several investigators have noted (e.g., Clark, 1974; Keenan, 1977; Snow, 1983; Stine and Bohannon, 1983), immediate imitation of adult speech can serve a variety of functions. If they are correct, there is no reason why we should expect to find a single individual difference dimension called "imitativeness." On theoretical grounds, the kind of imitation that *should* relate most to the various second-strand variables is the immediate imitation of something entirely new, before the child has had an opportunity to observe at length, "mull things over," and come to some understanding of the concept that has just been introduced.

In the present study, we spend a brief 5 minutes introducing a novel object concept to the child, together with an associated nonsense name, an associated nonsense action, and a nonsense verb for that action. Measures of vocal and gestural imitation during this brief introductory period should provide our best index to date of the kind of imitation hypothesized to underlie the various second-strand language variables.

Method

The novel object concept was introduced to the children during the 20-month home session. These objects, called "fiffins," consisted of various configurations of plastic pipe fittings with brightly colored fur screwed into the pipe openings. (The term "fiffin" is in honor of Keith Nelson's pioneering work on novel-concept acquisition, Nelson and Bonvillian, 1978). The fiffins were introduced to the child in an informal training session averaging 5 minutes in length. The Experimenter begins by removing one fiffin from the box, saying some variant of

> Do you know what this is? This is a FIFFIN. And do you know what I can do with it? I can GLOOP it. Watch! (Experimenter places the fiffin on her forehead and pushes it forward in a downward arc saying "GLOOOOP.")

This procedure is repeated three or four times, with different fiffins, handing a fiffin to the child after each demonstration to determine whether the child would imitate the gesture and either the novel object name or the glooping sound. Since we did not have sufficient time or resources within this larger study to present several different novel objects, in various counter-balanced presentations, we decided not to standardize the presentation beyond the restrictions just described. Instructions could be paraphrased or repeated, depending on the child's interest and attention. In this way, we tried to approximate as much as possible a relatively natural situation in which a child at this age might encounter a new lexical item for a new object concept.

From the videotapes of this introductory segment, we analyzed any instance in which a child (1) carried out the new gesture, (2) said "fiffin," or (3) said "gloop." We also noted behaviors that seemed to be partial versions of the modeled gestures and sounds, as well as efforts to do something with the fiffins regardless of whether a successful imitation was produced. From these behaviors, children were given a 0–3 score for gesture and sound, respectively 0 = absolutely no interest or effort to interact with the fiffins; 1 = obvious interest, with handling and/or sounds produced, but no detectable approximations of the target gesture and/or words; 2 = partial versions of the target behaviors (e.g., moving the fiffin upward in the direction of the head, without successful placement on the forehead; uttering fricatives approximating the "f" sounds in "fiffin," or "ooo" sounds approximating the vowel in "gloop"; 3 = clear and successful imitations of the glooping gesture and/or either of the target words. Children were given a score for the highest level reached along this 0–3 point scale for gesture and for word, respectively. This is, then, a qualitative measure that is only indirectly related to imitation frequency. We had originally intended to keep separate verbal counts for the new noun and for the new verb. However, children produced so few successful verbalizations overall that we decided to collapse the two new words and award verbal imitation scores for the highest level produced on either word.

In the laboratory session that followed 2–3 days later, we administered fiffin analogues to the multiple-choice word-comprehension test and to our elicited symbolic play sequences. The multiple-choice task was administered first. Within tasks, the fiffin items were always administered after testing with more familiar toys was complete. For the multiple-choice task, there were two trials in which a fiffin was the target object, permitting scores of 0–2 on name comprehension. Another type of comprehension was tapped in elicited play. Both a toy kitten and a real fiffin were presented, and the child was asked "Can you make the kitty gloop the fiffin?" This procedure was repeated a minimum of two times, a bit more often if the child responded positively and became thoroughly involved with the toys. Scoring criteria for the behaviors produced in response to this question were the same 0–3 quality ratings that we used for the home imitation sequence, one score each for production of the glooping gesture, and repetition either of the noun "fiffin" or the verb "gloop." To summarize, fiffin measures included (1) imitation in the home, verbal and gestural, (2) comprehension of the object's name in the multiple choice task, and (3) comprehension of the difficult question "Can you make the kitty gloop the fiffin?"

Because of equipment failure, data were lost for four of the children in at least some portion of the home or laboratory fiffin sequences. Hence our total sample for this study is twenty-three children.

Results

Starting with qualitative ratings of the fiffin behaviors, a score of 2 or 3 means that the child has successfully executed at least a fragment of the new word or gesture. By this criterion, nine of the children produced the new gesture at home and eighteen produced it in the laboratory. Levels of word production (for either the noun "fiffin" or the verb sound "gloop") were somewhat lower: eight made efforts scoring 2 or better in the home, while nine made similar scores in the laboratory.

On the two fiffin trials in the multiple choice test, average scores were 75% correct; since chance performance would be around 33%, this means that most children could successfully choose the fiffin on command from a three-toy array. Finally, on the difficult command "Make the kitty gloop the fiffin," eighteen of the children gave an appropriate gestural response warranting a score of either 2 or 3. In general, we can conclude that most children in this age range can acquire a novel lexical concept quite rapidly, with broad generalization occurring several days later.

Correlational relations involving the fiffin measures and the other 20-month variables are presented in Table 17. These data provide further support for a dissociation between comprehension and "pure production," i.e., production that does not necessarily reflect any understanding or internal analysis of a symbolic form.

The first signs of dissociation can be found within the fiffin measures themselves. In particular, the comprehension and imitation measures were essentially unrelated. Within production, the home measures of gestural and vocal imitation were significantly correlated, although at a relatively low level: $+.44$, $p < .05$. Also, in the laboratory successful gestural responses correlated $+.54$ ($p < .01$) with successful production of either of the associated words. However, performance on the multiple-choice comprehension items did not correlate significantly with any other fiffin measures. Also, correlations were low between home performance and response to the command "Make the kitty gloop the fiffin." Out of four possible correlations among gesture and word at home, and gesture and word on this comprehension item, only one reached significance: a correlation of $+.46$ between vocal imitation at home and vocal production in the laboratory.

However, note that the critical element indicating comprehension of the laboratory test sentence is the glooping gesture, applied with the fiffin to the body of the toy cat. We might have expected children who were more involved with the fiffin at home to show more comprehension in the laboratory, as measured by this criterion. And yet imitation levels during training did not predict this critical behavior. Apparently many of the children understood the novel relationship between fiffins and glooping without acting out the new behaviors during training. Hence although fiffin activity measures are loosely predictive of one another, overt activity is not strongly correlated with understanding.

More support for a divergence between activity and understanding comes from the correlations between the fiffin measures and other 20-

Table 17. *Correlations with the Fiffin Measures*

	Imitation of Word During Training	Multiple Choice Comparison	"Make the Kitty Gloop the Fiffin"
20 months			
1. MLU	**.54	.16	.15
2. Interview clusters			
Nom. multiword	.27	*.52	**.55
Gramm. morpheme	.33	.31	.29
Sem.-conceptual	.08	**.64	*.52
Dialogue	-.01	~.35	**.56
3. Observational Clusters			
Nom. multiword	*.46	~.37	*.50
Gramm. morpheme	**.55	.24	.17
Sem.-dialogue	.18	**.61	**.66
4. Interview lexical			
Vocabulary total	.10	*.41	*.51
Open-class style	.02	*.48	*.49
Verb density	.12	*.47	.34
5. Observed lexical			
Vocabulary total	~.39	~.38	*.42
Open-class style	-.23	**.61	*.43
Verb density	.03	.07	-.08
6. Canonical commands	.23	*.51	**.59
Noncanonical commands	.34	*.68	**.62
13 months			
7. Interview			
Production total	~.35	.01	.27
% Nouns production	-.01	.20	**.55
% Flexible nouns	-.11	.31	*.42
Comprehension total	-.26	~.37	~.35
% Nouns comprehension	-.18	*.45	.04
8. Observations			
Spontaneous production	**.61	.19	.11
Imitative production	.20	.13	.04
Comprehension	-.20	*.45	.31

~ $p < .10$.
* $p < .05$.
** $p < .01$.

month variables. First, gestural imitation in the home failed to correlate significantly with any of the other language variables, although a correlation of +.40 with the observational morphology cluster did approach significance ($p < .06$). Vocal imitation at home correlated significantly with MLU (+.54), observational morphology (+.55), and the observational nominal cluster (+.46), with a near-significant relationship involving observed vocabulary ($p < .06$). In short, then, fiffin imitations tend to relate more to the second strand.

By contrast, the fiffin comprehension tasks correlated primarily with the first strand. For response to "Make the kitty gloop the fiffin," there were significant relationships with reported and observed vocabulary, with all the clusters except the two involving grammatical morphology, and with multiword comprehension. Correlations involving comprehension on the fiffin multiple-choice items were weaker, but in precisely the same direction.

To clarify these patterns further, we carried out two reciprocal sets of partial correlations, examining the predictive value of fiffin comprehension and fiffin imitation, respectively, when all their overlapping variance is removed. The results were so clear that there is no need to report them in detail: The patterns reflected in the raw correlations in Table 17 remained the same. *Fiffin comprehension continues to align with the first strand, fiffin imitation with the second.*

Another set of partial correlations clarified the relationship between acquisition of a new lexical concept and our two different measures of 20-month vocabulary. Recall that in Study 3 the two 20-month lexical scores entered into mirror-image relationships when their shared variance was removed. Reported vocabulary aligned with the first strand, while the more frequency-sensitive measure of observed vocabulary aligned most clearly with the second strand. We repeated the same kind of analysis here in relation to the fiffin measures: correlations with observed vocabulary when interview vocabulary is removed, and vice-versa. Under these conditions, observed vocabulary is correlated positively and significantly only with vocal imitation in the home (+.56). Reported vocabulary, by contrast, correlates significantly and *negatively* with vocal imitation in the home (-.43).

This indicates quite clearly that immediate imitation of a new word is a poor index of the child's overall lexical knowledge—at least at this age, with this sample. Imitation is, however, a much better indicator of the child's tendency to use the vocabulary that he does have in a series of brief observations, with strangers. Once again, the contrast between knowledge and use seems to be involved in the individual differences observed and dissociable mechanisms inferred at 20 months of age.

Finally, we correlated the various fiffin measures with the major language variables at 13 months (also reported in Table 17). Although these longitudinal correlations were relatively weak, they fell into the two-strand pattern that we would expect, given the findings reported so far. *Fiffin comprehension is related primarily to early comprehension, and to flexibility and referential style in early production. Fiffin imitation, instead, shows continuity primarily with early production totals.*

Conclusion

Novel concept training tasks can, if properly designed, serve as a kind of microcosm in which we can observe more closely the acquisition processes that apply in the outside world (Nelson and Bonvillian, 1978; Schwartz, 1978). Because we were able to present only a single new concept in the present study (albeit a complex one, with object, action, noun, and verb), the findings should be interpreted with caution. As they stand, however, the fiffin results provide further support for the idea of two dissociable mechanisms in language acquisition: an analytic mechanism reflected in the degree to which the child understands a new form and generalizes it across contexts, and a more "holistic" mechanism that seems to result in the rapid but relatively unanalyzed use of formulas and rote forms. This is also the first time that we have found confirmation for the oft-claimed link between imitation and the second strand (e.g., "expressive style," "pronominal style," "noun leavers").

There is, however, an apparent contradiction between our findings and a report by Leonard et al. (1979). These investigators presented several novel objects and associated labels to children in the one-word stage, classified as "referential" or "expressive" on the basis of their vocabulary composition. They report that imitation of novel object names was more typical of the *referential child,* in contrast with claims in the literature and with our own findings here.

Our results also conflict with a study by Nelson et al., (1985). These investigators report the existence of a single "imitative-referential style" at 22 months of age, based, among other things, on the tendency to imitate during a novel-concept acquisition task. In fact, their measures of imitation fall into a set of correlations that is almost indistinguishable from our "first strand" of analytic variables. By 27 months, their findings look much more like ours, where imitation is more indicative of a rote/pronominal approach to language.

Why does research on imitation produce such completely contradictory results? One reason may be, as noted earlier, the fact that imitation is a cover term for repetition in the service of many different functions. In our study, fiffin imitations were restricted to the very first moments in which the concept was presented. The Leonard et al. study was more extensive, carried out over a more protracted period of time. Thus, their index of imitation must include repetitions that occur further on in "the word game," perhaps reflecting understanding at a more general level (i.e., "This is the man who is here to teach me names for things. . . .") But this explanation cannot handle the contradictions in Nelson et al., since they focused primarily on immediate imitations that do not play any obvious discourse role. The meaning of "imitativeness" seems to change from child to child, from sample to sample, and from one stage to another, in the same group of children.

When linear relationships change so much from one study to another, we may want to consider the possibility that nonlinear factors are at work. In fact, imitativeness is a particularly good candidate for nonlinear status in development. As Kinney and Kagan (1976) noted, children are most likely to imitate when the model lies right at the boundary of their understanding (see also Harnick, 1978; Hebb, 1949; McCall and Kagan, 1967; McClelland, Atkinson, Clark and Lowel, 1953). If the display is too simple and obvious from the child's point of view, it is unlikely to be imitated at all; if the display is too difficult, all but the most adventurous children may shrink back and wait until things become clearer before they try out their own version. We have found several examples of this kind of U-shaped function for imitation in our own laboratory.

One example comes from Shore, Bates, Bretherton, Beeghly, and O'Connell (in press), in a study of gestural comprehension in the same sample of children that we have been discussing here. At 28 months, these children were presented with a multiple-choice comprehension task similar to the one discussed in the previous chapter—except that, this time, they were asked to pick the object that matched an empty-handed pantomime of an associated action scheme. For example, the Experimenter would make the gesture of brushing her hair while saying "Get the one that goes like this"; the child was then asked to choose among a hairbrush, a necklace, and a shoe. Although the study focused on gestural comprehension, we immediately noticed a peculiar bimodal distribution in imitation of the Experimenter's gestural model: Some children imitated the gesture on more than half the trials, while others never imitated at all. And yet the two groups did not differ significantly on any other measures, including many of the language measures that we have studied here.

The reason for all these nonsignificant differences became clear when we inspected the composition of the nonimitative group more closely: This group was made up of both the most and the least precocious children in our sample. By contrast, the imitative group was made up primarily of children in the middle range. A series of curvilinear analyses of the imitation and comprehension data confirmed this picture: imitation of the gestural model was most likely to occur among children in the middle of the distribution for language and/or gestural comprehension on the same task. Those who knew exactly what the model was doing usually responded by labeling her action ("Brush!"), without carrying it out themselves. Those who had absolutely no idea what the model was doing also failed to imitate. It is as though the imitators were using their action to "figure out" the meaning of a difficult but nevertheless familiar activity.

A similar finding appeared in a study of 13–15-month old children by Bates, Whitesell, Oakes, and Thal (1987). The Experimenter modeled a series of familiar actions for the child (e.g., brushing the hair, cuddling a pretend babydoll, drinking from a pretend cup), and asked the child to imitate after each demonstration. The actions were all carried out with a plain wooden block, i.e., a "placeholder" that bore no recognizable relationship to the object usually associated with the action. The focus of this study was on the 1-year-old's ability to integrate gestural and linguistic cues. Hence some of the models were accompanied by a disambiguating word (e.g., "Look at the brush!"), some by neutral language (e.g., "Look at this!"), and others by a contradictory verb cue (e.g., "Look at the cup!" said while carrying out a brushing movement). Overall there was an effect of language on the child's reproduction of familiar gestures, in the expected direction, demonstrating that 13–15 month old children can integrate cues across modalities in their efforts to understand adult action. However, this effect reached significance *only* when we carried out our analyses factoring out the total amount of imitation carried out by each child across all language conditions. In other words, a confound between linguistic ability and total imitativeness obscured the expected effects. In a series of post hoc analyses, we were able to demonstrate once again that overall imitativeness is typical of children in the middle range of language ability. Children were less likely to imitate if they could not understand language at all or if they understood it very well.

We suggest that the relationship between imitativeness and language ability is best understood as an inverted U-shaped curve: At any given level of language development, imitation is most likely to occur when children are right in the middle of figuring out what is going on. This presents a real problem for studies that rely on linear statistics, including correlation, multiple regression, t-tests, analysis of variance—in short, most of the statistical methods used in psychological research. Our likelihood of obtaining a linear result depends entirely on how our sample is distributed around the underlying U-shaped function. To illustrate, consider the following three hypothetical outcomes in a study of the relationship between imitation of nouns and overall understanding of high-frequency object names:

1. **Outcome 1: Significant positive correlation.** This result would occur if the least sophisticated children in the sample have no understanding or interest in object names at all, while the most sophisticated children are just beginning to struggle with the idea that things have names. The most advanced children would be in the middle of the U-shaped imitation function, while slowest children would not imitate at all. Hence the relationship between language ability and noun imitation will fit a positively sloping line.

2. **Outcome 2: Significant negative correlation.** This result would occur if we were to choose our sample as they are exiting the U-shaped imitation curve for this language function. The most precocious children would understand the stimuli so well that imitation is unlikely, while the slowest children are still in the middle of the U-shaped curve, hence more likely to imitate. Under these circumstances, the relationship between language ability and noun imitation would fit a negatively sloping line.

3. **Outcome 3: No significant correlation.** If our sample straddles the full range of the hypothetical U-shaped function, imitation will be most likely among the children in the middle. As a result, our data would not fit either a positively or a negatively sloping line, resulting in an apparent lack of correlation between language ability and frequency of imitation. The "true" relationship between our target variables would become apparent only through the application of exploratory curve-fitting procedures—something psychologists rarely do unless they have theoretical grounds for expecting a nonlinear result.

We have now begun to expect nonlinear relationships in any study in which imitation plays an important role. Even so, it is difficult to specify a priori the shape and location of an idealized U-shaped function in an age range in which many things are happening very fast. We can say with some confidence when an ability isn't there at all and when it has reached a stable endpoint. But how do you specify in advance where the "true" underlying midpoint should be on a language development measure (or for that matter, on any other measure)?

For research on imitation, the matter is complicated still further by the fact that children imitate for many different reasons. The U-shaped relationship between imitation and understanding we have been discussing here seems to account for some proportion of the data on imitation we have obtained in laboratory studies. But there are no doubt other factors including temperament, the demand characteristics of the situation, the extent to which a given child likes and identifies with a particular Experimenter, and so forth. At this point, we are simply trying to understand the rather marked disparities between our study and others in the literature (in particular Nelson et al., 1985 and Leonard et al., 1979). We suggest that imitativeness may be involved in a characterization of language style, but the relationship is so complex that imitativeness should probably *not* be used as a marker variable. We will return to this point again in Chapter 16 (Study 12).

It is always wiser to conclude that "more research is needed." Nevertheless, the findings from 13 to 20 months do present a reasonably coherent picture so far, supporting our suggestion that Strand 1 reflects analysis and internal segmentation of new forms, whereas Strand 2 reflects a tendency toward "production for its own sake," resulting more often in holistic, formulaic, and perhaps imitative use of language. Now we can turn to findings at 28 months—when most of the children begin to show productive control over their grammar—to determine how the two style strands at the early stages map onto the acquisition of linguistic structure.

Chapter 10: Study 6
The Meaning of Mean
Length of Utterance at 28 Months

The purpose of this study is to investigate some properties of that classic measure of linguistic structure, Mean Length of Utterance (MLU), at 28 months of age. This study will parallel Study 2 at 20 months in several ways, exploring the internal composition of MLU variance through a series of raw and partial correlations and regression analyses using various semantic and grammatical measures from the earlier stages as predictors. However, there is an important difference. At 20 months, there was good reason to believe that much if not all of the grammatical morphology produced by children was based on rote or formulaic structures; at 28 months, most of the children have entered a stage in which they have achieved at least some productive control over aspects of English syntax and morphology. This means that we can finally tie the partially-dissociable strands of language development observed at the earlier stages into the "true" acquisition of grammar.

This also means that we can test some competing hypotheses about the processes that underlie the two style strands. In the previous studies, we offered a characterization in terms of two different acquisition processes (1) an analytic process, responsible for lexical comprehension and productive naming at the early stages, and for semantic-conceptual sophistication at 20 months, and (2) a rote learning process, including immediate imitation of new material, responsible for relatively unanalyzed vocabulary at the early stages and for the unanalyzed or formulaic use of grammatical morphemes at 20 months.

If this characterization is correct, the variables in the first strand should be the best predictors of MLU at 28 months, i.e., of grammar that has been subjected to the same kind of internal analysis that the child applied to single words in the early stages.

There are, however, some competing hypotheses that cannot be discarded yet, involving a partial dissociability between grammar and semantics. By one such model, the first strand would be primarily responsible for lexical-semantic development, at every stage. We might call this the "function module." The second strand would instead reflect the operation of a separate "form module." In the earliest stages, this form module would pick up single words and phrases before they have been subjected to functional analysis; in the later stages, this same module would be responsible for the analysis of grammatical morphemes and phrase structures, independent of the meanings or functions conveyed by those aspects of the grammar. If this hypothesis is correct, the second strand should be the best predictor of structural complexity at 28 months of age.

There is also a third possibility, preserving the grammar/semantics distinction by a different route. This model agrees with the first one with regard to the identities of Strand 1 and Strand 2: The first strand is indeed responsible for semantics, whereas the second strand reflects the operation of a rote device that is relatively independent of the grammar/semantics distinction. In this case, however, the true precursors of a "grammar module" would be traced back to yet a third strand, one that did not appear in the longitudinal data until 20 months of age. One candidate for this hypothetical third force is "telegraphic language," i.e., the 20-month measures of nominal multiword speech and comprehension of novel multiword combinations. Remember that these telegraphic language measures failed to align in any clear way with either of the two style strands, although they did bear a particularly strong relationship to one another. Telegraphic language might very well, then, represent the first accomplishments of an independent grammar acquisition device.

Another candidate for this third force lies in the verb density measures discussed in Study 3. These measures also fell outside of the two-strand picture, discontinuous with style measures at the earliest stages. We suggested there that verbs may offer a shortcut into the new linguistic system at 20 months, a means by which children who have not performed particularly well in the one-word stage can move ahead more rapidly into multiword speech. If 20-month verb density is a particularly good predictor of grammar at 28 months, over and above the variance shared with general lexical development, we would have further evidence for the independent emergence of a separate grammar module.

In addition to MLU, we tried unsuccessfully to develop some more detailed and informative structural complexity indices at 28 months, including ancillary cluster analyses and analyses of propositional complexity. These efforts are described briefly in the method section.

Method

In contrast with the other three age levels, at 28 months we must rely exclusively on observational measures of language, including free speech and structured tests. By this age, children are producing enough speech to permit robust assessments of their language ability without supplementary information from maternal reports. In fact, most children have advanced so far by this point that it is no longer realistic to expect parents to keep track of overall language progress. We did conduct a particular type of language interview with the mother, involving the child's use of language referring to emotions and other internal states (Bretherton, McNew, and Beeghly-Smith, 1981b). However, results of that rather specialized interview will not be discussed here.

Both the home and the laboratory visits were videorecorded at 28 months. In the home visit, we recorded the mother and child interacting freely in two contexts: having a snack, and looking at a book that we had brought with us. We also recorded the child playing alone with a standard set of experimental toys for 15 minutes, while the mother and the Experimenter went over the internal-state language interview. Structured tests administered at the home session included a word-order comprehension task and the Peabody Picture Vocabulary Test. Finally, the mother filled out a checklist concerning the child's personality and social behavior, the Rowe and Plomin Temperament Scale (Rowe and Plomin, 1977).

In the laboratory visit, we again recorded the mother and child interacting freely, playing with the same set of standard toys that the child had manipulated the day before. Structured tasks included an elicited symbolic play session with the Experimenter, a second word-order comprehension task, and a test for comprehension of morphology. There were two other structured tasks at this session that will not be described in this monograph: a gestural comprehension task (Shore, et al., in press), and a test for comprehension of emotion words (Bretherton et al., 1981b).

Free-speech analyses were based on transcriptions from all free play situations and structured interactions with the mother, as well as speech during elicited symbolic play. Responses during structured language tests were excluded from these analyses. (See Study 2 for more details on our procedures for training coders and obtaining reliability.) MLU in morphemes was calculated following the procedures recommended by Brown (1973).

The same transcripts were analyzed from several other points of view, discussed in the studies that follow: lexical development and lexical style (Study 7), and morphological productivity (Study 8). For the present purposes, two analyses of semantic/grammatical complexity are particularly relevant.

First, we coded the transcripts according to the same categories used in the 20-month cluster analyses described earlier: types of multiword constructions, imitation and labeling frequency, ability to discuss absent objects, past and future events, various semantic case relations, question answering in dialogue, and so forth (see Study 2, and Bretherton et al., 1983). The results of this effort can be summarized with no further ado: So many ceiling effects were obtained, in so many of the categories required for the cluster analyses, that we abandoned the enterprise. These clusters are a useful and reliable way of representing language developments at 20 months; by 28 months they are no longer relevant.

Second, we applied two different codings of propositional content and complexity to the transcripts, similar to coding schemes developed by Kintsch and Keenan (1973) for adults, and by Johnston and Kamhi (1980) for young children. The most important point for the present purposes is this: All of the propositional complexity indices derived for the 28-month sample are so highly correlated with MLU that they add no information at all to a study of individual differences. As Johnston and Kamhi have noted, propositional analyses and MLU yield quite different information at later stages of language development. At this stage, however, the two measures are statistically identical. *Despite its well-known flaws, Mean Length of Utterance seems to be the best index of structural complexity that we can derive for individual difference analyses at 28 months.*

Results

The results are divided into three sections: descriptive statistics for the MLU measure itself, relationships with the first-word measures, and relationships with grammar and semantics at 20 months.

Descriptive Statistics

There is a great deal of variation in MLU at this age level: a mean of 2.43, with a range of 1.16 to 3.43. These results place our group approximately 2 months ahead of the norms reported by Miller and Chapman (1981); in their sample, an average MLU of 2.43 was reached around 30 months of age. However, our least advanced child performs on a level with the average 20-month-old in the Miller and Chapman sample, whereas our most sophisticated child is comparable to their average 36-month-old.

In Brown's terminology (1973), the MLU stage breakdown for our children is as follows: two children in early Stage I (MLU = 1.0–1.5), five in late Stage I (MLU = 1.5–2.0), eight in Stage II (MLU = 2.0–2.5), six in Stage III (MLU = 2.5–3.0), and six in early Stage IV (MLU = 3.0–3.5). If Brown's original conclusions apply to our sample, this means that twenty of our children have at least begun to acquire productive control over English morphology (see Study 8).

Furthermore, six children are in a stage in which we might expect to find complex sentence constructions. There has, then, been considerable advancement in the 8 intervening months since our last session, when only one child had arrived at Stage II.

In terms of total output, the average child produced at least 100 utterances. The mean number of morpheme tokens produced was 220, with a range of 44 to 426. In other words, language output has increased in quantity as well as structural complexity.

The internal reliability of MLU at this age, in this sample, has been assessed independently in a study by Beeghly (1981; also reported in Beeghly and Bates, 1984). Beeghly compared the MLU scores for our children in three different situations: book reading, a snack, and free play with the mother. Despite the fact that each of the within-situation MLU scores were necessarily calculated on a rather small sample of utterances, the three situations yielded very similar results. First, there were no significant differences in the size of MLU across the snack, book reading, and free play. Second, correlations among the three MLU measures were quite high: .76 between reading and snack, .73 between reading and free play, and .69 between free play and snack (all significant at $p < .001$). These findings suggest that MLU is a surprisingly stable index of structural complexity in middle-class 2-year-olds. Quite comparable results can be obtained with only 5–10 minutes of language in a variety of different naturalistic situations.

From First Words to 28-Month MLU

Table 18 reports the simple correlations between 28-month MLU and the ten first-word measures discussed in Study 1: comprehension and production at 10 months, five interview and three observational measures at 13 months.

The first thing to note is the high degree of continuity and stability in the language measures over an 18-month period (see also Bretherton and Bates, 1984). Even the brief 10-month interview shows some predictive value over time: 28-month MLU correlates at $+.39$ ($p < .05$) with 10-month comprehension and $+.34$ ($p < .10$) with 10-month production.

The 13-month language measures are considerably better predictors of later MLU. However, all the significant correlations come from the parental reports. In general, this pattern offers particularly strong validation of parental report methods. *If an interview is carried out properly in the early stages of language development, it is ultimately a better predictor of things to come than 2–3 hours of observation by an itinerant investigator.*

The strength of the overall prediction from first words to grammar was assessed in a regression analysis using the five 13-month interview

Table 18. *Correlations of First-Word Measures with 28-Month MLU*

10 Months		13-Month Interview		13-Month Observations	
Comprehension	*.39	Comprehension	*.44	Spontaneous prod.	.09
Production	~.34	% Nouns comp.	**.54	Imitative prod.	.31
		Production	*.42	Comprehension	~.33
		% Nouns prod.	~.34		
		% Flexible nouns prod.	**.58		

~ $p < .10$.
* $p < .05$.
** $p < .01$.

Table 19. *Regression of all 13-Month Interview Measures on 28-Month MLU*

13-Month Predictors	Unique r^2	Total r^2
Total comprehension	.000	
% Nouns in comp.	.005	
Total production	.045	
% Nouns in prod.	.066	
% Flexible nouns in prod.	~.111	
		*.484

~ $p < .10$.
* $p < .05$.

measures as predictors (Table 19). Taken together, these first-word measures accounted for 48.4%, or just under half of the variance in 28-month MLU ($p < .01$). In this full analysis, none of the individual 13-month measures made a significant unique contribution when entered last, although the breakdown did tend to favor referential flexibility: 1.3% for total comprehension, 5.2% for total production, 1.1% for referential style in comprehension, 8.9% for referential style in production, and 11.3% ($p < .10$) for referential flexibility.

The pattern of contributions from individual predictors was examined in more detail with three pairs of regressions (Table 20), parallel to the ones reported in Study 2. The first compared the unique and joint contributions of *observed* comprehension and production at 13 months. As one might expect, given the low raw correlations going into the equation,

Table 20. *Pairs of 13-Month Regressions on 28-Month MLU*

13-Month Predictors	Unique r^2	Joint r^2
1. Observed production	.006	
Observed comprehension	.111	
		.121
2. Interview prod. totals	.098	
Interview comp. totals	*.114	
		*.293
3. Interview prod. totals	.023	
Interview % flexible nouns	*.184	
		**.364

* $p < .05$.
** $p < .01$.

neither the joint nor the unique variance explained by these early free-speech measures reached significance. In the second analysis, however, we compared unique and joint contributions by *reported* comprehension and production totals at 13 months. In this case, a significant 29.3% of the variance in MLU was accounted for overall; the unique contribution of 11.4% from comprehension reached significance, but the unique contribution of 9.8% from production did not. Finally, we used the two different *aspects* of early reported production as predictors of later MLU. With 36.4% of the variance accounted for overall, a significant 18.4% was uniquely contributed by referential flexibility, compared with only 2.3% for early production totals. In other words, 28-month MLU is continuous not with *how much* a child says at the one-word stage, but with *how she understands and uses the words she has*. This is exactly the opposite of the pattern obtained for 20-month MLU.

To summarize so far, there is a great deal of stability in our language measures over time, stretching from the meager comprehension and production vocabularies of the 10-month-old to the grammatical structure of 2-year-old speech. More important for our purposes, the pattern of relationships from first words to grammar suggests that 28-month MLU is more strongly associated with measures in the first strand, i.e., with the understanding and productive use of single words. But of course the "third-strand" candidates are not available at 10 and 13 months. For a further test of the hypotheses outlined above, let us move on to relationships between the 20- and 28-month session.

From 20-Month Grammar and Semantics to 28-Month MLU

Table 21 lists the simple correlations between 28-month MLU and the major 20-month variables discussed in Studies 2–5. Note first the continued evidence for stability of individual differences in language development. Out of twenty-one possible correlations, all but four are significant at $p < .05$. The four that fail to reach significance are fiffin imitation (both vocal and gestural), the multiple-choice test of single-word comprehension (an admittedly unreliable measure), and verb density in free speech (permitting us to eliminate at least one candidate from the hypothetical third strand).

One of the most important findings in Table 21 has to do with the differential predictive power of 20-month MLU and 20-month vocabulary. Even though MLU was calculated the same way at both age levels, the correlation between 20-month and 28-month MLU is not particularly high: $+.48$ ($p < .05$). In other words, MLU means different things at different age levels.

By contrast, 28-month MLU correlates at $+.73$ ($p < .01$) with 20-month observed vocabulary, and $+.83$ ($p < .01$) with 20-month reported vocabulary. *It looks as though variation in structural complexity at 28 months has more in common with early lexical development than with early word combinations.*

To examine this possibility further, we carried out a series of partial correlations, also reported in Table 21. When 20-month MLU was partialed out of the 20 x 28 matrix, almost nothing changed; the only variables that dropped markedly in predictive power were the two 20-month morphology clusters. By contrast, when either of the 20-month vocabulary measures were partialed out of the matrix, almost all of the relationships between 20-month language and 28-month MLU disappeared.

However, as described in Study 3, these data reflect more than a single monolithic "lexical factor." We concluded there that the two different assessments of vocabulary at 20 months are sensitive to different aspects of the variance: Reported vocabulary taps into what the child *knows,* while free-speech vocabulary has more to do with what the child typically *does.* Which of these bears the strongest relationship to grammatical complexity 8 months later? When 20-month reported vocabulary is partialed out, the correlation between 20-month observed vocabulary and 28-month MLU drops to a nonsignificant $+.17$; however, when 20-

Table 21. *Full and Partial Correlations of 20-Month Measures on 28-Month MLU*

20-Month Measures	Simple r	Partialing out		
		20-Month MLU	20-Month Observed Vocabulary	20-Month Reported Vocabulary
1. MLU	*.48	—	-.25	.05
2. Interview clusters				
Nominal multiword	**.69	**.61	~.39	.25
Grammatical morpheme	**.63	*.48	.23	.27
Semantic-conceptual	**.62	**.58	~.36	.08
Dialogue	**.61	**.60	~.34	.16
3. Observational clusters				
Nominal multiword	**.66	**.53	.06	.14
Grammatical morpheme	**.55	.33	-.24	.10
Semantics-dialogue	**.75	**.70	*.44	~.39
4. Interview lexical				
Total vocabulary	**.83	**.78	**.60	—
Open-class style	**.64	**.66	*.46	.23
Verb density	**.62	**.58	*.44	~.35
5. Observed lexical				
Total vocabulary	**.73	**.66	—	.12
Open-class style	*.46	**.52	~.37	.07
Verb density	.22	.01	-.15	.17
6. Comprehension				
Single-word	.22	.21	.06	-.03
Canonical commands	*.42	.31	.12	-.03
Noncanonical commands	**.64	**.52	.26	.20
7. Novel concept				
Imitation during training	.09	-.22	-.31	.01
Single word comprehension	*.42	~.39	.21	.14
Sentence comprehension	*.44	*.43	.22	.04

~ $p < .10$.
* $p < .05$.
** $p < .01$.

month observed vocabulary is partialed out, the correlation between 20-month reported vocabulary and later MLU is still a significant $+.57$ ($p < .01$). In other words, structural complexity in 2-year-old speech has more in common with *lexical knowledge* than with *lexical use* at 20 months. The same pattern obtains if we compare the contributions of the two respective 20-month vocabulary measures in regression analysis. Jointly, the lexical measures account for 68% of the variance in later MLU ($p < .01$); observed vocabulary increases the prediction by less than 1% when entered last, whereas reported vocabulary increases the prediction by 14.3% ($p < .01$).

So far we have still more support for the conclusion that productive grammar is continuous with the first-strand variables in early language development, i.e., with variables reflecting lexical/conceptual analysis. These results also support our conclusion in Study 2 that the second-strand variables in general—and 20-month grammatical morphology in particular—involve the use of rote, formulaic structures. Children who make great use of inflectional morphology and function words at 20 months can "buy" longer MLUs in the short run; in the long run, however, such a strategy apparently offers no advantages in breaking into grammar.

However, we still need to consider contributions from the hypothetical "third strand" at 20 months of age. For example, we suggested in Study 3 that verbs may provide a special route into first word combinations. Does the discovery of verbs represent the first stirrings of an independent grammar module, giving early "verb specialists" an advantage in grammatical development at the later stages? The correlations in Table 21 provide little support for that view. The verb-density measure in the 20-month free-speech data (i.e., early "verb use") does not correlate at all with 28-month MLU. The interview verb-density measure (i.e., early "verb knowledge") does correlate significantly with later MLU. However, this relationship disappears when variance in total vocabulary is partialed out. A similar conclusion emerges if we compare the contributions of verb density and reported vocabulary totals in a regression analysis: With fully 71% of the variance in MLU accounted for, a highly reliable 34.3% is uniquely contributed by 20-month reported vocabulary totals when entered last; the interview verb-density measure, when entered last, contributes only a nonsignificant 4%. *In other words, the relationship between early verbs and later grammar seems to be mediated by general lexical development.*

There is another candidate for "third strand status" in the origins of grammar: the two telegraphic language measures discussed in Study 5 (i.e., nominal multiword combinations in production, and comprehension of novel multiword commands). Remember that these two aspects

Table 22. *20-Month Cluster Score Regressions on 28-Month MLU*

Interview Clusters		Observational Clusters	
Joint variance (r^2)	**.567	Joint variance (r^2)	**.620
Unique variance to:		Unique variance to	
1. Nominal multiword	.023	1. Nominal multiword	.018
2. Grammatical morpheme	.013	2. Grammatical morpheme	.011
3. Semantic-conceptual	.017	3. Semantics-dialogue	**.156
4. Dialogue	.028		

$**p < .01.$

of language were highly related to one another, but failed to align consistently with either the first- or second-strand variables. If telegraphic language makes a unique contribution to 28-month MLU, over and above the first-strand variables discussed so far, we might have better evidence for the early operation of a "grammar module" that is partially dissociable from lexical/conceptual development. If, instead, the "nonaligned" variance in 20-month telegraphic language is unrelated to developments later on, there is further support for the alternative interpretation raised in Study 4. That is, individual differences in the ability to combine content words at 20 months, in comprehension and/or production, may reflect the linguistic effects of a more general but age-specific shift in "chunking" or working memory (Case and Khanna, 1981; Shore et al., 1984; Shore, 1981).

To consider this question, let us turn first to regression analyses involving the various 20-month cluster scores (Table 22). If the third-strand hypothesis is correct, we would expect the respective interview and observational nominal multiword clusters to contribute significant unique variance to later MLU. The first round of analyses used the three observational clusters as predictors. These three measures together accounted for a healthy 62% of the variance in 28-month MLU ($p < .01$). However, the only unique contribution came from the semantics/dialogue cluster (15.5%, $p < .01$). The morphological and nominal multiword clusters each uniquely accounted for only 1% of the variance.

The next set of analyses used the four interview clusters as predictors. In this case, the total variance accounted for was 56.7% ($p < .01$). However, none of the four clusters made a significant unique contribution to this equation (each accounting for less than 3% of the variance when entered last).

In Study 2, 20-month MLU loaded heavily on the respective interview and observational morphology clusters. 28-month MLU seems instead to "grow out of" the joint variance shared by the different cluster scores. In particular, the two nominal multiword clusters bear no privileged or unique relationship to individual differences in structural complexity at 28 months of age. This finding is consonant with the partial correlations reported in Table 21: When general lexical development is partialed out of the matrix, none of the purported "third-strand variables" correlate significantly with later grammar.

To summarize, the "nonaligned variance" in the ability to process combinations of content words at 20 months does not seem to predict anything unique about later grammatical complexity. The "special" relationship between nominal multiword combinations and comprehension of novel multiword commands may well reflect changes in information processing capacity that are specific to the 20-month level, i.e., a passage from "one chunk" to "two chunks." Once all of the children have passed this frontier, the measures have no further predictive validity beyond the variance shared with general lexical/conceptual progress.

Conclusion

The evidence reviewed here suggests that the mechanisms controlling variability in MLU at 28 months are the same ones involved in lexical/conceptual development from the very beginning of language, i.e., the so-called "first strand" of language measures. There is little continuity between the "pseudo-grammar" of first word combinations and the "true grammar" that underlies structural complexity at 28 months. In particular, the "second-strand" measures of MLU and morphology during Stage I seem to reflect a reliance on rote processes; children who rely primarily on these processes gain no advantage whatsoever when grammar becomes productive.

Several aspects of 20-month language failed to align with either the rote or the lexical/conceptual strands of early language. These included verb expansion and the ability to process telegraphic combinations of content words in comprehension and production. It seemed feasible that these variables might reflect the early operation of a grammar module, partially dissociable from lexical development, feeding separately into the acquisition of grammar later on. However, the correlations between these third-strand measures and structural complexity at 28 months were accounted for entirely by 20-month vocabulary scores.

In fact, the correlations between 20-month vocabulary and 28-month grammar could not possibly be higher, on mathematical grounds. No single measure can predict anything else better than it predicts *itself.* As we pointed out earlier, three separate calculations of 28-month MLU were intercorrelated around +.73 (Beeghly, 1981). The correlations between 28-month MLU and the two estimates of 20-month vocabulary averaged +.78. In other words, we are at the reliability ceiling; with estimates of early lexical development, we have accounted for *all* the variance in later MLU that is theoretically possible. We do *not* mean to suggest that grammar and vocabulary are "the same thing." However, individual differences in these two content areas do seem to be controlled by the same factors.

Before we accept this conclusion, there are still some further conceptual and empirical issues we have to consider. For example, MLU may not be the best index of grammatical progress, even in a 2-year-old. As described in the methods section, we tried to develop several other indices of structural development in this study: analogues of our 20-month clusters and two measures of propositional complexity. The clusters were of no use at all, because so many of the associated variables were at ceiling by 28 months. And the propositional indices were completely redundant with MLU from a statistical point of view. So far, MLU appears to be the best measure we have of grammatical development around Brown's Stage II.

In the next three studies we will examine several other aspects of 28-month language as they relate to or "grow out of" the earlier stages. Study 7 considers lexical development and lexical style—including a contrast between open class morphemes (i.e., content words) and closed class morphemes (i.e., function words and bound morphemes). Study 8 examines evidence for the productivity of specific grammatical morphemes, comparing several different criteria for determining productivity. Study 9 compares the results of lexical and grammatical comprehension testing, including tests of word order and morphology. These three studies will complement our findings for MLU and provide further clarification regarding the relationship between lexical and grammatical development.

Chapter 11: Study 7

Lexical Development and Lexical Style at 28 Months

Study 3 presented our examination of lexical development and lexical style at 20 months. The story was, to say the least, complex. The nature and meaning of lexical style seemed to change markedly from first words to first word combinations. In this study, we will examine many of the same variables at 28 months, when grammatical development is finally under way. The story is still quite complicated, but some consistent themes will emerge concerning the changing nature of lexical composition and its implications for qualitative and quantitative differences among children.

We will, once again, provide some useful normative information about changes in the size and composition of vocabulary, including a marked increase in the kinds of open- and closed-class lexical items necessary for grammatical constructions. We will also demonstrate again that lexical and grammatical development are strongly intertwined within and between stages. And we will provide some clarifications about the rote nature of closed-class usage at 20 months, compared with a much more productive use of the same forms by 2 ½ years of age. Indeed, as we shall see, there is a significant *negative* relationship between closed-class proportion scores at 20 and 28 months—suggesting that the children who were leaving those forms out of their early speech are at an advantage in the long run.

All these findings are both reasonable and understandable. The complications come in our effort to elucidate the meaning and function of lexical style. At 13 months, overall lexical advancement was characterized by "nouniness," in particular the use of context-flexible object names. At 20 months, lexical progress involved a more general expansion of the open-class (i.e., nouns, verbs, and adjectives), with a particular emphasis on "verbiness." This finding underscored the heterotypic nature of early language development—particularly measures of lexical style.

At 28 months, children are continuing to add new items to the open-class—as they will for the rest of their lives. However, there is also a new emphasis at this age level on the acquisition of closed-class morphology, i.e., grammatical function words and bound morphemes. Hence we might expect yet another shift in the lexical style preferred by the most advanced children from a noun bias, to a verb bias, to a bias in favor of grammatical morphology. To the extent that this is true, we can offer a sensible, unifying explanation for individual differences in lexical style from first words to grammar:

> The "best" children at any given age are the ones who concentrate on the most important milestones at that age level.

However, if we do find support for this view, the whole motivation for studying lexical style will have to change. That is, lexical style proportion scores may have more to do with *rate* of development than with qualitative differences in acquisition strategies.

To test this hypothesis, we will compare 28-month lexical development with the earlier stages, by deriving the three proportion scores that proved most useful in Study 3: open-class style, closed-class style, and verb density within the open-class. The results will suggest that lexical style does reflect the rate at which a child passes through basic stages of language development, which, in turn, accounts for the heterotypic nature of lexical style measures. Hence lexical style is not a pure and constant index of qualitative differences in language development. But as we shall see, this does *not* mean that *all* qualitative variation reduces to differences in rate. In particular, the patterns associated with verb acquisition at both 20 and 28 months returns us to a qualitative, two-strand approach to early language development.

There are some other analyses that might also prove informative at 28 months, when the structure of the lexicon is much richer than it was in the earlier stages. The contrast between open- and closed-class vocabulary has played an increasingly important role in recent psycholinguistic studies, of both adults and children (e.g., Berndt and Caramazza, 1980; Gleitman and Wanner, 1982; Gleitman et al., 1984). The suggestion has been made that the two vocabulary types involve separate underlying mechanisms, in adult processing and in acquisition. If this is true, we might expect to find at least a partial dissociation in the development of open- and closed-class morphemes at 28 months, with some children emphasizing one vocabulary type more than another. We did see such a dissociation at 20 months, but our data so far suggest that this was merely a by-product of a more general contrast between analyzed and rote forms. Because 28-month-old children are acquiring productive control over *both* vocabulary types, a dissociation between open- and closed-class forms at this age level would be much more informative. Such a dissociation would provide another kind of evidence for the idea of a "special" acquisition mechanism devoted to grammar.

Proportion scores of the kind involved in calculating lexical style may not constitute the best test of this question, since by definition they force the vocabulary data into an "either/or" format whether it fits the data naturally or not. A better test is provided by cluster analysis, to determine whether different kinds of closed- and open-class items "hang together" in two natural groupings. If two separate clusters do emerge, their relationship to the different strands of variables at the earlier stages will be particularly interesting.

Finally, the 28-month lexical data will be analyzed from the point of view of "type-token ratios," i.e., the total number of different lexical types produced by each child divided by the absolute number of lexical items produced, including repetitions. This is an old-fashioned measure, with a long history. For decades, language practitioners and developmental psychologists have used type-token ratios as a measure of vocabulary development from 2 years of age onward (e.g., McCarthy, 1954). The assumption has been that a high type-token ratio reflects a richer and more varied vocabulary. More recently, Miller and Chapman (1981) stated that

> The consistency of this measure makes it enormously valuable as a clinical tool. For example, if a normal hearing child's TTR is significantly below .50 we can be reasonably certain that the sparseness of vocabulary use. . . . is probably indicative of a language-specific deficiency. (p. 41)

As we shall see, our study of lexical style in 28-month-olds places some developmental qualifications on the use of this classic measure. Type-token ratios—like everything else that is developing around this time—reflect basic principles of language structure.

Method

All lexical measures were taken from the same transcripts described in Study 6, i.e., the transcripts used to calculate MLU. For each child, a list was made of the different bound and free-standing morphemes used (types), and of the number of times that each morpheme occurred (tokens). Three measures of lexical style were derived, calculated precisely as described in Study 3 for the 20-month data: *open-class style* (total different open-class nouns, verbs, and adjectives divided by the total number of different morpheme types), *closed-class style* (total different closed-class morphemes, including bound morphemes and free-standing function words, divided by the total number of different morpheme types), and *verb density* (total different open-class verbs divided by the total different open-class nouns, verbs, and adjectives).

For the lexical cluster analyses, the list of different morphemes produced by each child was divided into the following parts-of-speech
categories:

1. content words, further divided into nouns, verbs, adjectives, and
   certain open-class adverbials (e.g., "yesterday")
2. pronominal terms, subdivided into personal pronouns (e.g.,
   "he/him"), pronominal adjectives (e.g., "his/her"), demonstrative
   pronouns (e.g., "this/that"), and a remaining class of pronouns
   (e.g., "everybody," and "someone")
3. quantifier terms (e.g., "some," "all," "every," "more")
4. articles (e.g., "a," "an," "the")
5. interrogative terms (e.g., "who," "what," "where," "when,"
   "why," and "how")
6. adverbials, subdivided into demonstrative/locative adverbials (e.g,
   "there/here") versus a heterogeneous class of adverbials that
   modify adjectives, (e.g., "like," "kinda," "almost," "very,"
   "not," "so," etc.)
7. locatives, including prepositions like "on" and locative particles
   (e.g., "down" in "get down")
8. various verbal auxiliaries subdivided into copulas (main verb and
   auxiliary forms of the verb "to be"), sundry forms of "do" (e.g.,
   "do," "does," "don't," "doing"), and a remaining set of modal
   auxiliaries (e.g., "could," "can," "will," "wanna," "lemme,"
   "gonna")
9. conjunctions (coordinates like "and," "but," and subordinates like
   "that" in "the one that I like")
10. bound morphemes, subdivided into noun inflections and verb
    inflections
11. a remaining miscellaneous category that includes interjections (e.g.,
    "oh-oh") and animal sounds.

For each of these categories, the child received one score for types (i.e.,
the total number of different morphemes produced in that category) and
another for tokens (i.e., the absolute number of morphemes produced in
that category, summing over types).

Most of these categories seem a priori to belong to the closed-class.
However, as we noted at the outset, there is little consensus among
linguists about the border between the open- and closed-classes. For
example, quantifiers and prepositions carry considerable semantic content, and they may also occasionally receive heavy contrastive stress.
These two criteria are often used to define the open class. And yet
quantifiers and prepositions each form a small, closed set of high-
frequency words that are used primarily for their relational function;

furthermore, these words are almost always pronounced with minimal stress. These criteria are typically used to define the closed-class. If two distinct clusters do emerge in our data, reflecting the extent to which children can emphasize closed- versus open-class items in vocabulary development, we may be able to determine on empirical grounds where these "in-between" categories belong.

Another rationale for this particular classification scheme was to permit a possible differentiation between "noun-phrase expansion" and "verb-phrase expansion." Horgan (1981) has suggested that the nominal/pronominal distinction in Stage I continues to manifest itself at later stages of grammar, when "noun lovers" spend more time elaborating noun phrases, while "noun leavers" concentrate on the elaboration of verb phrases. This would lead us to expect a modest dissociation *within* the closed-class. For example, noun lovers might show a relatively greater use of articles, adverbials that modify adjectives in noun phrases (e.g., "very" in "a very big boy"), subordinating conjunctions like "that" in a relative clause modifying a noun phrase, and prepositions used in clauses that expand noun meanings (e.g., "in" in the phrase "a bird in the snow"). Noun leavers would, instead, make greater use of verb auxiliaries and various pronominal forms used as substitutes for more explicit and elaborate noun phrases.

The parts-of-speech subscores were analyzed with the same clustering procedures adopted by Bretherton et al. (1983) for the 20-month interviews and observations (Tryon and Bailey, 1970). Two separate cluster analyses were carried out: one on the type scores and another on the token scores.

Finally, overall type-token ratios were calculated in the traditional way: the total number of different morphemes in the transcripts for each child divided by the absolute number of morphemes produced.

Results

The results are divided into four sections: (1) size and composition of 28-month vocabulary in relation to 28-month MLU and to earlier language measures; (2) lexical-style analyses within and across ages; (3) results of the open- and closed-class clustering procedure; and (4) type-token ratios.

Size and Composition of 28-Month Vocabulary

An average of 86.9 distinct morpheme types (including both bound and free morphemes) were produced in the 28-month sessions, with a range of 26–129. Compare this with the thirty-six-morpheme average observed at 20 months, with a range of 4–121. For children at the "top of the class," the number of different items produced in a 2–3-hour period has not increased very much. The major changes in observed vocabulary have occurred for the children further down in the rankings.

These developmental patterns in vocabulary provide an interesting contrast with growth in structural complexity. Vocabulary development is stabilizing, with children at the bottom catching up. Grammatical development is, instead, undergoing a kind of explosion; the most advanced children are surging ahead with no end in view. This is the reverse of the 20-month pattern, when the most advanced children were sharply expanding their vocabularies without necessarily expanding phrase length.

This surge in grammar is accompanied by some important changes in the composition of the lexicon from 20 to 28 months. Most striking is a shift from 23.4% closed-class items at 20 months to 46.9% in the later transcripts. At a group level, this change reflects the move from Stage I to Stage II, and the general diminution of telegraphic speech (among children who used that kind of speech in the first place).

There are some corresponding changes in the composition of the open-class. As a proportion of total vocabulary at 20 months, the averages were 46.8% nouns, 8.3% verbs and 7.5% adjectives. The analogous proportions at 28 months are 31.6% nouns, 15.6% verbs and 5.5% adjectives. It appears, then, that the proportion of nouns and noun modifiers has decreased in the past 8 months, while the proportion of open-class verbs has doubled. Because grammatical complexity is increasing much faster than vocabulary in the 20- to 28-month period, these changes in the composition of the lexicon are exactly what we ought to expect. Verbs and closed-class morphology express relational information that is essential to the expansion of sentence structure.

Although the growth curves for MLU and vocabulary are different at this age level, there are still strong correlations between the two domains. In particular, the correlation between MLU and vocabulary continues to be very high: $+.73$. Before we conclude that lexical and grammatical development are inextricably entwined, however, we have another problem to consider. Because 28-month MLU and vocabulary are drawn from the same transcripts, it could be argued that their high correlation reflects nothing other than "general talkativeness," i.e., children who talk a great deal are likely to receive high scores on everything. We did not face this problem at 20 months, because the interviews permitted an estimate of vocabulary that was independent of the amount of speech children produced in the experimental sessions. To estimate the effects of "general talkativeness" at 28 months, we can use the total number of morpheme tokens produced by each child as a control. When the variance from this measure is partialed out, the correlation between

MLU and vocabulary is still a significant $+.42$ ($p < .05$). In other words, lexical and grammatical development do keep pace with one another in the third year of life, even when we control for the total amount of speech produced by each child.

There is one more piece of information in this three-way relationship of MLU, vocabulary, and total output. That is, the size of the speech sample seems to have a greater influence on vocabulary scores than it has on MLU: Total output in morphemes is correlated at $+.66$ with MLU and $+.89$ with vocabulary. To explore this apparent difference further, we first examined the partial correlation between vocabulary and total output when variance shared with MLU is removed. This left a significant positive correlation of $+.80$. Thus, our assessment of a given child's vocabulary is strongly affected by the total amount of speech we manage to elicit, even when differences in utterance "packaging" are taken into account. Next, we correlated total output with MLU, removing the effects of vocabulary size, resulting in a nonsignificant partial correlation of exactly $+.01$. In other words, if we equate children for estimated vocabulary size, grammatical complexity is unrelated to the sheer amount of speech produced.

This contrast in the "sampling sensitivity" of vocabulary and MLU provides still more evidence for the reliability and validity of MLU at this age level. This is also the exact reverse of the pattern 8 months earlier, when lexical development was the most reliable and sensitive indicator of overall progress in language. Although this finding may seem trivial from a theoretical perspective, it leads to a prediction that may seem more surprising:

> There should be stronger longitudinal correlations between early lexical development and later grammar (i.e., heterotypic continuity) than between early lexical development and later vocabulary (i.e., homotypic continuity).

The longitudinal data support this "heterotypic continuity" prediction. Table 23 compares correlations of the 13- and 20-month variables with 28-month MLU and vocabulary, respectively, with and without a control for total output. Starting with the findings for first words, the 13-month lexical measures predict 28-month MLU better than they predict 28-month vocabulary, whether or not total output is controlled. Regression analyses confirm this picture. In the last study, a regression of the five 13-month interview measures against 28-month MLU accounted for a significant 48% of the variance. In a parallel analysis here using 28-month vocabulary as the target, the same five 13-month predictors account jointly for a nonsignificant 24.6%. Furthermore, none of the individual predictors contributes significant unique variance to this equation. *In short, there is more continuity from first words to grammar than from first words to later vocabulary.*

The picture from 20 to 28 months is similar. With or without a control for total output, 28-month MLU is correlated with most 20-month variables, particularly with the lexical/conceptual strand. In the raw correlations, 28-month vocabulary is also highly related to most of the 20-month measures. However, when total output is partialed out of the matrix, most of these relationships drop below significance.

Given the huge overlap in variance between vocabulary size and the talkativeness control (i.e., almost 80% of the variance), it is perhaps surprising that anything is left at all. However, the relationships that remain are quite consistent: Lexical diversity at 28 months, controlling for amount of speech produced, is best predicted by earlier measures of *language comprehension* and *semantic–conceptual sophistication.* There is, then, a robust "lexical analysis" strand that reaches from first words to both lexical and grammatical abilities in the 2-year-old. However, this lexical strand has—ironically—more in common with grammar than vocabulary in the 2-year-old.

One final analysis illustrates this difference between MLU and vocabulary particularly well. In the last study, we showed that MLU is better predicted by 20-month reported vocabulary than 20-month observed vocabulary—consonant with our view that these two measures reflect *lexical knowledge* and *lexical use,* respectively. Here we performed an analogous pair of regressions using 28-month vocabulary as the target and the two respective 20-month vocabulary assessments as predictors. With a significant 54% of the variance jointly accounted for ($p < .01$), 20-month observed vocabulary contributed a significant and unique 11.9% of the variance when entered last, compared with a nonsignificant .5% for reported vocabulary. This is the opposite of the pattern for 28-month MLU.

To summarize, both MLU and vocabulary at 28 months are continuous with a strand of lexical-conceptual variables reaching back to the time that words first emerge. However, MLU at the later stages has more in common with *early lexical knowledge,* whereas later vocabulary shows more continuity with *early lexical use.*

Lexical Style at 28 Months

Table 24 lists the within- and between-session correlations involving open-class style, closed-class style, and verb density at 28 months, with and without a control partialing out the effects of total output.

The first and most obvious finding is that there has been a complete reversal from 20 to 28 months in the meaning of open- versus closed-

Table 23. *Full and Partial Correlations of Earlier Language Measures with 28-Month MLU and Vocabulary*

20-Month MLU and Earlier Measures	Simple Correlations		Controlling for Total Output in Morphemes	
	Vocabulary	MLU	Vocabulary	MLU
1. 20-month MLU	*.47	*.48	.05	.21
2. Interview clusters				
Nominal multiword	*.68	**.69	.22	*.44
Grammatical morpheme	**.61	**.63	.04	~.34
Semantic-conceptual	**.55	**.62	*.39	*.48
Dialogue	**.57	**.61	.19	*.38
3. Observational clusters				
Nominal multiword	**.67	**.66	.24	*.40
Grammatical morpheme	**.51	**.55	.21	~.35
Semantics-dialogue	**.76	**.75	**.56	**.57
4. Interview lexical				
Total vocabulary	**.64	**.83	.31	**.73
Open-class style	**.56	**.64	~.38	**.50
Verb density	*.48	**.62	*.42	**.57
5. Observational lexical				
Total vocabulary	**.73	**.73	*.43	**.52
Open-class style	*.45	*.44	~.39	.32
Verb density	~.34	.22	.00	-.03
6. Comprehension				
Single word choice task	.20	.22	**.50	.32
Canonical commands	~.33	*.42	.31	~.38
Noncanonical commands	**.52	**.63	*.39	**.54
7. Novel concept task				
Imitation during training	-.03	.09	-.05	.16
Word comprehension	~.39	*.42	**.60	*.43
Sentence comprehension	*.49	*.44	.21	.21
8. 13-Month interviews				
Total comprehension	~.32	*.44	*.45	*.46
% nouns in comprehension	*.44	**.53	*.44	*.49
Total production	.30	*.42	.03	.29
% nouns in production	.20	~.33	.10	.29
% flexible nouns in production	~.36	**.58	.08	*.49

Table 23. *Continued*

20-Month MLU and Earlier Measures	Simple Correlations		Controlling for Total Output in Morphemes	
	Vocabulary	MLU	Vocabulary	MLU
9. 13-Month observations				
Spontaneous production	.15	.09	-.01	-.02
Imitative production	.28	.31	.19	.22
Comprehension (choice task)	∼.34	∼.33	∼.38	.27
10. 10-Month interview				
Comprehension	.05	*.39	.15	**.54
Production	.08	∼.34	.11	*.43

∼ *p* <.10.
* *p* < .05.
** *p* < .01.

class style. At 20 months, the most advanced children had relatively high proportions of open-class items in their observed and their reported vocabularies. Furthermore, these were the same children who used high proportions of flexible object names at 13 months. In contrast, the same open-class proportion score at 28 months is correlated significantly and *negatively* with other languages measures, within and between age levels.

Conversely, at 20 months the closed-class style measure was either unrelated or negatively related to the rest of the language battery. At 28 months, closed-class style correlates significantly and *positively* with other aspects of language. When total output at 28 months is partialed out of these relationships, the results are weaker but the pattern is the same: Open-class style is characteristic of the less advanced children; closed-class characterizes the more advanced children. Furthermore, the longitudinal predictions of later closed-class style come primarily from variables in the lexical-conceptual strand: referential style in comprehension and referential flexibility in production at 13 months; semantic-conceptual clusters, the interview nominal cluster, reported rather than observed vocabulary, and open-class style at 20 months.

One correlation in Table 24 makes this reversal particularly clear: a significant *negative* correlation of -.41 between closed-class style at 20 months and closed-class style at 28 months (where both measures are taken from free speech). Obviously the same measure means very

Table 24. *Full and Partial Correlations with 28-Month Lexical Style*

13- to 28-Month Correlates	28-Month Lexical Style Measure			
	Simple Correlations		Partialing Out Total Output in Morphemes	
	Closed-class Style	Verb Density	Closed-class Style	Verb Density
28 Month				
1. MLU	*.50	*.44	*.46	.25
2. Vocabulary	.25	*.39	.08	.10
3. Total output	.24	*.39	—	—
20 Month				
4. MLU	.02	.14	-.11	-.07
5. Interview clusters				
Nominal multiword	*.40	.29	.32	.04
Grammatical morpheme	.27	*.39	.15	.18
Semantic-conceptual	**.52	~.33	*.48	.19
Dialogue	.18	~.36	.05	.18
6. Observational cluster				
Nominal multiword	.13	.11	-.04	-.21
Grammatical morpheme	.12	.22	.00	.03
Semantics-dialogue	*.42	*.44	~.35	.26
7. Interview lexical				
Total vocabulary	*.39	.28	.31	.06
Open-class style	*.40	~.34	~.33	.19
Closed-class style	.16	.07	.11	-.02
Verb density	*.39	.15	~.34	.01
8. Observed lexical				
Total vocabulary	.21	.30	.07	.06
Open-class style	**.57	**.55	**.53	*.49
Closed-class style	*-.41	**-.55	*-.41	**-.58
Verb density	.21	**.51	.13	*.43
13 Month				
9. Interview				
Total comprehension	.29	.23	.26	.19
% nouns in comprehension	**.56	*.38	**.53	.31
Total production	.12	~.36	.04	.27
% nouns in production	.25	.02	.22	-.05
% flexible nouns in production	**.56	.23	**.52	.10

~ $p < .10$
* $p < .05$
** $p < .01$

different things at Stage I and Stage II. At 20 months, closed-class style is typical of children with a high proportion of rote forms; at 28 months, the same proportion score reflects a more productive morphological system. *In the long run, then, children who leave closed-class items out of their first word combinations seem to be at an advantage.*

Why should this be? We suggest that children who omit function words from their speech at 20 months have had to carry out a significant amount of morphophonological analysis in order to figure out (1) the boundaries of content words, and (2) the general shape and position of expendable function words and inflections. In order to write a telegram, a native speaker has to know which items are essential and which items he can afford to leave out. The telegraphic 20-month old has a much more rudimentary knowledge of the language, and probably has very little understanding of the functions conveyed by grammatical morphemes. However, if she wants to omit poorly understood items from her own speech, she will at least be forced to locate the boundaries of recognizable content words in the language input, isolating them from surrounding bits of sound. For example, she has to figure out that "kiss" is a free-standing subcomponent of input sentences like "Mommy will kiss it" and "Give grandma a kiss." We do not know the basis by which a child carries out this kind of segmentation. It might be semantic (i.e., "this is a piece I don't understand"), phonological (i.e., "I couldn't quite hear that preceding bit"), grammatical (i.e., "This chunk of sound is clearly not a noun or a verb"), or some combination thereof (cf. Pinker, 1986; Wanner and Gleitman, 1982). The point is that a segmentation of the sound stream into content and function words provides an important starting point for both lexical and grammatical development. The sooner a child makes this kind of discovery, the sooner she will also discover the structure and function of the excluded material.

Because this last finding is particularly important, we need to be very cautious in its interpretation. The negative correlation between 20- and 28-month closed-class style *not* mean that the use of rote forms is bad. Proportion scores like these reflect the child's *relative* emphasis on one strategy versus another. Hence this finding suggests that, in the long run, a *disproportional* reliance on rote forms does not pay off. We will return to this point later on.

So far we have a clear and sensible characterization of lexical style from first words to grammar: The most advanced children tend to concentrate on object names at 13 months, the full range of open class terms at 20 months, and closed-class morphology at 28 months. Furthermore, for the measures we have discussed so far, these seem to be the same children across age levels—another case of heterotypic continuity from first words to grammar. This pattern also suggests that lexical style reflects nothing other than rate of normal language development. There is, in short, nothing qualitative or "stylistic" about it.

Once again, however, the pattern is far less clear when we look at individual differences in the development of verbs. Within the open-class, high verb density correlates with *both* vocabulary size and MLU at 28 months. This parallels the finding for verb density 8 months earlier. In addition, verb density is correlated with closed-class style even when total output is controlled (with a partial correlation of +.41). There seems, then, to be a continuing relationship between acquisition of main verbs and acquisition of closed-class morphology.

This finding is also quite sensible. The confusions regarding verb style result not from the within-age correlations but from the pattern of longitudinal relationships. In the raw correlations, 28-month verb density bears a particularly unsystematic relationship to the earlier language measures, compared with any of the other longitudinal analyses that we have carried out so far: positive correlations with the morphology cluster in the interview (but not in the observations), with the semantics-dialogue cluster in the observations (but not the semantic-conceptual cluster in the interview), with open-class style and verb density in the observations (but not in the interview). Among the 13-month measures, the only first-word variable that correlates with verb density in the last session is referential style in comprehension. In other words, early understanding of *nouns* predicts later specialization in *verbs*. But when the effect of general talkativeness is removed, virtually all these relationships disappear. The only remaining longitudinal relationships involve three 20-month variables: positive correlations with both observed open-class style and verb density, and a negative correlation with observed closed-class style.

There is no easy way to summarize this uneven pattern of findings. High levels of verb use are relatively stable from 20 to 28 months, and verbs appear in larger proportions among the more advanced children at each age level. But there is little consistency over time with regard to exactly *who* concentrates on verbs, and to what purpose. At 20 months, verb use is related to morphology but verb knowledge is related to telegraphic speech and lexical-conceptual analysis. At 28 months, verbs bear a continuing relationship to grammatical morphology when the latter is coming under productive control. Thus both the stability of "verbiness" and its relation to grammar seem well established. But here the confusion arises. There is no relationship between early morphology (which is related to 20-month verb use) and later morphology (which is related to 28-month verb use). We suggest the following solution:

Verbs feed into morphology in two entirely different ways. They play a role in the productive analysis of the grammar; but they are also implicated heavily in rote processes.

Once again, then, we go back to a two-strand characterization of early lexical development.

From a universalist perspective, the analysis of main verbs must play an important role in the acquisition of grammar for *all* children. Verbs are the key elements in predication, they form a bridge from semantics to grammar, and they are the carriers of most English morphology. However, from an individual differences perspective, there seems to be considerable variation in the *relative* importance of verbs in acquisition. The "main line" of individual differences runs from productive naming at 13 months, through general expansion of the open-class at 20 months, to grammatical morphology at 28 months. These are the developments emphasized by children "at the top of the class" across the second and third years of life. The verb density measures in this study seem to be sensitive to a "second line" of individual differences. Verbs seemed to offer a few children an opportunity to catch up with the others in Stages I and II. But it does not seem to be necessary for children to declare a verb major at any point in development.

The optional status of verb specialization becomes clear in a final set of partial correlations. We examined the relationships between 28-month closed-class style and its two strongest correlates at 13 months (referential flexibility in naming and referential style in comprehension), when variance from all three verb-density measures is removed. Since several degrees of freedom are lost in this partial correlation, the odds of wiping out a first-words-to-grammar relationship are high. Nevertheless, the correlations that remained were still significant: $+.40$ with referential style in comprehension ($p < .05$) and $+.50$ with referential flexibility in naming ($p < .01$). Regardless of individual variation in the acquisition of verbs at 20 and/or 28 months, 1-year-olds who understand the idea that things have names are also making more progress in morphology 1 1/2 years later.

How, then, should we summarize the role played by "verbiness" in early grammar? First, verbs do seem to play a special role in the acquisition of grammatical morphology. Second, there is some evidence for discontinuity of individual differences in the passage from nouns to verbs. These two points combined offer the best evidence to date in our study for the separation of grammar and semantics. And yet the "verbiness effect" is entirely secondary to a strong and continuous line of individual differences from early lexical development to grammar. Verb specialization seems to have a kind of optional status, a "booster rocket" some children use in Stages I and II to catch up (at least temporarily) with those children who have exploited the use of lexical-conceptual analysis at every stage. This pattern—or at least, this kind of pattern— should become clearer in Chapter 14, when we use factor analytic techniques to test the two-strand notion across measures and across ages.

Parts of Speech Cluster Analysis

As reported in Study 6, the cluster analyses applied to our 20-month data proved irrelevant by 28 months, because most of the children had reached ceiling on most of the relevant subcategories in those analyses. Nevertheless, there were good reasons to expect some kind of style difference to emerge in the children's relative emphasis on closed and open-class morphemes—a difference that would hopefully transcend the "forced-choice" proportion scores we have discussed so far.

For this reason, we applied cluster analysis to the various subcategories yielded in the parts-of-speech coding at 28 months. Through a fine-grained categorization of the morphemes produced by our children, we hoped to obtain an *empirical* grouping of the parts-of-speech categories, corresponding to the closed- and open-class distinction and/or to a relative elaboration of noun-phrase and verb-phrase morphology.

The results can be summarized quite succinctly. *No clusters emerged among the various parts-of-speech categories, either in the analysis across types or in the analysis across tokens.* Instead, everything tended to correlate highly and reliably with everything else, forming a single and insistent cluster that can only be described as "general lexical ability."

From one point of view, this result is comforting. Critics of both cluster and factor analysis have argued that these multivariate techniques frequently produce false positives, i.e., spurious and unreplicable groupings of the data (although individual researchers may be ingenious enough to find a way to interpret them anyway). This possibility was already greatly attenuated in the case of our 20 month clusters, because the same patterns appeared in both the interview and observations. However, the apparent reliability of the 20-month clusters provides no immunity against spurious groupings in the 28-month data. The single lexical fluency factor that did emerge at 28 months is unexciting; but it is utterly sensible and believable. *We suggest that, at 28 months, the processes used to acquire closed-class morphology are now by and large the same ones that are used to acquire open-class lexical items.* Furthermore, at this particular age level, there is little evidence for a split between noun lovers and noun leavers with their associated morphology.

Type-Token Ratios

It has generally been assumed that a high type-token ratio reflects relatively greater diversity in vocabulary, holding the amount of output constant. However, there appears to be a ceiling on type-token ratios. For example, Templin (1957) reports that variation from 3 to 7 years hovers within a constant range from .43 to .47, regardless of age. Furthermore, unlike other measures of vocabulary size and diversity, the type-token ratios in Templin's study did not seem to vary with birth order or social class. Even among adults, type-token ratios rarely go beyond .50.

In our 28-month sample, we obtained an average type-token ratio of .43, very much within the range that Templin reports for older children and adults. To determine whether variations in type-token ratio do reflect relative advancement in language, these scores were correlated with all the 10- to 28-month variables in the full data set (including many that we have not yet described). These results can be summarized briefly without providing correlation tables: Contrary to the prediction in the literature, type-token ratios at 28 months are either unrelated or significant *negative* indicators of language development as a whole. For example, these scores correlated at -.53 with MLU ($p < .01$), and at -.66 with vocabulary ($p < .01$).

Why should high diversity imply relatively slow development in language? The answer to this question may be related to the findings just reported for lexical style. At 28 months of age, the most advanced children have a high proportion of closed-class items in their observed vocabularies. Stages II to III are by definition the stages in which English-speaking children begin to elaborate the set of bound morphemes and grammatical function words. Hence the closed-class style measure tends to differentiate between children in Stage I (with a predominance of telegraphic utterances without closed-class forms) and children in Stages II, III, and IV (who have begun to supply closed-class terms at the appropriate points in sentence structure). The type-token ratio is sensitive to precisely the same difference between stages. In fact, there is a significant negative correlation of -.43 between closed-class style and the type-token ratio. *In other words, type-token ratios at 28 months are an indirect measure of the passage from telegraphic speech to grammar.*

Furthermore, it is likely that variations in the type-token ratio will be heavily constrained by grammatical structure from this point onward. Note that this ratio rarely exceeds .50, even among adults with full mastery of English. There seems to be a ceiling on the ratio of new content to closed-class morphology that is permissible in fully grammatical speech. Even for fluent adults, who use a wide range of sophisticated lexical items, each content word that is introduced must be accompanied by the required closed-class morphology (e.g., articles, prepositions, pronouns, auxiliary verbs). And each of these closed-class terms, in turn, adds to the token count without increasing the total vocabulary types. There are only two ways to break the .50 boundary and achieve a higher ratio of types to tokens. One way is to avoid any repetitions within the open class, i.e., never use the same noun, verb, or adjective twice. In this way, there can be a slow increase in the diversity of vocabulary within the heavy latticework of grammar. This kind of high-density language is surely atypical anywhere outside of the *Encyclopedia Brittanica*. The other way is to speak telegraphically, an option elected by many of the least advanced children in our 28-month sample. If this interpretation is correct, it would explain why high type-token ratios are negative indicators of language development at 28 months, even though the same measure is a positive indicator of language ability in later years.

Although the mean ratio at 28 months was not very different from the corresponding adult average, the range was quite large: .26–.74. As noted, a very high type-token ratio probably indicates that the child is still speaking telegraphically. But a slowly developing child might also obtain a very low ratio, if she produces a large number of uninformative and repetitious utterances (e.g., "No! Want dat one! Want dat one! Dat one!"). In other words, it seems likely that type-token ratios are a *nonlinear function* of the child's linguistic age. We think this small finding provides a useful developmental qualification on the clinical utility of type-token ratios, as discussed by Miller and Chapman (1981). Furthermore, this developmental pattern for type-token ratios fits within the more general pattern of findings regarding lexical style, i.e., measures of vocabulary composition that are tied to different language milestones at different points in language acquisition.

Conclusion

The main findings from this complex study can be summarized as follows:

Size and composition of the lexicon. By 28 months, rate of lexical growth has stabilized somewhat, compared with a massive spurt of development in grammatical complexity. Changes in the composition of the 28-month lexicon reflect this structural shift: a marked increase in the range and frequency of closed class morphemes, accompanied by an increase in the range of verbs within the open-class.

Lexical style. Lexical style analyses reflect these normative changes. At 13 months the most sophisticated children tended to specialize in nouns. At 20 months the more advanced children are expanding the open-class as a whole, with a particular emphasis on verbs. At 28 months, overall rate of development is correlated instead with expansions of the closed-class—although, within the open-class, verb development is still a hallmark of language progress. Hence, at each stage, lexical style reflects a new set of developmental problems. From this point of view, we might conclude that lexical style has nothing to do with *qualitative* differences among children; instead, it is an epiphenomenon of the rate at which children progress through basic developmental stages. However, a detailed analysis of verb-density patterns at 20 and 28 months suggests that a two-strand theory of some kind is still needed to account for the lexical style data. Verbs play a special role in both a rote and an analytic approach to grammar.

Grammar and semantics. Studies 6 and 7, taken together, provide still more evidence for a close developmental relationship between grammar and semantics. A cluster analysis of various parts-of-speech categories provided no evidence whatsoever for a dissociation between open- and closed-class items at 28 months. Furthermore, variance in the use of grammatical morphemes at 28 months is strongly associated with lexical-conceptual development at every preceding stage.

Note, however, that this last conclusion is based on the assumption that morphology is productive by 28 months, i.e., the use of these items reflects "true" grammar. In the next study we will provide a more direct test of this assumption, by applying productivity criteria to the grammatical morphemes used by the children in this sample.

Chapter 12: Study 8

Morphological Productivity at 28 Months

Because they are so frequent in the language environment, closed-class morphemes are particularly likely to occur within "frozen forms," amalgams, formulaic phrases that the child has not yet submitted to an internal analysis. For this reason, it is difficult to determine exactly when a child has really mastered the morphological rules of her language. Child-language researchers have been aware of this problem since the mid-sixties, well before the question of formulaic speech became an individual differences issue, and have developed several methods to establish whether or not a morphological rule is productive. In this study, we will compare the results obtained when four different productivity criteria are applied to the 28-month free-speech data—from both a normative and an individual differences perspective. To our knowledge, this is the first time that alternative measures of productivity have been compared with one another, and the first time that these measures have been examined from a psychometric point of view.

Although a comparison of productivity measures is useful in its own right, the major purpose of this study is to provide a further test of the relationship between grammar and semantics that has emerged in our data so far. There are very strong relationships between first words and 28-month grammar. And yet, paradoxically, the relationship between first sentences and 28-month grammar is very weak—even when we calculate structural complexity in exactly the same way at the 20- and 28-month age levels (i.e., MLU and closed-class style). We explained this lack of continuity between "identical" measures by arguing that grammatical morphology at 20 months is embedded within holistic, rote and/or imitative phrases. At 28 months, the same morphemes are more often used in a rule-governed fashion. Hence the lexical-conceptual variables that comprise the "first strand" are continuous with grammar only after grammatical forms have been subjected to the same kind of analytic process.

This interpretation deserves a more direct test. If we are correct, then the various measures of grammatical productivity should be highly correlated with MLU and closed-class style at 28 months; but the same productivity measures should not correlate with MLU and closed-class style at 20 months. Furthermore, the productivity measures should align with the "first strand" of language development from 13 through 20 months—i.e., with variables that reflect lexical-conceptual analysis.

What productivity measures should we choose to test this hypothesis? The best and most unambiguous test is an experimental one: Provide the child with a novel root form that he has never heard before (e.g., the noun "wug" or the verb "sib"), and observe whether he applies the requisite morpheme to this novel item (e.g., Berko, 1958). In analysis of free-speech data, we must take a more indirect route. The literature on morphological development suggests four options: the Brown criterion, the Bloom criterion, a hybrid measure from several different sources that we shall term the "contrast criterion," and a simple count of the presence and absence of the target bound and free morphemes. In the next section, we will consider some of the advantages and disadvantages of each method.

Method

The Brown Criterion

In Brown's classic longitudinal study of morphological development in three children, a given suffix or function word was assumed to be productive when it was used 90% of the time in obligatory contexts (Brown, 1973). An utterance provides an obligatory context for a particular morpheme if the omission of that morpheme would result in an ungrammatical sentence, from an adult point of view. One advantage of this measure is that it controls for the probability that a given morpheme will be needed at all. Some suffixes and function words are simply more frequent than others in natural conversation, for adults as well as children (e.g., the pronoun "I" compared with the pronoun "they"). Thus high-frequency morphemes may *seem* to be acquired earlier by children just because they come up more often in conversation. Brown's productivity criterion takes into account the absolute probability that a morpheme will be needed.

However, Brown's method does have some disadvantages. For one thing, the obligatory context criterion is not always easy to apply (Kuczaj, 1979; Maratsos, 1983). Take, for example, an utterance like "Mommy make dinner." Clearly something is wrong here. However, to determine exactly *what* morpheme is missing, we have to use contextual information to determine what target meaning the child had in mind. Did she mean to say "Mommy is making dinner," "Mommy makes dinner," "Mommy made dinner," or "Mommy is going to make dinner?'' Clearly, any use of the Brown criterion presupposes use of the ''method of rich interpretation'' (e.g., Howe, 1976). Parents and investigators are very often right when they guess what the child meant to say, as subsequent statements and reactions by the child often show (cf. Parisi, 1974; Golinkoff, 1983; Golinkoff and Kerr, 1978). But there is not always enough information to make an unambiguous interpretation.

Another problem pertains not to the obligatory context criterion per se, but to the list of elements to which that criterion has been applied. Brown's pioneering study was really the first of its kind to be carried out on the development of English—a language notorious for the irregular and relatively degraded status of its morphological system. One has to begin somewhere, and Brown chose to begin by studying a heterogeneous but fairly representative set of fourteen bound and free-standing morphemes: noun suffixes (possessives and plurals), verb suffixes (regular past ''-ed,'' regular third person singular ''-s,'' regular progressive ''-ing,'' irregular past, and irregular third person singular), articles, pronouns, prepositions, copular verbs, and auxiliary verbs. As Maratsos (1983) points out, ''The morphemes do not belong to any coherent structural group. Instead, the morphemes appear to have been chosen because of their methodological amenability for the study of the sequence of acquisition.'' Some of the individual items on this list are actually classes with several members. For example, the class of articles (constituting a single morpheme in the count of fourteen) includes ''a,'' ''an,'' and ''the.'' So when we conclude that the child has productive control over ''the article,'' we actually mean that the child produces some sort of article in the appropriate position 90% of the time. Brown also divided both copulas and auxiliaries into two subcategories: contractible forms and noncontractible forms. Each of the resulting four categories includes within it all the possible conjugations of that set for person and number (e.g., ''is'' and ''are''). In short, Brown's list of fourteen morphemes actually covers a much larger number of possible inflections and function words. Each of these possibilities, in turn, belongs within a somewhat different ''obligatory context.''

Despite the heterogeneous nature of this English list, and the difficulty of applying the obligatory context criterion, the sequence of acquisition that Brown observed has been replicated several times, with larger samples (cf. DeVilliers and DeVilliers, 1973; Miller and Chapman, 1981). We applied Brown's methods to the set of fourteen morphemes in our study as well, and obtained quite comparable results. However, since Brown's list of fourteen morphemes was based more on methological convenience than on a theory of morphology, it seems more appropriate for our purposes to focus on individual differences in the development of a coherent and homogeneous subset. In particular, we will focus on the productivity of seven bound noun and verb inflections: plural "-s," possessive "'s," progressive "-ing," regular third person singular "-s," regular past tense "-ed," irregular past (e.g., "went," "came"), and the irregular third person singular (e.g., the contrast between "have" and "has"). With this more limited and homogeneous list, we can compare Brown's criterion directly with other means of assessing productivity.

The Bloom Criterion

In studies of verb development by Bloom and colleagues (e.g., Bloom et al., 1980), a morpheme was considered productive when it appeared for the first time across at least five different types in a single session. For example, the progressive "-ing" must appear at the end of at least five different verbs (e.g., "playing," "hugging," "making," "doing," "going"). This criterion is quite conservative, requiring a rather large corpus of utterances (i.e., even an adult might fail to meet the productivity criterion in a very short conversation). Furthermore, the Bloom measure does not control for the absolute frequencies of different grammatical forms in the language. For example, five instances of the verb suffix "-ing" may be far more likely than five instances of the plural noun suffix "-s," even in a normal conversation by adults. However, compared with the Brown measure, the Bloom criterion requires fewer inferences about the child's target meaning and is thus much easier to apply.

The focus on types in Bloom's research also yields some interesting additional information about the lexical range for individual inflections (as summarized in Bloom, 1981). For example, only a handful of high-frequency, irregular verbs appeared in her transcripts with all the major inflectional markings (i.e., "do," "go" and "make"). Otherwise, verb inflections seemed to "specialize" in the early stages, applying to only a small subset of possible verb roots: Some occurred almost exclusively with past tense, others with "-ing," still others only with the third person singular "-s." These "specializations" seemed to have a semantic motivation, interacting with the underlying categories of tense and aspect. So, for example, past tense morphology tended to be attached to verbs that usually denote a clear end point or result (e.g., "pushed" or "found"), whereas the progressive "-ing" was applied to verbs that denote ongoing or repeated actions with no obvious point of completion. Such findings have implications for the category structure that underlies grammatical morphology, suggesting that the child's early knowledge of grammar maps onto prototypic configurations of meaning, and not onto abstract syntactic categories like "verb" (see also Bybee and Slobin, 1982; Bates and MacWhinney, 1982).

An advantage of the Bloom method for our purposes is that it forces a consideration of the semantic range of individual noun and verb inflections. It is not yet clear, however, whether this method will work for a corpus like ours, with a relatively small sample of utterances from each child.

The Contrast Criterion

For one particular set of morphemes in Italian, Bates and Rankin (1979) classified an ending as productive only if one of two criteria were met: (1) the morpheme must appear on a stem that had also occurred in the same session with a different ending (e.g., the child would receive credit for the -ing in "playing" only if forms like "played" or "plays" had also occurred in the transcript); and/or (2) the morpheme must occur in a novel, overgeneralized form that the child could not possibly have memorized (e.g., the plural in "feets" or the past in "goed away"). This contrast criterion is similar to the one used by MacWhinney (1978) in analyses of morphological development in Hungarian and German, and seems particularly useful for languages that are more heavily inflected than English. It is not entirely clear whether this method will yield coherent results for very young English children. Furthermore, like the Bloom measure, the contrast criterion fails to control for frequency.

The major advantage of this method is that it focuses on *creativity* in the child's use of a new suffix, i.e., use of a contrasting range of acceptable forms and/or use of a novel overgeneralized form that never appears in the adult linguistic environment. In this sense, the contrast criterion taps into the kind of generative process that we usually have in mind when we talk about "rules" rather than "habits." Whether or not this measure proves useful as an individual difference measure remains to be seen.

In the present study, we used all three criteria to calculate morphological productivity for the above seven English bound morphemes. In addition, we compared these criteria with a simple frequency count for the same seven morphemes. All four measures were applied to the same 28-month free-speech transcripts described in Studies 6 and 7.

Results and Discussion

Table 25 presents the number of children reaching criterion for each of the seven bound morphemes, according to each of the four productivity criteria. To compare the productivity measures with one another, we carried out two kinds of correlations: rank-order correlations across the seven morphemes, and product-moment correlations across the twenty-seven children in the study (Table 26).

Table 25. *Number of Children Reaching Criteria for Productivity on Seven Bound Morphemes*

	Productivity Criteria			
Bound Morphemes	Brown	Bloom	Presence/ Absence	Contrast
1. Plurals	20	6	27	15
2. Possessives	3	0	4	3
3. Third person singulars	7	0	12	9
4. Progressive -ing	19	5	26	20
5. Irregular past	8	0	15	10
6. Regular past -ed	2	0	4	3
7. Irregular third person singular	3	0	3	2

For obvious reasons, the simple presence/absence measure yielded the most generous estimates of acquisition, ranging from twenty-five children who produced at least one plural to two children who produced at least one instance of an irregular third person singular verb. Estimates obtained with the Brown and contrast criteria were somewhat lower, but otherwise very similar. Bloom's criterion yields a different pattern. For five of the seven morphemes, no child produced the requisite five different types in a single session. Only six children met this criterion for the plural, and six for the progressive. Apparently Bloom's metric requires a much larger corpus for each child than we have available in the present study. Applied to our data (with an average of 100 utterances per child), this criterion is simply too conservative to yield statistically meaningful data.

Similarities among these productivity criteria are underscored by the rank-order results across items. Spearman correlations among the Brown, presence/absence, and contrast criteria range from .88 to .96. And even though the Bloom method yielded very few data in our study, findings were in the same direction as the other three measures, with rank-order correlations ranging from .76 to .80. *In short, the sequence of acquisition for seven English bound morphemes seems to be quite stable, no matter how it is measured.* And for normative purposes—that is, for estimates of morphological productivity across a group of children—the first three measures are almost interchangeable.

Table 26. *Productivity Criteria: Full and Partial Correlations with Each Other and with Major Longitudinal Measures*

Longitudinal Measures	Productivity Criteria					
	Simple Correlations			Partialing Out Total Output		
	Brown	Presence/ Absence	Contrast	Brown	Presence/ Absence	Contrast
28-Month						
1. Productivity Criteria						
Brown	—			—		
Presence/absence	**.72	—		**.52		
Contrast	**.64	**.77	—	*.39	**.55	—
2. MLU	**.67	**.60	**.65	*.46	.21	~.37
3. Vocabulary	**.61	**.70	**.73	.21	.11	~.38
4. Total output	**.59	**.75	**.68	—	—	—
5. Closed-class style	*.40	.29	*.45	~.33	.16	*.40
6. Verb density	*.44	~.36	**.54	.28	.11	*.40
20-Month						
7. MLU	.27	.26	.29	-.04	-.20	-.08
8. Interview clusters						
Nominal multiword	**.54	**.64	**.54	.24	.27	.16
Grammatical morpheme	*.38	**.64	**.58	-.03	.29	.23
Semantic-conceptual	~.35	**.56	**.51	.12	*.38	.31
Dialogue	~.35	**.50	*.47	.02	.15	.15
9. Observational clusters						
Nominal multiword	~.37	.32	.33	-.03	~-.35	-.21
Grammatical morpheme	.26	.23	~.35	-.03	-.22	.03
Semantics-dialogue	*.44	*.44	**.61	.09	-.06	.30
10. Interview lexical						
Total vocabulary	**.57	**.52	**.52	~.33	.14	.19
Open-class style	~.36	*.39	~.36	.13	.07	.07
Verb density	*.43	~.34	~.35	.30	.13	.18
11. Observational lexical						
Total vocabulary	~.36	~.37	*.45	-.03	-.26	.02
Open-class style	*.41	~.38	~.38	.29	.22	.23
Verb density	.23	.22	.28	.01	-.10	.03
13-Month						
12. Interview						
Total comprehension	.02	.25	.32	.07	.26	~.36
% nouns in comprehension	~.33	~.36	**.58	.21	.23	**.55
Total production	.00	.28	.28	-.22	.02	.15
% nouns in production	.23	*.43	**.50	-.13	.22	.22
% flexible nouns in production	.14	.28	~.36	.02	.27	~.38

~ $p < .10$.
* $p < .05$.
** $p < .01$.

However, relative agreement across *items* does not necessarily mean that the different criteria will yield the same results across *children* (Clark, 1973). In analyses across children, we are focusing on the utility of each productivity criterion as an individual difference measure. This is a different kind of question and, as we shall see, the results are different as well. Table 26 lists the product-moment correlations of the productivity measures with one another and with the major language variables in this study. (Because the Bloom method yielded so little information across children, it failed to meet the assumptions of product-moment correlation and was excluded from all further analyses.)

First of all, the three remaining productivity measures are all significantly related to one another, with coefficients ranging from +.64 to +.77. Second, all three measures correlate highly with MLU, vocabulary, and total output, with coefficients in the +.60–.70 range. So far, there is little reason to choose among the different productivity metrics. However, when variance due to total output is removed, the patterns change. The Brown criterion is still related to MLU at above chance levels (+.46, $p < .05$), but the contrast measure and the presence/absence measure both drop below chance. In short, an analysis of grammatical productivity depends heavily on the size of the speech corpus. Note, however, that Brown's productivity criterion and MLU—which was also Brown's original measure of structural complexity—are related even when the size of the corpus is controlled.

Correlations with lexical style yield a slightly different pattern. When total output is controlled, the contrast criterion is still correlated reliably with closed-class style and with verb density. Relationships of the other two productivity measures to closed-class style and verb density drop below chance. These differences between the Brown criterion (which bears more relation to MLU) and the contrast criterion (which bears more relation to lexical style) are rather small. Nevertheless, they raise the interesting possibility that different productivity measures are sensitive to different aspects of sentence structure. These differences are more compelling when we look at the longitudinal patterns in Table 26.

From the raw correlations, grammatical productivity seems to align more with the "first strand" of lexical-conceptual variables: referential flexibility and comprehension at the stage of first words, and semantic-conceptual sophistication and lexical development at 20 months. When total output is partialed out, most of these relationships disappear— attesting again to the "output sensitivity" of the productivity measures. However, one pattern clearly remains: The contrast criterion for morphological productivity is continuous with referential flexibility and referential comprehension at 13 months. *In other words, there is a developmental relationship between variation in referential productivity at the*

Table 27. *Regressions of 20-Month Clusters on 28-Month Grammatical Productivity*

Predictor Variables	Productivity Criteria		
	Brown	Presence/Absence	Contrast
Interview clusters			
Joint variance (r^2)	.246	*.471	*.397
Unique variance:			
Nominal multiword	.093	.000	.001
Grammatical morphology	.002	.084	.048
Semantic-conceptual	.001	.011	.019
Dialogue	.001	.006	.006
Observational clusters			
Joint variance (r^2)	.206	.202	*.401
Unique variance:			
Nominal multiword	.007	.000	.026
Grammatical morpheme	.000	.000	.013
Semantics-dialogue	.066	.097	**.259

* $p < .05$.
** $p < .01$.

beginning of language development, and variation in grammatical productivity 15 months later.

This link between the contrast criterion and earlier lexical-conceptual measures is made clearer by a set of regression analyses using each of the three productivity measures as targets, with the different 20-month cluster scores as predictors (Table 27). When the observational clusters are used, a significant 40% of the variance in the contrast criterion is accounted for; the only significant unique contribution came from the semantics-dialogue cluster (25.9%, $p < .01$). In analogous regressions on the Brown productivity measure, the total variance accounted for was not significant (20.5%), nor did any of the clusters contribute significant unique variance. The same was true in regressions on the presence/absence measure (with 20% of the variance accounted for overall). When the four interview clusters were used, significant predictions were obtained for both the contrast criterion (39.7%) and the presence/absence criterion (47.1%). However, there were no unique contributions in any of the regressions by any of the interview clusters. In short, Brown's measure bears much less relationship to linguistic events at 20 months. The contrast criterion is consistently related to language at the earlier stages, particularly to the lexical-conceptual strand.

How should we interpret these differences among productivity measures that are supposedly aimed at the same thing, i.e., the degree to which children control morphological rules? The contrast criterion seems to tap into how *creatively* the child applies his understanding of a rule: creating novel overgeneralized forms and/or talking about the same object or event (e.g., play) from several different points of view (e.g., "play," "played," "plays," "playing"). In other words, the contrast criterion reflects an in-depth analysis of the meaning and range of a given grammatical form. This emphasis on "depth of analysis" may be the reason why the contrast criterion is predicted by lexical-conceptual analysis from the beginning of language acquisition.

Conclusion

To summarize, we have confirmed once again the close developmental relationship between lexical development and the acquisition of grammatical productivity. By contrast, the early appearance of grammatical morphemes at 20 months seems to reflect the operation of rote learning mechanisms that are unrelated to the single analytic strand that connects first words with later grammar. *Above all, grammatical morphology at 20 months is unrelated to productive control of morphology at a later stage.*

We may well begin to ask whether this unbroken line of analytic measures reflects anything other than general intelligence (if there is such a thing). In the next study, we will compare measures of morphological and syntactic comprehension with these productivity measures, and with a more general measure of lexical comprehension, the Peabody Picture Vocabulary Test. The PPVT is often used as a kind of "short form" for the measurement of IQ, because it does correlate so highly with standard intelligence measures. For that reason, it will provide a useful control for many of the patterns that we have observed so far.

One final point here concerns the question of *syntactic productivity,* i.e., the degree to which a child controls the word-order principles of her native language. It would certainly be useful to compare word-order with grammatical morphology to determine whether both aspects of grammar are mastered together or whether children can "specialize" in these two different aspects of the grammar. However, there is simply no way to calculate word-order productivity in the small speech samples that we have for these children.

Using much larger corpora, for a smaller set of children, Braine (1976) was able to derive an interesting contrast between "word-based" ordering principles (e.g., the More + NOUN pattern) and more abstract ordering rules that govern whole semantic and/or syntactic classes (e.g., the AGENT + ACTION pattern). There were also some interesting individual differences within his sample in the degree to which children relied on a heterogeneous set of narrow word-based patterns vs. a more systematic and homogeneous set of abstract principles. Note, however, that Braine's analyses were made possible by two factors: the large speech samples for each child, and (perhaps more important) the fact that many of his corpora were drawn from languages other than English. The word-order patterns of English are so rigid and so stable that word order variations or "errors" are rare in English-speaking children—even at the earliest stages. In our own sample, there were essentially no examples of "creative misorderings" at 28 months. Children tended to place verbs after subjects and before objects, prepositions before noun phrases, modifiers before their nouns, and so forth, with extraordinary regularity. If there are individual differences in the breadth of the categories that underlie these regularities, they are difficult if not impossible to detect in our children. However, in Study 10 we will at least be able to compare morphology and syntax in comprehension, and relate those respective measures of grammatical understanding to the morphological productivity scores described here.

Chapter 13: Study 9
Lexical Comprehension and the Question of Intelligence

In this study, we will take our first look at a traditional standardized test, the Peabody Picture Vocabulary Test (PPVT). In contrast with our other, "homemade" comprehension tests, the PPVT has an established record of reliability in this age range. However, its meaning is far from clear. It is basically a measure of how well children understand open-class vocabulary items (nouns, adjectives, action verbs). However, the PPVT is also often treated as a general intelligence test, on the basis of its high correlations with other standard IQ tests (in particular the verbal intelligence portions of the Stanford-Binet and the Wechsler).

Our primary interest here is in the use of the PPVT as a lexical comprehension measure. As such, this measure should align with the first-strand of language variables that we have tracked from 10 through 28 months of age. In addition, we would like to know whether the degree of dissociation that we have observed between lexical comprehension and production at the earlier stages is carried over into the third year of life.

Use of the PPVT as an intelligence test puts things in a very different perspective, presenting both an additional confound and an additional opportunity, depending on how we look at it. Suppose that we find very strong correlations between the PPVT and other Strand 1 measures at every age, perhaps correlations so high that performance on the PPVT can be said to *define* whatever it is that we mean by an analytic or lexical-conceptual style of language acquisition. If those who regard the PPVT as a general intelligence measure are correct, haven't we trivialized the findings of the last eight studies?

This is both an empirical and a theoretical question. We are not at all convinced that there is such a thing as "general intelligence." However, it does appear to be the case that the PPVT correlates with other so-called intelligence tests, and those tests in turn correlate with success in school and a variety of other markers that our society holds dear. For that reason, it will be useful to use the PPVT as an indirect control for whatever our society means by "IQ." In part, this may help us understand better just what "general intelligence" means in this age range.

Method

The Peabody Picture Vocabulary Test was administered using standard PPVT instructions (Dunn and Dunn, 1981). This is a multiple-choice test in which children are shown sets of black-and-white drawings with four pictures on each item. The items are presented in a picture book, ordered by increasing difficulty. The child's task on each item is to point to the object or action named by the Experimenter.

Results and Discussion

The results are divided into two sections: (1) results using the PPVT as a variable in its own right, focusing on lexical comprehension, and (2) results using the PPVT as a control for something like general intelligence.

The PPVT as a Comprehension Measure

Children completed a mean of 27.9 items on this test, ranging from 7 to 55. This means that our subjects are performing at or somewhat above age level, according to the PPVT norms.

Table 28 lists the raw correlations of the PPVT with major language variables at 28 months and at the earlier age levels. Let us start by considering correlations among the 28-month measures.

The Peabody correlates with observed vocabulary at $+.45$ ($p < .05$). This relationship is significant (unlike the comprehension-production correlation at 13 months), but it still means that the two lexical measures share only 20% of their variance. In other words, there is still considerable dissociability between receptive and expressive vocabulary. Furthermore, the correlation with total output in morphemes does not reach significance at all ($+.32$, $p < .10$). If we view the Peabody as a lexical comprehension measure, we can thus conclude that comprehension abilities are reflected in the *content* of speech but not in sheer *amount* of speech produced. This is consonant with dissociations obtained in the earlier studies.

A much higher correlation is obtained between the PPVT and MLU ($+.54$, $p < .01$). There are also significant correlations with each of the grammatical productivity measures (ranging from .41 to .48), and with closed-class style (.48). There does, then, seem to be a relationship between lexical comprehension and grammatical development. But the relationship is probably not direct. When we partial variance from lexical production out of these correlations, most of them drop below significance (see Table 28). The only one that remains is a partial correlation of +.42 with closed-class style. In other words, the relationship between the Peabody and grammatical development is primarily mediated by the variance shared with expressive vocabulary. This lends still more support to the notion of a partial dissociation between production (both lexical and grammatical) and comprehension.

Further evidence for this dissociation comes from the longitudinal correlations in Table 28. The PPVT is not correlated significantly with any of the 13-month observational measures, although (appropriately) a relationship with early comprehension testing approaches significance (+.36, $p < .07$). However, correlations involving the 13-month interview are considerably more robust and very specific: +.56 with total comprehension, +.72 with referential style in comprehension, and +.45 with referential flexibility in production. These comprehension-to-comprehension correlations are maintained even when 28-month productive vocabulary is partialed out of the matrix.

In our view, this pattern constitutes particularly clear evidence for developmental continuity in the lexical-conceptual strand of language development. This is also excellent evidence for the validity of parental-report measures at 13 months. If the predictive value of interviews rested solely on an uninteresting genetic confound (i.e., the bright parents have bright children and also give good interviews), there is no reason why these cross-age correlations should be restricted so specifically to comprehension measures. Viewed as a measure of child intelligence (in children with bright parents who say a lot in interviews), the PPVT should be just as likely to correlate with interview production as with interview comprehension. However, viewed as a measure of the child's lexical comprehension, it makes very good sense that the Peabody should be best predicted by another, earlier assessment of lexical comprehension. It is even more interesting that the correlation with referential style in comprehension is so strong, since this is presumably the best assessment that we have at the early stages of the child's receptive control over open-class content words (i.e., the same kinds of words that are tested in the PPVT months later).

To subject these correlational relations to a stronger test, we also repeated some of the regression analyses described in earlier studies, with the PPVT as the target measure. When early comprehension and production totals are the only predictors, they jointly account for 32.35% of the PPVT variance (multiple-r = .56). The unique contribution of production to this equation is only 0.1%; the unique contribution of comprehension is fully 30.8%, or almost all of the joint prediction. In another pair of regressions, we used two aspects of 13-month production as predictors, i.e., referential flexibility and total vocabulary. Neither the

Table 28. *Full and Partial Correlations of the Peabody Picture Vocabulary Task with Major Language Measures*

	Correlations with PPVT	
	Partialing out Simple Correlation	28-Month Expressive Vocabulary
28 Months		
1. MLU	**.54	~.33
2. Vocabulary	*.45	—
3. Total output	~.32	.22
4. Closed-class style	*.48	*.42
5. Verb density	.24	.07
6. Morphological productivity		
Brown criterion	*.41	.19
Contrast criterion	*.48	.24
20 Months		
7. MLU	.09	-.16
8. Interview clusters		
Nominal multiword	.22	-.13
Grammatical morpheme	.15	-.18
Semantic-conceptual	**.67	**.56
Dialogue	*.45	.26
9. Observational clusters		
Nominal multiword	.18	-.19
Grammatical norpheme	.15	-.11
Semantics-dialogue	*.45	.18
10. Interview lexical		
Total vocabulary	**.51	.31
Open-class style	**.59	*.45
Verb density	*.46	.31

Table 28. *Continued*

	Correlations with PPVT	
	Partialing out Simple Correlation	28-Month Expressive Vocabulary
11. Observational lexical		
Total vocabulary	~.34	.01
Open-class style	*.42	.27
Verb density	-.07	-.28
12. Comprehensive testing		
Single word	.19	.11
Canonical commands	.04	-.12
Non-canonical commands	.20	-.04
13. Novel concept		
Imitation in Training	-.31	-.33
Single-word comprehension	*.41	.28
Sentence comprehension	.15	-.10
13 Months		
14. Interview		
Total comprehension	**.56	**.49
% nouns in comprehension	**.72	**.64
Total production	.12	-.02
% nouns in production	.27	.20
% flexible nouns	*.45	~.35
15. Observations		
Comprehension	~.36	.24
Spontaneous production	-.18	-.28
Imitative production	.06	-.07
16. 10-Month interview		
Comprehension	~.34	~.36
Production	.14	.11

~ $p < .10$.
* $p < .05$.
** $p < .01$.

joint nor the unique contributions reached significance in this analysis. In short, the cross-age variance leading to performance on the PPVT seems to be restricted quite specifically to comprehension. This contrasts markedly with similar regressions on 28-month MLU (see Study 6).

Turning to the 20–28-month findings, we find still more evidence for a comprehension strand in early language development. None of the multiword measures at 20 months predicts performance on the PPVT (see also Bretherton et al., 1983). The significant relationships are restricted to reported vocabulary, all three of the semantic-conceptual-dialogue clusters, and certain aspects of lexical style and single-word comprehension.

When 28-month productive vocabulary is partialed out of these 20–28-month findings, only one significant relationship with the PPVT remains: a high positive correlation of +.56 with the semantic-conceptual cluster in the 20-month interview. It seems fair to conclude that lexical comprehension in 2-year-olds grows out of the first-strand of lexical-conceptual measures in the early stages of language; but it most certainly does *not* define that strand. Instead, the PPVT seems to reflect the "outer edge" of progress in language comprehension. Although it belongs more to the first-strand than the second, it may well represent a "third strand" of pure comprehension, a kind of minor harmonic on the major themes we have derived so far. We will return to this point later.

The PPVT as a General Intelligence Measure

The findings so far all fit with an interpretation of the PPVT as a language measure, specifically a measure of single-word comprehension. But, as we have noted, some investigators have chosen to view the PPVT as a measure of general intelligence. If this assumption is warranted, what can we learn by using the PPVT as a control variable? Table 29 summarizes a series of partial correlations among early and late language measures: first removing variance shared with the Peabody, then removing variance from total output at 28 months, and a final set controlling for both the PPVT and total output.

Starting at 28 months, when performance on the PPVT is controlled, the partial correlation between vocabulary and MLU is $+.65$ ($p < .01$). Thus, the relationship between lexical and grammatical development, as reflected in these two measures, involves more than general intellectual development, and/or lexical comprehension. However, when we partial out *both* control measures, the correlation drops to a nonsignificant $+.29$. In some sense, then, the relationship between vocabulary and MLU at 28 months is a product of the independent dimensions underlying receptive vocabulary and total speech output.

This result can be tied to the general framework of the present study as follows. First, let us assume (for the moment) that the PPVT may be the best indicator at 28 months of a comprehension-driven, analytic mode of processing. Conversely, total output in morphemes may be the best indicator that we have at 28 months of speech production for its own sake. From this point of view, we can use regression techniques to ask about the unique and joint contributions of these two indicators to MLU and vocabulary, respectively.

In a first regression analysis, we used MLU as the target variable and the PPVT and total output scores as predictors. The two predictors together account for 56.6% of the variance in 28-month MLU (multiple-r = .75). When the PPVT is entered into this equation last, it adds a significant 11.7%. When total output is entered last, it adds 27.2%. If we are correct in our characterization of the two predictor variables, we can conclude that *both* of our hypothetical acquisition mechanisms contribute to utterance complexity at 28 months. That is, MLU is a product of both "first-strand" and "second-strand" processes.

In the second regression analysis, we used vocabulary as the target variable, and (again) the PPVT and total output scores as predictors. This analysis gave rather different results. The two predictors together accounted for a very large 83.9% of the variance in 28-month vocabulary (multiple-r = .91). When the PPVT is entered into this equation last, it adds only a nonsignificant 3.1% unique variance. When total output is entered last, it adds a more substantial 62.7% unique variance. Hence we may conclude that second-strand processes contribute more to vocabulary than to MLU at 28 months, in line with our earlier suggestion that 28-month vocabulary is more affected to the size of the speech sample. Note, however, that this is a reversal of the MLU/vocabulary contrast at 20 months. At that age, MLU was clearly more influenced by whatever processes underlie "production for its own sake." Vocabulary (particularly reported vocabulary) received greater contributions from the joint variance underlying various language measures, and from variance specific to comprehension and to lexical-conceptual productivity in speech. This is one more bit of evidence for the heterotypic nature of individual differences in language development. The very same language measures are controlled by different processes at different points in time.

Unfortunately, there is a much less interesting way of looking at the partial correlations in Table 29 if we accept the Peabody as an intelligence test. Are the two strands of language that we have traced through all these studies reducible to nothing but IQ and general talkativeness? As "modular components of language processing," these two candidates would not carry us very far. Just how much is left in Table 29 when these two controls are applied? Although this is a *very* strong set of

Table 29. Longitudinal Relations Among Major Language Variables Controlling for PPVT and Total Output at 28 Months

| | 28-Month Variables | | | | | | | | | | | |
| | Removing PPVT | | | | Removing Output | | | | Removing Both | | | |
	MLU	Vocabulary	Closed-Class Style	Morpheme Production	MLU	Vocabulary	Closed-Class Style	Morpheme Production	MLU	Vocabulary	Closed-Class Style	Morpheme Production
28 Months												
1. MLU	—	**.65	.32	**.53	—	*.42	*.46	~.37	—	.29	.32	.24
2. Vocabulary	**.65	—	.04	**.65	*.42	—	.08	~.38	.29	—	-.11	.27
20 Months												
3. MLU	**.51	**.49	-.01	.28	.21	.05	-.11	-.08	.29	.10	-.08	-.05
4. Interview clusters												
Nominal multiword	**.70	**.66	~.34	**.51	*.44	.22	.32	.16	*.49	.24	~.36	.17
Grammatical morpheme	**.66	**.61	.23	**.58	~.34	.04	.15	.23	*.43	.09	.21	.28
Semantic-conceptual	*.41	~.38	.31	.29	*.48	*.39	*.48	.31	.28	.19	.29	.11
Dialogue	*.49	*.46	-.04	.32	*.39	.19	.05	.15	.27	.06	-.11	.02
5. Observational clusters												
Nominal multiword	**.68	**.67	.04	.28	*.40	.24	-.04	-.21	*.48	.28	-.03	-.21
Grammatical morpheme	**.56	**.51	.05	.32	~.35	.21	.00	.03	~.40	.23	.00	.04
Semantics-dialogue	**.67	**.70	.26	*.49	**.57	**.56	~.35	.30	*.49	*.49	.24	.20

20 Months Continued

6. Interview lexical

Total vocabulary	**.77	**.54	.19	~.36	**.73	.31	.31	.19	**.66	.17	.16	.04
Open-class style	*.47	*.40	.16	.11	**.50	~.38	~.33	.07	~.34	.21	.13	-.15

7. Observational lexical

Total vocabulary	**.69	**.68	.06	~.35	**.52	*.43	.07	.02	*.50	~.40	-.01	-.05
Open-class style	.28	.32	*.46	.22	.32	~.39	**.53	.23	.19	.29	*.45	.11

13 Months

8. Interview

Total comprehension	.19	.09	.02	.12	*.46	*.45	.26	~.36	.28	.30	.02	.20
% nouns comprehension	.25	.18	~.35	*.38	*.49	*.44	**.53	**.55	.26	.25	~.35	*.43
Total production	*.42	.28	.07	.30	.29	.03	.04	.15	.32	.03	.04	.15
% nouns production	.23	.09	.14	.18	.29	.10	.22	.22	.21	.01	.13	.15
% flexible nouns production	*.44	.19	*.43	~.36	*.49	.08	**.52	~.38	~.38	-.07	*.42	.27

~ $p < .10$.
* $p < .05$.
** $p < .01$.

manipulations, removing vast amounts of variance across the board, some strong and consistent relationships do remain.

Starting with MLU, most of the correlations involving the 20-month measures withstand all three partialing procedures. The correlations with 20-month vocabulary are particularly strong ($+.50$ with observed vocabulary and $+.66$ with reported vocabulary), suggesting that a strong link between lexical and grammatical development remains despite powerful control procedures. Also, although the 13-month predictions of MLU do drop below significance when both controls are applied together, the relationship with referential flexibility falls just short ($+.38, p < .10$).

Turning to 28-month vocabulary, we again obtain a different pattern. The 20-month predictions in Table 29 are relatively unaffected when the PPVT is controlled. However, when both the PPVT and total output are removed, only two significant correlations remain. Furthermore, the single 13-month prediction (from referential style in comprehension) disappears when variance from the PPVT is removed. Clearly, longitudinal predictions of vocabulary at 28 months are accounted for to a much greater extent than MLU by these two control variables.

Third, the longitudinal correlations involving 28-month closed-class style and morphological productivity generally disappear when the PPVT and total output are partialed out. Nevertheless, both morphological measures still retain significant relationships with at least one aspect of the "first-strand" at 13 months. In particular, a significant and continuous strand of variance remains from referential flexibility at 13 months, through open-class style at 20 months, to closed-class style at 28 months.

To summarize, a few rather consistent patterns of correlation do remain over time even when we remove variance shared with two powerful control measures (the PPVT and total output in morphemes). In particular, structural complexity at 28 months (i.e., MLU) retains connections with both "first-strand" and "second-strand" variables at 20 months. Furthermore, closed-class style and morphological productivity are still linked to certain aspects of lexical-conceptual analysis through the one-word stage.

Given the large amount of variance contributed by the two 28-month controls, it is perhaps surprising that anything is left at all. Even if we accept the dubious use of the PPVT as a measure of "g," and if we accept the idea that the total morphemes produced by the child reflect an uninteresting dimension of "talkativeness," the two dissociable strands of language development discussed in previous studies can still be detected in the data. Above all, a strong relationship between lexical and grammatical development remains, within the 28-month session and over time.

Conclusion

There are two main conclusions to take with us from this particular study. First, the PPVT functions more as a lexical-comprehension measure than as a test of general intelligence within this study. Even if we do accept this test as a control for IQ, the "two-strand" picture of language development still stands, with particularly strong ties between lexical development and grammar.

The second conclusion is less comforting and complicates the picture a bit more. The Peabody not only fails to *define* the first-strand of lexical-conceptual measures, it actually seems to stand apart from both rote and productive versions of expressive language development. We may actually have a situation of "strands within strands." On the one hand, there is a partial dissociation between rote and analytic processes in language development. On the other hand, there is a partial dissociation between comprehension and production, even within the first strand of lexical-conceptual analysis. We will be able to explore this possibility in more detail in Study 11—after we have compared measures of comprehension and production entirely within the domain of grammar.

Chapter 14: Study 10
Grammatical Comprehension at 28 Months

We have found very little evidence so far for a dissociation between lexical and grammatical development. We have, however, found evidence for a partial dissociation between lexical comprehension and lexical production, forming two strands that map onto different aspects of multiword speech. In this study, we can at last compare comprehension and production *within* the domain of grammar. Specifically, we would like to know whether tests of grammatical comprehension have more in common with production of grammatical forms or with comprehension of single lexical items. Is there a "grammar factor," a unified set of comprehension and production variables that can develop out of synchrony with lexical progress in the same children?

There are three measures that we will consider in this section: a test for comprehension of grammatical morphology, word-order comprehension assessed through enactment, and word-order comprehension assessed through picture choice. Unlike the Peabody Picture Vocabulary Test (PPVT), these grammatical comprehension tests are experimental procedures with essentially unknown psychometric properties. There are no published norms for grammatical comprehension by children this young. Furthermore, we know very little about the internal reliability and validity of these three grammatical comprehension tests. As noted in Study 4, comprehension tasks with very young children are particularly vulnerable to such sources of noise as toy preference, motivation, and obedience (Bridges, 1979). Given all these problems, we present our findings here with particular caution. The question we are asking is an interesting one, but the answer is necessarily rather tentative.

Method

The morphology comprehension test was devised in our laboratories, because the available standard tests of grammatical comprehension seemed to reach a "floor" above the 28-month age level. Our test used large, brightly colored magazine pictures instead of the black-and-white drawings that are customary in clinical instruments, and perhaps for this reason we were able to hold the children's interest and complete testing in the majority of cases. The morphology items, summarized in Table 30, each involved a pair of pictures contrasting along such dimensions as past versus present (a boy drinking his milk, compared with a boy smiling and holding an empty glass), male versus female actors carrying out the same activity (for a "he" versus "she" contrast), various locative contrasts (e.g., "on" versus "under"), and plural versus singular (e.g., a picture of a single towel versus a pile of towels). There were fifteen pairs in all, placed in random order within a looseleaf test book, with "distractor" pictures intervening between the test pages. On each item, the Experimenter would read two possible descriptions, with an exaggerated intonation marking the critical morphological contrast; she would then request the child to point to only one of the two descriptions, as follows:

The boy IS TAKING a bite; the boy IS GOING TO TAKE a bite. Show me The boy IS TAKING a bite.

Each child was taken through the book twice. On the first run-through, one of the two possible descriptions was asked for (randomly selected). On the second run-through, the alternative description was requested instead. For any picture pair, a child would receive a correct score only if he chose the correct alternative on both presentations. This reduces the likelihood of false positives based on such irrelevant factors as picture preference.

As can be seen from Table 30, our morphology test taps only a small subset of the grammatical morphemes that are produced spontaneously by children in this age range. There is, then, only a partial overlap between these items and measures of morphological production in the same children (e.g., closed-class style in Study 7; morphological productivity in Study 8). To permit a more direct comparison between comprehension and production of morphology, we went back to the transcripts and determined, for each child, whether the two contrasting forms tested on each morphology item were both spontaneously produced (e.g., whether the child produced both "he" and "she," both "on" and "under," both "is x-ing" and "are x-ing").

There were two tests for comprehension of word-order, each derived from experimental techniques that other investigators have used successfully with 2-year-old children. The first was a picture choice task adapted from Horgan (1981), with six pairs of pictures illustrating reversals of agent-patient relationship (e.g., a picture of a boy chasing a girl,

Table 30. *Number of Children Reaching Criterion for Comprehension and Production of Target Morphology Items*

Item Contrast Involving	Comprehension	Production	Both
1. She*	19	15	12
2. They	17	9	7
3. He	14	21	10
4. His	9	6	3
5. Her	9	5	0
6. Under	19	0	0
7. On	19	18	12
8. Inside	8	2	0
9. Outside	8	7	1
10. Third person singular-s	12	12	4
11. Doesn't	12	4	0
12. Cannot/(can't)	9	4	2
13. Can	9	11	6
14. Singular	14	27	14
15. Plurals	14	25	14
16. Progressive -ing*	7	23	6
17. Going to _____	9	17	6
18. Irregular past	3	13	3
19. Is (copula)	14	25	13
20. Was (copula)	14	2	2
21. Not	17	11	8

*A form that was contrasted in two different comprehension items

versus a girl chasing a boy). On each trial, the child was asked to point in response to a sentence describing only one of the two possibilities, e.g., "Show me THE BOY IS CHASING THE GIRL." As with the morphology task described above, the picture pairs were each shown twice: on the first run through the picture book, the sentence matched one randomly selected member of the pair; on the second run-through, the sentence matched the other picture. On our morphology test, we required that the child perform correctly on both members of an item pair. However, because there were fewer items on this test, we feared that the correct-pairs criterion might be too conservative. We therefore calculated the total number of correct choices across the task for this particular measure.

The other word-order comprehension task involved an enactment procedure (e.g., Chapman and Kohn, 1978). In the warmup phase of the task, five stimuli (a toy bear, a female doll, a kitty, a cup, and a bottle) were first introduced to the child individually. This helps ensure that children know the words for the word-order test items that follow later on. A different set of objects (a toy duck, dog, and fork) were then used to familiarize the child with the demands of the enactment procedure and the specific actions to be enacted (hitting, pushing, and kissing). Three demonstrations were given, in which the Experimenter would utter a phrase with canonical word-order such as "The fork is hitting the duck" while carrying out the action described (e.g., picking up the fork and making it hit the duck). Then the Experimenter would invite the child to do the same, asking "Can you make the fork hit the duck? Show me THE FORK IS HITTING THE DUCK." This general procedure was repeated two more times. Each of the three demonstration trials used a different verb, and there was one trial of each of three types: one involving two animate nouns, one involving an animate subject acting on an inanimate object, and another involving an inanimate subject acting on an animate object. We varied the three demonstration trials in this way to avoid biasing the child in favor of a particular animacy strategy. All children included in the analyses were able and willing to produce these actions, following the Experimenter's demonstration.

After the demonstration trials, each child received 16 experimental presentations with the original set of objects (bear, doll, kitty, cup, and bottle). This time the Experimenter uttered the sentence to be acted out (e.g., "Show me THE BEAR IS PUSHING THE GIRL"), but did not act the sentence out herself. On each trial, the two objects were placed equidistant from the child, with left-right side of presentation randomized across trials. The sixteen experimental trials involved eight contrasting pairs (e.g., "The bear is pushing the girl" versus "The girl is pushing the bear"), in random order (with the constraint that contrasting pairs were never presented in adjacent order). Half of the items were in the canonical Noun-Verb-Noun (NVN) order; the other half were evenly divided between two noncanonical word-orders (VNN and NNV). Thus, although half the stimuli represented noncanonical orders, each of these orders was represented only half as often as the canonical NVN. This was because pilot testing had established that the limits of the children's interest and tolerance were surpassed when the total number of trials was extended beyond sixteen to the twenty-four necessary to present all orders equally.

Finally, within each word-order type, animacy was varied systematically. In one-fourth of the items, an animate object was mentioned first and an inanimate was mentioned second; in another fourth of the items, these orders were reversed (e.g., "The bear is pushing the cup" versus "The cup is pushing the bear"). For the remaining half of the items, all the nouns were animate. These were also divided into reversed pairs (e.g., "The girl is kissing the kitty" versus "The kitty is kissing the girl"). This results in a 2×4 design: two levels of word-order (canonical versus noncanonical) and four levels of animacy (animate-inanimate, inanimate-animate, $animate_1$-$animate_2$, $animate_2$-$animate_1$), with two items within each cell, yielding sixteen items total.

The group data for this experiment are reported elsewhere (Bates et al., 1984). Briefly summarized, there was a significant effect of word-order at 28 months of age. Children were significantly more likely to use the first noun mentioned as the agent of an action if that noun appeared in first position in a canonical NVN sentence; their behavior on the non-canonical NNV and VNN sentences was random. In other words, 28-month-olds are sensitive to the SVO (Subject-Verb-Object) structure of English. However, the animacy manipulation did not make a difference. So, for example, 28-month-old English-speaking children are just as willing to make cups act on bears as they are to make bears act on cups. For our purposes here, this means that the scores for "percent choice of the first noun" in this experiment reflect the degree to which the child follows canonical subject-verb-object word-order in sentence interpretation.

Ideally, we would like a direct comparison between comprehension and production of word-order to parallel the direct comparison made here between comprehension and production of specific morphological forms. However, for the reasons outlined in Study 8, word-order relationships do not lend themselves to such a direct test in English, at least not for a relatively small corpus of utterances (see MacWhinney, 1978, Ingram, 1979, and Braine, 1976, on calculating the productivity of word-order patterns).

Results and Discussion

The results are presented in three sections:

1. The 28-month test of morphological comprehension, in relation to an analogous measure of morphological production, and to the other major language variables within and between sessions.

2. The two word-order comprehension tasks, as they relate to other language variables in the study, particularly morphological and lexical comprehension.

3. A factor analysis of all the 28-month grammar measures taken together, to provide one final look at the patterns of association and dissociation that emerge entirely within the domain of grammar.

Comprehension of Grammatical Morphology

Table 30 lists the number of children who responded correctly to each item pair in the morphology comprehension test. Next to each item, we have also listed the number of children who produced both of the forms contrasted in that item in their spontaneous speech.

By the conservative criterion of requiring correct choice on both presentations of an item, 28-month-old children as a group did not fare well in the morphology comprehension task. If the child responded on every trial (which did not always happen), both pairs would be correct by chance 25% of the time. This would yield scores between 4 and 5 on the test as a whole. In fact, the average number of correct pairs was 6.4, with a range 0 to 12. Eighteen out of twenty-seven children obtained scores of 5 or better—a number that falls below significance by a sign test, indicating that the group as a whole failed to grasp the point of this experiment.

Nevertheless, there were marked individual differences among children in performance on this task. Many were indeed in the chance range, and their behavior during testing also indicated that they enjoyed the pictures but did not understand the point of the game at all. Other children obtained two to three times as many correct scores as we would expect by chance; their behavior during testing indicated a clear understanding of the task, as they carefully compared the pictures back and forth, hesitated before making a choice, and occasionally corrected their initial errors. We must distinguish, then, between the use of this task as a normative measure and its use as a measure of individual differences.

There seems to be an interesting parallel here between comprehension and production. At 28 months, a large number of children are still in Stage I, a period in which Brown (1973) and others conclude that grammatical morphemes are not yet used productively. Others have begun to use inflections and function words correctly in their speech, at least some of the time. Are the same children crossing the threshold out of Stage I in both comprehension and production? Or will we find a dissociation between modalities similar to the dissociation observed in lexical development at the beginning of the one-word stage? As can be seen from Table 30, the relationship between comprehension and production is not very high across items or across children.

Across items, the rank-order correlation is nonsignificant and in the negative direction (-.22). This means that the most difficult items in one domain are actually slightly easier in another. Specifically, children did particularly badly on the comprehension of verb morphology (i.e., contrasts in tense, person, and aspect); these same items were among the most frequent in production. Conversely, children performed quite well in comprehension of certain preposition and pronoun contrasts; the same items were relatively infrequent in production. Of course since the negative correlation across items is not significant, these particular differences might well prove to be random. The important point is that the most difficult contrasts in comprehension are *not* necessarily the last to appear in free speech.

Across children, the product-moment correlation is significant and positive but not very high: +.38 ($p < .05$). In fact, this correlation is smaller than the relationship between morphological comprehension and the PPVT (+.46, $p < .05$). And when performance on the PPVT is partialed out (as a control for lexical comprehension, or general intelligence, or simple test-taking skills), the correlation between morphological comprehension and its production analogue drops to a nonsignificant +.27.

Finally, Table 31 lists correlations between the morphology comprehension test and other major language variables in this study. Briefly summarized, this test fails to correlate with any of the other measures of grammar discussed so far, including 28-month MLU, closed-class style, and the various indices of grammatical productivity. It also bears no relationship to language measures at 13 months. The test does correlate with many of the 20-month variables: observed vocabulary, the nominal multiword clusters and the semantic-conceptual clusters, as well as single- and multiword comprehension tests and some aspects of lexical style. Furthermore, many of these relationships remain even when variance shared with the PPVT is partialed out. Note, however, that comprehension of morphology is entirely unrelated to earlier measures of morphological production. Instead, it seems to have most in common with the first strand of lexical-conceptual variables, particularly with other comprehension tests.

By contrast, the production analogue of our comprehension test does correlate with many other aspects of grammatical production, including MLU and the various productivity indices at 28 months (though not closed-class style or verb density). Like the corresponding items in comprehension, this morphology production list is not continuous with 13-month language. But it is systematically related to many of the 20-month measures: MLU, vocabulary, all the cluster variables, lexical style indicators, and comprehension of multiword commands. Most of these relationships remain when variance shared with the PPVT is removed. Indeed, an unusual relationship with fiffin imitation (see Study 5) reaches significance *only* after the PPVT is partialed out. These findings—particularly the correlation with fiffin imitation—suggest that at least some of the variance in production of grammatical morphology at 28 months is still the result of rote processes. This is not true for comprehension of the very same grammatical forms.

The best summary of these patterns is the following: When we focus on the same set of morphemes in both comprehension and production, the comprehension version is primarily related to lexical development in general and to lexical comprehension in particular; the production version receives input from both the first and second strand of language development, but is uniquely affected by the second strand of variables involving rote/holistic learning and imitation. *It seems fair to conclude that we have found another dissociation between comprehension and production, in the domain of morphological development.*

We can never obtain a "pure" measure of morphological comprehension, out of a sentence or phrase context, independent of the child's understanding of content words. For this reason alone, a strong association between lexical and morphological comprehension tests might have been expected—evidenced here in the correlation between our test and the PPVT. However, this fact in itself does not explain the lack of concordance, across items or children, between comprehension and production *within* the grammar.

Early in the one-word stage, similar dissociations were caused primarily by a group of children who understood much more than they produced. Is the same thing happening here? Apparently not. A few children obtained markedly higher scores on the receptive task; but just as many children diverged in the opposite direction. So the comprehension-production dissociation observed within the grammar is not due to the expected developmental "lag" or "decalage" between modalities.

There are entirely different reasons why we might expect a dissociation in the opposite direction, with better performance in spontaneous production than in comprehension testing. There is most assuredly a *pragmatic* difference between laboratory comprehension tests and spontaneous speech. The test situation requires cooperativeness, test-taking skills, and a certain amount of metalinguistic awareness outside a normal conversational context (for discussion, see Bridges, 1979). The use of morphology in conversation is "scaffolded" by the ongoing context, and it is motivated by the child's own communicative interests. It is not obvious, however, why verb morphology is scaffolded by conversation but hard to think about on demand, while pronouns and prepositions receive

Table 31. *Correlations with the Grammatical Comprehension Tests and the Morphology Test Production Analogue With and Without Control for PPVT*

	Morphology		Morphology Production Analogue		Word Order Test			
					Pictures		Enactment	
	r	-PPVT	r	-PPVT	r	-PPVT	r	-PPVT
28 Months								
MLU	.28	.05	**.68	**.63	*.45	~.38	.32	.11
Total vocabulary	*.39	.22	**.71	**.67	~.37	.29	.11	-.10
Total output	.20	.06	**.73	**.70	.21	.14	.03	-.12
Closed-class style	.05	-.21	.19	.04	.11	-.02	.20	.00
Verb density	.08	-.02	.20	.13	.29	.24	.14	.04
Productivity								
Brown	.19	.00	**.55	*.48	~.34	.26	.00	-.21
Contrast	.16	-.08	**.50	*.42	.21	.10	.04	-.20
Presence/absence	.19	.00	**.68	**.64	.12	.01	.01	-.20
Comprehension								
Morphology	—	—						
Production analogue to morphology	*.38	.27	—	—				
Word order								
Picture choice	*.45	~.38	.18	.10	—	—		
Enactment	.24	.05	.19	.06	*.46	*.40	—	—
20 Months								
MLU	.29	.28	**.51	**.51	.18	.16	.01	-.06
Interview clusters								
Nominal multiword	**.49	*.44	*.71	**.69	*.45	*.42	.18	.09
Grammatical morpheme	.32	.28	**.66	**.65	~.35	.33	.18	.13
Semantic-conceptual	**.58	*.41	**.55	*.48	~.36	.25	*.48	.28
Dialogue	*.41	.26	*.41	.32	**.53	*.48	.29	.12
Observational clusters								
Nominal multiword	*.39	~.35	**.69	**.68	*.40	~.37	.31	.26
Grammatical morpheme	.31	.27	*.47	*.46	.26	.23	.05	.00
Semantics-dialogue	*.42	.27	**.51	*.43	**.54	*.49	~.35	.20

Table 31. *Continued*

	Morphology		Morphology Production Analogue		Word Order Test			
					Pictures		Enactment	
	r	-PPVT	r	-PPVT	r	-PPVT	r	-PPVT
20 Months *Continued*								
Interview lexical								
Total vocabulary	~.35	.16	**.53	*.46	*.43	~.36	~.34	.16
Open-class style	**.50	.32	*.43	.31	*.48	*.42	*.47	.29
Verb density	**.58	*.47	**.61	**.55	.18	.07	*.39	.24
Observational lexical								
Total vocabulary	*.46	~.36	**.62	**.58	*.44	~.38	.29	.17
Open-class style	.23	.04	.23	.11	~.39	.32	*.49	~.37
Verb density	.07	.12	.29	~.34	-.08	-.06	-.11	-.09
13-Month interview								
Total production	.23	.20	.26	.23	.10	.07	.21	.18
Total comprehension	.32	.08	.04	-.18	.17	.02	.26	.03
% Nouns in production	.11	.00	.00	-.09	.06	.00	.06	-.06
% Nouns in comprehension	~.32	-.01	.14	-.13	~.36	.25	.27	-.05
% Flexible nouns	.09	-.14	.10	-.04	.24	.13	.15	-.05

~ $p < .10$.
* $p < .05$.
** $p < .01$.

less conversational support but are much easier to think about in a test within and across children. In short, there is no simple explanation for the comprehension-production dissociation in terms of task difficulty.

This brings us to the relationship between morphology and another aspect of grammar, control over word-order principles. Here we can at least determine whether there is unity among different *aspects* of receptive grammar, separate from the variance shared with lexical comprehension.

Comprehension of Grammar: Word Order

Starting with the enactment procedure, the group results reported by Bates et al. (1984) did show that 28-month-olds have some sensitivity to canonical English word order. That is, children were significantly more likely to choose the first noun as the actor on noun-verb-noun sentences, compared with sentences in the verb-noun-noun or noun-noun-verb orders. As an individual difference measure, however, this experimental procedure is quite weak. Out of sixteen possible, the mean number of items correct was 3.6, with a range of 0 to 8. It is difficult to state exactly what would constitute chance performance here, since so many children failed to respond at all on many items. But it is easy to see from these descriptive statistics that the enactment procedure is an extremely "noisy" measure from a psychometric perspective.

We should thus not expect very much from correlational analyses involving this word-order test, and indeed we found very little. As indicated in Table 31, the enactment procedure did not correlate significantly with MLU, vocabulary, total output, or with any other 28-month measure except the PPVT ($+.43$, $p < .05$). This last result is not surprising, since the enactment procedure (like the morphology test) presupposes an ability to decode the open-class lexical items (i.e., to understand "bear," "push," and "block" in "Show me THE BEAR PUSHES THE BLOCK"). Also, both the PPVT and the enactment task require general "test-taking abilities," i.e., an ability to listen to verbal input and comply in some fashion. In longitudinal analyses (Table 31), the enactment task was entirely unrelated to the 13-month measures (although a relationship with referential style in comprehension did reach the $p < .10$ level). A few relationships with the 20-month battery did reach significance, primarily involving lexical-conceptual variables. All these correlations disappeared when performance on the PPVT was partialed out.

Assessments of word-order comprehension using the Horgan picture-choice technique did not fare much better. Out of a total of twelve items, correct choice averaged 6.65, with a range of 3 to 12. Since there were two pictures to choose from on each item, we might have expected 6 correct choices purely by chance. Fourteen of the children, or approximately half the sample, achieved scores of six or lower. And yet there were children who did extremely well, including one child with a perfect score. Given this distribution, we should expect the picture-choice task to serve as a weak albeit nonrandom measure of individual differences. As indicated in Table 31, it did indeed fail to correlate with most of the language measures in the study, including measures of morphological production.

However, this same task was at least correlated significantly with MLU (+.45), the morphology comprehension test (+.45), and the enactment procedure (+.46). Surprisingly, its relationship to the PPVT did not reach significance (+.26). We nevertheless decided to follow the control procedure of partialing PPVT performance out of these same correlational relations. After partialing, the relationships with MLU and vocabulary did drop below significance (although the correlation with MLU remained at the $p < .10$ level, +.38). But the correlations between the Horgan task and the other two grammar tests still stood: +.40 with morphology, +.40 with the enactment procedure.

There is some limited evidence, then, that grammatical comprehension may constitute a skill that is partially independent of "garden variety" lexical comprehension. On these grounds, we tried several procedures for pooling the variance shared by the grammar tests. We hoped in this way to obtain a more reliable estimate of grammatical comprehension for use in more detailed longitudinal analyses.

We began by constructing a summary measure for the two grammar tests alone, adding together *z*-scores for the enactment and the picture-choice procedures. However, the joint word-order comprehension measure fared no better than either of the individual tests. There were a few correlations within and across age levels, almost exclusively with the lexical-conceptual aspects of language. When variance on the PPVT was controlled, most of these disappeared. The ones that remained revolved primarily around lexical development at 20 months.

A second summary measure was constructed by adding the *z*-scores for all three grammatical comprehension tests (two for word-order, one for morphology). In general, these relationships were slightly stronger than those obtained with the individual tests taken separately. But the patterns are exactly the same: Grammatical comprehension testing is primarily related to lexical-conceptual measures, and not to the emergence of grammar in production. Furthermore, most of these correlations are lost when performance on the PPVT is controlled.

Factor Analysis across Grammar Measures

All the patterns that we have examined so far suggest that early grammatical development—like early lexical development—dissociates along comprehension-production lines. Factor analysis, a technique that is usually applied in exploratory data analysis, can also be used as a summary statistic for data of this kind.

Nine measures of grammatical development at 28 months were entered into a factor analysis set to extract all orthogonal factors with

Table 32. *Factor Loadings on 28-Month Grammar Analysis*

	Factor 1 (eigenvalue 3.80)	Factor 2 (eigenvalue 1.08)
28-Month Grammar Measures		
1. MLU	.74	.47
2. Closed-class style	.40	.16
3. Morphology comprehension	.22	.46
4. Word-order comprehension (enactment)	.00	.61
5. Word-order comprehension (picture choice)	.15	.75
6. Production analogue to morpheme comprehension test	.67	.24
7. Productivity criteria		
Brown	.81	.07
Presence/absence	.90	-.01
Contrast	.78	.16
% Variance accounted for	77%	23%

eigenvalues greater than 1.0. The nine measures were: MLU, closed-class style, three productivity measures (based on the Brown, presence/absence, and contrastivity criteria), the three grammar tests just described, and the production analogue to the morphological comprehension test. Two factors emerged: one accounting for 69.9% of the variance (eigenvalue = 3.86) and another accounting for 20.3% of the variance (eigenvalue = 1.12), with a residual factor accounting for 9.8% of the variance (eigenvalue = .54). To maximize fit to these first two factors, the analysis was then rerun setting the number of factors to be extracted at two. As summarized in Table 32, the two factors that fell out of this analysis are exactly what we might expect, given the correlational results discussed so far.

The first and largest factor loads highly on measures of grammatical productivity. The three grammar-comprehension tests are completely unrelated to what we are justified in calling the "production factor."

The second factor loads most highly on word-order comprehension (.60 for enactment and .76 for picture choice), with smaller contributions from morphological comprehension (.47) and MLU (.46). The other production measures make no contribution at all, permitting us to infer that this constitutes a "comprehension factor."

Table 33. *Longitudinal Correlations with 28-Month Grammar Factors*

	Grammar Factors	
	Comprehension	Production
28 Months		
1. MLU	**.52	**.78
2. Vocabulary	~.32	**.75
3. Total output	.14	**.77
4. PPVT	~.37	*.48
20 Months		
5. MLU	.25	~.34
6. Interview clusters		
Nominal multiword	*.43	**.66
Grammatical morpheme	~.32	**.64
Semantic-conceptual	*.47	**.56
Dialogue	**.49	**.52
7. Observational clusters		
Nominal multiword	**.54	*.42
Grammatical morpheme	~.34	~.37
Semantics-dialogue	**.58	**.57
8. Interview lexical		
Total vocabulary	**.51	**.64
Open-class style	**.59	*.44
Verb density	*.43	*.45
9. Observed lexical		
Total vocabulary	**.56	*.49
Open-class style	*.40	*.40
Verb density	-.06	.28
13 Months		
10. Interview		
Total comprehension	.25	~.35
% Nouns in comprehension	~.35	*.46
Total production	.21	.32
% Nouns in production	.07	.31
% Flexible nouns	.21	**.52

~ $p < .10$.
* $p < .05$.
** $p < .01$.

This factor analysis is nothing more than a convenient way of summarizing what we have already learned about grammatical development at 28 months, i.e., that grammar and the lexicon both dissociate along comprehension-production lines. There is one exception: MLU shares variance with both factors. In other words, those children who have achieved the greatest structural complexity in their spontaneous speech excel at both the production *and* comprehension of grammar. This was not true at 20 months of age, when variance in utterance length seemed to be controlled primarily by rote factors independent of comprehension and/or productive grammatical rules. We have reached a similar conclusion regarding 28-month MLU in several studies: This structural complexity index is a product of both first-strand and second-strand variables in language development.

This brings us back to the issue raised at the end of Study 9. Do we actually have two consistent strands of individual differences across language development? Or are there really several strands representing rote versus analytic processing, comprehension versus production, and (perhaps) single- versus multiword speech? Table 33 summarizes longitudinal predictions of the two grammatical factors. If these factors reflect a crisp dissociation among the same two strands that we have followed from 10 months onward, we should find that grammar comprehension correlates primarily with variables in Strand 1, grammar production correlates primarily with variables in Strand 2. But this is *not* what we find at all. Cross-age predictions of the two grammar factors are in fact remarkably similar. Both factors enter into more correlations with Strand 1 variables, suggesting that *all* aspects of grammatical variation at 28 months grow primarily out of individual differences in lexical-conceptual growth. Although there is a clear dissociation between comprehension and production in grammar, it is not the same dissociation that we traced through the one-word stage.

Conclusion

We are now at a critical point in this longitudinal study. There are no new language measures to be introduced. We have found repeated evidence for qualitative dissociations in language development, including a crisp dissociation between comprehension and production within 28-month grammar. Nevertheless, the Two-Strand picture that seemed to fit the data so well in the earlier studies begins to look much too simple. In the next study, we will extend the use of factor analysis as a descriptive tool and a source of summary statistics, testing the Two-Strand theory that emerged in previous studies against a model in which multiple dissociations in language functioning are possible.

Part III
A Summary View

Chapter 15: Study 11
A Factor Analytic Approach

We have presented evidence in the last ten studies for qualitative dissociations in language development. These dissociations seem to be continuous in the age range from first words to grammar, forming strands of variance that are relatively stable over time. Nevertheless, there are changes from one age to another in the content of each strand, forcing us to consider a variety of alternative interpretations of the processes and representations that underlie all this variation: rote versus analytic mechanisms, comprehension versus production, knowledge versus use, reference versus predication, verbs versus the rest of the lexicon, and perhaps grammar versus semantics. In the last few studies, we have been confronted with the possibility of "strands within strands," a system of major and minor harmonics that may be considerably more complex than we might have thought given the current literature on individual differences in child language. In this study we will use factor analysis as a descriptive device and a summary statistic, testing the two-strand picture of dissociation over time against various multistrand solutions that might emerge empirically from the data.

Why didn't we just start with factor analysis in the first place, as an exploratory procedure, putting all our variables in together to see what comes out? There are both practical and theoretical reasons why we opted against such a traditional psychometric approach.

The first reason is quite simple: No factor analysis may contain more variables than there are subjects in the study, and the number of variables we have considered far exceeds our sample size of twenty-seven. There are good reasons why the number of measures is so large. First, we were asking a lot of different questions. Second, where possible we sought to replicate effects in two data sets, observational and interview. This provided validation of the measures themselves, and a strong cross-check for resulting patterns of association and dissociation. Third, we tried to repeat the same measures at different developmental levels whenever feasible, to see whether the meaning of those measures had changed over time (e.g., MLU at 20 versus 28 months, referential style at 13, 20, and 28 months). The major disadvantage in this proliferation of measures is the one encountered here: an a priori, across-the-board use of factor analysis is impossible. We need some principled way to reduce the number of variables in order to use this technique properly, which means that separate studies were required before factor analysis made sense.

This brings us to the conceptual grounds for these measures. We preferred to examine specific subsets of measures in detail, as separate studies, because each subset had its own theoretical motivation and its own empirical consequences. For example, a separate consideration of lexical style was warranted, within and across age levels, because there has been so much speculation and so little data concerning the *meaning* of notions like referential style. As we found, lexical style is a paramount example of "homotypic discontinuity," i.e., superficially similar variables whose content and meaning change over time. At 13 months referential style was a positive predictor of progress in language, at 20 months its predictive value stood near zero, and at 28 months the very same measure was a negative indicator of overall language ability. Patterns like these would have been confusing and opaque if everything had been lumped together in one large factor analysis. Similarly, Study 5 on imitation and novel concept acquisition and Study 8 comparing methods of calculating grammatical productivity each asked a distinct set of questions that needed to be considered in their own right.

At this point, however, we are intimately acquainted with each measure, and with the general shape of individual differences as they develop over time. It is appropriate now to take a summary view of all these measures, to determine how they hang together or come apart when they are considered as a group. We are asking a very specific theoretical question here as well: Are there indeed two strands of variance in language acquisition that have roughly the same content and the same meaning over time? Or does the two-strand picture that emerged "locally" among specific subsets of variables mask the operation of several distinct strands of variation that can only be seen on a summary view?

As it has been characterized in the studies so far, Strand 1 seems to reflect the operation of some kind of lexical-conceptual analysis, loading highly on both lexical and grammatical comprehension and on productive or "rule-governed" aspects of single- and multiword speech. Strand 2 is characterized almost exclusively by expressive language variables that do *not* correlate with comprehension, leading us to suggest that this strand involves rote, holistic, and/or imitative use of language, perhaps in the service of "output matching," i.e., trying to sound like other people.

But there are already problems for this characterization. Certain variables refuse to fall into line across the course of the study. For example, comprehension and production of multiword utterances at 20 months split their variance across the two supposed developmental strands, providing the best evidence that we have in this study for a dissociation between single- and multiword speech. Verb density in free-speech at 20 months failed to correlate with much of anything except free-speech totals, in contrast with verb density in the parental reports, a Strand 1 variable par excellence. And 28-month MLU—our best index of structural complexity in the last session—consistently refused to accommodate this two-party system, taking contributions from both developmental strands (although the contribution of Strand 1 variables generally seems to be higher).

The most important discrepancy showed up in the last two studies. There was, again, no evidence for a dissociation between grammar and semantics. A very crisp dissociation did emerge between comprehension and production within the grammar. This seems on the surface to be quite parallel to comprehension-production dissociations that the same children showed at the lexical level, especially at 13 months. However, longitudinal predictions of the two grammar factors suggested that *both* the comprehension and production of grammar at 2½ years of age emerge primarily out of Strand 1. In other words, there seem to be dissociations nested within dissociations, related both to a comprehension-production contrast (at every age level), and a rote-analytic contrast (that may disappear, at least temporarily, by 28 months).

Clearly the two-factor notions laid out in the previous studies need to be reassessed.

Method

In an effort to clarify the dissociability issue, factor analysis will be employed in four separate steps.

1. At three age levels (collapsing 10 and 13 months), we will extract the first principal component, i.e., a single factor representing maximal progress across the board at that age. Longitudinal correlations among the first principal components will give a global view of continuity in rate of language development over time.
2. We next turn to structural analyses at each age level, entering the same variables used in the principal component analysis, with the number of orthogonal factors to be extracted set at two. By this "top down" procedure, we maximize the fit of these data to the hypothetical two-factor solution suggested in the last ten studies.

We can then compare the content of the two factors extracted at each age to determine whether they seem to reflect similar underlying mechanisms.

3. In the next round of analyses, the number of factors to be extracted will be determined empirically, setting the minimum eigenvalue at the conventional 1.0 level. If our two-strand theory is correct, this "bottom-up" analysis should obtain results quite similar to those obtained in Step 2, with two and only two significant factors emerging at each age level. If, instead, a solution with three or more factors seems preferable at any single age, then we need to reconsider the two-strand model at every age. Suppose, for example, that a two-factor solution is optimal at 13 and 28 months, but a three-factor solution provides a better fit at 20 months. It might be useful at this point to impose a three-factor solution on the other two age levels. This would show us whether a weaker version of the 20-month three-way pattern is detectable at an earlier and/or a later stage.

4. After both the "bottom-up" and "top-down" factors have been extracted at each age, longitudinal correlations among those factors will be calculated. This will tell us, for example, whether Strand 1 at 10–13 months links up most strongly with the "same" strand at 20 months (i.e., the strand with superficially similar content), with some other language factor, or, indeed, with nothing at all.

Results and Discussion

Step 1: First Principal Components

In these analyses, we were interested only in the first principal component, i.e., the factor that shares maximal variance with all the measures at a given age level. Each analysis was set to extract only one factor with an optimal fit to all the data.

The 10- and 13-month data were combined in a single analysis, with the following ten measures entered: 10-month comprehension and production (both from interviews), five 13-month interview measures (total comprehension, total production, referential style in both comprehension and production, and referential flexibility in production), and three 13-month observational measures (single word comprehension, number of words produced spontaneously, number of words produced in imitation). Loadings of these ten measures on the resulting principal component are listed in Table 34. They range from a low of .45 (from observed spontaneous production) to a high of .86 (from referential flexibility).

In the 20-month analysis, the following twenty measures were entered: MLU, free-speech and interview vocabulary totals, the four interview clusters, the three observational clusters, single-word comprehension, comprehension of plausible and of implausible multiword commands, two separate comprehension measures and one measure of vocal imitation from the fiffin study, and four measures of lexical style (open-class style and verb density, in the observations and the interviews, respectively). Loadings of these twenty measures on the 20-month principal component are also listed in Table 34, ranging from a low of .28 (for free-speech verb density) to a high of .89 (for free-speech vocabulary totals).

Finally, the 28-month analysis included the following thirteen variables: MLU, total vocabulary, total output in morphemes, the Peabody Picture Vocabulary Test (PPVT), closed-class style and verb density, three grammatical productivity measures (Bloom, Brown, and the contrast criterion), three grammatical comprehension tests (one for morphology and two for word-order), as well as the production analogue to the morphology comprehension test. Loadings on the first principal component extracted from these measures are in Table 34, with a range of .26 (for the enactment measure of word-order comprehension) to .89 (for total vocabulary).

As we might expect, given the cross-age correlations discussed in the previous studies, the three principal component scores were also highly related. The highest correlation $(+.79, p < .01)$ occurred between the 20- and 28-month factor scores. The combined 10–13-month principal component correlated significantly with both of these measures: $+.63$ $(p < .01)$ with the 20-month factor and $+.46$ $(p < .05)$ with the 28-month factor. In short, individual differences in overall rate of development are stable in the period from first words to grammar.

Finally, we constructed a composite "good-language" measure by averaging scores on the three principal component factors. Table 34 includes correlations of all the individual measures with this single global index of rate of language development. The variables that relate most strongly to this summary measure are referential flexibility at 13 months $(+.73, p < .01)$, reported vocabulary development at 20 months $(+.88, p < .01)$, and MLU at 28 months $(+.87, p < .01)$. This provides one more perspective on the close developmental link between early lexical development and later grammar.

Step 2: "Top-Down" Two-Factor Analyses

Table 35 summarizes the factor loadings at each age level, when the analysis is set to maximize fit to a two-factor solution.

Table 34. *First Principal Component Factor Loadings and Correlations with Global Scores*

	Factor Load	r with Global
10–13 Months		
10-Month comprehension	.61	*.41
10-Month production	.69	*.49
13-Month interview		
Total production	.72	**.62
Total comprehension	.67	**.55
% Nouns in production	.81	**.58
% Nouns in comprehension	.70	**.66
% Flexible nouns	.86	**.73
13-Month observation		
Spontaneous production	.45	~.37
Imitative production	.63	**.52
Comprehension test	.55	*.46
20 Months		
MLU	.61	*.49
Interview clusters		
Nominal multiword	.85	**.81
Grammatical morpheme	.72	**.72
Semantic-conceptual	.79	**.84
Dialogue	.64	**.70
Observational clusters		
Nominal multiword	.83	**.66
Grammatical morpheme	.67	**.60
Semantics-dialogue	.87	**.86
Interview lexical		
Total vocabulary	.86	**.88
Open-class style	.70	**.60
Verb density	.67	**.63

Table 34. *Continued*

	Factor Load	r with Global
20 Months Continued		
Observational lexical		
Total vocabulary	.89	**.80
Open-class style	.55	**.72
Verb density	.27	.21
Comprehension		
Single word	.40	.31
Canonical commands	.66	**.51
Noncanonical commands	.85	**.72
Novel object concept		
Imitation in training	.32	.12
Single-word comprehension	.63	**.53
Sentence comprehension	.63	**.58
28 Months		
MLU	.87	**.87
Total vocabulary	.88	**.77
Total output	.83	**.68
Closed-class style	.50	**.50
Verb density	.56	*.47
PPVT	.62	**.57
Productivity		
Brown	.79	**.54
Contrast	.83	**.70
Presence/absence	.82	**.66
Comprehension		
Morphology	.40	*.47
Production analogue to morpheme comp.	.76	**.61
Word order		
Picture choice	.44	*.43
Enactment	.26	.32

~ $p < .10$.
* $p < .05$.
** $p < .01$.

Table 35. *"Top Down" Factor Analyses: Two Factors*

	Factor 1	Factor 2
10–13 Months		
10-Month comprehension	.62	.11
10-Month production	.33	.60
13-Month interview		
Total production	.21	.88
Total comprehension	.83	.01
% Nouns in production	.60	.49
% Nouns in comprehension	.75	.13
% Flexible nouns	.78	.39
13-Month observation		
Spontaneous production	-.12	.84
Imitative production	.20	.66
Comprehension test	.58	.07
20 Months		
MLU	.11	.93
Interview clusters		
Nominal multiword	.74	.41
Grammatical morpheme	.43	.62
Semantic-conceptual	.87	.11
Dialogue	.58	.19
Observational clusters		
Nominal multiword	.50	.71
Grammatical morpheme	.19	.92
Semantics-dialogue	.81	.34
Interview lexical		
Open-class style	.80	.08
Verb density	.66	.18
Observational lexical		
Open-class style	.74	-.16
Verb density	.00	.46

Table 35. *Continued*

	Factor 1	Factor 2
20 Months Continued		
Comprehension		
Single-word	.40	.08
Canonical commands	.61	.24
Noncanonical commands	.73	.45
Novel object concept		
Imitation in training	.02	.57
Single-word comprehension	.68	.10
Sentence comprehension	.66	.10
28 Months		
MLU	.72	.50
Total vocabulary	.84	.27
Total output	.87	.08
Closed-class style	.35	.30
Verb density	.44	.24
PPVT	.37	.58
Productivity		
Brown	.74	.20
Contrast	.82	.17
Presence/absence	.88	.04
Comprehension		
Morphology	.18	.48
Production analogue to morpheme comp.	.70	.22
Word order		
Picture choice	.16	.62
Enactment	-.06	.70

In the combined 10–13-month analysis, the first factor accounted for 71.9% of the variance (eigenvalue 4.29), while the second factor accounted for the remaining 28.1% (eigenvalue 1.67). Since both factors exceed the conventional 1.0 eigenvalue cut-off, this means that *at least* two orthogonal factors are needed to account for the data. The factor loadings in Table 35 support the two-strand characterization discussed in Study 1. The larger factor loads most highly on comprehension and on referential style and referential flexibility in production. The second strand loads, instead, on expressive language totals in both the interview and the observations.

In our first structural factoring of the 20-month data, all the variables used in the principal component analysis were included. However, because vocabulary totals correlate so highly with virtually everything else, the matrix could not be inverted and no orthogonal factors could be found. We then repeated the two-factor analysis with a total of eighteen variables, excluding both the interview and free-speech vocabulary totals. Results of this procedure are summarized in Table 35. The first factor accounted for 76.5% of the variance (eigenvalue 7.92) and a second factor accounted for the remaining 23.5% (eigenvalue 2.43). Since both these factors exceed the conventional 1.0 cutoff point, it is clear that *at least* two factors are needed to characterize the 20-month data.

The content of these two factors also supports the two-strand theory. The larger factor loads most highly on comprehension, semantic-conceptual and dialogue clusters, open-class style, and verb density in the interview data. The second factor loads primarily on MLU, closed-class morphology, fiffin imitation, and verb density in free-speech.

Although the respective observational and reported vocabulary totals could not be included in the search for orthogonal factors, it was possible to correlate both vocabulary measures with the two-factor scores. The results are consistent with claims in Study 3, that free-speech totals reflect more variance from rote production, while reported totals reflect more analysis and understanding. Specifically, free-speech vocabulary correlated more with the second factor (+.71) than it did with the first (+.52); conversely, reported vocabulary correlated more with first factor (+.68), while its relationship to the second, "rote output" factor barely reached significance (+.38, $p < .05$).

The only problem for the two-strand picture at 20 months lies in measures that split their variance between the two factors: the interview version of the morphology cluster, both the interview and observational clusters for nominal multiword combinations, and comprehension of implausible multiword commands. If these multiword "outliers" form a separate factor in the "bottom-up" analyses below, it would provide at least some support for an independent multiword strand separate from both rote output and lexical analysis.

Finally, the 28-month analysis also produced two significant factors: one accounting for 82.2% of the variance (eigenvalue 1.26), and another accounting for the remaining 17.8% (eigenvalue 1.26). Once again, at least two factors are needed to characterize the data at this age level.

These 28-month factor loadings (see Table 35) are similar to the grammar-only factors reported in the last study, reflecting a clean dissociation between comprehension and production. The larger factor loads highly on vocabulary and total output, morphological productivity, and MLU, with much smaller positive loadings from verb density and closed-class style. The smaller factor is characterized by both lexical and grammatical-comprehension testing. Only two measures split their variance across these two factors: MLU, which loads highly on both, and closed-class style, which makes very weak positive contributions on both. This means that MLU and closed-class style might form a third factor in a more extended design. In general, however, the findings are compatible with the two-strand claims that we have made so far. They also provide still more support for a comprehension-production dissociation that cuts across both lexical and grammatical development.

Step 3: "Bottom-Up" *N*-Factor Analyses

In the next round of analyses, no a priori limits were set on the number of factors to be extracted. At each age, the variables entered were the same ones used in the two-factor design.

At the 10–13-month level, only two factors with eigenvalues greater than 1.0 emerged from the analysis: one accounting for 63.2% of the variance (eigenvalue 4.37), and a second factor accounting for 25.7% (eigenvalue 1.78). A residual factor (eigenvalue .77) accounted for the remaining 11.1%. These results suggest that either a two-factor or a three-factor solution could be justified, but a two-factor solution provides a better characterization of the data.

At 20 months, this analysis yielded *three* significant factors. The first accounted for 64% of the variance (eigenvalue 8.01), the second for 20.2% (eigenvalue 2.52), and the third for 8.8% (eigenvalue 1.10), with a residual factor accounting for 7% (eigenvalue .87). In other words, the two-factor solution obtained in Step 2 does *not* provide the most informative characterization of the 20-month data. Since only three factors reached significance, we reran this analysis to maximize fit to a three-factor solution. The results are summarized in Table 36.

The first factor accounted for 69.6% of the variance (eigenvalue 7.97). All the 20-month clusters except observational morphology contribute

Table 36. *Factor Analyses: Three Factor Designs*

	Factor 1	Factor 2	Factor 3
10–13 Months			
10-Month comprehension	-.04	.26	.73
10-Month production	.50	.06	.54
13-Month interview			
Total production	.80	.09	.36
Total comprehension	-.01	.69	.42
% Nouns in production	.36	.25	.73
% Nouns in comprehension	.14	.90	.20
% Flexible nouns	.28	.49	.66
13-Month observation			
Spontaneous production	.95	-.01	-.09
Imitative production	.65	.21	.17
Comprehension test	.09	.68	.11
20 Months			
MLU	.09	.13	.93
Interview clusters			
Nominal multiword	.66	.41	.38
Grammatical morpheme	.60	.03	.62
Semantic-conceptual	.70	.52	.07
Dialogue	.81	.04	.15
Observational clusters			
Nominal multiword	.43	.32	.68
Grammatical morpheme	.17	.16	.90
Semantics-dialogue	.68	.47	.30
Interview lexical			
Open-class style	.65	.47	-.02
Verb density	.26	.72	.15

Table 36. *Continued*

	Factor 1	Factor 2	Factor 3
20 Months Continued			
Observational lexical			
Open-class style	.57	.46	-.19
Verb density	.04	-.01	.46
Comprehension			
Single-word	.05	.55	.06
Canonical commands	.21	.69	.21
Noncanonical commands	.34	.74	.43
Novel object concept			
Imitation in training	-.10	.17	.57
Single word comprehension	.40	.57	.07
Sentence comprehension	.49	.45	.07
28 Months			
MLU	.61	.45	.41
Total vocabulary	.87	.16	.29
Total output	.88	.17	.08
Closed-class style	.10	.75	.13
Verb density	.28	.53	.10
PPVT	.26	.42	.50
Productivity			
Brown	.63	.43	.12
Contrast	.68	.54	.04
Presence/absence	.81	.31	.00
Comprehension			
Morphology	.24	-.06	.59
Production analogue to morpheme comprehension	.76	.04	.27
Word order			
Picture choice	.15	.12	.62
Enactment	-.08	.17	.65

heavily, as do both the interview and the observational versions of open-class style. In other words, this factor cuts across both single- and multiword measures. However, there was very little contribution from comprehension testing, and no relationship at all to verb density, MLU and observed morphology, or fiffin imitation. Given this pattern, we can interpret this as an "analyzed speech" or "productive-output factor."

The second factor loads most heavily on both single- and multiword comprehension testing, the semantic-conceptual cluster in the interview and the semantics-dialogue cluster in the observations, with weaker contributions from open-class style and the interview nominal multiword cluster. Given the emphasis on comprehension and understanding, we will refer to this as a "comprehension factor."

The third and smallest factor loads very heavily on MLU, both morphology clusters, the nominal multiword cluster in the observations, and fiffin imitation. Weaker contributions came from verb density in free-speech, comprehension of implausible commands, and the interview nominal multiword cluster. Because this factor is dominated by imitation and rote output, we will refer to it as the "rote output factor."

Although, again, vocabulary totals could not be included in the factor analyses themselves, we did calculate simple correlations of free-speech and reported vocabulary with the three 20-month factor scores. Given the findings reported in Studies 2–5, we should expect 20-month reported vocabulary to correlate more highly with comprehension and analyzed output; 20-month observed vocabulary should have more to do with rote output. This is, in fact, exactly what we found. Free-speech vocabulary correlated most highly with the rote output factor $(+.63, p < .01)$, followed by analyzed output $(+.50, p < .01)$, while its correlation with the comprehension factor missed significance $(+.32, p < .10)$. Reported vocabulary correlated highest with the analyzed output factor $(+.65, p < .01)$, followed by comprehension $(+.44, p < .05)$, while its correlation with the rote output factor was not significant $(+.29)$. These patterns lend more support to our interpretation of the three-strand solution at 20 months.

To summarize the 20-month results, there is still no evidence at all for a grammar/semantics division or a single-word/multiword division. Multiword comprehension and production, though highly correlated, did not form a factor separate from comprehension or production of individual lexical items. Instead, the multiword measures seem to distribute themselves across the three factors in a mix with other aspects of lexical development. However, the two-strand characterization that we offered in earlier studies is apparently misleading at this age level. Instead, we find a basic division between receptive and expressive language, with expressive language breaking into two further parts: analyzed or productive output, and imitative or rote output.

This brings us to 28 months, where the bottom-up analysis yielded only two significant factors: the first accounted for 73.2% of the variance (eigenvalue 5.91), the second for 16% (eigenvalue 1.28), with a residual factor accounting for 10.8% (eigenvalue .87). Similar to the findings at the earliest age level, either a two- or a three-factor solution could be justified, but a two-factor design provides a better fit.

So the two-strand picture is not upheld at every age level, although it provides a good fit to the data at the first and last sessions. The three-way dissociation that emerged at 20 months could be a peculiarity confined to that particular transition point in language development. But we might also find a "shadow version" of those three strands at the other ages. To explore this possibility, we imposed a three-factor solution at 10–13 months and again at 28 months, to see whether a similar (albeit weaker) three-way pattern emerged. Results for both analyses are summarized in Table 36.

At the youngest age level, we did indeed find some evidence for a rote output factor, a comprehension factor, and a factor loading primarily on analyzed or productive single-word speech. The largest factor (63% of the variance) loaded most highly on simple production totals, in the 10- and 13-month interviews and in the 13-month observations. This seems, then, to be an early analogue of the 20-month rote output strand. The second factor (25%) loaded most heavily on referential style in comprehension, followed by 13-month comprehension totals in the interview and laboratory comprehension testing. A smaller positive contribution comes from only one expressive measure, referential flexibility. Given the heavy loading on comprehension, this could be viewed as an early version of the 20-month comprehension strand. Finally, the third and smallest factor seems to reflect production of words that the child really does understand, loading primarily on referential flexibility and referential style in production at 13 months, as well as both expressive and receptive language at 10 months. This may represent, then, the first appearance of an analyzed or productive output strand.

The three-factor solution at 28 months can also be interpreted in ways that are analogous to three-strand patterns at the earlier age levels. The largest factor loads most heavily on total output in morphemes, with very strong contributions from vocabulary, MLU, and all measures of morphological production. Of the morphology measures, the strongest contribution comes from the simple presence/absence count (+.81), and from the production analogue to the morphology comprehension test (+.76). These measures simply reflect whether the child produced

certain forms *at all*. Smaller contributions came from the Brown measure
$(+.63)$ and the contrast criterion $(+.68)$ — productivity criteria which,
we have argued, require a greater degree of analysis and creativity on the
child's part. It could be argued, then, that this large cluster represents a
28-month version of "pure production."

The second factor loads most heavily on closed-class style and verb
density, followed by MLU, the three grammatical productivity measures,
and the Peabody. Note that the productivity measures load on this factor
in a descending order corresponding roughly to the amount of creativity
or analysis that each seems to require: the contrast criterion $(+.54)$, the
Brown criterion $(+.43)$, and the presence/absence criterion $(+.31)$. The
production analogue of the morphology comprehension test contributes
nothing to this factor at all. Given this pattern and the contribution from
the PPVT, this could be interpreted as a 28-month version of an
"analyzed production" strand.

Finally, the third factor loads primarily on both lexical and grammatical comprehension testing. Only one expressive language measure makes
a contribution: MLU once again fails to align with any one strand and
distributes its variance across all language factors, including this one.
However, given the heavy loading of comprehension measures on the
third 28-month factor, it seems fair to view this as a 28-month version of
the earlier comprehension strand.

To summarize, a three-factor solution provides an optimal fit only for
the 20-month data. Otherwise, a two-factor solution seems adequate.
Nevertheless, when three-factor designs are imposed at every age, there
is a compelling similarity across age levels in the three-way patterns that
emerge. Specifically, each analysis seems to yield one receptive factor,
and two expressive factors reflecting a dissociation between "pure" and
"analyzed" production. At no point is there anything resembling a
grammar/semantics split.

Step 4: Correlations among Factors

There are two kinds of questions that we are asking here. First, how
do the two- and three-strand solutions map onto one another *within* age
levels? In other words, when variance is broken out of the two-strand
design to form a third factor, where does it come from?

The second question pertains to relationships among supposedly
analogous factors *between* age levels. In terms of content, the two- and
three-factor solutions that we have imposed seem to yield similar patterns at every age. But similarity of content does not necessarily reflect
similarity in the underlying mechanisms responsible for that content.
Longitudinal correlations among the various factor scores can tell

Table 37. *Two Strand by Three Strand Factor Correlations with Ages*

	Two-Strand Factors	
Three-Strand Factors	Analytic/Comprehension Factor	Rote/Production Factor
10–13 Months	10–13 Months	
Rote output	-.06	**.94
Productive output	**.64	.30
Comprehension	**.75	-.05
20 Months	20 Months	
Rote output	-.12	**.98
Productive output	**.74	-.15
Comprehension	**.70	.08
28 Months	28 Months	
Rote output	.00	**.94
Productive output	.31	*.41
Comprehension	**.94	.00

*p< .05.
**p< .01.

us whether or not superficially similar measures are reliably linked over time.

In answer to the first question, within-age correlations among the two- and three-strand factor scores are reported in Table 37. At the first two age levels, results are extremely clear. The lexical-conceptual factor from the two-strand design is highly correlated with both analyzed production and comprehension in the three-strand analysis. The second factor in the two-way design correlates only with rote output in the three-way analysis. *In other words, both comprehension and analyzed production are broken out of a single lexical-conceptual factor similar to what we have called Strand 1 in the last ten studies.*

At 28 months, things have reorganized. Remember, first of all, that the supposed lexical-conceptual factors are much larger at the first two age levels than they are in the last session: Strand 1 accounts for 72% of the variance in the two-way analysis at 13 months, for 76.5% of the variance in the analogous results at 20 months, but for only 18% at 28 months. There is reason enough right here to suspect that things have changed. This is confirmed by the correlations in Table 37. At this age,

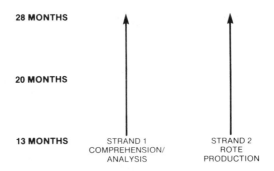

Figure 2a: Two Strand Design: Ideal Patterns.

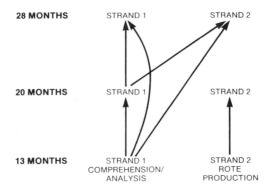

Figure 2b: Two Strand Design: Observed Patterns.

the lexical-conceptual factor from the two-strand design correlates significantly only with the comprehension factor in the three-strand analysis ($+.94$, $p < .01$). The much larger production factor from the two-strand design now correlates most with "pure production" ($+.94$), followed by "analyzed production" ($+.41$), while its correlation with the small comprehension factor is almost precisely zero.

To summarize, the deepest dissociation in the data from 10 to 20 months falls between rote production on the one hand, and an alliance between comprehension and analyzed production on the other. This is compatible with our characterization of Strand 1 and Strand 2 throughout the past ten studies. In contrast, the deepest dissociation in the data at 28 months pits *all* forms of production against an alliance between lexical and grammatical comprehension (at least as they are assessed in a self-

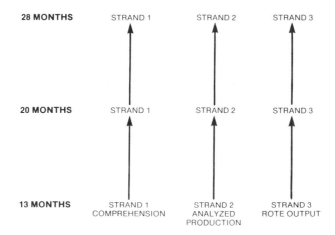

Figure 3a: Three Strand Design: Ideal Patterns.

conscious laboratory situation). This is quite different from the two-strand picture we painted for the earlier age levels.

Given this clarification of the two-strand theory, we should expect the longitudinal correlations to yield similar discontinuities within the "same" strands. And indeed, idealizations based on a single two-strand theory are not upheld.

Figure 2a presents the pattern that we would expect among the two-strand solutions in a longitudinal analysis, if we really were tapping the "same thing" at every age. In this idealization, children who score highly on Strand 1 from the earliest stages continue to do particularly well on this kind of content at every age. Similarly, children who score highly on Strand 2 measures from the beginning of language development are Strand 2 specialists across the course of the study. Figure 2b presents the pattern that we really do find, reflecting cross-age correlations among factors from the two-strand design at each age level.

The idealization in Figure 2a holds only between 10 and 13 months and at 20 months, where "Strand 1 leads to Strand 1" and "Strand 2 leads to Strand 2." After that point, we find that *both* comprehension and production at 28 months are predicted by the lexical-conceptual strand at the earlier ages. Strand 2 leads nowhere.

Figure 3a presents a similar idealization for the three-strand designs. If these three-way results at every age really did reflect "the same things," we would expect comprehension to lead primarily to comprehension, rote output to rote output, and analyzed output to analyzed output at every age. Figure 3b illustrates the actual situation, as indicated by the cross-age correlations in Table 38. This pattern is considerably more complex.

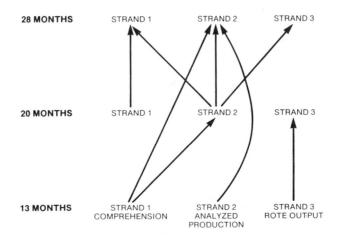

Figure 3b: Three Strand Design: Observed Patterns.

First, the rote output strand at 13 months leads to its analogue at 20 months, and then goes no further. It seems to reflect an isolated developmental pathway that plays no role at 28 months, when grammaticization is rampant and all children are involved in at least some degree of generative analysis. Whether this strand is ever picked up again, at later stages, is an open question.

Second, there is a peculiar disjuncture in the supposedly unified comprehension strand. The 10–13-month version leads not to comprehension, but to analyzed production at both 20 and 28 months. The 20-month version leads into its 28-month analogue, but nowhere else. *In other words, comprehension variance does not form a continuous and unbroken line over time, but weaves back and forth into production as children begin to say what they know.*

The most complex pathways in Figure 3b involve analyzed production. The earliest version of this factor "skips" 20 months and leads directly into its analogue at the last session. The 20-month version of analyzed production leads "backward" only to comprehension at 10–13 months, but moves "forward" into *everything* at 28 months: comprehension, analyzed production, and so-called "pure production." Confusing as this may be, it represents the only "single pathway" across the three-way design.

The best summary view of the data should represent the "true" or "optimal" solutions at every age: from two factors at 10–13 months to three factors at 20 months, to two factors again at 28 months. These correlations (in Table 39) are illustrated in Figure 4.

Table 38. *Cross-Age Correlations in the Three-Factor Design*

	10–13 Months			20 Months			28 Months		
	Rote	Productive	Comprehension	Rote	Productive	Comprehension	Rote	Productive	Comprehension
10–13 Months									
Rote	—								
Productive	—	—							
Comprehension	—	—	—						
20 Months									
Rote	*.44	.00	-.21	—					
Productive	.25	.31	**.53	—	—				
Comprehension	.29	.30	.11	—	—	—			
28 Months									
Rote	.15	.10	.20	-.03	**.61	.05	—		
Productive	-.03	*.40	**.53	-.08	*.43	.09	—	—	
Comprehension	.14	.06	~.36	.07	*.40	*.43	—	—	—

* $p < .05$.
** $p < .01$.

Table 39. Correlations for the "Best Solutions" Across Ages

	10–13 Months		20 Months			28 Months	
	Analytic	Rote	Comprehension	Productive Output	Output	Comprehension	Productive Output
20 Months							
Comprehension	.29	.27	—				
Productive output	**.53	.30		—			
Rote output	-.15	*.42			—		
28 Months							
Comprehension	*.42	.11	*.40	*.46	.07	—	
Production	*.40	.21	.07	**.68	-.05	—	—

* $p < .05$.
** $p < .01$.

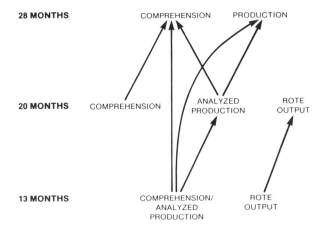

Figure 4: Pattern of Best Fit to the Observed Longitudinal Data

From this point of view, we can see two isolated developmental pathways flanking one "main line." The major pathway runs from Strand 1 at 10–13 months (i.e., lexical-conceptual analysis), through analyzed production at 20 months, to both comprehension and production at the last age level. One secondary path leads from Strand 2 at 10–13 months to the rote production factor at 20 months, and then disappears. Another small pathway does not get under way until 20 months, connecting the comprehension factor at that age level with the closest thing to a comprehension factor at the last session.

Conclusion

To summarize, the two-factor theory that we provided in the last ten studies is only partially correct. The picture is actually more complex, involving two distinct *kinds* of developmental dissociations, which have their major effects at different points in time.

— From first words to first word combinations, the major dissociation lies between lexical-conceptual analysis and rote output.
— From first word combinations through grammar, the cleft lies instead between receptive and expressive language.
— The 20-month transition point serves as a kind of waystation, where one dissociation drops off and another begins.

In the past ten studies, we found several instances of "homotypic discontinuity," where the same content means different things at different ages. The changes we found in referential style (Studies 1, 3, and 7) and MLU (Studies 2 and 6) are good illustrations. There are also several instances in our data of "heterotypic continuity," where stability of individual differences cuts across different content domains at different points in time. The strong link between early lexical development and later grammar is a particularly good example of this principal. It is clear now that similar longitudinal shifts operate at the summary level. So, for example, a "rote output" or "comprehension factor" at 13 months does not link up directly with its analogue 15 months later. Instead, we find patterns like those in Figure 4, where variance in comprehension weaves into production and then into comprehension again.

We started with a two-factor theory and ended with something richer but more difficult. Before we move into a final consideration of all these findings, there is one last piece of empirical work left to do. So far we have dealt with relationships among language *variables*. Now we want to take a brief look at the *children* who have given this shape to the data. This will include a consideration of the role played by the social-environmental context in creating, enhancing, and/or discouraging particular styles of language.

Chapter 16: Study 12
Social Contributions to
Individual Differences

The data presented in Studies 1–11 reflect *clusters of variables*, and not *clusters of children*. We have argued that the patterns of dissociation observed among these variables involve a dissociation between universal mechanisms that are available to every normal child. If we are correct, individual children differ not in the presence or absence of strategies, but in the degree to which they rely on different modes of learning. In this final study, we want to consider some characteristics of the children and their environments that may be associated with this "choice" of language styles.

We will begin with a consideration of three social variables: gender, birth-order, and temperament. Because all three reflect an unknown and perhaps inextricable mix of endogenous and exogenous factors, they are perhaps best referred to as "biosocial" rather than social influences on language development. In fact, it should become clear that these particular factors contribute very little to the strands of variation described in the last eleven studies. There is, however, a theoretically coherent relationship between sociability and rote-imitative style, even though the magnitude of the relationship is rather small.

Next we will review the more general case for environmental effects on individual differences in language in reference to other studies that we have carried out with this sample. Our null results for maternal style and other environmental phenomena are compared with more positive findings in studies by other investigators. We will try to outline some of the confounding factors that make environmental effects difficult to find and even more difficult to replicate.

We will conclude with a look at the different *profiles* of abilities that are possible for individual children within the model of dissociable mechanisms presented in Studies 1–11. In other words, we will end by looking at children instead of measures. This will include presentation of a single longitudinal case, a diary study of linguistic style in Bates's daughter Julia from 9 to 27 months of age. The Julia study validates many of the group findings presented here, outlining developments from prespeech to grammar in a particularly extreme version of referential-analytic style. But at the end of that study we will present some very surprising findings regarding Julia's encounter with a second language at 20 months of age—findings that help clarify the role of environmental factors in encouraging the use of different acquisition mechanisms.

Before proceeding, we must reiterate that this is a very homogeneous sample: healthy children from middle-class families, growing up in the privileged environment of a beautiful university town. We do not have a representative test for the influence of demographic and/or biosocial factors on individual differences in language. Nevertheless, we do have substantial and reliable patterns of variation within language development. If biosocial factors played a *major* causal role in the creation of qualitative differences in style, they should be detectable whenever we find the expected stylistic dissociations in our sample. But if robust patterns of variation can be found in the absence of associated social-environmental variance, we are justified in concluding that these social factors are not *necessary* for the development of linguistic style—although they may serve to enhance or discourage the development of a particular style once it is under way.

Method

We will present only a small amount of new data here: gender-related differences, correlates of birth-order, and correlations with five subscales from the Rowe and Plomin Temperament Inventory administered to the mothers in the 28-month session (Rowe and Plomin, 1977). In the present study, birth-order was treated two ways: as a dichotomous variable (comparable to gender), and as an interval measure of ordinal position (varying from 1 to 6 in this population).

Gender and birth-order are characteristics of the child; but they also reflect characteristics of the family ecology in which the child acquires his or her language. However lacking these two variables may be in *explanatory* value, they do appear to have a certain amount of *predictive* power in developmental research. When gender-related differences in language development are reported, they typically favor girls (Maccoby and Jacklin, 1974). And when birth-order effects are found, in language or in any other domain of cognitive development, they invariably favor first borns (see Bates, 1975, for a review). In the literature on individual differences in language, there are a few suggestions concerning both gender and birth-order effects (Nelson, 1973; Starr, 1975; Bloom et al, 1975). Specifically, the analytic/referential/nominal style is reported more often for girls and first borns; the holistic/expressive/pronominal style is reported more often for boys and later borns. If analytic/referential/nominal style is associated with more precocious language development (as it appears to be in our sample as well), this pattern of gender and parity differences is precisely what we should expect. Applied to the present study, we can make the following predictions (permitting a series of one-tailed tests): Females and first borns should score more highly on analytic/receptive variables at each age level; males and second borns should score more highly on rote-imitative measures.

Temperament is also, by definition, a characteristic of the child. But respective roles of genes and the social environment in child temperament are hotly debated (Campos, Barrett, Lamb, Goldsmith, and Stenberg, 1983). There is, to our knowledge, no evidence to date showing a link between individual differences in language and temperament. There is, however, a growing literature linking certain aspects of temperament to styles or strategies in problem solving (Kogan, 1983; Kagan, 1981; Reznick and Kagan, 1983). For example, Kagan and colleagues report that shy children are more likely to show a cautious, analytic approach to cognitive problems; very sociable children, on the other hand, are more likely to "leap before they look" when presented with various intellectual tasks in the laboratory. Findings like these have led to the speculation that there will be a link between the sociability/shyness dimension in temperament and the various dimensions of language style discussed here. Specifically, the holistic/expressive/pronominal style may be more typical of very gregarious children, i.e., children who are particularly anxious to be *with* and to be *like* their fellow human beings.

The Plomin and Rowe Temperament Inventory yields five subscales of infant temperament: emotionality, soothability, activity level, attention span, and sociability. Although we examined correlations of all five scores with the various language measures, our predictions pertain primarily to the sociability subscale; hence we will use two-tailed tests for the first four subscales, and one-tailed tests for sociability. Specifically, the sociability scale should correlate positively with rote/holistic/imitative measures and negatively or not at all with analytic/receptive measures.

We have considered a range of other nonlinguistic factors in the language development of these children in a series of separate publications. These include studies of the relationship between language and cognition, particularly symbolic play (Bretherton et al., 1981b; Bates et al., 1983; Bretherton and Bates, 1984; Shore, 1981; Shore et al., 1984; O'Connell and Bretherton, 1984; Bretherton, O'Connell, Shore, and Bates, 1984), as well as studies of the relationship between child language and the mother's social/communicative style (Beeghly, 1981;

Bates et al., 1982a; Bretherton et al., 1981b; O'Connell and Bretherton, 1984). Those results will be discussed very briefly here, insofar as they help us to understand the effects and non-effects of biosocial factors.

Results and Discussion

Gender and Birth Order

For the major individual language variables discussed in the previous studies, and for all the factor scores discussed in Study 11, we carried out simple Pearson product-moment correlations (one-tailed), for gender and for the two birth-order indices (i.e., a dichotomous classification into first borns and only children versus later borns, and an interval measure of ordinal position).

Correlations involving the two dichotomous variables are equivalent to a series of t-tests of the difference between the means for each of the language variables in question. The results of so many individual tests should be interpreted quite conservatively. As it turns out, however, there was little need for such a warning here. Whether we considered the individual measures or the factor scores, there were no more significant correlations involving gender or birth-order than we would expect entirely by chance. (In the interests of space and the reader's patience, we will not list this large matrix of random relationships.)

We also considered the possibility that boys may vary more in their *range* of variation even if there are no gender-related differences in the *mean*. On a host of biological indices from conception onward, males tend to be more variable or unstable (Maccoby and Jacklin, 1974). A cursory look at our sample suggested that this might well be the case here, since the two children scoring highest across the course of the study were boys, despite the fact that the mean scores for boys and girls did not differ. To test this hypothesis, we divided the variance in the male sample by the variance in the female sample for each of the factor scores and for several of the major individual language measures (e.g., MLU at 20 and 28 months; total vocabulary and lexical style at every age). This procedure yields a ratio that is distributed like the F-ratio in an analysis of variance. Once again, results were largely negative. Although the variance in the male sample was frequently larger on individual measures, the F ratios obtained with this test did not reach significance more often than we might expect by chance.

As one final control for possible gender-related differences, we separated data for the boys and the girls and computed correlations among the major language variables within and between age levels. In studies of the relationship between language and handedness, investigators have reported different patterns of correlation within the two genders, even though means on the respective language and handedness measures did not differ by gender (e.g., Gottfried and Bathurst, 1983). And in a separate study of language and handedness in our own sample, we also find gender-related differences in the relationship between language and lateralization (Bates, O'Connell, Vaid, Sledge, and Oakes, 1986). However, there are no such differences in patterning within language proper. When the size of the sample is cut in half, we should expect some correlations to disappear. Not surprisingly, then, the correlations among language measures were considerably weaker within the respective male and female halves of the sample. But the direction of effects (i.e., the various strands discussed in Studies 1–11) was quite similar for girls and for boys.

At face value, these findings disconfirm previous claims concerning gender and parity in language development. However, once the study was well under way, we noticed a confound between these two predictor variables in our sample. The children had been carefully selected for age in days and birthweight, with an even balance between the sexes and a representative range of birth-orders. However, in the final sample of twenty-seven who participated at all four age levels, only two of the fourteen girls were first born, compared with eleven of the thirteen boys. If there is a tendency for girls to elect an analytic strategy but for later borns to elect a holistic strategy, these tendencies might have canceled each other out in the present study.

Because there is a confound between gender and birth-order in this sample, we present these negative findings with caution. However, this is not the first time that gender-related differences have failed to appear in a relatively large study of early language development (e.g., Bates et al., 1979; Kagan, 1981; Gottfried and Bathurst, 1983; Macauley, 1978). McCall (1981) has suggested that gender-related differences may fail to appear before two years of age, because early developments are "buffered" against environmental effects. This assumes, of course, that gender-related differences are enhanced if not caused by the social environment. We will not take a stand on this vexed issue, except to point out that gender-related and birth-order differences in language development appear to be rather small and unreliable (Maccoby and Jacklin, 1974). They are, in any case, too small to play a major explanatory role in the robust individual differences in language development that occur between 1 and 3 years of age.

Temperament

For four of the five temperament indices (emotionality, soothability, activity, and attention span), there were no more significant correlations with language measures than we would expect by chance. This was true

Table 40. *Language Variables and Sociability (One-tailed tests)*

"First Strand"	"Second Strand"	
	1. 10-Month total production	-.01
No significant		
correlates	13 Months	
of 39 tested		
	2. Total production (int.)	*.36
	3. Imitative production (obs.)	**.50
	4. Spontaneous production (obs.)	.25
	20 Months	
	5. MLU	*.40
	6. Observed vocabulary	*.37
	7. Int. grammatical morpheme	.19
	8. Obs. grammatical morpheme	*.45
	9. Obs. verb density	~.32
	10. Closed-class style (int.)	*.36
	11. Closed-class style (obs.)	-.12
	12. Novel concept imitation	.17
	13. 28 Month total output	*.35
	Factor scores	
	14. 13-Month production	*.39
	15. 20-Month rote output	.20
	16. 28-Month production	.09

$\sim$ $p < .10$.
* $p < .05$.
** $p < .01$.

whether we looked at the myriad individual measures within age levels or at the factor scores reported in Study 11. Again, we will spare the reader a table of random results.

For the sociability scale, things were at last more interesting. One-tailed correlations were calculated for fifty-seven language variables: forty-six individual measures and eleven factor scores. Results are briefly summarized in Table 40. With the alpha level set at $p < .05$, eight correlations or 14% reached significance—two to three times as many as we might expect by chance.

But of course these were one-tailed tests, and positive relationships were expected with only a theoretically-specified subset of these fifty-seven measures. Specifically, sociability should correlate primarily with the rote/holistic/imitative variables that we previously described as "Strand 2." (Although Study 11 showed us that the Two-Strand theory is too simple to account for the data, we will use Strand 2 as shorthand for the rote/imitative variables that form a strand from 13 to 20 months, and as the closest thing we have to pure production measures at 28 months.) As indicated in Table 40, sixteen measures were designated as Strand 2 variables: reported vocabulary totals at 10 months, three different vocabulary totals at 13 months (reported word totals, observed imitations, and observed spontaneous speech), MLU, observed vocabulary, morphology clusters, fiffin imitation and aspects of lexical style at 20 months (including observed and reported closed-class density, and verb density in free speech), total morphemes produced at 28 months, and three factor scores (the single production factor at 13 and 28 months, and the rote output factor at 20 months). Out of these sixteen, eight correlations with sociability reached the .05 level of significance. In other words, our predictions were confirmed on half of the variables, ten times the level that would be expected by chance. Furthermore, there were *no* significant correlations with sociability for *any* of the language measures outside of the designated Strand 2 set.

These correlations are not particularly strong. If sociability is partialed out of the correlations among language measures, the pattern of within-language results does not change very much. In other words, the relationship between sociability and language style is too weak for us to conclude that individual differences in language are *caused* by differences in temperament. Nevertheless, the results obtained with this sociability subscale are consistent and theoretically coherent. This provides further justification for the view that rote/holistic style is not necessarily a default process, i.e., something that one does in the absence of adequate analytic skills. It may, instead, reflect a child's inherent need to be *with* and be *like* other human beings. All normal children have those needs; but some children make those needs a primary theme. These differences in temperament can *enhance* or *facilitate* reliance on rote/imitative processes in language-learning—even though temperament alone cannot account for either the existence or use of this language learning strategy.

Nonlinguistic Factors in Other Studies

To summarize so far, there is little evidence here for either gender-related or birth-order effects in styles of language learning. There is, however, some modest but consistent evidence for a relationship between language style and temperament, particularly sociability.

In our other studies of nonlinguistic factors in language acquisition (with these children and in other samples), we have found fairly consistent evidence for "intraorganismic" correlations, i.e., nonlinguistic factors *in the child* that seem to vary consistently with aspects of language development. Most of the successful nonlinguistic predictors of language are cognitive measures, particularly measures of symbolic play: Use of single gestural schemes in play correlates with single-word development (e.g., Bates et al., 1979; Bretherton et al., 1981b), and use of multischeme combinations in play correlates with multiword combinations in language (e.g., Shore et al., 1984; Shore, 1981). With separate samples of 20-month-old children, Shore and Bauer (1983; see also Bauer, 1985) have also reported differences between nominal- and pronominal-style children in the nature of their symbolic and combinatorial play and in the pattern of correlations observed between indices of play and language. Given these findings, we feel fairly sure now that individual differences in language development are associated with aspects of cognitive processing outside the boundaries of language proper. Notice, however, that these are all endogenous measures, so that in every case we are correlating the child with herself and not with some aspect of the environment.

In several other studies, we instead sought "extraorganismic" correlations, i.e., factors in the child's linguistic input and in the immediate social environment that predict both rate and style of communicative development (e.g., Bretherton, Bates, Benigni, Camaioni, and Volterra, 1979; Beeghly, 1981; O'Connell and Bretherton, 1984). In contrast with the cognitive studies, this search for social correlates of language has been largely disappointing. For example, Beeghly (1981) examined a large array of maternal style characteristics and measures of dyadic interaction. The nonlinguistic measures of style included both "macro-level" variables (e.g., subjective ratings of dyadic harmony and pace) and "micro-level" variables (e.g., the establishment and maintenance of eye contact and smiling during play). Linguistic/communicative measures included structural complexity of the mother's speech, repetitions, and a variety of speech adjustments that are typically associated with "motherese." Each of these measures was motivated by claims in the mother-child interaction literature, proposing some kind of teaching, structuring, or motivating relationship to the child's progress in language development. The results can be summarized succinctly: There were no more relationships between maternal style and child language than we would expect by chance. As reviewed by Bretherton et al. (1979) and again by Bates et al. (1982a), this kind of negative finding is quite common in studies seeking the effects of environmental factors on language development.

The picture is not entirely bleak. There are certainly some positive results in the literature on social-environmental inputs to language (e.g., McCartney, 1984; Nelson, Carskaddon, and Bonvillian, 1973). For example, Keith Nelson and colleagues have carried out several experiments demonstrating the positive teaching effects of "recasts," i.e., utterances in which the adult models a target grammatical structure by casting it within a "real" conversational response to a point raised by the child herself. Also, as we noted in the literature review, there are some positive relationships between maternal behavior and the child's linguistic style. The mothers of referential/nominal/analytic children are more responsive to object-oriented communications and are more likely to name and/or describe objects that catch the child's attention. The mothers of expressive/pronominal/Gestalt children do less to encourage object-oriented games, are more likely to communicate within social-regulatory sequences (e.g., caretaking, discipline, face-to-face games and routines), and are more likely to repeat rather than elaborate their child's preceding utterance. Such findings are consistent with the idea that maternal input "causes" or at least encourages the child's selection of style. However, even in the best studies, social factors account for only a small proportion the variance in child outcome measures.

As we have noted in some detail elsewhere, this is no doubt due, at least in part, to some profound methodological problems in the analysis of dyadic exchange (Bates et al., 1982a). Here is a partial list.

Bidirectionality of effects. In any naturalistic study of parent–child interaction, adults are responding to their child at or above the level of contingent behavior displayed by the child. In other words, it is often hard to know who is in charge. This direction-of-effects problem makes it difficult to draw causal inferences from correlations between parental style and child outcome measures.

For example, take the finding that the mothers of referential children respond more positively to object-oriented communications. This might occur simply because the mother knows what "turns her child on." She knows what kind of exchange is likely to be successful. Hence she can anticipate her child's preference by responding enthusiastically—and perhaps by seeking out a potentially successful exchange when the situation calls for it (e.g., trying to amuse and distract a child with available objects while sitting before the camera in a psychology laboratory). In other words, the child has taught her mother what to do to keep her entertained.

From this point of view, any correlation between parental and child speech forms is also suspect. Parents frequently echo their child's speech, with or without a subsequent elaboration or "recast" of the sort studied by Nelson and colleagues. In either an echo or a recast, we are likely to find a repetition of the particular linguistic forms chosen by the child. Furthermore, parents sometimes get into the habit of using their child's favorite structures and current form of address, even when they are initiating a new topic. For example, a parent is more likely to say

"Does Julia want Mommy to help?" if the child typically refers to her-self and her listener by name. Such "reactive" and "proactive" parental habits could lead to a significant positive correlation between parent and child speech—even on very specific structures like the use of auxiliary verbs (Newport et al., 1977).

A slightly different argument applies to the tendency for parents of pronominal/expressive children to repeat their child's speech. The logic goes something like this:

— Expressive children tend to have relatively inconsistent phonological systems.
— This lack of consistency in phonology may result from the fact that expressive children are trying to reproduce fragments of adult speech as they occur, "on line," without reflecting on the internal composition of the input or its relationship to things that they have heard before. Because the expressive child is aiming broadly at acoustic targets as they come in, without imposing a consistent set of phonological principals, the resulting speech may be very difficult for an adult to understand.
— If a child's speech is unclear (e.g., "Dah a beah deh"), the parent is more likely to repeat the utterance in order to understand or clarify what was said (e.g., "That's a bear there, yes").
— This situation would result in a positive correlation between adult repetition and rote/imitative style in the child, tempting us to con-clude that adult imitativeness "caused" the child to develop a mirror-image approach to language. But in fact, the actual causal route might run in the opposite direction: from child imitativeness, to child unintelligibility, to adult repetition.

We don't mean to argue that parents have no effect on child language. But style correlations are particularly difficult to interpret from a causal point of view. In fact, the bidirectionality confound is even more serious for studies that *fail* to show a relationship between child and adult language. It is now reasonably well established that parents and other adults respond to child comprehension failures by adjusting their speech "downward"—exaggerating their phonology, simplifying their choice of syntactic and lexical forms. This fact has very important implications for the analysis of cause and effect in dyadic exchange. *Simply stated, any index of motherese is an indirect measure of child failure—in short-term interactions and over longer time intervals.*

In many cases, this situation actually leads to a negative correlation between "teaching" style and child language (Bates et al., 1982a). How-ever, if the mother's speech adjustment does have a facilitative effect, the *positive* effect of teaching and the *negative* information that elicited that teaching will cancel each other out. As a result, we will find a nonsignificant correlation between two variables that are in fact strongly related in a system of homeostatic causes and effects.

In our view, the best way to get around bidirectional effects is to break into the natural cycle of dyadic exchange through various kinds of experimental manipulations (e.g., Nelson's experiments with recasts). As long as we are restricted to naturalistic data, we are likely to learn relatively little about causal relationships between maternal style and child outcomes.

Gene/environment confounds. Positive correlations between parent and child measures may also be due, at least in part, to genetic confounds. For example, if there is a genetic component to what we vaguely call "verbal fluency," it is entirely possible that a mother could pass that tendency on to her child even if they are separated at birth. If referential style and verbal fluency have anything in common (something that is by no means established at this point), then we might see the genetic confound expressed in a series of rather specific style relationships between parent and child speech (e.g., object-oriented communication). Hardy-Brown, Plomin, and DeFries (1981) have presented results from children adopted at birth, suggesting that variance in language ability at 1 year of age is better predicted by measures of the biological parent than by corresponding measures of the adoptive parents. So the genetic confound issue does have to be taken seriously if we want to understand the route by which parents encourage or discourage the development of linguistic styles.

Differential reliability of organismic and environmental variables. It is a simple but sad statistical fact that no measure can predict anything else better than it can predict itself. From this point of view, Beeghly (1981) notes that maternal style and dyadic exchange variables are frustratingly unreliable. Whereas 5 minutes of child language correlates quite highly with another 5 minutes taken 2 days later, 5 minutes of maternal style (at the microlevel of smiles and eye contact, or at the macrolevel of control and harmony) is often quite unrelated to 5 minutes of the same measure even in the same session. This is not because mothers are unstable beings, but because they are sophisticated, complex, and sensitive to a wide variety of changing conditions. Nevertheless, the low reliability of dyadic variables has serious consequences for any application of a correlational design. It may look as though environmental factors play no role in the creation and maintenance of linguistic style, simply because we cannot find a reliable way to measure them.

We do not wish to suggest that the search for social correlates of language development is doomed. First of all, the usual contrast between social and nonsocial is not the issue here. Temperament is a social variable—but it seems to be a variable that originates inside the child, although it can be amplified or attenuated by many external factors (e.g., Campos et al., 1983). And although the correlations between sociability and language style reported here are modest, they are considerably more consistent and robust than the many exogenous social factors that we have pursued in other studies. The real problem lies not in the absence of social factors, but in the difficulty in building a case for *exogenous* social factors.

If a thicket of methodological problems can be overcome, a causal role for exogenous social factors will undoubtedly be found—as we shall see in our report on Julia. We are probably also more likely to find environmental effects on language style if we move outside the privileged middle-class environment (e.g., Cohen and Beckwith, 1979). We know that quantitative aspects of intellectual development (including language) can be affected by drastic differences in education, nutrition, the nature of time spent with adults, and perhaps just the motivation to live. The same may be true for qualitative differences in language style. However, the normal range of variation in language development that we have described here seems to be a product, as far as we can tell, of "natural" or "endogenous" dissociations of learning mechanisms. That is, they come from somewhere inside the child. Differences in linguistic input and social environment may modulate these effects; but they probably do not create the initial preference. This is essentially the conclusion reached by Goldfield (1985), in a demonstration of how parents can reinforce or discourage an object-oriented language style that is already apparent in the child's orientation toward objects during the prespeech era.

Profiles of Individual Children

Insofar as we have talked about individual children at all, we have talked about the logical extremes. And yet most children fall somewhere in between, with a mix of styles or strategies. Let us consider for a moment some profiles of language abilities that are possible if we are correct about the dissociable mechanisms that underlie individual variation.

Although Study 11 tells us that more than two strands of variance are involved, we will restrict ourselves to two hypothetical mechanisms to simplify the discussion: analysis for understanding (associated with comprehension) and analysis for reproduction (associated with imitation and rote output). However, the same logic of profile analysis would apply whether we were talking about two, ten, or a hundred separate strands of development.

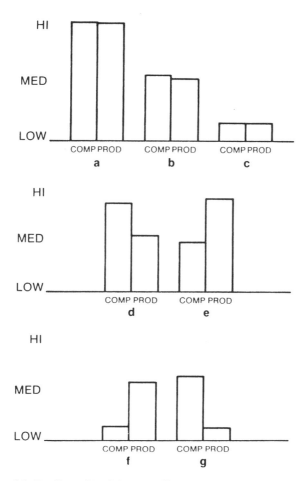

Figure 5: Possible Profiles of Individual Differences in Language Development.

Figure 5 represents some of the different processing "profiles" that are possible, assuming only two partially dissociable dimensions. Notice that complete dissociations are not represented. Within our normal sample, we find no case of a child who is at the top of one dimension while occupying the bottom percentile in another—although more severe dissociations might be found in the clinical literature (e.g., Curtiss and Yamada, 1978; see also concluding chapter of this volume).

The more typical cases in our data are represented in Figure 5a–c: children who are high, low, or medium on both aspects of language. For all the talk of style typologies, these are the garden variety patterns in a sample of middle-class children. Their early vocabularies have a lot of nouns, but other forms also occur frequently. In first word combinations, they may use a mix of nominal and pronominal forms (e.g., sentences like "Kathryn milk" and "I wan' dat" may be found in the same session). Sometimes they imitate, sometimes they don't, and they may change in their propensity to imitate from one stage to another. If the individual differences reported in the literature reflected a true dichotomy, a discrete "parameter setting" of some kind, then these middle-of-the-road patterns would not be so common.

Figure 5d–g represents the dissociative patterns that do seem possible in the normal range, the kinds of dissociations that make the individual-difference literature interesting.

The first of these (Fig. 5d) we will refer to as *high analytic style*. This is a hypothetical case in which the child performs adequately in rote learning for reproduction, right in the normal range. However, her analysis for understanding is exceptional: Receptive vocabulary is excellent, and single-words and simple phrases are often remarkably sophisticated in their lexical-conceptual content.

The second case (Fig. 5e) shows the reverse pattern, which we will call *high rote style*. Although analysis for understanding is quite satisfactory, this child is even better at mimicry, with an unusual interest in the surface forms of language (e.g., Horgan's daughter Kelly). This high rote ability could come from at least two different sources:

— **Social motivation**. The high rote child may have a particularly avid interest in sounding like and being with other people. Hence the heavy reliance on reproduction of forms would be brought about by the desire to find a "short cut" to grownup styles of social interaction.
— **Verbal memory**. The high rote child may have a greater-than-normal capacity to remember relatively long segments of discourse. This could include short-term memory (i.e., a capacity for instant replays) and/or long-term memory (i.e., storage and retrieval of interesting fragments of conversation, jingles, formulas, odd novel forms, that occurred hours or even days and weeks before).

Social motivation and verbal memory are both inherently positive attributes. There is no reason to conclude that high analytic style is "smarter" than high rote style. These two hypothetical children are simply good at different things.

By contrast, the last two profiles represent children with complementary problems. The child in Figure 5g illustrates what we will refer to as *low rote style*. Her comprehension-driven processing is adequate. However, she has difficulty reproducing large segments of input from memory. This might occur because of memory limitations. It might also occur for temperamental reasons, perhaps because the child is nervous around adults and unwilling to "rehearse" adultlike behavior out loud when anyone is watching. As a result, the adult model disappears before she has had a chance to encode it for later consideration. This child may rest at the one-word stage for some time, and rely on telegraphic output for a longer than average period after that. However, her understanding is fairly good. Because there is an upper limit on the length of normal conversational turns, memory limitations of this kind will become less important as time goes by. Eventually the everyday language of a low rote child will be difficult to distinguish from the middle-of-the-road profile represented in Figure 5b.

The profile in Figure 5f represents a different kind of problem, a hypothetical case of what we will call *low analytic style*. This fictional child is able to reproduce aspects of the linguistic input at adequate levels; but she is well below average in the internal analysis of linguistic forms. The child does well to rely on her strengths. Using formulaic speech as a compensatory device, she can function reasonably well in many social settings while she works on language structure at a slower pace. In that respect she is better off than the child in Figure 5c with across-the-board weaknesses. Nevertheless, it will take her considerably longer than average to acquire productive control over linguistic forms. And a continued analytic weakness may pose a problem in many other aspects of learning and development.

It is only in the contrast between low rote and low analytic profiles that the relationship between style and rate of language learning is an issue. In the early stages, the low analytic child may seem more advanced, pulling out routine phrases on demand and impressing friends and visiting relatives. But ultimately, the low rote child will "seem smarter," because she is better at following instructions and keeping up with the topic of conversation. In particular, she will do better on standardized measures like the Peabody Picture Vocabulary Test. Receptive vocabulary does seem to correlate highly with total IQ scores, which in turn correlate highly with many other indices of success in Western middle-class societies. We place a high value on this particular set of skills, and reward each other accordingly. Regardless of her performance in other domains, the child who is unskilled at this comprehension-driven mode of information processing will encounter problems in a society that values this ability.

Because this is a particularly important point, it is worth repeating. *In our view, it is only the low analytic child who represents any kind of problematic "lag" in development.* Correlations between style and precocity are an artifact of proportion scores (e.g., noun/pronoun ratios, lexical style). This kind of scoring forces the data into a kind of arbitrary choice between two mechanisms that are both necessary for normal language-learning. Children who are roughly equal in both styles can contribute nothing of interest to the variance, whether they display high-high, medium-medium or low-low profiles (Fig. 5a–c). As a result, a child with particularly severe delays in the segmentation and internal analysis of language will contribute disproportionately to our findings.

If we did not force a choice between styles through proportional scoring, we would find that the low analytic/low rote children are considerably worse off. Conversely, the children who make the greatest progress overall are making ample use of both rote and analytic skills. This point has implications for clinicians as well as psycholinguists. Our findings should not be used to argue that imitation and/or formulaic speech are "bad." Natural languages are full of irregularities and completely unanalyzable forms that have to be learned through some kind of process of implicit (and sometimes explicit) memorization. Because languages always contain a mix of rules and exceptions, children have to use a mixture of learning strategies in order to acquire their language on schedule. We think it unlikely that senseless drills will get a clinician very far in dealing with a language-disordered child. But if a child is spontaneously drilling himself, using a rote/imitative approach to language to compensate for weaker mechanisms, he should be encouraged to build on whatever strengths he has.

We have now generated seven types instead of two. But that is not the point. If individual differences in language acquisition are brought about by the dissociability of mechanisms or "modules," many different patterns are possible. A child can look like a referential or expressive "type" because he is bad at X but good at Y; he may also look like a referential or expressive "type" because he is merely good at X but outstanding at Y.

The positive aspects of pronominal/expressive/rote/imitative style (whatever it may be) are made particularly clear in our own study by a consideration of two children at the top of the sample. These two boys had the highest scores overall on the first principal component factors described in Study 11. Both were producing complex sentences with ample morphology at 28 months of age. In fact, both were very good at everything. Nevertheless, they still differed in some interesting ways.

Boy One (the superstar) had forty-five words at 13 months, more than 400 words at 20 months, and topped the charts on most expressive language measures throughout the study (including a 28-month MLU of 3.43, on a par with most 4-year-old children). He was not, however, at the top of the class in comprehension, although he did very well.

Boy Two had only nine words at 13 months, with a 20-month reported vocabulary of 294. So his early expressive language was good but not exceptional—certainly below the superstar's level. However, he scored at the top of the sample on comprehension measures from the very beginning. By 28 months, Boy Two had caught up with Boy One in expressive language (including an MLU of 3.30), and had even edged ahead on a few measures.

What is our message here? Still waters run deep? Hard work pays off in the end? Yes, and no. One of the clear messages in the last few studies is that comprehension is ultimately a better predictor of success in language than early talking (i.e., vocabulary totals at 1 year). Boy Two is obviously contributing to this picture. However, when we returned to the original transcripts for these two children, another compelling difference between the two emerged, suggesting that Boy Two never really "caught up" with our superstar at all. Boy Two was just as sophisticated in his speech as the numbers suggested he should be, but the ideas he expressed were entirely normal and even mundane. By contrast, Boy One displayed a kind of poetic genius, insofar as it is fair to burden a small boy with that label. For example, in the 28-month snack scene, he engaged in a long conversation with his cracker about eating rights, changing voices as he played each part (e.g., "Why you drink all my orange juice, cracker?" . . . "I'm a cracker, don't eat me up . . ."). And as he sat among our standard experimental toys, he set up a game of grocery store and planned out a list that included a new dish invented on the spot: cranberry whipped cream.

In short, there are advantages to a high-rote profile in which production exceeds comprehension, as long as comprehension is very good. Fragments of remembered language are accessed quickly, and new amalgams are forged rapidly without excessive monitoring. The impression of wit and poetry in Boy One's transcripts has a lot to do with his ability to reproduce old bits of adult input rapidly, in new situations and in new combinations (cf. Horgan, 1981; Snow, 1983; MacWhinney, 1982).

This qualitative impression was certainly not contained in any table of numbers; we had to go back to the transcripts to understand what these profiles look like "in vivo." This brings us back to a point raised in the introduction concerning the relative utility of descriptive case studies. By quantifying results across children and applying multivariate techniques, we have learned things that we could not otherwise have known. But the converse still holds: certain kinds of qualitative information are lost in group studies, and can only be obtained by looking directly at children and their language.

From this point of view, let us take a final look at individual difference issues by examining one detailed diary study of language development in a referential child.

Julia

Bates's daughter Julia was born in March of 1983, when this monograph was still being written and some subsidiary analyses still remained to be done (not surprisingly, the monograph and the analyses sat on the shelf for approximately a year after this point). Starting in January of 1984 (when Julia was 9 months old), Bates began a computer diary of her daughter's communicative, gestural, and linguistic development. The diary ends at 26 months when, just as our mothers told us here, it became very difficult to keep track of the child's exploding language abilities. Hence these Julia notes cover the period from first words to grammar, permitting us to compare the "coarsely cut" findings for our larger sample with a fine-grained longitudinal examination of language development and language style in a single child.

One caveat is in order right away: The mother/observer in this study was certainly not naive about the hypotheses and conclusions that we have presented here. If it is possible to induce a style of development in one's child, this mother might have been tempted to try (hoping, perhaps, for the high/high profile displayed in Figure 5a). The child's father was not so informed (it is hard to find time to talk in detail about one's work when a child arrives), nor was the babysitter who spent a good proportion of each week with Julia from 5 months of age onward. Nevertheless, those who believe the environment can have a strong impact on choice of style might be suspicious that Bates induced referential style in her daughter. In any case, Julia did develop into a rather clear example of high analytic, referential/nominal style in her acquisition of English. But as we shall see, she displayed a very different pattern in her later acquisition of Italian. Let us go over the data briefly by stages.

Prespeech. Julia engaged in prolific giving, showing, and pointing to objects from 9–11 months onward, in line with Goldfield's characterization of a "proto-referential" child. Bates may well have had something to do with encouraging these events, given her long-standing interest in the problem (Bates et al., 1975). It is, after all, no accident that the diary begins at 9 months of age, the point at which these communicative gestures start to appear in most normal children. More unexpectedly, however, Julia proved to be quite uninterested in imitation, vocal or gestural, at this or at any other stage of development. This is recorded in the opening pages of the diary, in a retrospective account of Julia at 12 weeks:

> The first week that Julia began to respond to vocal imitation, volleys of vocalization up to 12 turns long took place for several days—only to disappear with essentially NO other signs of imitation for many months to come.

In fact, Julia was often quite resistant to on-line imitation of parental models—despite strong encouragement to the contrary. The following excerpt from the diary at 10 months illustrates this point:

Pattycake has emerged at last. Three weeks ago Julia received a book of nursery rhymes with a pattycake page, and we modelled pattycake at every reading. She would not imitate, and resisted when we tried to mold her hands while reciting the rhyme. Last week, however, we sneaked in to watch her chattering in bed alone after a nap—and found her surreptitiously practicing at clapping her hands! Within a few hours, she clapped spontaneously on seeing the patty-cake page in the book, and has given us the book (rejecting other books) several times while clapping and looking expectant.

Julia was either unwilling or unable to try out new models on line. This tendency persisted into the next few stages, showing up in phonological and lexical acquisition.

First words. By 13 months of age, Julia had an expressive vocabulary of thirty-four words, and a receptive vocabulary of eighty-four words (according to the diary and to self-administration of our maternal interviews). Both of these vocabulary totals are two standard deviations above the mean for the group data described in Study 1—although Julia still fell well below the records established by Boy One and Boy Two (proving that there is only so much a mother can do to move those numbers around). The two vocabularies were both quite clearly specialized in object naming. In particular, twenty-seven (or 79%) of Julia's first words were names for common objects; eighteen of these items (or 67%) met the criteria described in Study 1 for contextually flexible use. In other words, Julia would be classified as a strong example of early referential style.

Throughout the single word stage, Julia's phonology consisted of a small stock of consonant-vowel patterns, first restricted primarily to monosyllables (e.g., BAH, TEH, CAH), and ultimately branching off into a set of systematic contrasts between monosyllables (e.g., BABA for "bottle") and disyllables (e.g., BAH for "ball" and "balloon"). At 13 months, the thirty-four words recorded by the mother contained a considerable number of homophones. For example the single sound BAH was used to name bottles and balls and babies. Because all three words were used flexibly to name appropriate referents in each category, and because Julia seemed to understand the contrasts among BALL, BOT-TLE and BABY in her receptive language, it seemed appropriate to classify these as separate albeit homophonic lexical entries. However, for many of her monosyllabic words at 13 months, Julia did seem to make a series of subtle vowel contrasts that made one word noticeably different from another (e.g., BUH for BIRD, contrasting with BAH for BALL, BOTTLE and BABY). Somewhere between 14 and 15 months, many of these distinctions disappeared. Julia carried out a factor analysis of some kind on the phonological variations in her repertoire—a great weeding out in which she eliminated many of the subtle contrasts that had been detectable in her speech during the preceding weeks. Her set of thirty-four words, including twenty-seven object names, reduced temporarily to a handful of distinguishable forms. Furthermore, the reduction was carried out on phonological rather than semantic grounds: All initial-B words were now pronounced as BAH, initial-G words were conflated into a single GAH, and so forth.

This Draconian phase lasted for 2 or 3 weeks, ending with the emergence of contrasting monosyllabic and disyllabic forms. In the new disyllabic stage, Julia also began to produce words with two contrasting syllables (e.g., WADOO for WATER) and a few consonant-final forms (e.g., DIS). Her analytic approach to phonology during this cross-over period is made clear in the following exchange:

> A new event is the tendency for her to try and name things with something very like a questioning intonation, looking straight at me as if for confirmation. A particularly interesting exchange in this regard occurred in the car yesterday, waiting for George to come out of the post office. Trying to forestall an impatient tantrum, I kept pointing out pigeons and other birds flying nearby from roofs to wires to ground. At first she kept providing the usual label BUH. I kept repeating with very clear and even caricatured enunciation BIRD, stressing the last phoneme in particular. She started to stare at me, and back at the birds, and said DAH several times. Fearful of having caused backsliding, I repeated BIRD stressing the first letter. She looked at me intently and pressed her lips together twice in a sustained start of a B, and alternated back and forth between BA and DA for a minute or two. I continued to provide a clearly enunciated BIRD, and at one point she seemed to pick up on neither the first nor the final consonant, but on the medial sound pattern, saying RWA several times. I take this as further evidence of a new and explicit interest in phonological analysis, at a level as close to consciousness as anything else that Julia does.

This kind of on-line analysis is an imitation of a kind, but its focus seems to be on the internal structure of the sound rather than an effort to match the general contours of her mother's speech.

An example later in the one-word stage, at 17 months, illustrates the extent to which Julia is unable (or unwilling) to incorporate new material into her sound system without mulling things over in her own good time.

> Last night I challenged her recent pronunciation of HORSIE as SHEESHEE, by repeatedly saying HORRRRSIE back to her. After repeating SHEESHEE back to me about 10 times, she finally tried a

compromise: HAH-SHEESHEE. Today, however, she seems to be trying to work my midwestern "r" (the same one I belabored last night in HORSIE), into her pronunciation of CAR. The result is something like CAH-RWRWRWRWRW.

Word Combinations. At 20 months of age, Julia's reported vocabulary weighed in at 290 words (by self-administration of our parental checklist). Independent interviews taken by father and mother were in close agreement on these figures—which, once again, are high but still below the records set in our larger sample (so much for the efforts of a stagedoor mother . . .). At this point, Julia's total vocabulary contained 87% open-class words, of which 17.4% were verbs. This qualifies her at 20 months as a continued example of referential/analytic style.

This tendency was also reflected in the structure of Julia's first word combinations. A handful of multiword constructions first appeared at irregular intervals between 14 and 16 months: AHGAH BABA (or "all-gone bottle"), AHGAH GAGA (comments on the repeated disappearance of pets in the house during a three-day visit to a friend in Chicago), WADOO BABA (or WATER BOTTLE, a comment made after throwing a little boy's bottle into his wading pool), DIS WADOO (meaning something like THIS IS WATER, while pointing at the ocean as we came down over a hill and the port came in view), and TADOO BABA (said while stroking a beloved babydoll—TADOO being a word apparently derived from GENTLE to mean something like LOVE/HUG/STROKE). Notice that these early combinations involve only a very narrow subset of Julia's larger vocabulary—although they are among the most frequent and most talked-about items in Julia's extant linguistic world.

When multiword speech was finally in full flower at 18 months, nominal compounds and noun-verb constructions were by far the most common patterns she displayed. Within these and other constructions, she first referred to speaker and listener by name: DOODAH (her version of JULIA), DADA (a term originally used for both parents, now restricted to her father) and MOMMY, together with proper names for her babysitter and family and a few more significant others. Julia did use both MY and DOODAH to indicate possession. But in general, she fit the pattern that first inspired Bloom and her colleagues to distinguish between nominal and pronominal style.

Julia's comprehension seemed to be quite good during her lengthy telegraphic stage, supporting the view that nominal style is associated with higher receptive language abilities. Evidence relative to comprehension in the diary include examples of Julia's response to lengthy commands with four or five content words and her response to a variety of

implausible multiword commands that her mother tried out from time to
time across the second year. A particularly clear example of Julia's ability
to comprehend combinations of content words is reflected in the following entry at 22 months:

> We had an incredible exchange today, around the routine WHAT'S
> X'S Y'S NAME. She correctly answered the following questions:
> WHO IS DADDY'S BABY? SARA'S DADDY? VIRGINIA'S
> BABY? VIRGINIA'S GIRL? TRAUTE'S GIRLS? FRAN-
> CESCA'S DADDY? FRANCESCA'S MOMMY? FRANCESCA'S
> DOG? CINDY'S BABY? CINDY'S GIRLS? HEIDI'S SISTER?
> (she had to be prompted on that one, with the input "Heidi is Sara's
> sister"), and finally FRANCESCA'S DADDY'S DOG. We went
> through these literally dozens of times, every example I could think
> of, and she was at least 80% correct across the set.

Despite the evidence for good comprehension, Julia's telegraphic
approach to language production persisted for so many months that her
mother began to express concern. In the period between 20 and 23
months, Julia would often produce telegraphic sentences that were up to
four words long (e.g., DADDY BABA KITCHEN JULIA, meaning
"Daddy is making a bottle in the kitchen for Julia"). A few function
words like "more," "no" and "don't" were well established, and an
occasional preposition or pronoun could be heard from 20 months on
(see below). But overall, her language was virtually agrammatic. (One
waggish visitor, a neurolinguist working at an area veterans' administration hospital, pointed out the similarity between Julia's speech and
several of his patients on the ward—offering his referral services if the
problem did not resolve soon.)

Grammaticization. Maternal concern aside, Julia's apparent resistance to morphology posed an interesting question: After avoiding grammatical inflections for so long, how would this child begin her first forays
into the grammar? This answer was not available in our longitudinal
group study, because we had to skip the period between 20 and 28
months, when our initially telegraphic children produced their first
inflections and function words.

Pronominal forms came in slowly between 19 and 25 months, in
sporadic uses that seemed to be competing against the predominant
nominal mode of talking about people and things. By 19.5 months,
Julia's first recorded use of "I" appeared (I BABY in response to the
question "Who's a baby?"). As far as her diarist could determine, I and
DOODAH were in free variation for many weeks thereafter. The second
person pronoun YOU came in between 19 and 22 months, but Julia

consistently reversed its meaning. This is particularly clear in utterances like CARRY YOU, HELP YOU, and HOLD YOU, obviously intended to mean "Carry me," "Help me," "Hold me," etc. At 24 months, the pronoun problem was exacerbated by the appearance of ME in subject position. An apparent competition among I, ME, and JULIA continued for weeks. This tendency is clearly illustrated in the single utterance at 25 months I DO THAT . . . JULIA DO THAT. . . .ME DO THAT (followed by a puzzled frown, and silence). The use of her own name as a first-person subject disappeared shortly thereafter, but a competition between I and ME persisted well beyond the point where the diary notes end. Hence Julia did, like the original subjects studied by Bloom et al. (1975), replace nominal forms with the appropriate pronouns. But she took a long time sorting things out, and built a number of intermediate theories along the way.

Julia's way of breaking into other aspects of grammatical morphology also reflected an analytic approach, an effort to impose order similar to the way she treated phonology many months before. Some fledgling morphology is first recorded between 20 and 21 months in examples like the following:

> Some interesting contrasts: MY XXXX versus I HAVE A XXXX, both to indicate possession, and COOK IT versus PEAS COOKING (which suggest that -ING may soon be a productive ending). See also CUT IT, KISS IT, and several other XXXX IT constructions, suggesting that IT now serves as a kind of general accusative marker added to the imperative form of the verb.

These examples remained the exception rather than the rule until around 23 months, when Julia went to work very systematically on a contrasting set of English prepositions (e.g., IN, ON, FOR, TO, FROM). From the beginning, these were used to express a clearcut set of semantic relationships, resembling the case contrasts that first appear in children acquiring richly inflected case languages (i.e., locative, accusative, dative, and benefactive meanings). A particularly clear (and long) example recorded at 24 months was the utterance   I GIVE KISS TO LION ON EYES FOR GRANDMA.   In this utterance, and in all the other inflected sentences that appeared during this period, the prepositions carried the same full lexical stress accorded to content words (i.e., nouns, verbs, and adjectives). The resulting overuse of full stress gave Julia's speech an oddly "precious" sound, as though she were reading lines in an audition for a Shirley Temple role.

One might argue that Julia *still* refused to accept the existence of grammatical morphology at this point. On both phonological and semantic grounds, she seemed to be treating English prepositions as though they were non-cliticized content words like all the others in her repertoire. But of course the story is not quite so clear. Noun morphology did begin to come in during this same period, including plural "s," possessive "'s" and sporadic use of the definite and indefinite articles. Verb morphology seemed to lag behind; even the high frequency irregular verbs (e.g., GO, HAVE) appeared in the present tense whenever Julia was recounting some kind of past event.

Twenty-four months was a kind of watershed, where the pace of morphological development accelerated markedly. Julia's approach to verb morphology focused initially on some contrasting modal verbs (e.g., NEED TO, HAVE TO). She also began to produce the regular past tense, but still avoided most copular and auxiliary verb forms. The organizing principle seemed to be a focus on meaning, i.e., those aspects of verb morphology that had some kind of recognizable semantic-conceptual content.

The appearance of the regular past occurred before any of the high-frequency irregular past forms were used with any consistency. This is an apparent reversal of the usual pattern reported in the literature, where irregular but high-frequency past tense forms often precede the regular past tense "-ed" by weeks or months. Overgeneralizations also began with a vengeance, within weeks or even days from the point where bound morphology first appeared. This tendency toward overgeneralization is illustrated in the following entry just before 25 months:

> Having mastered the "s" plural and the "'s" possessive, Julia had just started moving into the use of "s" for the third person singular when she apparently decided that "-s" final was a much more general principal. Now she attaches it to all kinds of forms, including: NO'S (which came in symmetrically during the transfer from YEAH to YES this week), WANT UPS and GET DOWNS, and a variety of other odd spots that I can't remember. An interesting variant two weeks ago was the sentence DADDY MAKE JULIA'S CRY. I think maybe she was trying to form an analogy with possessive structures, as in DADDY TAKE JULIA'S BOOK.

The last entries are on May 23, when Julia was exactly 26 months old. They contain a list of sentences with accompanying observations, scribbled frantically onto notepads during the week, making it obvious why the diary had to end:

> THERE'S A CLEANING LADY THERE (the first existential clause that I remember hearing)

> I GET MESSY HANDS FROM IT (a sort of passive meaning)

I TOOK MY TEMPERATURE FROM THE DOCTOR (as above, pseudo-passive meaning)

WHAT ARE YOUR COLOR EYES? (There were two or three other examples of violations of WH extraction but unfortunately I didn't write them down and can't remember them)

I DON'T HOW DO THIS (meaning I DON'T KNOW HOW TO DO THIS)

MOMMY PUT AWAY IT (followed immediately by the self correction MOMMY PUT IT AWAY).

I MADE MESS IN LIVING ROOM. . . .I MAKE MESS . . . JULIA MAKE MESS (a nice example of competition between old and new forms).

IT TASTES NOT (a comment about mustard, building on a phrase IT TASTES that she has used for weeks to mean IT TASTES NICE/GOOD).

A period of rapid grammatical growth happens between 24 and 30 months for most normal children. The above examples are fairly typical of reports in the literature. They are of interest here primarily because Julia's long avoidance of grammatical morphology seems to have forced them into a space that is even shorter than usual. If we start with her first multiword combinations at 14–15 months, Julia seems to have stayed within Stage I for at least 8 months.

Julia's acquisition of Italian. Although we have reached the end of the diary, this is not the end of the story. What we have documented so far pertains to Julia's acquisition of English. However, in the period from 20 to 24 months in Julia's life, her parents whisked her off to Rome for a winter quarter sabbatical.

To understand how Julia approached a second language, it is important to clarify the contexts in which she was exposed to English and Italian during this period. Her parents spoke English in the home, and her Italian babysitter Francesca (a college student who had acquired some English in school) spoke to Julia in English most of the time. Julia's exposure to Italian was restricted primarily to the following four situations:

— One trial week in an Italian preschool in the second month (an effort that was abandoned because Julia seemed to dislike it so much);
— Daily trips to public places (the market, the park), where Italian adults and children occasionally tried to speak with Julia (efforts that were usually translated by parent or babysitter);

— Visits to the homes of Italian friends, where both languages were spoken in an uneven mix (Italian to Julia's mother; English to Julia and her father).
— Daily lunches during the week at the home of her babysitter's parents.

The lunch context was probably the most important, because it was the only situation in which Italian was the dominant language addressed to Julia herself. Francesca's parents spoke no English at all, but became extremely fond of Julia and tried hard to engage her in conversation during their daily visits. Francesca was always present to translate, but Julia was clearly motivated to join the party.

As far as her parents could tell, Julia picked up almost no Italian at all during this 4-month stay. She showed no interest in speaking Italian when they were around, though she did seem to attend to conversations when visiting friends. Nevertheless, Bates asked the babysitter to keep a log of any Italian words or expressions that Julia produced across the sabbatical period. The log was turned over on the day of departure, when Julia's parents saw it for the first time.

This log contained some major surprises: a total of seventy-five different Italian words, reduced to sixty-five if the closed-class items within frozen expressions are eliminated from the count. Table 41 documents these Italian diary entries, compared with the thirty-four words in Julia's English repertoire at 13 months of age. Table 42 presents a breakdown of lexical statistics for Julia in her 13-month English, 20-month English, and 20–24 month Italian.

In size, Julia's Italian vocabulary falls in between her English scores at 13 and 20 months. However, a total count of seventy-five is well beyond the fifty word boundary that often marks a vocabulary burst in the second year. Particularly in view of the short amount of time that Julia was exposed to Italian, a total count of seventy-five definitely suggests that she was approaching her new language with the lexical abilities of a 20-month-old. In other words, she is not just starting from scratch. In the acquisition of verbs, Julia's Italian also seems to reflect the developmental abilities of a 20-month-old: 14% of her open-class items consisted of action verbs, compared with 17.4% verbs in English at 20 months, and no verbs at all in English at 13 months.

In every other respect, however, the data in Tables 41 and 42 seem to come from two completely different children, at opposite ends of the style spectrum.

Julia's acquisition of English was consistently referential/nominal/analytic in style at every stage of development from prespeech through grammar. She rarely imitated on line, mulled new things over at length before producing them, and winnowed out forms that failed to meet her current efforts to make language orderly. Jingles, formulas, and frozen social expressions were all rare in her early acquisition of English. New forms were welcomed primarily when Julia had finally figured out what they were for and how they worked.

Julia's acquisition of Italian appears to be the outcome of a passionate Roman holiday, with a tourist phrase book in hand. Only 24% of her lexical items are common nouns—compared with 79% at 13 months and 56.5% at 20 months in English. Counting all kinds of open-class forms together (nouns, verbs, and adjectives), she achieved an open-class style score of 82% at 13 months and 87% at 20 months in English. Compare this with a low of 37.3% open-class items in her new Italian.

Furthermore, many of the open-class items in Italian are actually embedded within social games and routines, most of them recognizably associated with a typical Italian lunchtime ritual. All of the verbs occur in the imperative form (e.g., WAIT! DON'T CRY! LOOK!), and the adjectives also occur within characteristic expressions of rebuke or praise (HOW DISGUSTING! BEAUTIFUL! NAUGHTY! QUIET!). In fact, there are three different forms of QUIET in the list: STA ZITTO (a harsher form of SHUT UP addressed to the family dog), SILENZIO (more like HUSH!), and PIANO (which means both QUIET and SOFTLY). This proliferation of terms of silence may have something to do with the siesta that Francesca's father takes after lunch, in the Italian fashion, before returning to a long evening of work. The nouns in the list are also fairly utilitarian, including JACKET and SHOES (which are the items most likely to be taken off around lunch time, and hence the object of a group search), TOWEL (always needed before and after lunch), and a predictable set of food words (BREAD, GELATO, FRAPPE, BEANS, CARROT, MANDARINS, PARMESAN, PROSCIUTTO, WATER). Others like MOUTH and NOSE are an understandable part of conversation during lunch with a 2-year-old.

A script-based analysis accounts for most of the content in the Italian list. But the same life routines were operative when Julia was acquiring English, without dominating the composition of her lexicon. Why did she behave so differently in her second language?

First of all, Julia did not seem to realize that Italian is a separate language at all. According to Volterra and Taeschner (1977), bilingual children come to the realization that they are learning two languages early in the second year. In their first fifty-word vocabularies, it is rare for a bilingual child to have two equivalent terms for the same referent (e.g., if the child has a German word for "glasses," she will not produce its Italian translation). Equivalents proliferate soon thereafter, as though the child has at last understood that the same referent can have two

Table 41. *Julia's First Words in English and Italian*

ENGLISH
Common Nouns

apple	peas
juice	cookie
cheerios	cheese
bottle	ball
blocks	book
doll	baby
car	tree
shoes	socks
bellybutton	eyes
nose	dog
bear	fish
horse	lion
monkey	sheep (behbeh)
rooster (cococo)	

Proper Nouns

Dada (mother and father)	Virginia

Nonnominals

down	this (dis)
hi	bye
nice	

ITALIAN
Common Nouns

pane (bread)	gelato (ice cream)
parmigiano (parmeasan cheese)	fagioli (beans)
carota (carrot)	mandarino (mandarin orange)
acqua (water)	frappe (seasonal cookies)
prosciutto (ham)	un altro pezzettino (another little piece)
bimbi (babies)	uomo (man)
naso (nose)	bocca (mouth)
giacca (jacket)	scarpe (shoes)
lana (yarn)	asciugamano (towel)

Proper Nouns

Mamma (mommy)	Papa (daddy)
Fulvio	Giada
Ianus (family dog)	Papa Giovanni (Pope John's picture)
Federica	Marco
Bruno	

Table 41. *Continued*

Nonnominals

ancora (again)	va bene (okay)
a cuccia (sit down, to dog)	managgia (darn it!)
che schifo (how disgusting)	aspettqa (wait!)
ciao (hi and bye)	grazie (thanks)
silenzio (hush)	ecco fatto (there, done!)
non piangere (don't cry)	metti a posto (put away)
salute (to your health)	buono (good)
buongiorno (good morning)	buona sera (good evening)
arrivaderci (good bye)	aiuto (help!)
allora (so now)	dunque (well then!)
bello	dispettoso (disrespectful)
cattiva (naughty)	guarda (look!)
sta zitto (shut up)	piccolo (little)
piano (quiet, slowly)	eccomi (here I am!)
uno, due (numbers from one to ten)	

names. They also engage in spontaneous translation from this point on, and can answer questions like HOW DO YOU SAY XXX IN GERMAN?

Of course the Volterra and Taeschner subjects were acquiring two languages simultaneously, from the very beginning. Julia was already well beyond the vocabulary burst in English when the family sabbatical began, but she gave no evidence whatsoever of a "bilingual insight." She never engaged in spontaneous translation, and seemed quite puzzled by translation requests like HOW DO YOU SAY "PANE" IN ENGLISH? or HOW DO YOU SAY "MOUTH" IN ITALIAN? Very few of the words in her Italian diary had equivalents in her concurrent English speech. Many of the named foods were new to her (e.g., FRAPPE, a kind of Italian holiday cookie), or they named foods appearing in a form that she had never seen in America (e.g., the great grey slices of Italian bread that bear virtually no resemblance to the products we buy in U.S. grocery stores). Two Italian words, BOCCA and ACQUA, showed up in her English speech; but in doing so they actually replaced their English equivalents for weeks beyond the time that the family returned to America (resulting in utterances like IN MY BOCCA, said while pointing to a candy in her mouth).

It seems fair to conclude that the referential functions of language play almost no role at all in Julia's acquisition of Italian. She did not use Italian to label, categorize, classify, or organize her cognitive world. Her

Table 42. *Lexical Statistics for Julia*

	13-Month English	20-Month English	20–24 Month Italian
Total	34	290	75
Percent common nouns	79%	56.5%	24%
Percent open class Nouns, verbs and adjectives	82%	87.2%	37.3%
Percent closed class	5.5%	7.5%	9%
Percent verbs in open class	0%	17.4%	14%

repertoire consisted almost entirely of social-regulatory expressions with no equivalent in English, and enough Italian nominals to meet her lunchtime needs. Clearly, Julia's acquisition of Italian was designed to fulfill a completely different set of functions, compared with her acquisition of English.

There are several possible explanations for an outcome of this kind. They are not mutually exclusive, and they all may have played a role.

Input. Julia's Italian vocabulary clearly reflects the lunchtime situation in which most of it was acquired. However, the input situation may account for more than vocabulary content. Italian families generally live up to their reputations: warm, lively, gregarious, centered around food and children. In cross-cultural work by Volterra, Bates and colleagues (Volterra, Bates, Benigni, Bretherton, and Camaioni, 1979), Italian 1-year-olds are often more precocious than their middle-class American counterparts; but the difference consists primarily of words and gestures acquired in social routines—the routines that are so broadly encouraged by an array of visiting relatives. Julia's English and Italian vocabularies reflect the same cultural split. Her parents used language largely as a medium of communication. In their lunches with Julia, Francesca and her family were more interested in the use of language to amuse and entertain. They cheered whenever she produced any Italian expression, engaged in explicit teaching of classic Italian baby routines, and thus ending up focusing more on linguistic form than linguistic content.

Age. We have noted that referential/nominal children tend to be somewhat more precocious in development, while pronominal/expressive children tend to be a little slower (e.g., the early and late talkers in Horgan, 1981). Julia began to acquire Italian at 20 months of age—

equivalent to some of the late starters in our English sample. The age at which a language is first acquired may play a role in determining the linguistic strategy that a child prefers to use.

Memory. One of the factors that does change with age is verbal memory: a 20-month-old can store and retrieve more linguistic material than she could at 1 year of age. This may be one explanation for the above relationship between style and age, and might account at least in part for the preponderance of multisyllabic social expressions in Julia's 20-month Italian, compared with her 13-month English.

Second language learning. Fillmore (1979) has pointed out that children who are acquiring a second language in an immersion situation tend to rely to an extraordinary extent on large formulaic frames (e.g., HOW DO YOU DO THAT MAKE TORTILLAS? GOTCHA ONE COWBOY!). These expressions allow them to "get by" in social exchange with their peers while they analyze the structure and content of the second language at their own pace. Age, memory differences, and social motivation could all account for some aspect of this second language learning phenomenon. But there may also be something special about second language learning that makes the acquisition process different the second time around. For one thing, the child already has a code available for private cognition, i.e., a way to label and categorize the world. The second language is needed for social exchange, but its referential functions are not crucial. This analysis would certainly apply to Julia's situation as well.

We are not going to opt for any of these explanations. We think they are all true, to some extent. The important point is that an extreme case of referential/analytic style can look entirely different if the context of language acquisition is radically changed—including endogenous factors like age and memory, but also exogenous factors like caretaker style and the social situation in which input is provided to the child. At no point in her Italian experience did Julia adopt a different personality or a different general theory of language. Her approach to Italian never spilled over into her doggedly analytic approach to English, even though both were going on simultaneously. Hence she represents a true dissociation between language styles, housed within a single child.

We still believe that endogenous factors play a major role in determining a child's relative emphasis on mechanisms of language learning. For example, we think it likely that Julia would have handled Italian differently if it had become her major language—for example, if she had continued to spend full days in an Italian preschool where no English was spoken. Nevertheless, her case shows that environmental factors can play a role in the development of language style that is probably underestimated by the data we have available for our longitudinal sample.

To summarize, we suggest that individual differences in early language development have to be explained at two separate levels. The underlying "base" of the individual variation observed from first words to grammar is a dissociation between two (or more) general learning mechanisms— an analytic mechanism whose primary function is to break the input down into its relevant parts, and a rote mechanism whose primary function is to store and reproduce whole forms. But we still need to explain how and why these mechanisms dissociate in normally developing children. Our current view is that the profiles illustrated in Figure 5 can be brought about in many different ways. Endogenous causes would include differential rates of maturation (associated, perhaps, with different brain systems), differences in temperament that cause the child to use one mechanism more than another (e.g., sociability or an unwillingness to make mistakes in public), differential growth in memory (which could encourage storage of whole forms), or even different auditory thresholds (i.e., a child with particularly acute hearing may tune in earlier to poorly-understood but ubiquitous closed-class words and inflections). Exogenous causes would include differences in linguistic input (e.g., exposure to speech by older children with high pronoun-to-noun ratios; exposure to input primarily from adults, with higher noun-to-pronoun ratios), and/or differences in interactive style (e.g., caretakers who engage in lots of object-oriented play; conversational partners who imitate the child's own speech). Any and all of these factors may contribute to a given child's choice of "styles," and to qualitative changes in the way the same child learns his language at different points in development. At the deepest level, however, all these separate causes operate by pulling apart basic learning mechanisms.

Chapter 17
Conclusion

We built our study around the issue of modularity, using individual differences as one way of testing theories about the componential structure of the language processor. And we want to end our discussion by reconsidering those issues in light of the present findings. However, the data are also relevant to a number of more general issues in language development. To meet all our obligations before the curtain comes down, this final chapter is organized as follows:

— First, we will present a brief summary of the findings in Studies 1–12, to refresh the reader's heavily taxed memory.
— Second, we will consider some of the more general developmental and methodological points touched on by our longitudinal results.
— Third, we will close with a discussion of the empirical evidence for and against modularity.

Summary of the Twelve Studies

We sympathize with the reader who has ploughed through twelve studies and hundreds of numbers to get to this point. If it is any comfort, it took us considerably longer to pull it all together (some of the children who started our study in 1978 may already be thinking about medical school). The following abstract of results may be helpful before we go on to a discussion of their implications for development in general and modularity in particular.

Study 1. Here we examined the emergence of first words, from 10 to 13 months, using a combination of observations and maternal report. The most important finding for our purposes was a dissociation between comprehension and production, detectable by 10 months and increasing markedly by the next session. Right away, however, the story is complicated by the fact that certain aspects of production do align with comprehension—notably the flexible use of object names across a variety of contexts. We argued that children who are high in comprehension, using their repertoire of nouns in a flexible way, have reached insight

261

into the idea that things have names. All children reach that insight eventually, but these children have arrived ahead of schedule. When comprehension and referential flexibility are partialed out, there is still considerable variance in production—apparently due to rote or routinized use of speech in the service of other social functions. **Punchline: dissociations in language functioning begin at the earliest stages of lexical development, and seem to involve rote production versus comprehension and analysis of words and their meanings.**

Study 2. Moving on to 20 months of age, we examined the psychometric structure of that classic language measure Mean Length of Utterance, or MLU. Using clusters of predictor variables from a previous study of lexical-structural development in this sample (Bretherton et al., 1983), we found that variation in 20-month MLU is due primarily to a rote or unanalyzed use of closed-class morphemes (i.e., bound inflections and grammatical function words). Our conclusion concerning the rote nature of early grammatical morphology was supported by the fact that 20-month MLU forms a continuous strand of development growing out of pure or rote lexical production at 13 months. By contrast, early comprehension and analyzed production form another continuous strand, leading into clusters that reflect semantic-conceptual sophistication in the way both single words and sentences are used at 20 months (e.g., range of semantic case relations expressed, talking about absent objects and events, answering questions in dialogue). One anomaly remained: At this point in our analyses, nominal or telegraphic constructions did not seem to fall easily into either strand. **Punchline: Variance in MLU at 20 months is contributed primarily by the rote use of closed-class morphology, and is tied to unanalyzed production from the earliest stages of lexical development.**

Study 3. Our two lexical style studies were by far the most complex and the hardest to summarize here. From a normative point of view, we showed that there is a sharp increase from 13 to 20 months in the proportion of verbs and other predicates in the lexicon. This shift is associated with the passage into multiword speech, suggesting some kind of causal relationship between the two. Verbs were also implicated in the individual difference patterns at 20 months. Referential style, or "nouniness," is no longer a characteristic of fast language learners. Instead, the most precocious children are now expanding the open class as a whole (i.e., nouns, verbs, adjectives, and certain adverbial modifiers). In general, these open-class specialists are the same children who adopted a referential style at 13 months. However, variance in early "nouniness" is not completely continuous with variance in later "verbiness." Some children in the middle ranks at 13 months seem to have used the discovery of verbs to move toward the head of the class. So verbs may afford an extra opportunity, a "booster rocket" effect that is not perfectly continuous with strands of variation at the earlier stages.

Some additional findings in Study 3 involve the relationship between reported and observed vocabulary. The two are very strongly correlated at 20 months. However, each contains some unique variance that projects off in separate directions: Parental report seems to tap into what the child *knows*, variance which is in turn associated with an analytic approach to language from the earliest stages; observed vocabulary taps into what the child typically *does*, variance that plugs into the rote production strand of development. Similar conclusions hold for the difference between verb knowledge (in the parental reports) and verb use (in the observations), although the longitudinal story is less clear.

Punchline: There is a switch in emphasis from nouns to verbs in the second year; this switch is implicated in the passage from first words to grammar in all children, but it is also a source of qualitative variations in style. In other words, verbs are "special."

Study 4. In this study, we tried to learn more about the nature of nominal style at 20 months by investigating the relationship between telegraphic speech and comprehension of plausible and implausible commands containing two or more content words (i.e., "telegraphic comprehension"). The implausible commands were particularly important, because they can only be understood by analyzing and recombining lexical items that have no a priori relationship (e.g., "Give the book to the piano"). We showed that children who produce a large number of nominal constructions are also more advanced in their comprehension of implausible commands. This correlation holds up even when various control measures are partialed out. Hence there is a "special relationship" between telegraphic production and telegraphic comprehension at 20 months. However, this small cluster of abilities did not align clearly with either of the two strands of variation that had emerged in the previous studies. At this point, we suggested two different explanations for the separate variance in telegraphic language: (1) it reflects the first stirrings of a separate grammar module that was undetectable in the first word stage, or (2) it reflects a change in working memory that occurs at 20 months, permitting children to make the passage from "one thing" to "two things" in a single cognitive act (including linguistic and nonlinguistic plans). If the first explanation were correct, we should subsequently find that children high in telegraphic language would pass more quickly into the productive use of grammar—which in fact proved not to be the case. **Punchline: There is something separate and special about telegraphic language, defined as the ability to combine content words in production and comprehension. But this special relationship seems to be specific to changes in cognitive ability at 20 months,**

changes that are in turn unrelated to grammatical development later on.

Study 5. This was our fiffin study, where we looked at individual differences in the acquisition of a novel lexical concept at 20 months. We found a dissociation between imitation of the new label and subsequent evidence for comprehension and generalization of the fiffin complex. Fiffin comprehension fell into the First Strand of language variation from first words to grammar, while fiffin imitation aligned with the Second Strand of rote processing. **Punchline: There is a link between imitation and rote processes in language acquisition. But the link seems to be restricted to imitation of a new label when it is first presented, i.e., imitation prior to understanding.**

Study 6. Here we examined MLU at 28 months, when grammatical forms are coming under productive control (i.e., in Brown's Stage II — Brown, 1973). We found very strong links between early lexical development and the structural changes reflected in later MLU. By contrast, the relationship between MLU at 20 months and the "same" measure at 28 months was very weak. Hence the meaning of MLU has changed markedly in 8-months time. We tried to derive some other structural indices to supplement the use of MLU, including two different analyses of propositional complexity. However, these indices added no new information from psychometric perspective. That is, MLU and propositional complexity at 28 months account for precisely the same variance, suggesting that the two are paced and shaped by common factors. **Punchline: Variation in structural development at 28 months is strongly predicted by variation in lexical development at the earlier stages. Because there is so much continuity from first words to grammar, we suggest that early lexical and grammatical development are paced by the same mechanisms.**

Study 7. In yet another difficult and complex study of lexical style, we found evidence for another shift in the style preferred by the most advanced children: a marked increase in the proportion of closed-class items in the child's observed vocabulary. This clearly reflects the acquisition of productive control over grammatical morphology, in the passage from Stage I to Stage II and beyond (Brown, 1973). Closed-class style at 28 months was correlated significantly and *negatively* with the "same" measure at 20 months. This constitutes further evidence that early morphology is controlled by rote mechanisms, which are at least partially dissociable from the analytic mechanisms required to attain productive control over grammar. Within the open class, the proportion of verbs has continued to grow from 20 to 28 months. Furthermore, "verbiness" is still associated with faster overall rates of learning. However, the verb effects disappear when general lexical progress is partialed out of the equation, suggesting that verbs have lost the "special," separate status they had at 20 months. **Punchline: The "main line" of lexical style from first words to grammar runs from flexible use of nouns at 13 months, to expansion of the open class as a whole at 20 months, to mastery of closed-class morphology at 28 months.**

Study 8. In this study we compared some alternative ways of calculating grammatical productivity for a set of seven bound noun and verb inflections. Each of the four criteria for productivity that we examined yielded a similar sequence of development over items, and they were also reasonably well correlated over children. In general, measures of morphological productivity fall into the First Strand of variation in language development, i.e., a lexical-conceptual strand that runs from first words to grammar. This was particularly true for a criterion that focuses on creative errors in grammatical morphology (i.e., the contrast criterion). This measure was predicted by flexible and productive use of object names at 13 months, even when variance in general vocabulary level was partialed out of the equation. **Punchline: Productivity in the use of grammatical morphemes at 28 months seems to be continuous with lexical development at every age level, including productivity in the use of object names at 1 year of age.**

Study 9. In this study we looked at the Peabody Picture Vocabulary Test at 28 months from two points of view: as a measure of lexical comprehension, and as a general control for intelligence. The measure did indeed align with variance in comprehension from 10 months onward. But it did not *define* the lexical-conceptual strand in language development. When variance in the Peabody was partialed out of correlational analyses, most of the major findings in Studies 1– 8 were unaffected. **Punchline: The strands of variation that appear in our longitudinal study are not artifacts of general intelligence—if there is such a thing.**

Study 10. Here we examined comprehension of word order and morphology at 28 months in three separate laboratory procedures. The three tests were moderately correlated with one another, but bore very little relationship to measures of grammatical production. This was true even when we restricted our analysis to comprehension and production of the same morphological structures. However, grammatical comprehension measures were predicted by measures of lexical comprehension. **Punchline: There is a sharp dissociation between comprehension and production within the domain of grammar. This dissociation maps directly onto a corresponding comprehension-production split in the lexicon.**

Study 11. This was a particularly important study, where we used factor analysis to test the Two-Strand model of development that had emerged in the ten previous chapters. At 13 months and again at 28 months, a two-factor solution does provide the best fit to the data. However, the composition of the factors changed between age levels. At 13 months, the largest factor involves comprehension and analyzed production; a second factor involves rote or unanalyzed production. At 28 months, the largest factor involves *all* measures of production, lexical and grammatical; the second, smaller factor involves *all* measures of comprehension. Twenty months seems to be a way-station between these two points. These data are best fit by a three-factor solution: a large factor composed primarily of measures that reflect lexical-conceptual sophistication in speech (i.e., analyzed production), a second factor composed primarily of comprehension measures, and a third factor made up of measures that seem to involve rote output.

We also carried out "bottom-up" factor analyses at each age level, with no limit placed on the number of factors that could appear. It was entirely possible for separate "outlier" factors to emerge in these analyses, e.g., factors based on verb use, telegraphic speech, or any other combination of lexical and structural variables. No such factors emerged. A handful of outlier measures contributed equal amounts of variance to two or more of the major factors, hence refusing to declare their party affiliation. But they did not go off on their own. Above all, there was no evidence at any point for a separate factor that could be construed as evidence for a dissociable grammar module. Instead, grammatical measures split up along the lines described above.

Turning to longitudinal analyses of these factor scores, a Two-Strand model would predict two continuous pathways of variance across age levels. But the story was in fact more complex.

One continuous pathway ran from comprehension and analyzed production at 13 months, through the isolated analytic production factor at 20 months, and linking up with both general comprehension and general production factors at the last session. This seems to be the developmental "mainline" from first words to grammar. Lexical and grammatical accomplishments share this common pathway, with comprehension weaving in and out of the factor structure as today's understanding turns into tomorrow's productive speech.

Two smaller pathways flank this main line. From 13 to 20 months, the two rote production factors were linked; but this pathway seems to disappear, unrelated to either of the summary variables at 28 months. From 20 to 28 months, there is a new and separate pathway linking the two comprehension factors. This path seems to start up fresh at 20 months, separate from the comprehension variance at the stage of first words; but it connects up with the first-word variance later on, when both factors tie into the 28-month comprehension factor.

Clearly a straightforward two-factor model is too simple to account for the results. We are left with the following: **Punchline: The factor structure from 10 to 28 months of age suggests the existence of three partially dissociable language acquisition mechanisms, which are emphasized to different degrees at different points in development. These are comprehension, rote production, and analyzed production. There is no evidence for a split between grammatical and lexical development within or across ages.**

Study 12. In the final study, we examined demographic and biosocial correlates of the language measures. Gender-related and birth-order differences were apparently not associated with language variables in this population. There was a modest relationship with temperament in the expected direction: a link between sociability and rote production, suggesting that some children use forms they do not yet understand because they want to be with and sound like other people.

In general, we found very little evidence to suggest that social factors play a major role in either rate or style of language development in this culturally homogeneous sample of children (see also Beeghly, 1981). But there is reason to believe that we may have underestimated the role of social context in our studies to date. We reviewed many of the methodological problems involved in studies of dyadic interaction, problems that may have masked social effects on language in this and other samples of children. We then went on to present a case study of one child, Julia, who had shown an extreme version of referential/analytic style from preverbal communication through the acquisition of syntax and morphology. This study validated in detail many of the conclusions we had drawn about the mechanisms responsible for style variation in early language. However, at the end we presented a surprise: a study of the first stages in Julia's acquisition of a second language, in a social context that differed radically from the one in which she first acquired English. In her acquisition of Italian, Julia was an extreme example of pronominal/expressive/formulaic style. Hence, if the context and timing of acquisition is sufficiently different, two distinct styles of language learning can clearly coexist within the same child.

The punchline for this chapter can serve as the punchline for all twelve studies:

The strands of dissociable variance observed in early language development reflect the differential operation of universal processing mechanisms that every normal child must have in order to acquire a natural language. For a variety of internal or external

reasons, children may rely more on one of these mechanisms, resulting in qualitatively different profiles of development. But all the mechanisms are necessary to complete language learning.

General Implications for Development

Normative Data

With the help of the twenty-seven children who participated in this study, we have provided a great deal of normative information about the passage from first words to grammar. Many of these findings simply confirm results from a wealth of longitudinal case studies in the language acquisition literature. Others add information that can only be obtained by examining group data. Relevant evidence in Studies 1–12 includes:

— information about the nature and range of first words in comprehension and production (Study 1);
— changes in the composition of vocabulary during the second year, from nouns to verbs to closed class morphology (Studies 1, 3, and 7);
— confirmation at the group level of an oft-suggested relationship between the vocabulary burst in the second year and a parallel shift from single- to multiword speech (Study 2);
— changes in the variables contributing to Mean Length of Utterance from Stage I to Stage II (Studies 2 and 6);
— a comparison of MLU at 28 months with two indices of propositional complexity, demonstrating a great deal of overlap between semantic and structural complexity at this age level (Study 6);
— information on the meaning of type-token ratios in the early stages of grammar (Study 7);
— a comparison of different methods for calculating grammatical productivity at 28 months (Study 8);
— a comparison of the Peabody Picture Vocabulary Test as a measure of lexical development and as a measure of general intelligence, with some general implications for the role of IQ (if there is such a thing) in language development (Studies 9 and 12);
— a detailed comparison of the inflectional morphemes that are mastered first in comprehension versus production (Studies 8 and 10).

These findings should be of some utility regardless of one's theory of the underlying developmental process. We humbly offer them to readers who are bored by our harangues about individual differences and modularity.

Continuity

We found substantial evidence supporting the case for continuity in intellectual development from infancy to early childhood (cf. Kagan, 1971; Emde and Harmon, 1984). The first principal components of our language measures were correlated from 10 through 28 months. A small set of first-word measures at 1 year of age predicted half the variance in MLU at 2 ½ years (see also Nelson, 1975; Baker and Nelson, 1984). And a combination of 13- and 20-month measures of vocabulary predicted essentially *all* the variance in this index of structural complexity during the "heart" of grammatical development.

As Bretherton and Bates (1984) have noted, language seems to be a great deal more stable than other cognitive or social measures during the infant to preschool years. And yet, as our technologies improve, evidence for continuity emerges in other domains as well. For example, tests of visual recognition memory in the first year of life predict performance on cognitive tasks several years later (Fagan and McGrath, 1981). Such findings are valuable on clinical/diagnostic grounds as early indicators of problems that might otherwise go undetected until the child enters the school system. But the growing evidence for continuity also has theoretical implications, increasing our respect for the structural integrity of the organism and the consequences of success on one task for performance on the next (Piaget, 1970).

In this regard, we have particularly good evidence for *heterotypic continuity* (Kagan, 1971; McCall, 1981) — that is, cross-age correlations between measures with superficially different content. The strong link between early lexical development and later grammar is one example. Lexical style is another. At 13 months, the most precocious children in our sample specialized in object names. At 20 months, the same children were expanding all aspects of the open class (including nouns, verbs, and adjectives). By 28 months, the most advanced children had changed their specialties once again, expanding various aspects of the closed class (e.g., pronouns, auxiliary verbs, prepositions). From this point of view, lexical style seems to have a content-independent status not unlike the notion of "fashion sense." A fashionable woman is not defined by the absolute length of her hemline, but by the length of her hemline relative to some moment in fashion history: short skirts in 1968, longer skirts in 1975, short again in 1983. Similarly, the most precocious children in our longitudinal sample are the ones who are working at the new frontiers of language at any given age level: object naming at 13 months, predication at 20 months, grammaticization at 28 months.

Conversely, these data also provide evidence for *homotypic discontinuity*, i.e., drastic changes in the meaning of a superficially similar measure at different points in time. Consider, for example, the negative correlation between closed-class style at 20 months and the same proportion scores at 28 months. Apparently this measure is picking up variance from different and perhaps opposing sources at different moments in development: an overreliance on unanalyzed or frozen forms at 20 months versus productive control of morphology at 28 months.

A similar point can be made with regard to referential style. The literature summarized in Table 1 suggested that "nouniness" would always be associated with linguistic precocity (Horgan, 1979). Instead, our data show that the meaning of "nouniness" changes over time. Referential style was a *positive* predictor of overall progress at 13 months, *unrelated* to overall progress at 20 months, and a *negative* predictor of linguistic advance at 28 months. And for all we know, the meaning of "nouniness" could change again later on. For example, Horgan's findings with 3–4-year-old children suggest that "noun lovers" are more precocious than "noun leavers" at later stages of development. Also, a high noun-to-pronoun ratio in adulthood is associated with use of the "elaborated code," i.e., the more explicit forms of speech used by middle- and upper-class adult speakers who are comfortable with written discourse (Bernstein, 1970). The point is simply this: There is no single dimension of referential style. The same measure means entirely different things, depending on when it is derived.

Methodology in Language Assessment

We hope to have convinced many skeptical readers that parental reports can be extremely useful in the early stages of language acquisition. Our 13- and 20-month interviews were validated repeatedly against concurrent behavioral data. And in many cases, these interviews were *better* predictors of later behavior than the short-term observations that are possible in a large sample study.

One reason why these interviews were successful is that they measured not only *what* the child says, but *how* he uses both lexical and grammatical elements. At 13 months, we measured total vocabulary in comprehension and production; in addition, however, we assessed the productivity and/or contextual flexibility of lexical items. Eventually, these two different aspects of the interview predicted quite different aspects of later language. Similarly, at 20 months we determined whether the child had made the transition into multiword speech, and calculated MLU. In addition, however, we also considered the function and patterning of the single- and multiword forms used by each child (i.e., the contrasts embodied in the 20-month cluster scores). Once again, these two aspects of the interview predicted different aspects of language later on. The contrasts that we sought made the interviews considerably longer and more difficult to administer. But they also gave us a richer and more valid assessment of early lexical and grammatical abilities.

Encouraged by these results, our research team has gone on to develop several different parental-report instruments for use in this age range, including modifications of the procedures used in the present study. Because we hope to develop a "Still Better Version" of our interview methods, we decided against the option of publishing the interviews we used here in an Appendix. But we would be happy to make these and subsequent parental-report instruments available to interested investigators.

A second methodological conclusion is also relevant to the issues of heterotypic continuity and homotypic discontinuity discussed above. The "same" measure can mean very different things at different points in development. Referential style at 13 months predicts grammatical development at 28 months because the two measures tap into some kind of shared mechanism, and/or because the two measures are both affected by the same external factors. Closed-class style at 20 months is negatively related to closed-class style at 28 months because the two measures tap into different and perhaps (to a limited extent) opposing factors. Type-token ratios can be positive or negative indicators of progress in language, depending on when we take the measure. *Findings like these challenge the simple linear assumptions that underlie so much developmental research.*

This point is easier to digest when we take measures at two distinct stages in development, because we expect to find changes in our sample as a whole. However, the same point can also apply to data taken within a single age, if the sample of children spans widely different developmental levels. Because our Boulder sample was so homogeneous from a medical and socioeconomic point of view, the variance within any single age level was fairly constrained. Suppose, however, that we had taken a sample of 227 children instead of 27, drawing from the greater Denver metropolitan area. And suppose, to push the point a little further, we had been fairly unselective about such factors as birth weight (including premature children under 4-5 pounds) and socioeconomic status (including children below the poverty line, with a history of inadequate nutrition and medical care). At 20 months of age a sample like this could end up spanning a much larger developmental range, including children who are the developmental equivalent of our Boulder 13-month olds. Similarly, at 28 months we might have a large number of children who are still at the stage of first words.

Under those conditions, what would happen to the pattern of linear correlations and regressions reported in this study? Some would be enhanced, but others would effectively disappear. Because our sample would contain children spanning the range from first words to grammar, predictor variables like referential style would be *positively* related to overall development (e.g., total vocabulary) at the lower end of the distribution, and *negatively* related to the same target measures at the higher end of the distribution. The resulting U-shaped relationship could not be detected by simple linear statistics, and we would end up concluding that referential style and total vocabulary are completely unrelated.

We made a similar point in Study 5 concerning the U-shaped relationship between immediate imitation and the child's level of understanding: children in the middle range are more likely to imitate "on-line," at least in certain tasks. Hence correlational studies of the relationship between imitation and some target measure may find positive results, negative results, or no results at all depending on where a particular sample falls along an underlying U-shaped distribution (see also Schwartz and Camarata, 1985).

We have argued that multivariate, psychometric studies can make an important contribution to our understanding of language and language development. But we must also add a note of caution regarding the use of linear statistics in developmental research. We have to be aware of the existence of nonlinear relationships in the data. These relationships are difficult to detect with "canned" programs; they require a detailed understanding of the developmental processes tapped by our variables and the distribution of any given sample of children around those processes.

Basic Information on Individual Differences

For those who are interested in individual differences in their own right, some new information has been offered. Like the normative findings listed earlier, these results will hopefully be of use whether or not the reader shares our interest in the modularity issue.

First, we replicated many of the dimensions reported by other investigators (e.g., referential/expressive style, nominal/pronominal style), and added information concerning their cross-age and cross-domain stability. This is a mop-up operation, to be sure, but useful nonetheless.

Second, some hypotheses concerning biosocial correlates of language differences were tested. This effort was in many ways the most disappointing. There was no evidence for either gender-related or birth-order differences, in contrast with some claims in the literature (although our finding is certainly not unequivocal). And, in reviewing other studies we have carried out with the same children, we find little evidence for strong effects of maternal style on either quantitative or qualitative dimensions of language development (cf. Furrow and Nelson, 1984). However, we did find some support for the notion that endogenous social factors like temperament may play a role in the degree to which children emphasize different language styles. And our follow-up study of Julia showed that extreme differences in the language learning environment can have a major effect on style, even in the very same child.

Above all, we provided a unified test of the Two-Strand theory proposed in most reviews of the individual differences literature. Although the two-strand notion received partial support, the total picture is much more complex (Study 11). At least *three* factors are required to account for the longitudinal data: *comprehension, analyzed production*, and *rote production*. And there may well be other dissociations that we missed because they simply were not measured adequately in our study. We think that we have brought a little more order and coherence to the range of proposals reviewed in Chapter 4. But there is still ample room for more exploratory research, including detailed case studies, to uncover other patterns of variation and their possible causes.

Cross-Linguistic Implications

The conclusions we have reached here are of course restricted to children learning English. But our model of the underlying processes responsible for these dissociations provides a series of clear hypotheses for cross-linguistic research (Snow and Bates, 1984).

To offer one example, consider the issue of verb use during the transition from first words to grammar. It has been noted that English children are particularly likely to omit verbs during the telegraphic stage (e.g., Bloom, 1970). At least two different explanations have been offered for this pattern:

— Verbs are morphologically more complex than nouns, and hence avoided until the problems of morphology are worked out.
— Verbs express complex semantic relationships that are relatively late in development. Because these relationships are so complex, the child first expresses them in a syncretic, unanalyzed form by simply naming one or more of the associated nouns (e.g., MOMMY SOCK).

However, the verb-omission pattern itself may not be universal. MacWhinney and Bates (1978) have shown that there are cross-linguistic differences in the frequency of verb omission, using an experimental situation in which all children were describing the same set of pictures. Verb omission was significantly less likely to occur in Italians, compared with either English or Hungarian children in the same age range.

Why should this be the case? Italian verbs are much more complex morphologically than the same verb forms in English, so these cross-linguistic differences in verb omission cannot be due to avoidance of difficult morphemes. And the pictures used in this experiment tapped verbs of equivalent semantic complexity in all three languages, so that the cross-linguistic differences cannot be accounted for on semantic grounds. The difference seems to be due to the informativeness of verbs in Italian, compared with the other two languages. Italian and Hungarian both permit a great deal of word-order variation compared with English. But Hungarian has case inflections on the noun that help the listener figure out "who did what to whom." Italian has no case inflections to compensate for variations in word order; instead, information about the identity of the subject is carried primarily by agreement markers on the verb. As a result, Italians cannot *afford* to omit the verb. The pressure to produce verbs is reflected in the behavior of children as young as 2 (see also Bates, 1976). It might also play a role during the second year, when verbs are first acquired. If there is heavy communicative pressure to acquire verbs and their associated inflectional morphology, we may find that verbs appear earlier in lexical development for Italian children. And we might also find considerably less stylistic variation among Italian 20-month-olds in proportions of verb use.

There are also reasons to expect cross-language differences in the relative use of nouns and pronouns. The nominal/pronominal contrast was first discovered by Bloom et al. (1975) in a study of the development of personal pronouns in English-speaking children during the first stages of multiword speech. If our analysis of these differences is correct, the use of personal pronouns by expressive/pronominal children reflects a reliance on rote processes. In his effort to sound like other people, the expressive child tends to reproduce the highest frequency forms in the linguistic input—whether he understands them or not.

In English, such a strategy would necessarily result in a proliferation of subject pronouns. But there are languages in which we might make very different predictions. For example, Italian is what is currently called a "pro-drop" language: If the identity of the subject of a sentence can be taken for granted, the subject is not mentioned at all. In roughly 70% of the utterances in informal discourse, Italian adults omit the subject altogether (Bates, 1976). In the remaining 30%, most of the subjects are full noun phrases that have to be mentioned for the listener to understand a point. So an Italian might say the equivalent of "Went to the store" or "John went to the store," but only rarely "He went to the store." When subject pronouns are used, they are typically used for emphasis of a particular kind, similar in function to the use of contrastive stress in a sentence like "Surely you don't mean that *I* have to go?"

The implications for a language-learning child should be clear: Because full pronouns are in fact not so frequent in Italian, they should not form part of the cluster of morphemes acquired by a rote/imitative mechanism at 20 months of age. In fact, because full pronouns are used for a highly informative and emphatic purpose, they may actually be acquired earlier by children who rely more on analysis for understanding.

These are only two examples of some directions for cross-linguistic research that follow from the individual difference literature. Many more are possible, and could add a great deal to our understanding of language variation. Cluster analyses similar to those reported by Bretherton et al. (1983) could be carried out in a variety of languages to determine the degree to which individual differences in language revolve around particular kinds of *content* (which could be constant across languages) or particular kinds of *mechanisms* (which might control different content depending on the structure of the language). What parameters of variation are possible in a language like Mandarin Chinese, where grammatical morphology is close to nonexistent? (Erbaugh, 1982). What happens in a language like Turkish, where case inflections are crucial for sentence interpretation, and cannot be ignored by an "information-sensitive" mechanism aimed at analysis-for-understanding?

Cross-language research gave us our first insights into the fact that normal children do not all acquire language the same way. Research in the last decade has also established the parameters for variation within a single language. It is now time to put the two research efforts together. By examining cross-linguistic "variations in variation," we may be able to specify the full range of patterns that are possible in the passage from first words to grammar.

Implications for Clinical Research

We have argued throughout that individual differences can provide evidence about the biological substrates of language. There is, for example, a particularly tantalizing parallel between the dissociations observed in early grammar (e.g., nominal versus pronominal style) and the dissociations observed in Broca's and Wernicke's aphasia. If these superficially similar dissociations do have a common neural basis, we should find analogous patterns in children with disturbances of language, tying together the literatures on normal children and adult aphasics.

Consider, for example, the clinical phenomenon of congenital dysphasia or specific language delay (e.g., Leonard, 1979; Snyder, 1978, 1982; Johnston, 1981). By definition, the congenitally dysphasic child is impaired in language despite apparently normal progress in other aspects of cognition. Most clinical investigators have concluded that the syndrome involves *delay* rather than *deviance.* That is, the children have normal profiles of language abilities for their "linguistic age." But if their patterns are indeed "normal," exactly which portion of the normal range are we talking about? One of the typical symptoms is telegraphic speech, i.e., omission of function words. In this sense, the congenitally dysphasic child seems like a slow motion version of referential/nominal style. Is the range of individual variation also normal in congenitally dysphasic children? Or does this syndrome represent a truly "Broca-like" pattern, a pathological extreme of the referential/nominal end of the continuum?

There is no early childhood version of a fluent Wernicke's aphasia (Hecaen, 1976). But there are two syndromes that could represent an extreme version of "pronominal style." First, there is the phenomenon of "echolalia," a tendency to repeat adult speech in a meaningless way, almost without modification. This rote/imitative form of language is particularly common in autistic children although some investigators have argued that echolalia often does serve a pragmatic purpose of some kind (e.g., Baltaxe, 1977). The existence of echolalia does certainly argue for the "separability" of imitation from other aspects of language development. However, the echolalic child tends to reproduce utterances intact, preserving both content and function words. In that sense, it is very different from the relatively empty formulaic speech of an extreme pronominal/expressive child. A second syndrome, sometimes called "the Cocktail Party Syndrome," seems to bear a closer relationship to the holistic/pronominal side of normal processing (Tew, 1975). This syndrome is often found in hydrocephalic children with relatively low IQs; in fact, it is less common among hydrocephalic children with IQs near the normal range. As described by Tew, the child with Cocktail Party Syndrome seems to chatter endlessly and inappropriately, with a high proportion of formulas, cliches, and empty pronominal forms, mixed in with apparently "novel" bits of conversation that might well have been derived from something overheard the day before. Although this speech is inappropriate, it is not echolalic; in particular, fragments of sentences are often modified grammatically to fit the current conversational context. Note that there is nothing like a Cocktail Party Syndrome in children as young as the ones that we have studied here (mentally, linguistically, or chronologically). Instead, it seems to happen in children who at least have a mental age of four years or more (a point that we will pursue in more detail shortly). Nevertheless, the syndrome may represent a pathological variant on expressive/pronominal style, involving a dissociation of neurobehavioral mechanisms similar to the ones used by normal children during language acquisition.

To learn more about the neural mechanisms controlling normal and abnormal development, it would be useful to study children with specific forms of focal brain damage. Although we know that children recover extremely well from early forms of brain damage, there are still residual forms of language dysfunction that show up in laboratory testing (Dennis and Whitaker, 1976). This is true even when the children have had many years to develop compensatory strategies for language processing. The differential effects of focal brain damage might be clearer still if we could study the *process* rather than the *products* of early language acquisition. There is, as we noted in Chapter 4, considerable speculation about the interhemispheric and intrahemispheric bases of differences in language style. If there is anything to these claims, we might expect variations in style (perhaps even extreme variations) as a function of lesion site. For example, left-hemisphere damage could predispose a child to develop something akin to pronominal/expressive style. Alternatively, variations in style might result primarily from the anterior-posterior locus of brain damage: a more telegraphic style in children with anterior lesions, and a more holistic style in a child with posterior damage.

Research with clinical populations has always given us information about the variations in language development that are possible outside the normal range. It has also given us information about the neural substrates of linguistic and nonlinguistic processors. This brings us at last to the case for modularity, in particular the case for an innate and hardwired division between grammar and semantics.

The Case for Modularity

We did find evidence for the idea that language acquisition is carried out by partially dissociable mechanisms. However, these mechanisms cut across the content domains of language: analytic versus rote processing, comprehension versus production. In Fodor's terms, these are *horizontal faculties*. There was no evidence whatsoever for a division between grammar and semantics, i.e., a division reflecting vertical faculties peculiar to language. Indeed, we found repeated evidence that lexical development and grammar are closely linked within and across stages of development.

Now and then the case for autonomous grammar seemed hopeful. For example, at 20 months there seemed to be something special and separate about multiword constructions, in both comprehension and production, setting them apart statistically from single-word semantics and from the two-strand picture that had emerged up to that point. It seemed possible that this might constitute the first stirrings of an independent grammar module. However, if this were the case, we would expect some continuity from the unique variance in telegraphic speech to structural complexity and grammatical productivity later on. But this just did not happen. All the correlations between telegraphic speech and later grammar were accounted for entirely by shared variance in lexical development.

This led us to offer another explanation for temporary "separateness" of multiword constructions. As noted by Shore et al. (1984) and Shore (1981), there is a special link at 20 months between nominal multiword speech and the ability to combine two gestures in a single act of symbolic play. The statistical relationship between these two abilities holds up when variance in single-word vocabulary is removed, so it is not just an epiphenomenon of "verbal fluency" or some vague notion of intelligence. By 28 months, this "grammatical" relationship between language and gesture has disappeared. Shore et al. conclude that the 20-month link derives from a general shift in working memory and/or motor planning, from "one thing" to "two things" (see also Sugarman, 1983). Hence the special status of multiword constructions at 20 months may constitute evidence for yet another kind of horizontal faculty, with effects that hold at only one stage of development. This is the kind of "local homology" that we have proposed for many years to characterize the relationship between language and nonlinguistic aspects of cognitive development (Bates et al., 1977 and 1979).

We also considered the possibility that verbs play a separate and special role in the development of grammar. As Bloom (1981) has pointed out, verbs serve as a bridge from semantics to grammar, providing a way of encoding the relational meanings that have emerged during the one-word stage. Of course this should be true for every child. However, our data suggest that some children make more use of this bridge than others. Specifically, some children in the middle ranks at the stage of first words seem to exploit the special properties of the English verb (which carry a large number of grammatical morphemes) to "bootstrap" their way into grammar and to move (at least temporarily) toward the head of the class on several related measures. However, this temporary advantage is short-lived and narrow in its range of application. That is, the "verb advantage" (such as it is) does not explain any variance in later grammatical development that is not accounted for entirely by vocabulary totals. Ultimately, then, this turns out to be one more aspect of a powerful lexical factor that controls most of the variance in grammatical development in this age range.

Yet another candidate for a "special" grammatical module was suggested in the dissociation between closed- and open-class morphology at 20 months (embodied in the contrast between the nominal multiword cluster and the grammatical morpheme cluster in both the interview and the observations). Gleitman and Wanner (1982) have argued that the child's ability to separate open- and closed-class morphemes constitutes a special kind of preparation for the task of language acquisition. If this is true, however, it is not clear how the early dissociation leads into grammar. First of all, there was (as noted) actually a *negative* correlation between closed-class style at 20 and 28 months, suggesting that the early "discovery" of grammatical function words offers no advantage at all in their eventual mastery. And by 28 months, when grammatical morphemes are finally used in a productive way, the dissociation between the two vocabulary types has disappeared entirely (evidenced in the fact that cluster analyses at 28 months yielded only a single lexical factor). We stick by our conclusion that the use of inflections and function words in Stage I reflects an overreliance on rote, unanalyzed forms that has little to do with later grammar and may actually impede progress (at least in the short run). In fact, this conclusion is buttressed by Gleitman and colleagues' own results (Gleitman et al., 1984). They have shown that certain closed-class morphemes (notably auxiliary verbs) are particularly vulnerable to frequency and type of modeling by the mother, a finding that they use to argue for the child's innate tendency to discover the separateness of open- and closed-class vocabulary. However, a careful examination of their findings suggests that most of this effect is located in their youngest subjects—at an age and developmental level corresponding roughly to our 20-month sample. In other words, the modeling effect may be temporary, and may be one more symptom of the tendency for some children to use inflections and function words inside of frozen or semianalyzed forms at the earliest stages of development. In short, their findings may also have nothing to do with the eventual conquest of "true" grammatical morphology.

This does not mean that rote processes are "bad for children." As we have stressed repeatedly, both rote and analytic factors are necessary to learn a natural language. The relationship that we have found here between analytic style and precocity derives not from the *presence* of rote learning in some children, but from the relative *absence* of deeper analysis in a few children with highly skewed proportion scores. In fact, high rates of early closed-class usage—combined with high usage of analytic processes—characterize our most precocious children. Our superstar Boy One, described in Study 12, achieved his near-poetic use of English at 28 months through a judicious combination of productive analysis and storage of long adult forms. For present purposes, the point is that he applied both of these learning mechanisms at every stage of development to a similar degree, from first words through the productive conquest of grammar.

We will conclude that there is no evidence for a division between grammar and semantics at the earliest stages of language development, up through 2 ½ years of age. To account for the strong link between lexical and grammatical development (despite dissociations along other "horizontal" lines), one or more of the following statements must be true:

1. Grammar and semantics proceed apace because they have to use each other's *products*.
2. Grammar and semantics are yoked together because they involve the same *processes*.
3. Grammar and semantics may each have unique products and/or unique processes; however, both of them are paced by and vulnerable to one or more shared "outside" mechanisms (e.g., some kind of horizontal resource or control mechanism that both must use, such as short-term memory or differences in temperament and a basic approach to problem solving).
4. Grammar and semantics are influenced to a similar degree by common environmental factors (e.g., variations in the richness of the child's linguistic input).

These four explanations are certainly not mutually exclusive. However, they all violate at least some of the criteria for modularity proposed by Gardner and Fodor—notably the criteria of mutual impenetrability and separate developmental histories.

One can never prove the null hypothesis. We certainly do not claim to have proven the *nonexistence* of vertical language modules. However, we have demonstrated some extraordinarily strong links between lexical and grammatical development at the early stages—despite robust evidence for other kinds of dissociations in language development. One might argue that we failed to look carefully enough at grammar, and that more interesting dissociations between grammar and semantics might show up on some kind of item-by-item basis. And yet, even when we examined inflectional morphemes one at a time in Studies 8 and 10, the most striking finding was a dissociation between comprehension and production—evidence which mitigates against the notion of a central, unified grammatical processor (Caramazza, Basili, Koller, and Berndt, 1981). There are only so many ways to measure grammar in a two-year-old child, and we tried in good faith to use them all: MLU, density of grammatical morphemes (i.e., closed-class style), various measures of morphological productivity, and structured tests of morphological and syntactic comprehension. As a group, these children were simply too young to give us any further information. If a grammar module is at work during the passage from first words to grammar, only two conclusions are possible:

— It cannot be measured in this age range.
— It cannot be dissociated empirically from lexical development.

In either case, the hypothesis becomes untestable—and Occam's razor dictates that we accept a theory that postulates fewer separate entities over a theory with untestable arguments.

Suppose, for the moment, we accept the conclusion that grammatical and lexical development are inseparable during the early stages. It is still entirely possible that some kind of modular division between grammar and semantics will appear further on down the road. To consider the implications of this argument, let us take a journey down three logical paths:

1. **The maturation hypothesis.** There are innate modules devoted especially to the different subcomponents of language, but they involve more complex aspects of grammar, and they mature much later in language development than the period we have covered here;
2. **The construction hypothesis.** Domain-specific language modules exist, but they are not innate; instead, they must be constructed and exercised over time in order to attain a modular status.
3. **Total interactionism.** There are no vertical modules within the language processor; evidence in favor of such modules can be reinterpreted in terms of horizontal architecture.

The Maturation Hypothesis

There is at least one kind of modern linguistic theory that is entirely compatible with our findings, in particular the class of *lexicalist grammars* (e.g., Bresnan, 1982; see Newmeyer, 1980, for a review). There is in fact a tendency in all the major syntactic theories, including recent versions of Government and Binding theory (Chomsky, 1980), to account for many grammatical phenomena in the lexicon. This is because so many grammatical rules seem to apply quite stubbornly to only a subset of possible lexical items. One example should suffice to make the point. Consider a rule called dative movement, which describes the relationship between the following two sentences:

John gave money to the church.

John gave the church money.

If grammatical rules were "blind" to lexical content, this rule should apply to any verb that takes three arguments (i.e., subject, direct object, and indirect object). And yet the rule apparently cannot apply to sentences like the following:

John contributed money to the church.

*John contributed the church money.

Apparently some verbs (e.g., "give") can take dative movement, but other verbs (e.g., "contribute") cannot. There seems to be no way to account for this difference without somehow building rules into the lexicon. As researchers in the generative grammar movement worked out the detailed implications of their theory throughout the 1970s, more and more examples like these cropped up. A variety of different theories were subsequently proposed to account for all these uncomfortable exceptions to the rule, but they all have one thing in common: A great deal of grammatical work has to be handled by the same "module" or "processor" or "unit" or "place" that handles the interpretation and assignment of individual lexical items or words. In other words, according to the lexicalist movement in modern grammatical theory, we should *expect* a close relationship between vocabulary learning and the acquisition of grammar.

But this argument can only be pushed so far. Although most modern theories, including Chomsky's own, contain a healthy measure of lexicalism, only the most radical theories have done away altogether with the division between lexical and grammatical structure. In particular, many of the phenomena that characterize recent work in Government and Binding theory pertain to constraints on *Wh*-movement and anaphora that supposed to hold for *all* sentences regardless of the lexical items that occupy a given sentence slot. For example, the "pure" grammatical component sets limits on the kinds of elements that can be moved "up the chain of command" to the *Wh*-word position in sentences like the following:

John saw Peter

Who did John see?

John saw Peter and Mary

*Who did John see Peter and?

Though many aspects of the grammar may indeed have to mingle with lexical assignment, Chomsky believes that these constraints on the "government and binding" of noun phrases operate on abstract grammatical symbols, without interference by or consultation with the lexicon.

Notice, however, that the structures and rules within the "pure" non-lexical component of the grammar are really very complex. That is, they tend to be forms that are simply not used by children under 30 months of age. There could be an independent grammar module responsible for "chain of command" phenomena in complex sentences, meeting all the criteria for modularity outlined by Gardner, Fodor, and others. However, such a module is not relevant in the age range we have examined here, and if it exists at all, we should expect it to "kick in" much later in language acquisition.

At the moment, evidence for a late-maturing syntax module is still rather slim. First of all, a maturational approach would dictate reasonable age limits on the point at which the requisite grammatical structures first appear in normal children. And yet the supposed maturation point for many of the target phenomena in Government and Binding theory has been reported at ages ranging from 2 to 3 years (Crain and McKee, in press) up into junior-high-school age (Wexler, 1986; Matthei, 1978). Second, the parameter-setting version of Government and Binding theory implies that new principles will appear rather suddenly in a given child's language. However, results by Matthei and by Deutsch, Koster, and Koster (1984), suggest that the course of development for many of the proposed binding phenomena is quite protracted and error-filled. Third, the current maturational version of the theory suggests that certain errors will *never* occur in child language, in particular errors that violate basic principles of Universal Grammar. The child will either (1) fail to produce the linguistic forms to which a principle applies, or (2) obey the principle completely once it has been invoked. And yet, there are already reports in the language literature suggesting that violations of universal principles do occur during language acquisition. Examples include

What are we cooking on a hot?

(one of many such violations of *Wh*-extraction reported by Peters, 1983), or

What do horses sweat through their?

reported by M. Bowerman (personal communication, 1985).

Even if the maturational course of grammatical development is not as clean as its proponents might hope, there is enough data on the relationship between grammar and semantics in adult native speakers to support the view that some kind of grammar module does eventually exist. This brings us to a second proposal, concerning the gradual construction of vertical language modules.

The Construction Hypothesis

Many forms of receptive and expressive grammatical processing seem to "run off" in an autonomous and unconscious way in normal adults; as Garrett notes, "parsing is a reflex" (cited in Fodor, 1983). For example, a skilled adult reader will slow down processing immediately after an error in grammatical morphology, even though he is unable to detect that error consciously when asked to "proofread" a passage presented rapidly on a CRT screen (Schweikert and Garrett, research in progress; Wright and Garrett, 1984). There is also some evidence from adult aphasics suggesting that a fluent control of grammatical form can be dissociated from semantic knowledge: Broca's aphasics have impaired access to grammatical morphology but normal or near-normal control over content words; Wernicke's aphasics produce long and fluent phrases with intact morphology even though their comprehension and production of content words is grossly impaired. How can we put this evidence for modularity together with our own developmental findings?

In our view, the best way to salvage the argument for vertical modules in language acquisition can be summarized in the dictum: *Modules are not born; they are made.*

An independent and ultimately "impenetrable" use of grammar is slowly constructed, piece by piece, practiced endlessly until it becomes as effortless and routine as any other fully acquired perceptual-motor skill. Only at this point will we find the kind of evidence for autonomy of grammar cited by Fodor and Gardner. Several different lines of evidence support this interpretation.

The conscious nature of language "practice" in young children. Weir (1962) was perhaps the first to note that young children tend to "practice" or play with possible word combinations and inflectional forms in crib speech, when the constraints of communication are removed and language becomes one of many toys. Although one can never prove that a process is "conscious," it is difficult to imagine what else to call the buildup and breakdown of grammatical forms evidenced in this and other studies of solitary speech. Apparently grammatical forms *are* accessible to consciousness in the phase in which they are acquired, although it may eventually be very difficult to "think about" those forms once they become automatic. Julia's heavy concentration on the internal structure of the word BIRD makes the same point in the domain of phonology (Study 11).

The nonautonomy of grammar in second language learning. More evidence has accumulated in the last few years to suggest that an automatic control over both lexical and grammatical processing has to be acquired all over again in a second language (Favreau and Segalowitz, 1983). If grammar has the status of a routinized grammatical skill, with an autonomy that is not innate but acquired, this is exactly what we ought to expect.

The developmental onset of jargon aphasia. The most impressive evidence for the potential autonomy of grammar comes from the hyperfluent but totally empty speech of Wernicke's aphasics. In this regard, it is very interesting that fluent aphasia does not appear to occur in very young children (Hecaen, 1976). And yet very early versions of Broca's aphasia have been amply documented. In other words, young children are capable of losing what grammar they have; but they are apparently not capable of producing that grammar in isolation, at least not until grammatical processes have been practiced long enough to function on their own.

Age limits on linguistic savants. There are a number of rare cases reported in the literature in which a child's linguistic abilities far outstrip his performance on other cognitive tasks (Kempler and Curtiss, 1984; Bellugi, Browning, and Blakemore, 1984). As Gardner notes, the existence of such "savants" constitutes particularly good evidence for the autonomy or modularity of an "intelligence." And yet there is an interesting limitation on the savant phenomenon in language: The child's remarkable abilities in language do not become evident until he reaches some baseline in cognitive abilities, equivalent to that of a normal child between 2 and 4 years of age. Perhaps one needs the cognitive abilities of a preschool child to "build" a grammatical module, mapping the grammar onto some minimal lexical-semantic support system. However, once that system is built it may break free of the cognitive yoke and burst forward.

Grammar and other skills in Alzheimer's disease. Several recent studies have shown that patients with Alzheimer's disease preserve a remarkable degree of control over grammatical morphology and word order long after they have degenerated to the point of having nothing further to say (Schwartz, Marin, and Saffran, 1979; Kempler, 1984). In fact, one patient studied by Schwartz et al. produced long strings of jargon with only one content word ("shopping center") serving as an all-purpose noun, verb, and adjective. However, Kempler also notes that this preserved use of "empty" grammar is accompanied by a preservation of many other over-learned motor skills (e.g., driving, dressing, certain simple aspects of cooking). He suggests that grammar may in fact *be* an overlearned perceptual motor skill. Of course the preserved grammar is productive, in the sense that the patient "tunes" morphology correctly to fit new utterances (even when he is repeating something that he doesn't understand at all). And yet, in some sense, the same thing is true for other motor skills: We adjust our driving, walking, and other movements to the particular demands of the situation without giving it any thought at all (e.g., avoiding other pedestrians on the sidewalk). In just that sense, the preservation of a modular grammatical processor may constitute a flexible and productive set of integrated reflexes. Like other motor skills, it has to be mastered with great effort and considerable experience; however, once mastered it is just like riding a bicycle—that is, very hard to lose.

In short, we might well find evidence for a new dissociation between grammar and semantics if we could follow our children for a few more years. The complex patterns of dissociation outlined in Study 11 show that dissociations do indeed come and go. There is, then, no reason whatsoever to deny the possibility that yet another dissociation could emerge down the line.

Our major point is, that the early stages of language acquisition are characterized primarily by dissociations among *horizontal faculties* in Fodor's terms: analytic versus holistic processing, comprehension versus production. Vertical faculties may develop later, but they are probably learned rather than innate. In this sense, they would meet Fodor's first six criteria, but not the biological criteria that he finds interesting. Similarly, Gardner was probably premature in concluding that syntax and phonology are separate and modular, while semantics lies closer to general intelligence. This may be true long after language acquisition is underway. In the early stages, however, there is a very close relationship between lexical and grammatical learning. And if Vihman (1981) is correct, the same can be said for the development of phonology, where individual differences in style of learning are correlated with analogous patterns in grammar and semantics.

Total Interactionism

At the moment, we tend to favor the Construction Hypothesis as a way of unifying developmental data with adult evidence for the separability of grammar and semantics. However, our own data is equally compatible with the Total Interactionism Hypothesis—that is, with the idea that all aspects of language functioning can be accounted for with a mix of horizontal faculties that are shared with other content domains. For that reason, we think that the Total Interactionist position deserves a fair hearing.

No one could deny that the content and organization of language is "special," qualitatively different from any other human activity. The question is, can we account for the acquisition and use of eccentric language structures without invoking a special and impenetrable set of processors to handle those structures? The question is still completely open. There are, however, those who believe that the question is entirely closed. Three of the strongest empirical arguments in favor of vertical language modules (constructed or otherwise) include the following:

— the dissociations between grammar and semantics observed in aphasia;
— the impenetrable and obligatory nature of lexical access in on-line studies of adult processing;
— the eccentric nature of phoneme perception in infants and adults.

Let us examine each of those arguments in turn, to determine whether or not the Analogy–Anomaly debate has finally been solved in the twentieth century.

Dissociations in Aphasia. Aphasiologists have long noted a striking contrast and an apparent complementarity between Broca's and Wernicke's aphasia. This contrast has provided some of the most compelling evidence in modern times for a dissociation between grammar and semantics.

Broca's aphasia is characterized by slow and effortful speech, reduced length and complexity of sentence structure, and omission and/or substitution of inflections and grammatical function words. The following example from Bates, Hamby, and Zurif (1983b) is typical, taken from an English-speaking patient trying to describe a three-picture sequence of a cat giving flowers to a boy, a dog, and a rabbit:

Cat is flower . . . give boy, dog, rabbit.

Despite their severe production deficits, these patients do seem to be able to understand most of the language addressed to them by their families and by clinical interviewers. The syndrome usually results from damage to a particular area in the left anterior quadrant of the brain, i.e., Broca's area. Because this area of cortex lies next to the motor strip, and because the syndrome seems to be restricted to difficulty with speech output, Broca's aphasia was traditionally viewed as a *motor aphasia.*

This characterization makes neuroanatomical sense, but it now appears to be too simple. In the 1970s a large body of evidence accrued suggesting that comprehension is *not* intact in these patients. When they are not allowed to rely on semantic and pragmatic information, Broca's aphasics demonstrate an inability to use precisely the same grammatical forms that are missing or impaired in their speech production (Caramazza and Zurif, 1978; Berndt and Caramazza, 1980). For example, they can understand a sentence like

The apple that was eaten by the boy was red.

but fail on semantically-reversible sentences of equivalent complexity, such as

The girl that was chased by the boy was tall.

As such, Broca's aphasia seems to constitute prima facie evidence for the selective impairment of grammar—and hence the best evidence to date for a separate, hard-wired grammatical module.

Wernicke's aphasia is characterized by fluent and sometimes hyperfluent speech, with a normal melodic line, in the presence of moderate to severe deficits in comprehension. This syndrome is usually associated with damage in the left posterior quadrant of the brain, i.e., Wernicke's area. Because Wernicke's area is located between auditory cortex and a variety of sensory association areas, and because comprehension seemed to be so seriously impaired, this syndrome was classically viewed as a *sensory aphasia*.

However, this sensible neuroanatomical characterization proves once again to be too simple. The expressive language of a Wernicke's aphasic is fluent, but it is far from normal. Patients with posterior damage suffer from particularly severe impairments in word finding. As a result, their speech tends to be semantically "empty"—filled with circumlocutions, pronouns, and other vague or nonspecific terms. In severe cases, the patient may produce what are called *paraphasias*, i.e., substitutions of an inappropriate word for the intended item, blends of two or more words associated with the target, and/or invented words that are uninterpretable hash. The following example from Bates et al. (1983b) illustrates the problem, taken from a patient describing the same three picture sequence of a cat giving flowers to a boy, a dog and a rabbit.

> The little boy is talking to the goody—no—it is a cappy—capatter, it is a cappy, no, cat. It is a cat, that's a cat. And he is taking the plowel, pull—no—follow—flower, flower. The catty is giving the flower and there is a dog that likes the—the dog is giving the flower to that—it is a . . . a dog, flower, and a bunnet, bun . . . bunker, bunther, bun, banther, bather, batter [*Experimenter cues "bunny rabbit"*]. And the dog is doing with the flower, the dog is doing the flower to the bagette, rabbit—and this rabbit, he has a flower which he is giving to the dog.

Given such severe problems of lexical access, coupled with a comprehension problem, researchers in the 1970s argued that Wernicke's aphasia may constitute a *semantic* rather than a *sensory* disorder. Hence the existence of both Broca's and Wernicke's aphasia seemed to constitute a double dissociation between grammar and semantics.

Other forms of aphasia have been reported, but these do not fit easily into the same linguistic framework (Lesser, 1978). For example, conduction aphasia is a syndrome characterized by impairment in the patient's ability to repeat linguistic material—despite sparing of both comprehension and production in spontaneous language. Repetition also plays a role in two other aphasias: transcortical sensory aphasia (spared repetition despite comprehension impairments) and transcortical motor aphasia (spared repetition despite impairments in spontaneous production). This three-way dissociation of comprehension, production, and repetition made sense within the classic neuroanatomical/connectionist view of aphasia. They seemed to reflect all the logically possible forms of damage and disconnection among a speech-motor component of some kind (around Broca's area), an area of auditory-sensory associations (around Wernicke's area), and relays connecting auditory inputs directly into their articulatory equivalents (permitting repetition with or without an ability to understand and produce the associated content). However, once aphasiologists began to characterize the two major aphasias in terms of grammar and semantics, it became less obvious how to classify dissociations involving repetition—unless, perhaps, they could be shown to involve a phonological module of some kind.

This linguistic characterization of aphasia was widely accepted in Britain and the United States until very recently, when the whole concept of "agrammatism" came under fire (Badecker and Caramazza, 1987; Miceli and Mazzucchi, in press; Goodglass and Menn, 1985). As stated succinctly by Caramazza et al., (1981a, p. 348):

> Although it is possible that Broca patients may suffer from deficits in addition to this syntactic processing deficit, it should be the case that all patients classified as Broca's aphasics will produce evidence of a syntactic impairment in all language modalities.

This is an exceptionally clear prediction—but it is also a prediction that has been rapidly falsified. There are several case studies of patients who show agrammatic symptoms in production, but not in comprehension (Naeser, Haas, Auerbach, Helm-Estabrooks, and Levine, 1984; Miceli, Mazzucchi, Menn, and Goodglass, 1983; Kolk, Van Grunsven, and Keyser, 1985). There are also reports of patients who show agrammatic symptoms in comprehension even though their production is quite fluent (Caramazza, Berndt, Basili, and Koller, 1981b; Smith and Bates, in press; Bates, Friederici, Miceli and Wulfeck, 1985a; Bates, Friederici, Miceli, Wulfeck, and Juarez, 1985b). Finally, patients who are agrammatic in both comprehension and production have proven to retain a surprising degree of sensitivity to violations of grammaticality (Linebarger, Schwartz, and Saffran, 1983; Wulfeck, 1984). In view of findings like these, Badecker and Caramazza (1987) have recently suggested that "agrammatism is not a natural kind," i.e., there is no such thing as a unitary syndrome of grammatical impairment.

If grammar is not selectively impaired, what about evidence from posterior patients suggesting that grammar can be selectively spared? In fact, this case was never conclusively proven, because it is so difficult to prove the existence of an intact parser in a patient with severe receptive language problems. Some investigators report that Broca's aphasics actually perform better than Wernicke's aphasics on judgments of grammaticality (e.g., Milberg, Blumstein, and Dworetzky, 1985), and on comprehension tasks that require the patient to make use of strictly grammatical cues (Bates et al., 1985a, 1985b). Other investigators have claimed that Wernicke's do perform better than Broca's aphasics, in a small set of carefully controlled studies of on-line sentence processing (Swinney, Zurif, Fosenberg, and Nicol, 1984). Still other reports have emerged suggesting that Broca's and Wernicke's are both impaired in grammar, but in qualitatively different ways (e.g., Linebarger, Schwartz, Saffran, and Pate, 1985; Pate, 1985).

Blumstein and colleagues have tried to unify these findings by proposing that Broca's aphasics do better on the more controlled or reflective aspects of language processing, while Wernicke's aphasics have the advantage in tasks that require an automatic, unconscious use of the same linguistic devices (Milberg et al., 1985; Blumstein and Milberg, 1983). Notice, however, that a dissociation between automatic and controlled modes of access is quite different from a dissociation between two linguistic content domains. Arguments concerning the modularity of grammar and/or semantics can be salvaged only by redefining each module in ways that are specific to particular modalities or modes of processing.

A similar conclusion is reached by Kempler (1984) in describing the spared grammatical abilities of Alzheimer's patients. These patients also demonstrate severe disruptions of lexical-semantic processing in both comprehension and production. However, their spontaneous speech is grammatically quite normal, compared with controls matched for age and education level. In this last respect, their abilities exceed those of Wernicke's aphasics, who generally produce a more restricted range of syntactic structures despite their apparent fluency. Nevertheless, Kempler's patients performed quite poorly on tests of grammatical comprehension and on a sentence repetition task that seemed to invoke some kind of metalinguistic awareness. As long as their grammatical performance is automatic, based on lifetime habits of speech, the demented patients do very well; but the same grammatical information is not accessible in all modalities, nor in tasks requiring some reflection.

Where does this leave us? The classic neuroanatomical characterization of aphasia actually provided a reasonably good fit to our own developmental data. The orthodox view involved a potential dissociation involving comprehension, production, and some form of repetition-without-understanding. Our data suggest that the possible lines of dissociation in young children involve comprehension, analyzed production, and rote production based on imitation and/or shallow forms of analysis. The new aphasia literature seems to be moving back in a similar direction: dissociations between comprehension and production that cut across grammar and semantics, and dissociations involving automatic versus controlled access over the same linguistic forms.

It is too early to say whether or not we will ultimately find a good fit between our developmental findings and the lines of dissociation observed in brain-damaged adults. The question is still open. But that is precisely the point: We cannot yet conclude, on the basis of dissociations observed in adult aphasics, that the brain is organized into hard-wired modules devoted to particular kinds of linguistic content.

Lexical Access in Normal Adults. In the 1970s, there was a veritable cottage industry devoted to demonstrating effects of context on language processing (Danks and Glucksberg, 1980; Clark and Clark, 1977). This included effects of word and sentence context on the perception of phonemes (e.g., Warren and Warren, 1970), effects of the sentence and discourse context on perception and/or anticipation of whole words (e.g., Marslen-Wilson, 1975), effects of semantic content on perception of syntactic structure (e.g., Slobin, 1966), and effects of a global narrative context on memory for sentence form (e.g., Bransford, Barclay, and Franks, 1972). "New Look" theories based on top-down language processing were so dominant for so long that it was difficult to envision how any kind of non-interactionist view of language would ever arise again.

The modular approach has become feasible again, despite evidence of context effects, because of two changes in our view of the way that language modules can interact.

First, for a variety of reasons we cannot review here, serial processing views have been abandoned for a parallel processing approach in which individual subcomponents go about their business and worry about getting together later. These parallel processes can be integrated into a single output in one of two ways: by sending their individual products to some kind of "general executor," or by communicating with one another directly (Marslen-Wilson and Tyler, 1980; Rumelhart and McClelland, 1982, 1986). The debate between modularists and interactionists focuses not on the existence of parallel processing (which is now almost universally accepted), but on the nature of the integration process—in particular, on the extent and timing of communication between various components.

In this light, modular theories have considerable heuristic value, by offering constraints on communication between separate parallel processing components (Chapter 2). But if the notions of "impenetrability" and "encapsulation" are to have any meaning at all, a certain amount of seriality must be retained. By definition, autonomous components can deal with each other's *products*, but they cannot interfere with or contribute to the internal computations required to arrive at those products. So, for example, a phonological speech processor must work in a completely "bottom-up" fashion, making decisions based on the acoustic data; context effects on phoneme perception should occur only after the first-pass results of phonemic analysis have been handed up the line. Similarly, a modular lexical processor should activate all the information associated with a particular lexical string, automatically and obligatorily; higher-order effects on word processing may occur very fast indeed, but only after the lexical processor has completed its first analysis. In the same fashion, a modular parser should build all the syntactic structures that fit with a given string of lexemes and morphemes; higher order context effects can begin to operate only after the parser has offered some results. The overall framework is one of "quasiparallelism," a cascade in which individual components make a rapid, data-driven analysis of the data and pass their products on to any other module that might be interested. The key point is that context cannot *pre-select* or *activate* a set of lower-order representations; instead, context operates to *select* (albeit very rapidly) from a set of representations that emerge from the reflexive and obligatory operation of various modular input systems.

Which brings us to the second reason why modular approaches are once again in ascendance: the development of so-called "on-line" techniques for studying the temporal course of language processing. The wealth of context effects that were demonstrated in the last two decades almost all involved what are now called "off-line" techniques. The subject was required to make some kind of decision, but there was virtually no information about the point in processing at which the requisite decision was made. Hence we cannot determine whether a given context effect involved top-down activation (in line with interactionist theories) or selection after bottom-up, data driven access (in line with modular theories). With the availability of micro-processors to control stimulus presentation and record response, experimenters are now able to ask questions about the moment-to-moment details of language processing (i.e., "What did the listener know, and when did he know it?"). So, in principle, it is now possible to tease apart the claims of modular and interactive theories.

Or so it seemed. In fact, the application of on-line techniques has been fraught with methodological and conceptual problems. The most serious problem is this: Proponents of modularity often find themselves predicting null effects, i.e., predicting that a given context effect will *not* occur, or that it will occur only at some later point in processing. Alas for the modularist, there are many unintended ways to obtain such a null effect. The contextual manipulation might be too weak to give the hypothesis a fair test. The number of items and/or subjects may be too few to yield the statistical power required to find an interaction. Or, worse still, the experimenter may be looking at processes that are down at the human reaction time floor, making it impossible to detect any subtle effects. An example comes from a series of studies by Seidenberg and colleagues (Seidenberg and Tannenhaus, in press; Seidenberg, Tannenhaus, Leiman, and Bienkowski, 1982). They have shown that context effects do occur when word processing is measured in a lexical-decision paradigm, where the subject decides whether a target string is a word in the English language; but the same contextual manipulation has no effect when subjects are simply asked to name the target letter string (i.e., read the string aloud—see also Stanovich and West, 1979). Because naming is much faster than lexical decision, Seidenberg et al. argue that naming reflects a "true" rapid, automatic lexical-access process; by contrast, the slower process of lexical decision is a kind of metalinguistic, post-access behavior that operates on the product of an encapsulated lexical module. But there is an alternative explanation: naming is much *too* fast, bringing us down to the reaction time floor where effects have to be extremely strong if we are going to detect them at all.

The case for modularity would be easier to establish if it involved some *positive* predictions. In this regard, let us consider an influential series of experiments on the processing of ambiguous words (Swinney, 1979; Onifer and Swinney, 1981; Oden and Spira, 1983; Seidenberg et al., 1982; Kintsch and Mross, 1985). According to the *multiple access model* of lexical processing, ambiguous words will automatically and obligatorily access all their associated meanings—regardless of the sentence context. Hence, in the first moments after an ambiguous word like BUG is perceived, it will prime or activate words associated with both of its meanings (e.g., SPIDER and ANT as well as MICROPHONE or SPY), resulting in faster reaction times to these target words compared with unrelated control words (e.g., CHAIR or STADIUM). Soon thereafter, however, context may select one of the two meanings and discard or inhibit the other. After that point, priming from the ambiguous word should affect only those words that are associated with the contextually appropriate meaning. This is, in fact, exactly what researchers have found in a series of experiments across modalities (e.g., visual-visual and auditory-visual) and across response paradigms (e.g., lexical decision and naming). They have concluded that lexical access is an automatic, completely obligatory bottom-up process that cannot be over-ridden or short-circuited by contextual expectations. This constitutes excellent positive evidence for lexical modularity.

But there are still two problems with this conclusion. The first has to do with an issue raised in Chapter 2 on the size of the module responsible for this effect. Proponents of the multiple-access view have assumed that the obligatory, automatic-access effect derives from the operation of a "macro-module," i.e., a large bounded processor with jurisdiction over all individual lexical items. Suppose, however, that each individual word operates as a self-contained processing unit or "micro-module," a word demon or word expert that listens for itself in the input and activates everything in its domain when its name is called (e.g., Morton, 1970). Thousands of these individual word modules would behave exactly like one large lexical module in experiments like the one described above, giving evidence of multiple access for ambiguous word stimuli.

The second problem is an empirical one, raised in a recent paper by Van Petten and Kutas (1987). These investigators used event-related brain potentials (ERPs) to investigate the time course of priming effects associated with ambiguous words. In their first experiment, they replicated the behavioral effects shown by other investigators for materials of this kind: priming for both meanings of an ambiguous word at a short stimulus onset time, but priming only for the contextually appropriate meaning with a longer interval between the prime and target words. In the second experiment, they studied the brain waves associated with priming at both the short and long inter-stimulus interval. The advantage of the ERP technique is that it permits us to watch the brain's reaction to stimuli during the complete interval *prior* to the 600–900 millisecond point at which a subject can register any kind of behavioral response (e.g., pressing a button, saying a word aloud). In this and other experiments by the investigators, priming effects for unambiguous words begin around 200 milliseconds, with a positive slow potential that grows in magnitude and continues for the next few hundred milliseconds. By contrast, unexpected or unprimed words elicit a negative potential that begins around the same time and reaches its peak magnitude somewhere between 300–500 milleseconds. In the ambiguous word experiment, if the multiple access view is correct, then evidence for priming (i.e., positive waves) should appear simultaneously for both the contextually appropriate and the inappropriate meaning of an ambiguous word prime in the short inter-stimulus condition. But results did *not* support this multiple access prediction. For the first 400 milliseconds, the brain showed priming effects (i.e., positive waves) only for contextually appropriate targets. Reactions to contextually inappropriate targets looked exactly like reactions to an unrelated control word (i.e., negative waves) up until around 400–500 milliseconds—when the waves suddenly began to move in a positive direction, as though the subject had noticed a relationship that had not occurred to him before. By the time the brain waves moved into the 700 millisecond region (i.e., the region at which multiple access effects are observed for both meanings of a word in behavioral experiments), both meanings did show the positive waves associated with priming.

Van Petten and Kutas suggest that this pattern is consonant with the phenomenon of "backward priming" (Kiger and Glass, 1983; Glucksberg, 1984; Glucksberg, Kreuz, and Rho, in press). In their interpretation of multiple access effects, Glucksberg et al. have argued that activation of the contextually inappropriate meaning of an ambiguous word does not begin until the subject reads a target word. For example, given a sentence context associated with electronic surveillance, the prime word BUG would only prime targets associated with its "hidden microphone" meaning. Hence there would initially be no recognition advantage for target words like SPIDER. However, *after* the reader is presented with the SPIDER target, activation flows backward to BUG and primes the INSECT reading—which in turn ricochets forward to speed up and confirm recognition of SPIDER. Because backward priming involves this kind of back-and-forth flow of activation, it should only be detectable when the interval between prime and target is very short—and hence the so-called multiple access effect would (as its proponents predict) take place only in the first few moments of lexical processing. This crucial processing window cannot be observed directly in behavioral studies, because so much time is needed to martial the requisite behavioral response. But it can be observed in the ERP paradigm, permitting us to choose between the multiple access hypothesis and the backward-priming alternative.

If the brain and mind first activate only the contextually appropriate reading for an ambiguous word, then multiple access is not an obligatory process. Instead, it can be viewed as an artifact created by the priming paradigm itself. And if multiple access is not an obligatory, encapsulated, automatic process, then modularists have lost some of the best evidence to date for their position.

However, the Van Petten and Kutas evidence is new, and the ERP technique has not yet been exploited to its full advantage in studying the temporal microstructure of language processing. It offers a considerable advantage in taking us down below the reaction time floor that we have reached with behavioral techniques like phoneme monitoring and naming. But it may present methodological and theoretical problems of its own that defeat this apparent challenge to modularity. Recently, Fodor (1985, p. 36) met some related criticisms of modularity with his usual panache, as follows:

> I think that [the critic] considerably underestimates the polemical resources available to the antiinteractionist position. This game isn't going to be won by flourishing a fact or two.

Despite the menacing tone of this remark (or perhaps because of it), the point is well taken. Facts change rapidly in the field of psycholinguistics, particularly when technologies are being applied for the first time. We would simply like to point out that the case for modularity remains to be established, one way or another, in research on real time language processing in normal adults.

Eccentricity. The two sources of evidence for modularity that we have just reviewed involve Fodor's criteria for dedicated neural processors (i.e., the evidence from aphasia), and the processing criteria of speed, encapsulation, and mandatory operation. A very different kind of argument for the psychological separateness of language or any other domain revolves around its *eccentricity*. Certain kinds of content may be so utterly peculiar and intractable that they can only be handled by special processors. This case is all the more compelling if the processes themselves have properties that distinguish them from garden variety perception and cognition.

A paradigm case for arguments based on eccentricity can be found in the study of human speech perception (Aslin, Pisoni, and Jusczyk, 1983; Kuhl, 1986). When investigators first began to examine the acoustic properties of human speech in the 1950s and 60s, they were surprised to find no obvious mapping between physics and experience, in contrast with the lawful psychophysical relationships that had been discovered in so many other perceptual domains (Liberman, 1982). The two major problems were a lack of *linearity* and *invariance*.

Linearity refers to the assumption that a physical stimulus unfolds in time in a way that corresponds to our phenomenal experience of that stimulus. So, for example, it sounds as though the noises that distinguish "ka" from "da" come at the front of the syllable. Unfortunately, this is not the case. Somewhere between the physical input and our phenomenal experience, there seems to be a process of transformation or recoding, so that bits and pieces of energy that come after the onset of the stimulus are made to sound as though they occurred at the beginning.

Invariance refers to the assumption that an invariant psychological entity (e.g., the "k" sound in both "ka" and "ku") corresponds to an invariant physical entity, i.e., a physical unit that is just as similar across contexts as it seems to be when we hear it. But this assumption is also violated by human speech. The burst of energy that distinguishes a "k" sound before an "a" does not look at all on spectographic analysis like the pattern that distinguishes a "k" before a "u." But unfortunately the "k" part of a "ka" *does* look like the burst that distinguishes a "d" before a "u." Furthermore, if any of these bursts is presented to human listeners with the vowel context that normally follows excised, the listener experiences something that sounds like an unrelated, nonlinguistic "chirp."

In short, the units of speech perception are quite unlike the units of sound, light, smell, etc. that have made psychophysics an orderly science. Corresponding to this peculiar domain, the process of speech perception in humans also seems to have some eccentric properties. Most notable is the phenomenon of *categorical perception*. Stimuli like "pa" and "ba" differ primarily along what is called Voice Onset Time (VOT), referring to the relationship between the time at which the listener opens her lips and the time at which the vocal chords begin to vibrate. VOT is a continuous dimension, and artificial stimuli can be created that arbitrarily vary the amount of time between these two pieces of the speech signal. Nevertheless, listeners are apparently unable to hear continuous differences between pairs of speech stimuli. Instead, they hear an abrupt change from "ba" to "pa" that occurs at a particular point along the VOT continuum (i.e., when the vocal chords start vibrating at +25 milliseconds after the burst). Stimuli that come from within the "ba" region all sound alike, as do stimuli from within the "pa" region. Hence human speech perception seems to involve sharp and discontinuous boundaries that are quite unlike the Gaussian distributions found for so many other perceptual categories (e.g., color).

Not only did the process of categorical perception appear to be an eccentric aspect of human speech perception, evidence on the perceptual abilities of very young infants suggested that the phenomenon is probably innate (e.g., Eimas, Siqueland, Jusczyk, and Vigorito, 1971). At this point, we seemed to have adequate evidence to conclude that human beings are born with special perceptual abilities adapted entirely for speech.

But of course, if categorical perception is indeed speech specific, then we would not expect it to occur in other species. In addition, if this phenomenon is truly unique to speech, then human beings should not show a similar pattern of response to stimuli from other domains. However, studies have appeared in the last decade that bring both of these claims into question. Kuhl and Miller (1975) showed that chinchillas have a sharp perceptual boundary for speech sounds, at roughly the same point where the boundary is located in human perception; the phenomenon has since been demonstrated in several other species, for several different phonemic contrasts (see Kuhl, 1986, for a review). Furthermore, categorical perception has now been demonstrated for several different kinds of nonlinguistic stimuli—including pairs of pure tones that differ in onset time and flicker-fusion boundaries in the visual modality (Aslin et al., 1983). The phenomenon now appears to be a general property of perceptual discriminations aimed at resolving the temporal difference between two discrete stimuli. Particular temporal resolution boundaries will be dictated by the absolute perceptual threshold for each stimulus together with the differential threshold in that modality. In other words, categorical perception is not, after all, an eccentric or inexplicable process. Nor is it unique to humans. It is innate in human infants for acoustic rather than linguistic reasons.

Because we could not understand how human infants perceive the speech signal, we rushed too quickly to the view that speech perception is special and innate. There are of course many other idiosyncratic properties of human speech perception, which deserve the same kind of rigorous test that was finally given to the phenomenon of categorical perception. It may yet prove to be the case that speech perception is an eccentric domain, and that it requires the application of special processors that evolved entirely for that purpose (Liberman and Mattingly, 1985). And the same may also be true for the acquisition and use of grammar. Nevertheless, the lesson of categorical perception should not be lost on us as we set about trying to explain language learning.

Punchline

Eccentricity should always be the argument of last resort in any science. If a scientist is actively looking for intractible phenomena, and wants to prove that his subject matter defies further analysis, then he will almost always succeed—at least in the short run. If nothing else, he can cast his phenomenon in a notation that obscures any possible resemblance to anything else that we understand. In the worst case, he may become so obsessed with the notion of eccentricity that he adopts an academic Scorched Earth Policy—refusing to leave anything behind that his opponents could possibly explain or use (cf. Chapter 2).

We think that it is better scientific policy to assume that any phenomenon can be shown to belong to a more general family of facts. This approach is particularly wise when we are dealing with biological processes that had to evolve from simpler beginnings. For this reason, we have cast our lot with Aristotle and the Analogists, trying to understand language development within a more general framework of cognition, perception, and learning. Anomalism is a defeatist philosophy, a bad place to start no matter where we ultimately have to end up.

In our efforts to understand the passage from first words to grammar we have applied a multivariate method that has at least as many critics as fans. The particular results presented here will have to undergo a process of replication, extension, and revision that may change the story as we have presented it here. It is entirely possible that our findings will, in a very short time, look just as quaint as the etymological speculations the Analogists used to prove their point. But we remain convinced that the patterns of variation shown by individual children contain rich information about universal mechanisms of language learning. By looking at the way that things come apart, under normal or abnormal conditions, we can see more clearly how they were put together in the first place.

REFERENCES

Anderson, J. R., & Bower, G. H. (1973). *Human Associative Memory*. Washington, D. C.: V. H. Winston and Sons.

Aslin, R., Pisoni, D., & Jusczyk, P. (1983). Auditory development and speech perception in infancy. In M. Haith & J. Campos (Eds.), *Handbook of Child Psychology: Infant Development*. New York: Wiley.

Badecker, W., & Caramazza, A. (1987). On considerations of method and theory governing the use of clinical categories in neurolinguistics and cognitive neuropsychology: The case against agrammatism. *Cognition*. 20, 97-115.

Baker, N., & Nelson, K. (1984). Recasting and related conversational techniques for triggering syntactic advances by young children. *First Language,* 5, 3–22.

Baltaxe, C. (1977). Pragmatic deficits in the language of autistic adolescents. *Journal of Pediatric Psychology,* 2, 176–180.

Barnes, S., Gotfreund, D., & Wells, G. (1983). Characteristics of adult speech which predict children's language development. *Journal of Child Language,* 10, 65–84.

Bates, E. (1975). Peer relations and the acquisition of language. In M. Lewis and L. Rosenblum (Eds.), *Friendship and Peer Relations*. New York: Wiley.

Bates, E. (1976). *Language and Context: The Acquisition of Pragmatics*. New York: Academic Press.

Bates, E., Benigni, L., Bretherton, I., Camaioni, L., & Volterra, V. (1977). From gesture to the first word. In M. Lewis and L. Rosenblum (Eds.), *Interaction, Conversation and the Development of Language*. New York: Wiley.

Bates, E., Benigni, L., Bretherton, I., Camaioni, L., & Volterra, V. (1979). *The Emergence of Symbols: Cognition and Communication in Infancy*. New York: Academic Press.

Bates, E., Bretherton, I., Beeghly-Smith, M., & McNew, S. (1982a). Social bases of language development: a reassessment. In H. Reese and L. Lipsitt (Eds.), *Advances in Child Development and Behavior,* Vol. 16. New York: Academic Press, 8–68.

Bates, E., Bretherton, I., Shore, C., & McNew, S. (1983a). Names, gestures and objects: symbolization in infancy and aphasia. In K. Nelson (Ed.), *Children's Language,* Vol. IV. Hillsdale, N. J.: Lawrence Erlbaum, 59–123.

Bates, E., Camaioni, L., & Volterra, V. (1975). The acquisition of performatives prior to speech. *Merrill-Palmer Quarterly*, 21, 205–226.

Bates, E., Friederici, A., Miceli, G., & Wulfeck, B. (1985a). Sentence comprehension in aphasia: a cross-linguistic study. Manuscript, University of California, San Diego.

Bates, E., Friederici, A., Miceli, G., & Wulfeck, B., & Juarez, L. (1985b). Word order and syntactic complexity in aphasia: Evidence from English, Italian and German. Manuscript, University of California, San Diego.

Bates, E., Hamby, S., & Zurif, E. (1983b). The effects of focal brain damage on pragmatic expression. In D. Kimura (Ed.), Special issue on neuropsychology. *Canadian Journal of Psychology*, 37:1, 59–84.

Bates, E., & MacWhinney, B. (1979). A functionalist approach to the acquisition of grammar. In E. Ochs and B. Schieffelin (Eds.), *Developmental Pragmatics*. New York: Academic Press.

Bates, E., & MacWhinney, B. (1982). Functionalist approaches to grammar. In E. Wanner and L. Gleitman (Eds.), *Language Acquisition: The State of the Art*. New York: Cambridge University Press.

Bates, E., & MacWhinney, B. (1987). Competition, variation and language learning. In B. MacWhinney (Ed.), *Mechanisms of Language Learning*. Hillsdale, N. J.: Lawrence Erlbaum.

Bates, E., MacWhinney, B., Devescovi, A., Caselli, C., Natale, F., & Venza, V. (1984). A cross-linguistic study of the development of sentence interpretation strategies. *Child Development*, 55, 341–354.

Bates, E., McNew, S., MacWhinney, B., Devescovi, A., & Smith, S. (1982b). Functional constraints on sentence processing: a cross-linguistic study. *Cognition*, 11, 245–299.

Bates, E., O'Connell, B., Vaid, J., Sledge, P., & Oakes, L., (1986). Language and hand preference in early development. *Developmental Neuropsychology*. 2(1), 1–15.

Bates, E., & Rankin, J. (1979). Morphological development in Italian: connotation and denotation. *Journal of Child Language*, 6, 29–52.

Bates, E., & Snyder, L. (1987). The cognitive hypothesis in language development. In I. Uzgiris and J. McV. Hunt (Eds.), *Research with Scales of Psychological Development in Infancy*. Champaign-Urbana: University of Illinois Press.

Bates, E., Whitesell, K., Oakes, L., & Thal, D. (1987). Integrating language and gesture in infancy. Manuscript, University of California, San Diego.

Bauer, P. (1985). *Referential and expressive styles in linguistic and non-linguistic domains*. Unpublished Doctoral Dissertation, Miami University of Ohio, Oxford, Ohio.

Beeghly, M. (1981). *Consistency and change in dyadic behavior: A developmental study of style and context*. Unpublished Doctoral Dissertation, University of Colorado.

Beeghly, M., & Bates, E. (1984). Situation differences in toddlers' use of grammatical and lexical forms. Paper presented to the Boston Conference on Child Language, Boston, October 1984.

Beeghly, M., Weiss, B., & Cicchetti, D. (1985). Structural parallels between symbolic play and language in children with Downs Syndrome. Paper presented at the Tenth Annual Boston University Conference on Language Development, Boston, October 1984.

Bellugi, U. (1967). *The acquisition of negation.* Unpublished Doctoral Dissertation, Harvard University.

Bellugi, U. (1984). Personal communication.

Bellugi, U., Browning, J., & Blakmore, A. (1984). A dissociation between language and visualspatial functioning in a child with William's Syndrome. Manuscript, The Salk Institute for Biological Studies, La Jolla, California.

Benedict, H. (1979). Early lexical development: comprehension and production. *Journal of Child Language,* 6, 183–200.

Berko, J. (1958). The child's learning of English morphology. *Word,* 14, 150–177.

Berndt, R.S., & Caramazza, A. (1980). A redefinition of the syndrome of Broca's aphasia: Implications for a neuropsychological model of language. *Applied Psycholinguistics,* 1, 225–278.

Bernstein, B. (1970). A sociolinguistic approach to socialization: With some reference to educability. In F. Williams (Ed.), *Language and Poverty.* Chicago: Markham.

Bickerton, D. (1984). The language bioprogram hypothesis. *The Behavioral and Brain Sciences,* 7:2, 173–187.

Block, E., & Kessel, F. (1980). Determinants of the acquisition order of grammatical morphemes: a reanalysis and reinterpretation. *Journal of Child Language,* 7, 181–188.

Bloom, L. (1970). *Language Development: Form and Function in Emerging Grammars.* Cambridge, Mass.: MIT Press.

Bloom, L. (1973). *One Word at a Time: The Use of Single Word Utterances Before Syntax.* The Hague: Mouton.

Bloom, L. (1981). The importance of language in language development: linguistic determinism in the eighties. In H. Winitz (Ed.), *Foreign and Native Language Acquisition. Proceedings of the New York Academy of Sciences.* New York: New York Academy of Sciences.

Bloom, L., Hafitz, E., & Lifter, K. (1980). Schematic organization of verbs in child language and the acquisition of grammatical morphemes. *Language,* 6, 386–412.

Bloom, L., Hood, L., & Lightbown, L. (1974). Imitation in language development: If, when, and why? *Cognitive Psychology,* 6, 380–420.

Bloom, L., Lightbown, P., & Hood, L. (1975). Structure and variation in child language. *Monographs for The Society for Research in Child Development,* 40 (Serial No. 160).

Bloomfield, L. (1933). *Language.* New York: Henry Holt. (Reprinted in 1961.)

Blumstein, S., & Milberg, W. (1983). Automatic and controlled processing in speech-language deficits in aphasia. Symposium on Automatic Speech. Academy of Aphasia, Minneapolis, October 1983.

Bohannon, J., & Marquis, A. (1977). Children's control of adult speech. *Child Development,* 48, 1002–1008.

Bowerman, M. (1973). Structural relationships in children's utterances: Syntactic or semantic? In T. Moore (Ed.), *Cognitive Development and the Acquisition of Language.* New York, Academic Press, 197–214.

Bowerman, M. (1982). Reorganizational processes in lexical and syntactic development. In E. Wanner and L. Gleitman (Eds.), *Language Acquisition: The State of the Art.* Cambridge: Cambridge University Press.

Bowerman, M. (1985). Personal communication.

Braine, M. D. S. (1976). Children's first word combinations. *Monographs of the Society for Research in Child Development*, 41:1, Serial Number 164.

Branigan, G. (1977). If this kid is in the one word stage, so how come he's saying whole sentences? Paper presented at the Second Annual Boston University Conference on Language Development, Boston, September 1977.

Bransford, J., Barclay, R., & Franks, J. (1972). Sentence memory: A constructive versus interpretive approach. *Cognitive Psychology*, 3, 193–209.

Bresnan, J. (Ed.) (1982). *Mental Representation of Grammatical Relations.* Cambridge, Mass.: MIT Press.

Bretherton, I., & Bates, E. (1984). The development of representation from 10 to 28 months: differential stability of language and symbolic play. In R. Emde and R. Harmon (Eds.), *Continuities and Discontinuities in Development.* New York: Plenum.

Bretherton, I., Bates, E., Benigni, L., Camaioni, L., & Volterra, V. (1979). Relationships between cognition, communication, and quality of attachment. In E. Bates, L. Benigni, I. Bretherton, L. Camaioni, & V. Volterra (Eds.). *The Emergence of Symbols: Cognition and Communication in Infancy.* New York: Academic Press.

Bretherton, I., Bates., E., McNew, S., Shore, C., Williamson, C., & Beeghly-Smith, M. (1981a). Comprehension and production of symbols in infancy. *Developmental Psychology*, 17, 728–736.

Bretherton, I., McNew, S., & Beeghly-Smith, M. (1981b). Early person knowledge expressed in gestural and verbal communication: When do infants acquire a "theory of mind"? In M. Lamb and L. Sherrod (Eds.), *Infant Social Cognition.* Hillsdale, N. J.: Lawrence Erlbaum.

Bretherton, I., McNew, S., Snyder, L., & Bates, E. (1983). Individual differences at 20 months: Analytic and holistic strategies in language acquisition. *Journal of Child Language*, 10, 293–320.

Bretherton, I., O'Connell, B., Shore, C., & Bates, E. (1984). The effect of contextual variation on symbolic play: Development from 20 to 28 months. In I. Bretherton (Ed.), *Symbolic Play: The Development of Social Understanding.* New York: Academic Press.

Brown, R. (1968). *Words and Things.* New York: Free Press.

Brown, R. (1973). *A First Language: The Early Stages.* Cambridge, Mass.: Harvard University Press.

Bridges, A. (1979). Directing two-year-old's attention: some clues to understanding. *Journal of Child Language,* 6, 211–226.

Bybee, J., & Slobin, D. I. (1982). Rules and schemas in the development and use of the English past tense. *Language,* 58, 265–289.

Campos, J., Barrett, K., Lamb, M., Goldsmith, H., & Stenberg, C. (1983). Socioemotional development. In M. Haith and J. Campos (Eds.), *Infancy and Developmental Psychobiology.* Vol. II of P. Mussen (Ed.), *Handbook of Child Psychology.* New York: Wiley.

Caramazza, A., & Berndt, R. (1978). Semantic and syntactic processes in aphasia: A review of the literature. *Psychological Bulletin,* 85, 898–918.

Caramazza, A., & Berndt, R. (In press). A multi-component deficit view of agrammatic Broca's aphasia. In M. L. Kean (Ed.). *Agrammatism.* New York: Academic Press.

Caramazza, A., Basili, A., Koller, J., & Berndt, R. (1981a). An investigation of repetition and language processing in a case of conduction aphasia. *Brain and Language,* 14, 235–271.

Caramazza, A., Berndt, R., Basili, A., & Koller, J. (1981b). Syntactic processing deficits in aphasia. *Cortex,* 17, 333–348.

Caramazza, A., & Zurif, E. (Eds.). (1978). *Language Acquisition and Language Breakdown.* Baltimore: Johns Hopkins University Press.

Carlson-Luden, V. (1979). *Causal Understanding in the 10 Month Old.* Unpublished Doctoral Dissertation, University of Colorado, Boulder.

Carroll, J. B. (1985). On Spearman's "problem of correlations." *Behavioral and Brain Sciences,* 8:1, 39–40.

Case, R., & Khanna, F. (1981). The missing links: Stages in children's progression from sensori-motor to logical thought. In W. Fischer (Ed.). *New Directions for Child Development.* San Francisco: Jossey-Bass.

Chapman, R. (1981). Exploring children's communicative intents. In J. Miller (Ed.), *Assessing Language Production in Children.* Baltimore: University Park Press, 111–139.

Chapman, R., & Kohn, L. (1978). Comprehension strategies in two- and three-year-olds: animate agents or probable events? *Journal of Speech and Hearing Research,* 21, 746–761.

Cattell, R. B. (1971) *Abilities: Their Structure, Growth and Action.* Boston: Houghton Mifflin.

Chomsky, N. (1957). *Syntactic Structures.* The Hague: Mouton.

Chomsky, N. (1959). Review of B. F. Skinner *Verbal behavior. Language,* 35, 26–57.

Chomsky, N. (1965). *Aspects of a Theory of Syntax.* Cambridge, Mass.: MIT Press.

Chomsky, N. (1980). *Rules and Representations.* New York: Columbia University Press.

Chomsky, N. (1981). *Lectures on Government and Binding: the Pisa Lectures.* Dordrecht: Foris.

Clark, E. (1985). The acquisition of Romance, with special reference to French. In D. I. Slobin (Ed.), *The Cross-linguistic Study of Language Acquisition.* Vol. I, 687–782. Hillsdale, N. J.: Lawrence Erlbaum.

Clark, E. (1983). Meanings and concepts. In J. Flavell and E. Markman (Eds.), *Handbook of Child Psychology, Vol. III.* New York: Wiley, 787–840.

Clark, H. (1973). The language-as-fixed-effect fallacy: a critique of language statistics in psychological research. *Journal of Verbal Learning and Verbal Behavior,* 12, 335–359.

Clark, H., & Clark, E. (1977). *Psychology and Language.* New York: Harcourt, Brace, Jovanovich.

Clark, R. (1974). Performing without competence. *Journal of Child Language,* 1, 1–10.

Clark, R. (1977). What's the use of imitation? *Journal of Child Language,* 4, 341–358.

Cohen, S., & Beckwith, L. (1979). Preterm infant interaction with the caregiver in the first year of life and competence at age 2. *Child Development,* 50, 767–776.

Corrigan, R. (1978). Language development as related to Stage 6 object permanence development. *Journal of Child Language,* 5, 173–189.

Crain, S., & C. McKee (in press). Acquisition of structural restrictions on anaphora. *Northeastern Linguistic Society Proceedings, Vol. 16.*

Curtiss, S., & Yamada, J. (1978). Language and cognition. Paper presented at the Third Annual Boston University Conference on Language Development, Boston, September, 1978.

Dale, P. (1976). *Language Development: 2nd edition.* New York: Holt, Rinehart & Winston.

Danks, J., & Glucksberg, S. (1980). Experimental psycholinguistics. *Annual Review of Psychology,* 31, 391–417.

DellaCorte, M., Benedict, H., and Klein, D. (1983). The relationship of pragmatic dimensions of mothers' speech to the referential-expressive distinction. *Journal of Child Language,* 10, 35–44.

Dennis, M., & Whitaker, H. A. (1976). Language acquisition following hemidecortication: Linguistic superiority of the left over the right hemisphere. *Brain and Language,* 3, 404–433.

Deutsch, W., Koster, J., & Koster, C. (1984). What can be learned from children's errors in understanding anaphora? Manuscript, Max Planck Psycholinguistics Institute, Nijmegen, Holland.

DeVilliers, J. G., & DeVilliers, P. A. (1973). A cross-sectional study of the acquisition of grammatical morphemes in chld speech. *Journal of Psycholinguistic Research,* 2, 267–278.

Dore, J. (1974). A pragmatic description of early language development. *Journal of Psycholinguistic Research,* 4, 423–430.

Dulay, H., & Burt, M. (1974). Natural sequence in child second language acquisition. *Language Learning,* 24, 37–53.

Dunn, L., & Dunn, R. (1981). Peabody Picture Vocabulary Test–Revised.

Eimas, P., Siqueland, E., Jusczyk, P., & Vigorito, J. (1971). Speech perception in infants. *Science,* 171, 303–306.

Emde, R., & Harmon, R. (eds.). (1984) *Continuities and Discontinuities in Development.* New York: Plenum.

Erbaugh, M. (1982). The acquisition of Mandarin Chinese. Unpublished Doctoral Dissertation, University of California, Berkeley.

Ervin, S. (1964). Imitation and structural change in children's language. In E. H. Lenneberg (Ed.), *New Directions in the Study of Language.* Cambridge, Mass.: MIT Press.

Fagan, J., & McGrath, S. (1981). Infant recognition memory and later intelligence. *Intelligence,* 5, 121–130.

Favreau, M., & Segalowitz, N. (1983). Automatic and controlled processes in the first and second language reading of fluent bilinguals. *Memory and Cognition,* 11:6, 565–574.

Ferguson, C. (1984). From babbling to speech. Invited Address to the International Conference on Infant Studies, New York, April 1984.

Ferguson, C., & Farwell, C. (1975). Words and sounds in early language acquisition. *Language,* 51, 419–439.

Fillmore, L. (1979) Individual differences in second language acquisition. In C. J. Fillmore, D. Kempler, and W. Wang (eds.), *Individual Differences in Language Ability and Language Behavior.* New York: Academic Press.

Fischer, K. (1980). A theory of cognitive development: The control and construction of hierarchies of skills. *Psychological Review,* 87(6), 477–531.

Fodor, J. (1983). *The Modularity of Mind.* Cambridge, Mass.: MIT Press.

Fodor, J. (1985). Precis of The Modularity of Mind. *Behavioral and Brain Sciences,* 8, 1–42.

Furrow, D. (1980). *Social and asocial uses of language in young children.* Unpublished Doctoral Dissertation, Yale University.

Furrow, D., & Nelson, K. (1984). Environmental correlates of individual differences in language acquisition. *Journal of Child Language,* 11, 523–534.

Furrow, D., Nelson, K., & Benedict, H. (1979). Mothers' speech to children and syntactic development: some simple relationships. *Journal of Child Language,* 6, 423–442.

Gardner, H. (1983). *Frames of Mind.* New York: Basic Books.

Gentner, D. (1982). Why are nouns learned before verbs: Linguistic relativity versus natural partitioning. In S. A. Kuczaj II (Ed.), *Language Development, Vol. 2: Language, Thought, and Culture.* Hillsdale, N.J.: Erlbaum.

Gleitman, L. R. (1983). Biological predispositions to learn language. In W. Demopolous and A. Marras (Eds.), *Language Learning and Concept Acquisition.* Norwood, N. J.: Ablex.

Gleitman, L. R., Newport, E., & Gleitman, H. (1984). The current status of the motherese hypothesis. *Journal of Child Language,* 2:1, 43–81.

Gleitman, L.R., & Wanner, E. (1982). Language acquisition: the state of the art. In E. Wanner and L. Gleitman (Eds.), *Language Acquisition: The State of the Art.* New York: Cambridge University Press, 3–51.

Glucksberg, S. (1984). On resolving lexical ambiguity: can context constrain lexical access? In J. Danks, I. Kurcz, & G. Shugar (Eds.), *Proceedings of the International Conference on Knowledge and Language,* Warsaw.

Glucksberg, S., Kreuz, R., & Rho, S. (in press). Context can constrain lexical access: implications for models of language comprehension. *Journal of Experimental Psychology: Learning, Memory and Cognition.*

Goldfield, B. (1982). Intra-individual variation: Patterns of nominal and pronominal combinations. Paper presented at the Seventh Annual Boston University Conference on Language Development, October 1982.

Goldfield, B. (1985). *The contribution of child and caregiver to referential and expressive language.* Unpublished Doctoral Dissertation, Harvard University.

Goldfield, B., & Snow, C. (1985). Individual differences in language acquisition. In J. Gleason (Ed.), *Language Development.* Columbus: Merrill Publishing Co.

Goldin-Meadow, S., Seligman, M., & Gelman, R. (1976). Language in the two year old. *Cognition,* 4, 189–202.

Goldin-Meadow, S., & Mylander, C. (1985). Gestural communication in deaf children: the effects and non-effects of parental input on early language development. *Monographs of the Society for Research in Child Development.*

Golinkoff, R. (1983). The preverbal negotiation of failed messages. In R. Golinkoff (Ed.), *The Transition from Prelinguistic to Linguistic Communication.* Hillsdale, N. J.: Lawrence Erlbaum, 57–78.

Golinkoff, R., & Kerr, J. (1978). Infants' perception of sematically-defined action role changes in filmed events. *Merrill-Palmer Quarterly,* 24, 53–61.

Goodglass, H., & Kaplan, E. (1972). *The Assessment of Aphasia and Related Disorders.* Philadelphia: Lea and Febiger.

Goodglass, H., & Menn, L. (1985). Is agrammatism a unitary phenomenon? In M. L. Kean (Ed.), *Agrammatism.* New York: Academic Press.

Gottfried, A., & Bathurst, K. (1983). Hand preference across time is related to intelligence in young girls, not boys. *Science,* 222, 1074–1076.

Greenfield, P., & Smith, J. (1976). *The Structure of Communic ation in Ec ·ly Development.* New York: Academic Press.

Hakuta, K. (1982). Interaction between particles and word order in the comprehension of simple sentences in Japanese children. *Developmental Psychology,* 18, 62–76.

Hakuta, K., & Diaz, R. (in press). The relationship between degree of bilingualism and cognitive ability: some longitudinal data. In K. E. Nelson (Ed.), *Children's Language,* Vol. 6. Hillsdale, N. J.: Erlbaum.

Harding, C., & Golinkoff, R. (1978). The origins of intentional vocalizations in prelinguistic infants. *Child Development*, 49, 33–40.

Hardy-Brown, K. (1983). Universals and individual differences: Disentangling two approaches to the study of language acquisition. *Developmental Psychology,* 19, 610–624.

Hardy-Brown, K., Plomin, R., & Defries, J. (1981). Genetic and environmental influences on rate of communicative development in the first year of life. *Developmental Psychology,* 17, 704–717.

Harnick, F. (1978). The relationship between ability level and task difficulty in producing imitation in infants. *Child Development,* 49, 209–212.

Harris, P. (1983). Infant cognition. In M. Haith and J. Campos (Eds.), *Handbook of Child Psychology,* Vol. II, 689–782.

Hebb, D. (1949). *The Organization of Behavior.* New York: Wiley.

Hecaen, H. (1976). Acquired aphasia in children and the ontogenesis of hemispheric functional specialization. *Brain and Language,* 3, 114–134.

Horgan, D. (1978). How to answer questions when you've got nothing to say. *Journal of Child Language,* 5, 159–165.

Horgan, D. (1979). *Nouns: Love 'em or Leave 'em.* Address to the New York Academy of Sciences, May 1979.

Horgan, D. (1981). Rate of language acquisition and noun emphasis. *Journal of Psycholinguistic Research,* 10:6, 629–640.

Howe, C. (1976). The meanings of two-word utterances in the speech of young children. *Journal of Child Language,* 13, 29–47.

Hull, C. (1943). *Principles of Behavior.* New York: Appleton-Century-Crofts.

Hyams, N. (1983). *The Acquisition of Parameterized Grammars.* Unpublished Doctoral Dissertation, City University of New York Graduate Center.

Ingram, D. (1979). Phonological patterns in the speech of young children. In P. Fletcher and M. Garman (Eds.), *Language Acquisition.* Cambridge: Cambridge University Press, 133–148.

Johnston, J. (1981). The language disordered child. In N. Lass, J. Norther, D. Yoder, & L. McReynolds (Eds.), *Speech, Language, and Learning.* Philadelphia: Saunders.

Johnston, J. (1985). Cognitive prerequisites: the evidence from children learning English. In D. I. Slobin (Ed.), *The Cross-linguistic Study of Language Acquisition.* Hillsdale, N.J.: Lawrence Erlbaum.

Johnston, J., & Kamhi, A. (1980). The same can be less: syntactic and semantic aspects of the utterances of language-impaired children. Paper presented to the Symposium on Research in Child Language Disorders. University of Wisconsin, Madison. (Revised version to appear in *Merrill-Palmer Quarterly.*)

Kagan, J. (1971). *Change and Continuity in Infancy.* New York: John Wiley and Sons.

Kagan, J. (1981). *The Second Year: The Emergence of Self-awareness.* Cambridge, Mass.: Harvard University Press.

Karmiloff-Smith, A. (1979). *A Functional Approach to Child Language.* Cambridge: Cambridge University Press.

Keenan, E. (1977). Making it last: Uses of repetition in children's discourse. In S. Ervin-Tripp and C. Mitchell-Kernan (Eds.), *Child Discourse.* New York: Academic Press.

Keenan, E. (1976). Towards a universal definition of "subject." In C. Li (Ed.), *Subject and Topic.* New York: Academic Press.

Kempler, D. (1980). Variation in language acquisition. *UCLA Working Papers in Cognitive Linguistics.* Los Angeles: UCLA Linguistics Department.

Kempler, D. (1984). *Syntactic and symbolic functions in dementia of the Alzheimer type.* Unpublished Doctoral Dissertation, University of California, Los Angeles.

Kempler, D., & Curtiss, S. (1984). The changing neuropsychological profile of Turner's Syndrome. Manuscript, University of California, Los Angeles.

Kempler, D., Van Lancker, D., & Hadler, B. (1984). Familiar phrase recognition in brain-damaged and demented adults. Paper presented to the Academy of Aphasia, Los Angeles, October 1984.

Kiger, J., & Glass, A. (1983). The facilitation of lexical decisions by a prime occurring after the target. *Memory and Cognition*, 11, 356–365.

Kinney, D., & Kagan, J. (1976). Infant attention to auditory discrepancy. *Child Development*, 47, 155–164.

Kintsch, W., & Keenan, J. (1973). Reading rate as a function of the number of propositions in the base structure of sentences. *Cognitive Psychology*, 5, 257–274.

Kintsch, W., & Mross, E. (1985). Context effects in word identification. *Journal of Memory and Language*, 24:3, 336–349.

Kogan, N. (1983). Stylistic variation in childhood and adolescence. In J. Flavell and E. Markman (Eds.), *Cognitive Development.* (Volume III of P. Mussen, ed., *Handbook of Child Psychology*).

Kolk, H., Van Grunsven, M., & Keyser, A. (1985). On parallelism between production and comprehension in agrammatism. In M. L. Kean (Ed.), *Agrammatism.* New York: Academic Press.

Kuczaj, S. (1979). Young children's overextensions of object words in comprehenson and/or production: support for a prototype theory of early object word meaning. Paper presented to the Society for Research in Child Development, San Francisco, March 1979.

Kuhl, P. (1987). The special-mechanisms debate in speech: Contributions of tests on animals (and the relations of these tests to studies using non-speech signals). In S. Harnad (Ed.), *Categorical Perception.* Cambridge: Cambridge University Press.

Kuhl, P., & Miller, J. (1975). Speech perception by the chinchilla: Voiced-voiceless distinction in alveolar plosive consonants. *Science*, 190, 69–72.

Lashley, K. (1950). In search of the engram. *Symposium of Social Experimental Biology, No. 4.* Cambridge: Cambridge University Press.

Lenneberg, E. (1967). *The Biological Foundations of Language.* New York: Wiley.

Leonard, L. (1979). Language impairment in children. *Merrill-Palmer Quarterly,* 25, 205–232.

Leonard, L., Newhoff, M., & Masalem, L. (1980). Individual differences in early childhood phonology. *Applied Psycholinguistics,* 1, 7–30.

Leonard, L., Schwartz, R., Folger, M., Newhoff, M., & Wilcox, M. (1979). Children's imitations of lexical items. *Child Developmental,* 59, 19–27.

Lesser, R. (1978). *Linguistic Investigations of Aphasia.* London: Edward Arnold.

Liberman, A. (1982). On the finding that speech is special. *American Psychologist,* 37, 148–167.

Liberman, A., & Mattingly, I. (1985). The motor theory of speech perception revised. *Cognition,* 21, 1–36.

Lieven, E. (1978). Conversations between mothers and young children: individual differences and their possible implications for the study of language learning. In N. Waterson & C. Snow (Eds.), *The Development of Communication: Social and Pragmatic Factors in Language Acquisition.* New York: Wiley.

Lieven, E. (1980). *Language development in young children.* Unpublished Doctoral Dissertation, Cambridge University.

Linebarger, M., Schwartz, M., & Saffran, E. (1983). Sensitivity to grammatical structure in so-called agrammatic aphasics. *Cognition,* 13, 361–392.

Linebarger, M., Schwartz, M., Saffran, E., & Pate, E. (1985). Using judgments of anomaly/plausibility to investigate the determinants of sentence interpretation in aphasia. Paper presented to the Academy of Aphasia, Pittsburgh, October 1985.

Loftus, E., & Loftus, G. (1976). *Human Memory: The Processing of Information.* Hillsdale, N. J.: Erlbaum.

Macaulay, R. (1978). The myth of female superiority in language. *Journal of Child Language,* 5, 353–363.

Maccoby, E., & Jacklin, C. N. (1974). *The Psychology of Sex Differences.* Stanford, California: Stanford University Press.

MacWhinney, B. (1978). The acquisition of morphophonology. *Monographs of the Society for Research in Child Development,* Serial No. 174, Vol. 43.

MacWhinney, B. (1982). Point-sharing. In R. Schiefelbusch & J. Pickar (Eds.), *Communicative Competence: Acquisition and Intervention.* Baltimore: University Park Press.

MacWhinney, B. (Ed.) (1987). *Mechanisms of Language Learning.* Hillsdale, N.J.: Lawrence Erlbaum.

MacWhinney, B., & Bates, E. (1978). Sentential devices for conveying givenness and newness. *Journal of Verbal Learning and Verbal Behavior,* 17, 539–558.

MacWhinney, B., Pleh, C., & Bates, E. (1985). The development of sentence interpretation in Hungarian. *Cognitive Psychology*, 17, 178–209.

Maratsos, M. (1983). Some current issues in the study of the acquisition of grammar. In J. Flavell and E. Markman (Eds.), *Handbook of Child Psychology*, Vol. III, 707–786.

Marslen-Wilson, M. (1975). Sentence perception as an interactive parallel process. *Science*, 189, 226–228.

Marslen-Wilson, M., & Tyler, L. (1980). The temporal structure of spoken language understanding. *Cognition*, 8, 1–71.

Matthei, E. (1978). On the acquisition of reciprocal expressions. In H. Goodluck and L. Solan (Eds.), *Papers in the Structure and Development of Child Language*. University of Massachusetts, Amherst.

McCall, R. (1981). Nature-nurture and the two realms of development. *Child Development,* 52, 1–12.

McCall, R., Eichorn, D., & Hogarty, P. (1977). Transitions in early mental development. *Monographs of the Society for Research in Child Development* Serial #171.

McCall, R., & Kagan, J. (1967). Stimulus-schema discrepancy and attention in the infant. *Journal of Experimental Child Psychology,* 5, 381–390.

McCarthy, D. (1954). Language development in children. In L. Carmichael (Ed.), *Manual of Child Psychology.* New York: John Wiley.

McCartney, K. (1984). Effect of quality of daycare environment on children's language development. *Developmental Psychology*, 20:2, 244–261.

McClelland, D., Atkinson, J., Clark, R., & Lowel, E. (1953). *The Achievement Motive.* New York: Appleton-Century-Crofts.

McClelland, J., & Rumelhart, D. (1986). *Parallel Distributed Processing: Explorations in the Microstructure of Cognition.* Vol. 1. Cambridge, Mass.: MIT Press/Bradford Books.

McNeill, D. (1970). *The Acquisition of Language.* New York: Harper and Row.

Miceli, G., & Mazzucchi, A. (in press). The nature of speech production deficits in so-called agrammatic aphasia: evidence from two Italian patients. In L. Menn, L. K. Obler, & H. Goodglass (Eds.), *Agrammatic Aphasia: Cross-language Narrative Source Book.* Baltimore: John Benjamins.

Miceli, G., Mazzucchi, A., Menn. L., & Goodglass, H. (1983). Contrasting cases of Italian agrammatic aphasia without comprehension disorder. *Brain and Language*, 19, 65–97.

Milberg, W., Blumstein, S., & Dworetzky, B. (1985). Sensitivity to morphological constraints in Broca's and Wernicke's aphasics: A double dissociation of syntactic judgment and syntactic facilitation in and lexical decision task. Paper presented to the Academy of Aphasia, Pittsburgh, October 1985.

Miller, J., & Chapman, R. (1981). Procedures for analyzing free-speech samples: syntax and semantics. In J. Miller, *Assessing Language Production in Children.* Baltimore: University Park Press, 21–73.

Miller, W., & Ervin, S. (1964). The development of grammar in child language. In U. Bellugi & R. Brown (Eds.), *The Acquisition of Language. Monographs of the Society for Research in Child Development*, Serial No. 92, Vol. 29.

Moerk, E. (1980). Relationship between parental input frequencies and children's language acquisition: A reanalysis of Brown's data. *Journal of Child Language*, 7, 105–118.

Morton, J. (1970). A functional model of human memory. In D. Norman (Ed.), *Models of Human Memory*. New York: Academic Press.

Naeser, M., Haas, G., Auerbach, S., Helm-Estabrooks, N., & Levine, H. (1984). Correlation between extent of lesion in Wernicke's area on CT scan and recovery of auditory language comprehension in Wernicke's aphasia. Paper presented at the Academy of Aphasia, Los Angeles, October 1984.

Nelson, K. (1973). Structure and strategy in learning to talk. *Monographs of The Society for Research in Child Development*, Serial No. 143, Vol. 38.

Nelson, K. (1975). The nominal shift in semantic-syntactic development. *Cognitive Psychology*, 7, 461–479.

Nelson, K. (1981). Individual differences in language development: Implications for development and language. *Developmental Psychology*, 17, 170–187.

Nelson, K. (1985). *Making Sense: The Acquisition of Shared Meaning*. New York: Academic Press.

Nelson, K. E., Baker, N., Denninger, M., Bonvillian, J., & Kaplan, B. (1985). "Cookie" versus "Do-it-again": imitative-referential and personal-social-synactic-initiating styles in young children. *Linguistics*, 23:3.

Nelson, K. E., & Bonvillian, J. (1978). Concepts and words in the two-year-old: acquisition of concept names under controlled conditions. In K. E. Nelson (Ed.), *Children's Language*, Vol. I. New York: Gardner Press.

Nelson, K. E., Carskaddon, G., & Bonvillian, J. (1973). Syntax acquisition: Impact of experimental variation in adult verbal interaction with the child. *Child Development*, 44, 497–504.

Newmeyer, F. (1980). *Linguistic Theory in America*. New York: Academic Press.

Newport, E., Gleitman, H., & Gleitman, L. (1977). Mother, I'd rather do it myself: some effects and non-effects of maternal speech style. In C. E. Snow & C. A. Ferguson (Eds.), *Talking to Children: Language Input and Acquisition*. Cambridge: Cambridge University Press.

Newport, E., & Maier, R. (1985). The acquisition of American Sign Language. In D. I. Slobin (Ed.), *The Cross-linguistic Study of Language Acquisition*. Vol. I, 881–938. Hillsdale, N. J.: Erlbaum.

Nicolich, L. (1975). A longitudinal study of representational play in relation to spontaneous imitation and development of multiword utterances. *ERIC Document--PS007-854*.

Norman, D., & Shallice, T. (1980). Attention to action: willed and automatic control of behavior. La Jolla: Technical Report, Center for Human Information Processing, University of California, San Diego. To appear in R. Davidson, G. Schwartz & D. Shapiro (Eds.), *Consciousness and self-regulation: Advances in research*, Vol. 4. New York: Plenum.

O'Connell, B., & Bretherton, I. (1984). Toddler's play alone and with mother: The role of maternal guidance. In I. Bretherton (Ed.), *Symbolic Play: The Development of Social Understanding.* New York: Academic Press.

Oden, G., & Spira, J. (1983). Influence of context on the activation and selection of ambiguous word senses. *Quarterly Journal of Experimental Psychology*, 35, 51–64.

Onifer, W., & Swinney, D. (1981). Accessing lexical ambiguities during sentence comprehension: effects of frequency of meaning and contextual bias. *Memory and Cognition*, 9, 225–236.

Oviatt, S. (1979). The developing awareness of linguistic generality in 9- to 17-month-old infants. Paper presented to the Society for Research in Child Development, New Orleans, April 1979.

Parisi, D. (1974). What is behind child utterances? *Journal of Child Language*, 1:1, 97–107.

Parisi, D., & Gianelli, W. (1974). Language and social environment at 2 years. Manuscript, Institute of Psychology, National Council of Research, Rome, Italy.

Pate, D. (1985) The syntactic sensitivity of a Wernicke's aphasic: A case report. Paper presented to the Academy of Aphasia, Pittsburgh, October 1985.

Peters, A. (1977). Language learning strategies: Does the whole equal the sum of the parts? *Language,* 53, 560–573.

Peters, A. (1983). *The Units of Language Acquisition.* Cambridge: Cambridge University Press.

Piaget, J. (1962). *Play, Dreams and Imitation.* New York: Norton.

Piaget, J. (1970). *Genetic Epistemology.* New York: Norton.

Piatelli-Palmerini, M. (Ed.) (1980). *Language and Learning: The Debate between Jean Piaget and Noam Chomsky.* Cambridge, Mass.: Harvard University Press.

Pinker, S. (1981). On the acquisition of grammatical morphemes. *Journal of Child Language,* 8, 477–484.

Pinker, S. (1982). A theory of the acquisition of lexical-interpretive grammars. In J. Bresnan (Ed.), *The Mental Representation of Grammatical Relations.* Cambridge, Mass.: MIT Press, 655–726.

Pinker, S. (1987). Constraint satisfaction networks as implementations of nativist theories of language acquisition. In B. MacWhinney (Ed.), *Mechanisms of Language Learning.* Hillsdale, N. J.: Lawrence Erlbaum.

Posner, M., & Snyder, C. (1975). Attention and cognitive control. In R. Solso (Ed.), *Information Processing and Cognition.* Hillsdale, N. J.: Erlbaum.

Radulovic, L. (1975). Acquisition of language: studies of Dubrovnik children. Unpublished Doctoral Dissertation, University of California, Berkeley.

Ramer, A. (1976). Syntactic styles in emerging language. *Journal of Child Language,* 3, 49–62. York: Academic Press.

Reznick, S. Personal communication.

Reznick, S., & Kagan, J. (1983). Dishabituation and category detection in infancy. In L. Lipsitt & C. Rovee-Collier (Eds.), *Advances in Infancy Research.* Norwood, N. J.: Ablex.

Reznick, S., Snow, C., & Wolf, D. (1985). Repeat of the New England Individual Differences Project. Summer Institute of the MacArthur Network on the Transition from Infancy to Childhood.

Robins, R. H. (1968). *A Short History of Linguistics.* Bloomington, Indiana: Indiana University Press.

Ross, E. (1981). The aprosodias: Functional-anatomic organization of the affective components of language in the right hemisphere. *Archives of Neurololgy,* 38, 561–569.

Ross, G., Nelson, K., Wetstone, H., & Tanouye, E. (1980). Concept acquisition at 20 months. Manuscript, Graduate Center of the City University of New York. Cited in K. Nelson (1981). Individual differences in language development. *Developmental Psychology,* 17:2.

Rowe, D., & Plomin, R. (1977). Temperament in early childhood. *Journal of Personality Assessment,* 41, 150–156.

Rumelhart, D., & McClelland, J. (1982). An interactive activation model of context effects in letter perception: Part 2. The contextual enhancement effect and some tests and extensions of the model. *Psych Review,* 89, 60–94.

Rumelhart, D., & McClelland, J. (1986). *Parallel Distributed Processing: Explorations in the Microstructure of Cognition.* Vol. 2. Cambridge, Mass.: MIT Press/Bradford Books.

Sachs, J., & Truswell, L. (1978). Comprehension of two-word instructions by children in the one-word stage. *Journal of Child Language,* 5, 17–24.

Schwartz, M., Marin, O., & Saffran, E. (1979). Dissociations of language function in dementia: A case study. *Brain and Language,* 7, 277–306.

Schwartz, R. (1978). Words, objects and actions in early lexical acquisition. Unpublished Doctoral Dissertation, Memphis State University.

Schwartz, R., & Camarata, S. (1985). Examining relationships between input and language development: some statistical issues. *Journal of Child Language,* 12:1, 199–209.

Schweikert, J., & Garrett, M. Research in progress.

Seidenberg, M., & Tanenhaus, M. (in press). Modularity and lexical access. In I. Gopnik (Ed.), *Studies in Cognitive Science: The McGill Workshops.* Norwood, N. J.: Ablex.

Seidenberg, M., Tanenhaus, M., Leiman, J., & Bienkowski, M. (1982). Automatic access of the meanings of ambiguous words in context: some limitations of knowledge-based processing. *Cognitive Psychology,* 14, 489–537.

Shiffrin, R., & Schneider, W. (1977). Controlled and automatic processing II: Perceptual learning, automatic attending and a general theory. *Psychological Review,* 84.

Shore, C. (1981). *Getting It Together: An Exploration in Cognitive Capacities Related to Multisymbol Combinations.* Unpublished Doctoral Dissertation, University of Colorado, Boulder.

Shore, C. (1986). Combinatorial play, conceptual development and early multi-word speech. *Developmental Psychology*, 22:2.

Shore, C., Bates, E., Bretherton, I., Beeghly, M., & O'Connell, B. (in press). Vocal and gestural symbols: Similarity and Differences from 13 to 28 months. In V. Volterra & C. J. Eating, (Eds.), *From Gesture to Language Hearing and Deaf Children*. New York: Springer Verlag.

Shore, C., & Bauer, P. (1983). Individual styles in language and symbolic play. Paper presented at the American Psychological Association, Anaheim, California.

Shore, C., O'Connell, B., & Bates, E. (1984). First sentences in language and symbolic play. *Developmental Psychology*, 20:5, 872–880.

Skinner, B. F. (1957). *Verbal behavior*. New York: Appleton-Century-Crofts.

Slobin, D. I. (1966). Grammatical transformations and sentence comprehension in childhood and adulthood. *Journal of Verbal Learning and Verbal Behavior*, 5, 219–227.

Slobin, D. I. (1973). Cognitive prerequisites for the acquisition of grammar. In C. Ferguson & D. I. Slobin (Eds.), *Studies of Child Language Development*. New York: Holt, Rinehart, and Winston.

Slobin, D. I. (1979). *Psycholinguistics: 2nd edition*. Glenview, Ill.: Scott, Foresman.

Slobin, D. I. (1982). Universal and particular in the acquisition of language. In L. R. Gleitman & E. Wanner (Eds.). *Language Acquisition: The State of the Art*. Cambridge: Cambridge University Press.

Slobin, D. I. (Ed.). (1985). *The Cross-linguistic Study of Language Acquisition*. Hillsdale, N. J.: Erlbaum.

Slobin, D. I., & Bever, T. G. (1982). Children use canonical sentence schemas: a cross-linguistic study of word order and inflections. *Cognition*, 1–37.

Slobin, D. I., & Welsh, C. (1973). Elicited imitation as a research tool in developmental psycholinguistics. In C. A. Ferguson & D. I. Slobin (Eds.), *Studies of Child Language Development*. New York: Holt, Rinehart & Winston.

Snow, C. (1981) The uses of imitation. *Journal of Child Language*, 8, 205–212.

Snow, C. (1983). Saying it again: the role of expanded and deferred imitations in language acquisition. In K. E. Nelson (Ed.), *Children's Language*, Vol. 4. New York: Gardner Press.

Snow, C. E., & Bates, E. (1984). Individual differences: a cross-language approach. Workshop presented at the Stanford Child Language Research Forum, Stanford, April 1984.

Snow, C. E., & Hoefnagal-Hohle, M. (1978). The critical period for language acquisition: evidence from second language learning. *Child Development*, 49, 1114–1128.

Snyder, L. (1978). Communicative and cognitive abilities and disabilities in the sensorimotor period. *Merrill-Palmer Quartery*, 24, 161–180.

Snyder, L. (1982). Communicative competence in children with delayed language development. In R. Schiefelbusch & J. Pickar (Eds.). *Communicative Competence: Acquisition and Intervention*. Baltimore: University Park Press.

Snyder, L., Bates, E., & Bretherton, I. (1981). Content and context in early lexical development. *Journal of Child Language*, 8, 565–582.

Spearman, C. (1937). *The Abilities of Man*. New York: Macmillan.

Stanovich, K., & West, R. (1979). Mechanisms of sentence context effects in reading: automatic activation and conscious attention. *Memory and Cognition*, 7, 77–85.

Starr, S. (1975). The relationship of single words to two-word sentences. *Child Development*, 46, 701–708.

Sternberg, R., & Powell, J. (1983). The development of intelligence. In J. Flavell & E. Markman eds., *Cognitive Development*. (Volume III of P. Mussen, (Ed.), *Handbook of Child Psychology*. New York: John Wiley.)

Stine, E., & Bohannon III, J. (1983). Imitations, interactions, and language acquisition. *Journal of Child Language*, 3, 589–605.

Sugarman, S. (1983). *Children's Early Thought*. New York: Cambridge University Press.

Swinney, D. (1979). Lexical access during sentence comprehension: (Re)consideration of context effects. *Journal of Verbal Learning and Verbal Behavior*, 18, 645–660.

Swinney, D., Zurif, E., Fosenberg, B., & Nicol, J. (1984). Modularity and information access in the lexicon: Evidence from aphasia. Paper presented to the Academy of Aphasia, Los Angeles, October 1984.

Templin, M. (1957). Certain language skills in children: their development and interrelationships. *Child Welfare Monograph No. 26*. Minneapolis: University of Minnesota Press.

Tew, B. (1975). The "Cocktail Party Syndrome" in children with Hydrocephalus and Spina Bifida. *British Journal of Disorders of Communication*, 14:2, 89–101.

Thurstone, L. L. (1938). Primary mental abilities. *Psychometric Monographs*, 1.

Tinbergen, N. (1951) *The Study of Instinct*. London: Oxford University Press.

Tomasello, M., & Todd, J. (1983). Joint attention and lexical acquisition style. *First Language*, 4, 197–212.

Tryon, R., & Bailey, D. (1970). *Cluster Analysis*. New York: McGraw-Hill.

Van Lancker, D. (1975). *Heterogeneity in Language and Speech: Neurolinguistic Studies*. Unpublished Doctoral Dissertation, University of California, Los Angeles.

Van Petten, C., & Kutas, M. (1987). Ambiguous words in context: An event-related potential analysis of the time course of meaning activation. *Journal of Memory and Language*, 26, 188–208.

Varma, T. L. (1979). Stage I speech of a Hindi-speaking child. *Journal of Child Language*, 6, 167–173.

Vihman, M. (1981). Phonology and the development of the lexicon: evidence from children's errors. *Journal of Child Language*, 8, 239–264.

Vihman, M., & Carpenter, K. (1984). Linguistic advance and cognitive style in language acquisition. Manuscript, Stanford University Department of Linguistics.

Volterra, V., Bates, E., Benigni, L., Bretherton, I., & Camaioni, L. (1979). First words in language and action: A qualitative look. In E. Bates, L. Benigni, I. Bretherton, L. Camaioni, & V. Volterra, (Eds.), *The Emergence of Symbols: Cognition and Communication in Infancy.* New York: Academic Press.

Volterra, V., & Taeschner, T. (1977). The origin and development of child language by a bilingual child. *Journal of Child Language*, 5, 311–326.

Wanner, E., & Gleitman, L. (Eds.). (1982). *Language Acquisition: The State of the Art.* New York: Cambridge University Press.

Warren, R. M., & Warren, R. P. (1970). Auditory illusions and confusions. *Scientific American*, 223, 30–36.

Weir, R. (1962). *Language in the Crib.* The Hague: Mouton.

Weist, R. (1983). The word order myth. *Journal of Child Language*, 10:1, 97–107.

Weist, R., & Koniecanza, E. (1985). Affix processing strategies and linguistic systems. *Journal of Child Language*, 12, 27–36.

Wetstone, H., & Friedlander, B. (1973). The effect of word order on young children's responses to simple questions and commands. *Child Development*, 44, 734–740.

Wexler, K., & Culicover, P. (1980). *Formal Principles of Language Acquisition.* Cambridge, Mass.: MIT Press.

Whorf, B. (1956). *Language, Thought and Reality.* J. Carroll (ed.). New York: Wiley.

Wolf, D., & Gardner, H. (1979). Style and sequence in symbolic play. In M. Franklin and N. Smith (Eds.), *Early Symbolization.* Hillsdale, N. J.: Erlbaum.

Wright, B., & Garrett, M. (1984). Lexical decision in sentences: Effects of syntactic structure. *Memory and Cognition*, 12, 31–45.

Wulfeck, B. (in press). Grammaticality judgments and sentence comprehension in agrammatic aphasia. *Journal of Speech and Hearing Research.*

Zurif, E., & Blumstein, S. (1978). Language and the brain. In M. Halle, J. Bresnan, & G. Miller (Eds.), *Linguistic Theory and Psychological Reality.* Cambridge, Mass.: MIT Press.

Zurif, E., & Caramazza, A. (1976). Psycholinguistic structures in aphasia: studies in syntax and semantics. In H. Whitaker and H. A. Whitaker (Eds.), *Studies in Neurolinguistics*, Vol. 1. New York: Academic Press.

AUTHOR INDEX

SUBJECT INDEX

adjective density, 98
agrammatism, 63, 289; *see also* aphasia
Alzheimer's disease, 285, 290
amalgams, *see* formulaic expressions
Analogy vs. Anomoly debate, 13–18, 287,
  298–9; and Piaget, 17
analysis, depth of, 175
analytic modes of learning, 8, 12, 28, 33, 78,
  108, 183, 218; and novel concepts, 124,
  126–31; vs. rote processing, 29, 64, 94,
  106, 135–6, 205, 219, 227, 264, 286
analytic style, 177; in Julia, 247–8; and social
  variables, 242
animacy in word order comprehension, 5, 192
Anomalists, 14; *see also* Analogy vs. Anomoly
  debate
aphasia, 25, 63, 275–7, 284–5, 286–91
Aristotle, 13, 298
articulation (*see also* phonology), 52
automatic vs. controlled processes, 24, 240
autonomy of grammar, 16, 18, 277–8

backward priming, 295
Bayley Test of Infant Intelligence, 40
Behaviorism, 16–17, 19
Berkeley Longitudinal Study, 40
bidirectionality of effects, 58–9, 237–8
bilingualism, *see* second language learning
biological bases of language, 3–4, 7, 21
biosocial factors: in acquisition, 59, 229,
  232–3, 258–60, 267–8; in individual differences, 56–60, 229–35, 267–8
birth order, 59, 229, 232–3, 267
Bloom criteria of morphological productivity,
  169–70 171–3, 209, 220
bound morphemes, 169, 171–2
brain damage, 22, 277
Brown criteria of morphological productivity,
  167–9, 171–3, 209, 220
Brown's fourteen grammatical morphemes,
  37, 168

Brown's stages of morphological acquisition,
  86, 138–9, 147, 193
by-product approach, 17

caregiver/caretaker style, *see* parental style
case studies, 31–2, 35, 245; of Julia, 229–30
categorical perception, 297–8
closed-class morphology, 88, 97–8, 262;
  defining criteria, 151–2
closed-class style, 61, 98, 100–1, 148–9,
  156–9, 178–9, 186, 262–4; *see also* open-
  class style; styles of acquisition
Cocktail Party Syndrome, 276
cognitive bases of language, 35, 235–40,
  263–4, 278
cognitive style, 52
comprehension: commands test of, canonical
  and non-canonical, 114–17, 209; experimental measures of, 113–14; of morphology, 137–8, 188–90, 193–4, 209; multiple-
  choice measure for single-word, 74, 84,
  115–6; and multiword comprehension,
  113–14, 114–17, 120–3, 194, 209; and
  novel concept test, fiffins, 124–33, 195,
  209, 264; from parental report, 45, 72–3,
  96–7; vs. production, 29, 41, 65, 77, 88–91,
  195, 199–200, 205, 208, 261–2, 265, 286;
  standardized tests of, 113; of word order,
  enactment test, 188, 191, 198–9, 209, 265;
  of word order, picture-choice test, 188–91,
  198–9, 209, 265
congenital dysphasia, 275–6
connectionism, *see* parallel distributed processing models
consciousness in language practice, 284
content: vs. frequency, 65; vs. process, 5, 20
contextual flexibility, 46, 76
continuity, 95–6, 107, 155, 264, 269–70
contrast criterion of morphological productivity, 170–6, 209